Organizing Women in Contemporary Russia

Engendering Transition

This book offers the first comprehensive analysis of the contemporary Russian women's movement and of the social, political, economic, historical, and international contexts that surround it. Valerie Sperling paints a vivid portrait of the women's movement's formation and development, paying particular attention to the key challenges facing a social movement in post-communist society, including the virtual absence of civil society, constant flux in political institutions, wrenching economic changes, and the movement's own status in a shifting transnational environment. The author also addresses the specific challenges facing women's organizations by discussing societal attitudes toward feminism in Russia. Based on participant observation, primary source materials, and dozens of interviews conducted in Moscow (as well as two smaller Russian cities), the narrative brings alive the activists' struggle to build a social movement under difficult conditions, and sheds new light on the troubled and complex process of Russia's democratization.

VALERIE SPERLING is Visiting Assistant Professor at Clark University, Massachusetts. She is the author of several journal articles on gender politics in Russia.

Organizing Women in Contemporary Russia

Engendering transition

Valerie Sperling

CAMBRIDGE
UNIVERSITY PRESS

PUBLISHED BY THE PRESS SYNDICATE OF THE UNIVERSITY OF CAMBRIDGE
The Pitt Building, Trumpington Street, Cambridge CB2 1RP, United Kingdom

CAMBRIDGE UNIVERSITY PRESS
The Edinburgh Building, Cambridge, CB2 2RU, UK   http://www.cup.cam.ac.uk
40 West 20th Street, New York, NY 10011–4211, USA   http://www.cup.org
10 Stamford Road, Oakleigh, Melbourne 3166, Australia

First published 1999

Typeset in 10/12pt Plantin   [CE]

A catalogue record for this book is available from the British Library

Library of Congress cataloguing in publication data

Sperling, Valerie.
Organizing women in contemporary Russia: engendering transition / Valerie Sperling.
  p.   cm.
Includes bibliographical references (p. 283).
ISBN 0 521 66017 3 (hbk). – ISBN 0 521 66963 4 (pbk.)
1. Feminism – Russia (Federation)
2. Women – Russia (Federation) – Social conditions.
3. Russia (Federation) – Social conditions – 1991–
I. title.
HQ1665.15.S685   1999
305.42'0947 – dc21   98–43642   CIP

ISBN 0 521 66017 3 hardback
ISBN 0 521 66963 4 paperback

Transferred to digital printing 2002

Contents

Tables

Acknowledgments

Writing a book about a social movement is a dicey undertaking. After viewing drafts of parts of this manuscript, some of the activists I had interviewed were livid: angry, upset, and afraid that my mention of conflicts within the movement would lead to immediate de-funding, and to dismissal of the movement as a gaggle of quarrelsome females. Other activists were thrilled that someone had given voice to their concerns and aired the conflicts that they had longed to see discussed in public. It is my sincere hope that readers of this book on a fascinating and valuable social movement will not leave the text with the first impression. My purpose in describing instances of conflict as well as of cooperation is not to display other people's dirty laundry in public, but rather to paint an honest portrait of a social movement, seen from the rare vantage point that participant observation allows. Naturally, social movements across the globe are riddled with conflict, interpersonal, tactical, strategic, and ideological. I argue in this book that the Russian women's movement, like all social movements emerging into a post-communist environment, encounters a particular set of challenges that would make smooth sailing nearly impossible.

Several institutions and countless people deserve and have my gratitude for the support and assistance they rendered me during the process of researching and writing this book. The International Research and Exchanges Board (IREX) made possible the trip to Russia during which much of the data was collected, the Social Science Research Council (SSRC) provided funding for the writeup of the dissertation in which this book had its genesis, and a postdoctoral fellowship from the Davis Center for Russian Studies at Harvard University provided institutional and financial support for the rewriting and rethinking process.

The countless people on whose advice (formal and informal) I have relied include: Gail Lapidus, George Breslauer, Henry Brady, Kim Voss, Jim Richter, and everyone who reviewed the book. I also thank editors Michael Holdsworth and John Haslam for their support and suggestions, and Karen Anderson Howes for her eagle-eyed copyediting skills.

Georgina Waylen and Vicky Randall provided constructive comments on an earlier version of chapter 4, which they published in their edited volume, *Gender, Politics and the State* (London: Routledge, 1998), as "Gender Politics and the State During Russia's Transition Period."

This book would never have been written or researched without the great help and kindness of a veritable slew of Russians, as well as several Ukrainians, Chuvash, Cossacks, expats, and so forth: you know who you are. I'm inexpressibly grateful to all of my interviewees, to everyone at the Moscow Women's Archive, to Natalia Abubikirova, Nadezhda Azhgikhina, Laima Geidar, Masha Gessen, Maia Kazmina, Olga Khas-bulatova, Oleg Kharkhordin, Elena Kochkina, Valentina Konstantinova, Elvira Novikova, Marina Regentova, Tatiana Troinova, Martina Van-denberg, and so many others without whose help, invitations to semi-nars and conferences, and networking advice I would never have met all the activists that I did manage to meet, nor would I have gathered all the written materials that now make up my own archive of sorts. Thanks also go to my friends, parents, and grandmothers for their bottomless well of emotional support. Finally, I want to express my appreciation to Sam Diener, for his truly endless willingness to read, edit, and argue; for his contributions, especially to the conclusion; and for his commitment: without these, this book and I would have suffered considerably.

Note on transliteration

I have used a modified Library of Congress system for transliteration. Diacritical marks appear in the notes and bibliography, but have been largely omitted from the text so as not to distract the reader. Thus, "Tatiana" in the text becomes "Tat'iana" in the notes. Diacriticals in the text remain in Russian words discussed or given as examples; they are also retained in occasional transliterated passages that serve to clarify my translations. Finally, well-known names are rendered in their familiar transliterated form (for example, Yeltsin rather than El'tsin, and Yabloko rather than Iabloko).

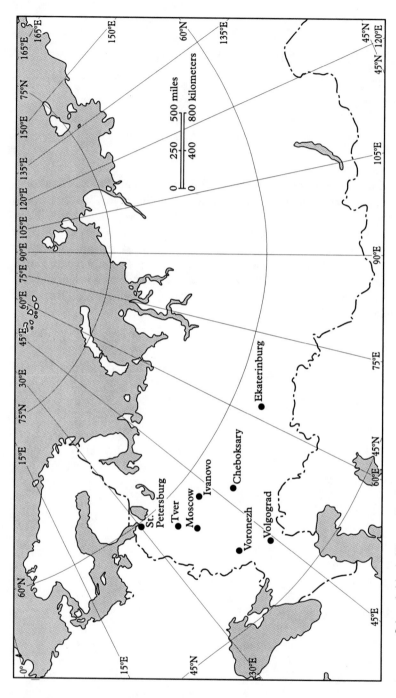

Selected cities in Western Russia

Introduction

Around noon on a chilly day in early March – International Women's Day, 1996 – a group of women gathers in Moscow's Pushkin Square. They are there for a demonstration: Women in Black Against Violence. The women mill around, waiting for the protest march to begin; they plan to walk to the Nikitskie Gates, a few blocks away. More women trickle into the square in twos and threes. Soon, the group has expanded to about sixty. A few stand silently, dressed in black, holding a banner reading "Women in Black Against Violence." Two young women hold a large blue banner with white felt letters, spelling out a slogan strange and unfamiliar to Russian passersby: "There are no free men without free women. Amazons: Women Smashing Stereotypes!" The "O" letters are drawn as woman-symbols, a little cross beneath each one. Representatives of the "Sisters" Rape Crisis Center circulate, handing out business cards and leaflets advertising their services for victims of rape. One woman holds a poster decrying Soviet agitprop about International Women's Day. It is a three-frame cartoon. In the first frame, dated "March 7th," a man is shown threatening a woman with his fist. The second frame, "March 8th," shows him presenting her with a bouquet of flowers. The third frame, "March 9th," simply repeats the image from the first frame. In a similar vein, a middle-aged woman carries a poster reading, "We demand the adoption of a law against domestic violence." These posters are a bitter response to the government's failure to do anything to stem the widespread violence against women in Russia, where approximately 14,000 women are murdered each year by their husbands and partners. A kind-looking woman with gray hair holds a hand-lettered sign: "TV creates new rapist-Chikatilos" (Chikatilo was a serial killer, rapist, and cannibal). A television camera crew strolls around, filming the banners and posters; in an attempt to be an anonymous observer, I try to avoid them (and, as it turns out, I fail).

When it comes time to march, we move out of the square and tramp down the snowy sidewalk in a relatively cheery mood: the sun is shining.

Passersby seem curious; a group of policemen turns and stares as we march past. I snap a photo of them. They ignore me completely.

The march concludes at the Nikitskie Gates. We form a circle, and someone hands out candles. We light the candles and cup them in our hands, trying to shield them from the wind: always a struggle at outdoor candlelight vigils. I look around the circle and notice that about a third of us are foreigners.

One of the organizers calls for our attention, and declares a moment of silence for all the women who have been victims of violence: in the home, on the streets, in Chechnia. Everyone falls silent. After a time, women begin to step forward, one by one, and speak a few words each about how violence against women has entered their lives. Someone mentions the origins of International Women's Day; another speaker talks about reclaiming International Women's Day to remember those who have died at the hands of violence. Someone says that, between violence on the streets and violence in the home, there is no safe place for women. There is a respectful silence as each woman speaks, their words quiet against the noise of passing streetcars.

Suddenly, a middle-aged man who has been lurking nearby breaks his way into the circle. As though making us a toast, the man gestures and then holds forth: "I want to wish *all* you women a happy International Women's Day, and wish you happiness, and love, and . . ." I cringe, silently pleading with him to get lost, to let this group of women have this one, temporary space to express themselves. And then, without missing a beat, Laima Geidar, a young activist, one of the "Amazons," interrupts him. She shouts: "Don't wish us happiness! Wish us *equal rights*!!!" She raises her fist in the air, and cries, "Hurrah!!!" She continues: "Wish us *equal opportunities*!!! Hurrah!!! Full-fledged *citizenship*!!! Hurrah!!!" Within moments, the whole circle is cheering.

The man seems dazed, shocked, and then crestfallen. A tall, willowy woman takes him by the arm, says a few soft words, and leads him out of the circle. I feel sorry for him. In his experience, International Women's Day has been a holiday, a time for men to praise women for their achievements, thank them for their tireless hard work in the economy and in the home, bring home a bouquet of flowers, and maybe even do the dinner dishes for once. Times have apparently changed. The women in this unusual circle are saying that International Women's Day has been a terribly whitewashed holiday, and that they will no longer participate in the lie. The rest of the demonstration passes peacefully and without interference.

That night, snatches of the protest are shown on the evening news. For many viewers, it might appear a curiosity, a man-bites-dog sort of story. Rather than the saccharine broadcasts shown on Women's Day in years past, this one portrays a group of women speaking out in public against oppression and discrimination in Russian society. Another piece of the truth has emerged from the Soviet skeleton closet. A new set of women's issues has come out into the public sphere.

April 17, 1995. Twelve women meet in the basement of a building not far from Moscow's renovated Tretiakov art gallery. They drink tea from mugs inscribed with their names – many worn to the point of illegibility. They snack on cookies and candies, and chat. After a time, they move into the next room, put on comfortable clothing, and engage in confidence lessons: vocalization, and a sort of posture-correcting aerobics. They are reclaiming their "femininity" in a post-totalitarian world – one whose ideology did its best to eliminate gender distinctions, while in reality it reinforced women's sense of inferiority in all areas of life: politics, society, the economy, the home. Welcome to Club Harmony (Klub Garmoniia), run by Mariia Arbatova, a dark-haired mother of twins, in her late thirties.

One newcomer explains that she is attending the club after having seen Arbatova on television. A playwright, Arbatova has taken on a new role, as the regular co-host of a television talk show called *I Myself* (*Ia Sama*). Each week, the show features a new female guest – for instance, a woman who has been married three times, and has decided that she has had enough of married life. On each show, Arbatova presents a "feminist" viewpoint (counterpoised to a "traditional" woman's viewpoint) on that episode's topic, bringing the word "feminist" into average Russian homes on a weekly basis. I ask the newcomer what she thinks of feminism. She is a high-school math teacher, with a daughter two and a half years old. She plans to go back to work in a few months, this time as a translator – more profitable by far than teaching. Her monthly maternity benefit from the state is laughably small – enough to pay for two cartons of milk. She tells me she has been to Germany, and seen women's feminist clubs there. She was impressed by the women's self-confidence and by the status women had achieved in German society: "Women even drive cars there," she tells me.

Arbatova's goal for Klub Garmoniia is to encourage self-confidence as well. A self-declared feminist, she aims to restore "what's female" to women, and thereby bring a form of equality to Russia's women, while spreading the idea that a feminist can be "feminine," even happy. This is not a popular idea in Russia. Outside the club, and off the air, Arbatova engages in a war of mutual trashing in the pages of one of Moscow's most reputable newspapers, *Nezavisimaia gazeta*. There,

Olga Lipovskaia, the director of Petersburg's Center for Gender Issues, criticizes Arbatova's sometimes "aggressive" style, and laments that Arbatova's image of a feminist is the only one available to Russian television viewers. She accuses Arbatova of hoarding the laurels that go along with being Russia's only "paid telefeminist." Arbatova responds with harsh words for Lipovskaia, accusing her and other women who have received Western grants to support their work in the feminist movement of being behind the times, concerned only about their own salaries, and not about bringing feminist ideas to the population.

June 20, 1995. Galina Klimantova, deputy of the Women of Russia (WOR) political bloc, and head of the Russian legislature's Committee on the Affairs of Women, the Family, and Youth, sits with Mariia Gaidash (also a WOR deputy), surrounded by a group of women activists from various Russian organizations. This is the first of what is supposed to be a series of monthly meetings to exchange ideas and hear proposals from women's groups, which could then be addressed or adopted by WOR, and brought up for discussion in the Duma. The activists raise several acute issues. One is the International Monetary Fund's policy of insisting that Russian enterprises end their tradition of providing social services. These policies have had a deleterious effect on women, as factory-based childcare centers and medical clinics have been shut down. The activists decry the state's failure to consider the effects of the IMF's policy on women. They argue that there is a desperate need for gender-based analysis of legislation in general. And they raise the new problem of abortion – still legal, but no longer provided free by the state. After the meeting, Klimantova writes a sort of "thank you" letter – not specifically to the Russian women with whom she met, but instead to an American-sponsored organization: the Winrock US–NIS Consortium, which arranged the meeting. It turns out to be the last meeting of its kind. A few months later, in the December elections, WOR fails to gain 5 percent of the vote, and is thus excluded as a faction from the parliament.

May 3, 1995. An organization called "Creativity" (Tvorchestvo), whose main business has become teaching women how to repair old clothes and make handicrafts for sale to tourists, gathers together twenty artistic survivors of World War II for a celebration. The women arrive at the first-floor office space of a residential building in Moscow, and sit around a U-shaped cluster of tables, laden with open-faced sandwiches, greens, and vodka. They reminisce about the war, and show each other various and extraordinary works of art, including one woman's portrait of Lenin that appears to be a line drawing, done in ink, but is in fact embroidered in fine black thread. At the time that the portrait was sewn, its creator could not exhibit it openly because it was not an "official" portrait; it lacked approval by the Communist Party.

Tvorchestvo was founded in 1988, one of the earliest women's groups to form and attempt to gain official recognition. Its original goal was to bring together women in the creative professions – artists, writers, journalists, composers, architects – to socialize and enjoy monthly "club days." As Russia's economy deteriorated, and as women, especially educated women, began to lose their jobs, Tvorchestvo started to offer courses to women, staving off unemployment through craft production and the sale of handmade goods. Tatiana Riabikina, the chairwoman of the organization, had originally dreamed of creating a center for the women's movement: a private residence in Moscow, with a movie theater, an exhibition hall, a library, and a cafe, where women could come together and socialize, share their experiences, support and learn from each other. "We were closer to that goal in 1988 than we are now," she told me. "Now if we teach someone to sew, that's almost good enough."

Until Gorbachev introduced his new policies in the late 1980s, making freedom of speech and association a possibility, rather than a criminal activity, women in the Soviet Union had been essentially voiceless. Before that time, none of the organizations and events described above would have been feasible. Severe penalties were imposed for unsanctioned political or social action. As late as 1986, a demonstration protesting violence against women would have been impossible, much less shown on the evening news.

Political opportunities for social movement organizing and protest in Russia have changed dramatically over the course of the last decade. In 1991, activists in the Soviet Union's nascent women's movement organized the first national women's conference independent of state and Communist Party control. The First Independent Women's Forum, as it was labeled, was a momentous event. Over 200 women descended on Dubna, a small town outside Moscow, for the conference. But state monitoring of grassroots organizing was not yet a thing of the past. On the eve of the conference, permission to hold the event was withdrawn by city authorities. Only after highly placed officials interceded on behalf of the organizers was the conference able to go forward. The First Forum was only the beginning. Women took advantage of their newfound freedoms, creating hundreds of new organizations.

Yet despite the blur of women's organizing activity in today's Russia, the International Women's Day demonstration in 1996 was atypical. Demonstrations are rare events in the contemporary Russian women's movement. Seminars and conferences are far more prevalent as a means of organizing. Moreover, the demonstrators' demographics revealed another fascinating element of the contemporary movement: the pervasive influence of non-Russians on the development of the women's movement. What was the reason for participation by so many foreigners? Was this a chance display of international sisterhood?

Duma deputy Klimantova's letter in response to the lobbying meeting also highlights the controversial role of foreigners in today's women's movement. How did an American-funded organization come to arrange a meeting between Russian legislators and Russian women's groups? The Russian women's movement is embedded in its international context. Mass communications systems and modern methods of travel have enabled social movements and activist networks to span the entire globe. Activists from countries thousands of miles apart can share literature, attend international conferences, and strategize online with the aid of electronic mail. Governments, foundations, and social movement organizations can share tactical advice across borders, and even fund initiatives abroad. The participation of foreign women in the International Women's Day demonstration was only the tip of the iceberg. International influences affect the Russian women's movement in diverse and complicated ways, sometimes useful, sometimes benign, and sometimes rather problematic.

The Tvorchestvo group's activity points to another axis of women's movement organizing, namely, groups driven by economic need. Economic collapse in Russia in the early 1990s produced a great wave of women's organizing, aiming to counteract the flood of unemployment and to provide mutual support. Tvorchestvo is not a political advocacy group, protesting the society-wide feminization of poverty. Instead, it operates at the individual level. Women bring their handicrafts in, show them to art experts, and discover whether or not there is a niche for them in the handicraft market, at home or abroad. Others take courses in craft production, with the same goal. Many such job-training programs for women exist, often focusing on sewing, embroidery, and handicrafts. Critics question the degree of market demand for such things, and worry that women will be reduced to piecework, deprived of a standard salary and insurance benefits, and excluded from the more organized and more profitable domains within the private sector. Meanwhile, the economic-related groups proliferate. Their chairwomen consider themselves part of a dynamic women's movement, while the women who attend their courses may be quite unconcerned about social movement participation per se; many have never given a moment's thought to feminism.

Arbatova's experience with Klub Garmoniia and the television program *Ia Sama* reveals some of the complexity of defining feminism in Russia. In Arbatova's view, the club was designed for the psychological rehabilitation of women. The point was to help each woman uncover her own self, and thereby recover her "femininity"; Arbatova believes this should be feminism's central concern. She opposes the idea of pursuing "equal rights," if that means "losing her sex," becoming a man, playing by male rules in a male game. Yet, for several of the club's participants, feminism meant standing up for women's rights. Meanwhile, Arbatova's television show enters average Russian homes, portraying her as a woman who freely calls herself a feminist. But to millions of Russian women, feminism has sinister and foreign overtones. "Gender" is a foreign word with no Russian equivalent. Some activists have imported it directly into Russian (for example, there are several research institutes in Russia called centers "for Gender Studies"), but the term is meaningless to 99 percent of the population. The challenge of spreading ideas about women's oppression and women's rights in a language that all can understand confronts women activists in Russia at every turn.

Also confronting women activists in Russia are the effects of recent political history. The Women of Russia faction that had agreed to meet with activists was in parliament for only two years – from December 1993 to December 1995. WOR's experience is emblematic of the shifting and unstable political alignments in Russia. In 1991, the Soviet Union collapsed, along with its political institutions. In 1993, the Russian parliament was destroyed in a hail of tank fire, and a new legislature created. The women's movement has had to struggle to keep its balance as the ship of state has been tossed around on the waves of reform and reaction. The rules of the political game shift; it is not easy for a social movement to make visible progress.

Today's Russian women's movement is spread far and wide across Russia's immense territory. It includes oldtimers from the pre-glasnost era, and newcomers; women on the left, and women on the right; a few young women, many women in their forties and fifties, and a number of extremely tough women in their sixties. They have joined the women's movement out of various motives, ranging from the desire to gain a political voice to finding a means to forestall personal economic ruin. Russia's transition from communism toward capitalism and a more democratic political arrangement has been both good and bad for women, presenting both obstacles and opportunities for organizing. The obstacles and opportunities are domestic as well as international. They are cultural, political, economic, and historical.

My personal experience with the Russian women's movement began in 1992, when I attended the Second Independent Women's Forum, the second national conference of the women's movement. Unlike the First Forum, this one took place in the new Russia – no longer under Soviet rule. It was an unforgettable experience. Like its predecessor, the Second Forum took place in Dubna. The conference organizers were overwhelmed by the number of attendees – over 500 women – far more than had been anticipated. They ran out of hotel rooms, and housed me with a local family. The hours of the conference were long. Lida, my host mother, woke me each day at 6 a.m. and hustled me off to the bus stop while it was still dark. The Forum itself took place a few miles away from Lida's apartment, at Ratmino, a "resort hotel" associated with Dubna's Institute for Joint Nuclear Research. I returned home every night utterly exhausted, but excited about the day's events. In the evening Lida fed me delicious chicken dinners, and I played with her daughter Dasha, who badly wanted a Barbie doll. It was the warmth and generosity of Lida's family, and of many of the women I met at the conference, plus their enthusiasm and drive to tell their stories (of organizational success and tragedy), that initially cemented my fascination with the Russian women's movement.

At the Second Forum, I formed a multitude of impressions, many of which centered around the weather. It was the end of November. It was freezing outside, and freezing inside. The Forum was divided into sections, or workshops. Groups of women met in classrooms, in all-purpose rooms, in hallways and lobbies, often wearing their coats.

I came to the Forum equipped with tape-recording equipment, a notebook, a few copies of an article I had written on rape and domestic violence in the Soviet Union, and a bag of political buttons, most bearing a single picture on a light blue background. On the top half of the button, a large black fish with its mouth wide open was chasing after a school of little fish. The lower half of the button sported an inspiring illustration: the little fish had arranged themselves into a large, fish-shaped school, and were going after the big fish. Around the top edge of the button, in large block letters, it said, "ORGANIZE!" The women attending the Forum loved my buttons. I handed one to whomever I sat next to, and, in exchange, met a large number of extremely pleasant and talkative women.

One woman donated a copy of her newly founded newspaper to me, called *Women's Games* (*Zhenskie igry*). It was sort of an erotic newspaper; the cover featured a black-and-white photograph of a naked man in a top hat, shown from the side. The paper was put out by a women's group in far-off Volgograd, and bore an odd motto: "For the Moral Equality of Men and Women." This was a far cry from the ever-present motto of Soviet newspapers, "Proletarians of the World, Unite!" She asked me to try and send her a copy of *Playgirl*. "It would be really helpful," she said. A few years later, at a large library just outside Moscow, I found recent copies of *Zhenskie igry* – it had apparently survived without ever receiving the desired copy of *Playgirl* from me. On an issue from 1994, an additional motto had been added to the masthead: "Humanity Began with a Matriarchy!" An issue from 1995 replaced both mottoes with a pithy summary of patriarchy: "Patriarchy is when men are favored in everything, and women feel guilty for everything."

The Second Forum was organized around a series of extended workshops on a variety of topics including women and business, unemployment, health, religion, politics, trade unions/the workplace, military conversion, nationalism, rural women, art, and violence against women. At the workshop on violence against women, I watched as Russian women who had been interested in this topic, working separately, on their own, met each other for the first time and began to talk about cooperation. Several of them were later among the founders of the "Sisters" Rape Crisis Center, established in 1993. One of the buttons I had brought to hand out at that workshop said simply, "If she says No, it's Rape." One woman laughed as she took it, saying to her friend, "I'm going to tell my husband about this, and put it right next to our bed!"

It was at the Second Forum that I began to realize how diverse the spectrum of women's organizing was in Russia. There were women providing support for women in business, including training, education, and placement; professional associations; mutual support associations for people with similar problems, such as soldiers' mothers, parents with handicapped children, and women who served in Afghanistan; groups concerned with defending women's rights during privatization; charities; rape crisis centers and shelter projects; and groups promoting feminism and conducting women's studies. A few organizations focused on training women for political leadership. At least eight groups were explicitly concerned with family welfare. One group from Ukraine was dedicated to the preservation of women's creativity and femininity in the face of the Chernobyl disaster. The variety was extraordinary.

The stated purpose of the Second Forum was to provide a strategy session for putting women's issues on Russia's national agenda: the slogan for the Forum was "From Problems to Strategy." The organizers felt that women's issues should be indivisible from the general social transformation that was taking place, not viewed as secondary problems that would be solved automatically *after* national economic conditions had improved overall. After all, the Bolsheviks, too, had promised that women's position would improve after the economic transformation of society was accomplished. Yet, the most useful service the Forum provided may have been the opportunity for women activists from across the country to engage in networking. Many hours were spent on welcoming ceremonies, where representatives of the more than sixty groups present introduced themselves, one by one, to the Forum participants gathered in a large, cold auditorium. Despite the shortage of time, nearly all the speakers recited their phone numbers, which were urgently scribbled down by other participants. This was the sole chance for these women to find out about each other's existence and exchange such basic information before the next Forum – and no one could predict with any certainty when that might occur.

One afternoon a few years later, while doing the fieldwork for this book, I was sitting in the Women's Archive (hidden away in one room of a scientific institute near Moscow's Semenovskaia metro stop), leafing through its collection on the Second Independent Women's Forum. I uncovered receipts, letters of invitation, and a list of foreign guests – with my own name on it. I held it and marveled for a moment, before getting up and showing it to one of the young women staffing the archive. "I was there!," I bragged. But now it was history. The movement I returned to in the mid-1990s had grown and, in growing, had started displaying some fairly serious growing pains. There were internal divisions – common to all social movements – but certainly shaped by Russia's political history. And there were complications stemming from the Russian movement's location in a politically and economically charged international context. Moreover, the domestic political and economic situation in which the movement was attempting to blossom was troubling at best.

The field research I conducted in Russia between 1994 and 1996 revealed a multifaceted set of opportunities and obstacles facing the contemporary women's movement, as well as a seemingly endless string of questions about the movement's form, and about activists' tactical and strategic choices. The bulk of these questions were addressed during in-depth, semi-structured interviews with sixty-three activists, representing fifty women's organizations (listed in the bibliography).[1] Additional interviews with journalists, academics, other professionals in the field, representatives of the state employment services and the Ministry of Social Protection's Women's Department, and several

---

[1] Shorter informal interviews were also conducted with a handful of additional activists.

female deputies to the Russian state legislature provided important data to complement the activist interviews.[2] The in-depth interviews ranged from forty-five minutes to over three hours. People were interviewed at their offices, in their homes, in my apartment, and, in two cases, in a public park. I conducted the interviews in Russian, and all translations of those interviews and Russian-language sources given here are my own (unless otherwise specified).[3]

My goals in the activist interviews spanned a broad spectrum. I sought to acquire information about the organizations, the movement as a whole, the leaders themselves and their opinions, and the main issues affecting women in Russian society. Specifically, my questions were designed to elicit information about the aims, tasks, activities, origins, problems, and structures of the most active women's organizations in the cities I visited; to find out what motivated group leaders to start their organizations, and why they created *women's* organizations in particular; to explore the extent of networking between organizations and the obstacles to it, including perceived divisions within the women's movement; to discover what activists thought were the main problems for women in Russia, and what could be done about them; to find out whether activists perceived discrimination against women in Russia as a problem; to explore what "feminism" meant to the activists; to uncover how they and their organizations related to Women of Russia and other political parties, and to other women's organizations in Russia; and finally, to learn about each activist's personal history of participation in women's organizing.

The set of activist interviews constitutes a representative sample of the range of goals, activities, and political tendencies within the women's movements of Moscow and two provincial Russian cities, Cheboksary and Ivanovo. The provincial cities were included in order to provide a more accurate and balanced view of women's organizing in Russia, one that travels beyond the capital, to explore local-level organizing.[4] The

---

[2] The organizations were distributed thus: Moscow, thirty-seven women's organizations; Ivanovo, five; Cheboksary, four. I also interviewed representatives of three women's organizations in Ekaterinburg, and the director of the main feminist organization in St. Petersburg. In total, I conducted seventy-three interviews. In three cases, I interviewed more than one person (separately) from each organization. In five cases, I interviewed several people together (two or three) from the same organization. The total number of interviewees was eighty.

[3] Two interviews – one with an American activist in Moscow, another with an official of the MacArthur Foundation – were conducted in English.

[4] This study does not address rural women's organizing. On rural women and the effects of the economic transition, see Sue Bridger, "Rural Women and the Impact of Economic Change," in Mary Buckley, ed., *Post-Soviet Women: From the Baltic to Central Asia* (Cambridge: Cambridge University Press, 1997), pp. 38–55.

number of women's groups in Cheboksary and Ivanovo was small enough that I was able to interview the leaders of every extant women's organization, except one, the Ivanovo city division of the Committee of Soldiers' Mothers, at that time consumed with work opposing the war in Chechnia. In Moscow, for which no comprehensive directory of women's organizations was available, I operated under the assumption that social movement activity could best be studied by interviewing and observing the most visible women's groups, although, for balance's sake, I also sought out groups whose leaders had a lower profile and who were only marginally if at all networked with other women's organizations. Organizations came to my attention through participation at varied women's movement events, personal introductions, references made to groups in the mass media, and partial lists of organizations compiled by several Moscow-based women's groups and the Russian Ministry of Justice.

With a few exceptions, I chose to interview only one person from each organization as an informant about the group: this was almost exclusively a group leader, rather than a rank-and-file member. Although many of the organizations were small, it seemed that only the organization's leaders had a grasp on the information I sought, whether it was about the organization's history, its membership, dues policies, or sometimes even its goals and activities. The organizations were uniformly of such recent vintage that, almost without exception, the founders of the organization were still in leadership positions.[5]

In addition to interviews, I relied on extensive participant observation at women's group meetings and events in all three cities. I observed attempts at coalition-building, and heard first-hand accounts of women's groups' lobbying activities. I also compiled internal organization literature, including charters; journals and newsletters produced and distributed by women's groups; small-run published volumes about

---

[5] One note about anonymity: out of the desire to get the most honest possible responses to my questions, and wishing to safeguard my respondents' privacy, I conducted the first twenty interviews – between September 19, 1994, and February 2, 1995 – with the understanding that the interviewees' names would be withheld entirely. Therefore it should not be inferred that people interviewed during that time period were being unusually paranoid or circumspect by not wanting to be cited directly. I have footnoted quotes from those interviews as "Interview, [date]." After repeated assurances from my interviewees that they were comfortable being quoted directly, I altered my policy and informed the respondents that I would keep the interview fully confidential if they wished, or that I could keep any given answer or part of an answer confidential. All the interviewees were more than willing to be identified, except on certain "taboo" topics, mostly regarding interpersonal and interorganizational disagreements. Thus, the interviews dated after February 2, 1995, are cited as "[Name], interview, [date]," except on the "taboo topics" quotes. The footnotes for those quotes appear as "Interview, name withheld."

feminism and women's economic and political status; and newspaper articles and television/radio reports on women's activism, feminism, and other relevant issues, from both the mainstream and the women's press. Finally, in order to gain a measure of the diffusion of feminist consciousness within and outside the activist community, the degree of collective identity among women, and the extent to which women consider collective action an effective way of solving their problems, I conducted a small-scale public opinion survey.[6] These diverse research methods enabled me to explore the views of a wide range of activists, attain a deeper understanding of the movement's internal dynamics, and gain a sense of the social, political, and economic contexts in which the movement's groups emerged and operated.

On the basis of this research, the chapters that follow illustrate the opportunities and obstacles inherent in women's movement organizing in contemporary Russia.[7] Chapter 1 provides a brief history of the contemporary Russian women's movement, surveys the women's groups and activists who constitute the movement, and explores some of the essential differences between organizing in Moscow and in the provincial cities. Chapter 2 elaborates the paradoxes of women's movement organizing in Russia, sets them in the context of social movement theory, and suggests a framework that can be employed to understand movements occurring outside the industrialized, capitalist, democratic regimes of Western Europe and the United States. The rest of the chapters use that framework as a means to organize the discussion of the women's movement in Russia, starting with the opportunities and obstacles that the movement confronts in the socio-cultural sphere (chapter 3), the political sphere (chapter 4), and the economic sphere (chapter 5). Chapter 6 explores the varied ways in which the movement has been shaped by the historical legacies of Leninism, and chapter 7 takes up the movement's emergence into an international context of direct and indirect aid. The conclusion addresses the implications of the study for our understanding of social movements in an increasingly globalized society, and suggests possible directions for the Russian women's movement.

---

[6] With a few exceptions, I was able to get the survey completed by at least one interviewee from each women's group in Moscow (thirty-three of thirty-seven groups), as well as by five activists in Ivanovo, twenty-four unemployed women in Ivanovo who were not affiliated with any women's organization, and twelve women from one Moscow women's club.

[7] Carol Nechemias used an "opportunities-and-obstacles" framework to evaluate the potential for women's movement development in the early perestroika years. See "The Prospects for a Soviet Women's Movement: Opportunities and Obstacles," in Judith B. Sedaitis and Jim Butterfield, eds., *Perestroika From Below: Social Movements in the Soviet Union* (Boulder: Westview, 1991), pp. 73–96.

In essence, this book argues that the women's movement in contemporary Russia confronts all the major hazards of organizing in a post-Leninist country: the absence of civil society and the difficulties of networking; a lack of economic infrastructure conducive to social movement growth and maintenance; disruptive economic changes and a decline in the social services that women relied upon; and the pervasive institutional and psychological legacies of the Soviet–Leninist regime. The movement is further challenged by the prevalence of ongoing sexist attitudes toward women, and by the denigration of feminism in the post-Soviet socio-cultural arena.

Simultaneously, the women's movement has emerged into an actively interventionist international and transnational environment, which provides intellectual contacts, financial support, and even a degree of domestic legitimation for activists in Russia. Driven by the lack of an economic infrastructure to support grassroots social movements, women's organizations in Russia are increasingly turning to international sources of support, which bring with them a host of benefits as well as unintended side effects.

These varied conditions interact, I argue, resulting in a movement that has grown substantially, from an initial handful of women independently challenging the Soviet state and Communist Party into a vibrant movement consisting of hundreds of groups engaging state and society on a multitude of levels. The women's movement of the mid-1990s is flourishing, even as it struggles within its social, political, economic, historical, and international contexts. Yet the Russian women's movement is traveling a trying path. The incentives provided by the international sphere, combined with the movement's domestic challenges, produce a movement that tends to avoid confrontational demonstrations, has not focused on mobilizing large numbers of women, and, like other post-Soviet social movements, has faced significant barriers to sustaining cooperative interactions between groups, particularly in Moscow. Seen from this perspective, the women's movement is best understood as an unfolding drama, one which sheds light on the dynamics of social movements worldwide, as well as on Russia's difficult democratization process.

1 Russian women's movement groups and activists

In 1985, when Mikhail Gorbachev was selected by his colleagues on the Politburo to become general secretary of the Communist Party of the Soviet Union, there was only one women's organization in Soviet Russia: the Soviet Women's Committee. It was a state-controlled organization, operating under the watchful eye of Communist Party apparatchiks. A decade later, there were hundreds of women's groups, clubs, initiatives, and projects officially registered and operating in Russia. Estimates put the number of unregistered groups at several thousand. Relative to the previous decades of Soviet rule, this increase represented a tremendous surge in civic action, spurred by the political and economic transitions that began in the late 1980s under Gorbachev and continued under Yeltsin's administration. Along with women's groups, a multitude of other "informal" organizations formed, including independent trade unions, a variety of noncommunist political groups, and environmentalist and antinuclear power movements. Emerging from decades of totalitarian[1] control into a chaotic political and economic environment, Russian society was attempting to organize itself.

Women activists had their work cut out for them. And, as though making up for lost time, women began to protest against the economic and political discrimination that seemed to intensify as the transition period wore on. Within a few short years, the single-organization Soviet women's movement had been replaced by a multifaceted spectrum of women's activism.

---

[1] Scholars have used the term "totalitarian" to represent a range of beliefs about the nature of politics under communist (and nazi) rule. Whereas I would not join those scholars who argued that the Soviet state was monolithic and unchanging, I find that the term captures the extent to which the state and Communist Party monopolized the public sphere in the Soviet Union, and employ it descriptively for that purpose. For a concise discussion of the scholarly debate over the accuracy and utility of the totalitarian model, see George Breslauer, "In Defense of Sovietology," *Post-Soviet Affairs*, vol. 8, no. 3 (1992), pp. 197–237.

A brief history of the contemporary Russian women's movement

Early Soviet history is hardly devoid of dedicated women activists. After the 1917 revolution, Alexandra Kollontai and other female Bolsheviks conducted organizational work among women, with the dual intent of mobilizing female support for the new Soviet regime, and ridding society of its "backward" manifestations that helped keep women subordinated to men.[2] In 1919, their efforts crystallized in the creation of the *zhenotdel* – the Women's Department of the Communist Party's Central Committee Secretariat. Local women's departments were established, and *zhenotdel* agitators traveled throughout the country carrying the message of women's liberation, meeting with women in factories, villages, and local bathhouses. Their concerns and activities ranged from politics to maternity care; from ending prostitution and illiteracy to eliminating what Lenin had called "stultifying and crushing [household] drudgery" with the establishment of collective childcare and eating establishments.[3] *Zhenotdel* activists also traveled to remote areas of Central Asia and the Caucasus, encouraging women to discard their veils and reject other patriarchal Muslim practices. Hundreds of newly "liberated" women were attacked and even murdered for their defiance of tradition. The *zhenotdel* activists were widely feared by local men, who opposed, often violently, the efforts of these strange emissaries of the new regime.[4]

From its inception, the *zhenotdel* met with opposition even from within the party: some feared that women's concerns would compete with workers' concerns.[5] In 1930, Stalin decreed that women in the Soviet Union were free, equal, and emancipated, having been liberated by the revolution. His Politburo promptly disbanded the *zhenotdel*.[6] According to the Soviet leadership, women had no further need of women's organizations; such autonomous groupings could only distract

[2] For a lively and detailed study of women revolutionaries, see Barbara Evans Clements, *Bolshevik Women* (Cambridge: Cambridge University Press, 1997). Also see *Alexandra Kollontai: Selected Writings*, trans. with intro. and commentary by Alix Holt (New York: W. W. Norton, 1980).

[3] V. I. Lenin, *The Woman Question* (New York: International Publishers, 1951), p. 56.

[4] Richard Stites recounts the experiences of *zhenotdel* activists in graphic detail. See *The Women's Liberation Movement in Russia* (Princeton: Princeton University Press, 1978), pp. 329–45.

[5] See Gail Lapidus, *Women in Soviet Society: Equality, Development, and Social Change* (Berkeley: University of California Press, 1978), chs. 1, 2; and Mary Buckley, *Women and Ideology in the Soviet Union* (Ann Arbor: University of Michigan Press, 1989), ch. 2.

[6] See Wendy Goldman, "Industrial Politics, Peasant Rebellion and the Death of the Proletarian Women's Movement in the USSR," *Slavic Review*, vol. 55, no. 1 (Spring 1996), p. 63.

women from the process of building communism "cheek by jowl" with men.[7]

Despite Stalin's proclamations, women in the Soviet Union experienced significant discrimination over the course of Soviet rule. Segregated in the labor force into the least-prestigious and lowest-paying jobs and industrial sectors, women were expected to perform all the domestic chores and childrearing tasks as well. This produced a female work week twice as long as men's, which became known as the "double burden." Although there was a quota of 33 percent for women in the Supreme Soviet, which functioned as a rubber-stamp legislature, women were few and far between in the Communist Party bodies that in fact ran the country. Communist rhetoric about equality between men and women was declarative, not reflective of reality.

By the late 1960s, Soviet policy debates had begun to reflect an awareness of these problems.[8] At that time, Communist Party leader Leonid Brezhnev had declared that the Soviet polity, while well on its way toward full-fledged communism, was still struggling with obstacles, labeled "nonantagonistic contradictions." Among these was an apparent conflict between women's productive and reproductive roles.[9] As birth rates fell and economic productivity declined, Soviet analysts openly concluded that the "woman question" had not, in fact, been solved.

The 1970s brought increasing debate over gender roles and sexual equality. Within the Soviet policy community, social scientists argued that women were having difficulty "combining participation in the workforce and in political life with domestic labor."[10] Fear that a declining birth rate would create problems of labor supply in the future drove a variety of policy prescriptions designed to facilitate women's combination of paid labor and household work. Yet, as Mary Buckley persuasively argues, the goal of these debates was to address the effects of women's double burden on economic productivity and the future supply of labor, and not to encourage women's "self-determination" per se.[11]

For the most part, women in the Soviet Union did not unite to protest against sex-based inequality or the double burden. Under Soviet rule, the formation of any organizations independent of the Soviet party-state was strictly forbidden. Whereas independent interest groups and social movement organizations abounded in the West, the Soviet Union – until

---

[7] See Olga Voronina, "Soviet Women and Politics: On the Brink of Change," in Barbara J. Nelson and Najma Chowdhury, eds., *Women and Politics Worldwide* (New Haven: Yale University Press, 1994), p. 728, quoting *Pravda*, March 8, 1936.

[8] For a thorough discussion of these policy debates, see Buckley, *Women and Ideology*, especially chs. 5 and 7.

[9] Ibid., pp. 162–63.   [10] Ibid., p. 161.   [11] Ibid., pp. 187–88.

glasnost and perestroika took root – tolerated only state-run organizations, such as the Soviet Women's Committee. And like the other "mass" organizations of the Soviet era, the Soviet Women's Committee was designed to mobilize the population to carry out party goals, rather than to address women's concerns as such.

After its inception in 1941, when it was founded as an "antifascist" organization, the Soviet Women's Committee remained for five decades the only legal organization said to represent women in the Soviet Union. The attempt by a small group of Soviet women to organize an underground women's journal, in 1979, was swiftly repressed; their editorial collective was forcibly disbanded by the KGB, and several of its members were deported.[12]

Glasnost and perestroika swiftly altered the opportunities available to women who wished to publicly express dissent over their treatment as women in Russian society. Under Gorbachev's new policies, it became legal to assemble in public; to organize groups; to register such organizations with the state; to publish newsletters and journals; and even to start independent political parties. Under these new conditions, women's accumulated frustration over being treated as second-class citizens erupted. In the late 1980s, the seeds of this dissidence took root and flourished in the form of tiny feminist organizations, especially in Moscow and St. Petersburg. These groups took on the function of consciousness-raising clubs.[13] In the early 1990s, another wave of women's organizing took place, this one motivated by the growing economic crisis and rapid reduction in social welfare benefits (such as state-subsidized childcare) that women had come to rely on during the years of Soviet power. A vast number of self-help groups and employment-training organizations formed, trying to bridge the gap that the collapse of the centrally planned welfare state had left behind. In essence, these pragmatically based groups sought to find the resources to perform the tasks that the state had chosen to abandon.

By early 1994, Russia's Ministry of Justice had officially registered over 300 women's groups (a process which enables an organization to open bank accounts and conduct financial transactions, rent office

---

[12] See Robin Morgan, "Foreword," in Tatyana Mamonova, ed., *Women and Russia* (Boston: Beacon Press, 1984), p. ix.

[13] Some of the earliest such groups included Preobrazhenie (Transfiguration; registered in 1990), Klub Garmoniia (Club Harmony; registered in 1990), LOTOS (founded in 1988), and SAFO (Free Association of Feminist Organizations; registered in 1990). See Valentina Konstantinova, "Women's Political Coalitions in Russia (1990–1994)," in Anna Rotkirch and Elina Haavio-Mannila, eds., *Women's Voices in Russia Today* (Brookfield, VT: Dartmouth Publishing, 1996), pp. 235–47.

space, and publish information under its name),[14] and many more existed, operating "unofficially."[15] These organizations ranged from small, local groups to larger national organizations with regional subdivisions, and also included several national-level networks of women's groups, headquartered in Moscow.

The activists leading these varied women's organizations viewed and described themselves as part of a small, emergent women's movement, advocating on women's behalf. They were conscious of and objected to pervasive discrimination against women, and engaged in a wide variety of movement activities attempting to raise women's political, economic, and social status in Russian society. Russian women's movement groups have lobbied the Supreme Soviet and its parliamentary successor, the Russian Duma, as well as local legislatures; campaigned on behalf of women politicians; organized large conferences involving hundreds of women, starting in 1991; held fairs and other charity events providing material assistance to women and children; organized self-help groups and consultation/support services in order to combat rising unemployment and the declining availability of daycare and other social services; organized employment-training, business-management, and leadership-training programs for women; created support groups for single mothers, women artists, and women entrepreneurs; held countless roundtables, seminars, and lectures on feminism and women's issues; established rape crisis and domestic violence hotlines; founded a women's radio station; conducted self-esteem workshops for women and other consciousness-raising activities; published and distributed women's publications (largely small-run newsletters and journals); conducted research on women; lobbied the media to cover women's issues and movement events more extensively; organized occasional pickets and small demonstrations; and, last but not least, registered their organizations – itself no small achievement in the labyrinthine bureaucracy of the Russian Ministry of Justice.

Russia's emerging women's organizations catalogued themselves with the state over a period of several years, beginning in October 1990, when it became legal to constitute an "informal" organization and register it with the Soviet government. In early 1991, the government of the Russian Republic passed its own law on the formation and registration of autonomous organizations. This registration process was

---

[14] On registration, see Kathleen E. Smith, *Remembering Stalin's Victims* (Ithaca: Cornell University Press, 1996), p. 117.

[15] Ol'ga Samarina, interview, March 24, 1995. Also, see "Doklad o vypolnenii v Rossiiskoi Federatsii Konventsii o likvidatsii vsekh form diskriminatsii v otnoshenii zhenshchin: chetvertyi periodicheskii doklad (predstavlen v sootvetstvii so stat'ei 18 Konventsii)" (Moscow: Ministry of Social Protection, 1994), p. 24.

"complicated and subject to arbitrary interpretation by officials."[16] Nevertheless, women's organizations took advantage of the new laws, and registered in increasing numbers. SAFO, the Free Association of Feminist Organizations (in reality, a small group of feminists, which later changed its name to FALTA – the Feminist Alternative), claimed to be the first openly feminist organization to have been officially registered. They achieved this status in fall 1990, and soon set about conducting consciousness-raising groups and seminars for women, publishing their occasional journal (*FemInf*), and helping to organize and sponsor the first national conference of independent women's organizations.[17] Others followed quickly.[18]

Despite obstacles to networking that have arisen and been exacerbated during the transition period, these nascent organizations were not completely isolated from each other. The first major opportunity for networking among women's groups independent of the state in the former Soviet Union arose in March 1991 at a national conference called the First Independent Women's Forum, which was followed by a second Forum in late 1992. Both of these were held in Dubna, a town on the outskirts of Moscow. The organizers labeled the Forums "Independent" to stress their identity independent of the Soviet state, the Communist Party, men, and the official Soviet Women's Committee. The Forums represented new opportunities for contact between activists from feminist-identified organizations and those from the economically oriented groups. Given the shortcomings of the Soviet and post-Soviet communications infrastructure, such national meetings provided rare opportunities for women activists to network and share information about their organizations' activities. National conferences, sponsored by independent women's movement networks (and also by the Russian government) in recent years have perpetuated these otherwise limited networking opportunities.

On the basis of such contacts, between 1991 and 1995 four separate (but in places, overlapping) networks of women's organizations appeared in Moscow. Out of the two Forums emerged a network of activists and women's organizations operating independently of the state, called the Independent Women's Forum (IWF), which maintained an aura of independence and radicalism. In 1993, the Women's League, also a nonhierarchical network of organizations that came

---

[16] M. Steven Fish, *Democracy from Scratch* (Princeton: Princeton University Press, 1995), pp. 59–60.

[17] Marina Regentova and Natal'ia Abubikirova, no title, unpublished typescript, Moscow, 1995.

[18] Of the registered organizations in my sample, three registered in 1990, ten in 1991, ten in 1992 (the peak for registration in Moscow), six in 1993, and eight in 1994.

together after a conference ("Women and the Market Economy," held in Moscow in 1992), was established. While the Women's League, like the IWF, was formed independent of the state, it was viewed as more establishment-oriented and less radical than the IWF (not pursuing, for example, issues like violence against women). In 1991, with the collapse of the Soviet Union, the Soviet Women's Committee (SWC) disappeared and was replaced in Russia by the Union of Russia's Women (URW). The URW was an umbrella network including numerous smaller women's councils, as well as independent, pragmatically oriented women's organizations operating under its aegis. Although the URW (unlike the SWC) was no longer supported directly by the state, it was nonetheless perceived by independent women's groups as being part of the state system and, thus, as nonindependent. The fourth network was a joint operation between women's organizations in the United States and the former Soviet Union (mostly in Russia), called the US–NIS Consortium and established in 1994. The Consortium, with Western funding and leadership, brought together members of the Women's League and the IWF in a somewhat uneasy coalition which later became transformed into a Russian-operated network, headed by one of the founders of the Women's League. Despite conflicts and disagreements, as of 1995, all the networks shared the goal of improving women's status in Russia, all were to varying degrees involved in politics, and all asserted their independence from the state.[19]

In the mid-1990s, the women's groups operating in Russia ranged in size from tiny groups of friends to organizations with branches in dozens of Russian regions boasting memberships of several thousand. Many of these groups were affiliated with one (or more) of the women's movement organizational networks in Moscow. This flowering of women's organizations in a country where nonstate organizations had been illegal until the mid-1980s is remarkable, both for its speed and its extent.

The Russian women's movement has been in many ways Moscow-centered.[20] As Russia's capital, Moscow is where lobbying and other forms of mobilization aimed at changing policies at the national level (such as Russia-wide women's conferences) tend to take place. Moscow's women's movement is complex, with dozens of active organizations focusing on consciousness-raising, employment training, professional

---

[19] Linda Racioppi and Katherine O'Sullivan See provide information on the history of three of these networks – the IWF, the URW, and the Women's League – as well as background information on some of the leaders of these networks in *Women's Activism in Contemporary Russia* (Philadelphia: Temple University Press, 1997).

[20] St. Petersburg also has a rich tradition of women's organizing. See Jane Berthusen Gottlick, "Organizations in the New Russia: Women in St. Petersburg" (dissertation, University of South Carolina, 1996).

support, violence against women, political advocacy, and more. Also, Moscow serves as the site for the headquarters of many "national" and "interregional" women's movement organizations (those with branches in other cities), as well as being home to local Moscow women's groups and the main women's movement networks mentioned above. Russia's vastness and diversity makes it inadvisable to generalize about the "Russian" women's movement purely on the basis of the movement as it appears in Moscow. Moscow is, however, the city with the largest number of women's organizations, the highest frequency of women's movement events, and many of the most politically oriented women's organizations in Russia.

This book explores two additional cities – Ivanovo and Cheboksary – that permit a more representative peek at the women's movement outside Moscow and Russia's other major urban centers. Ivanovo lies about six hours northeast of Moscow by train, and is dominated by the textile industry. Cheboksary is the capital of the ethnic republic of Chuvashiia, situated on the Volga river about midway between Moscow and the Ural mountains, over fifteen hours by train away from Russia's capital.

The three cities are characterized by several important differences which affect their women's movements. Both Ivanovo and Cheboksary are much smaller than Moscow, with populations of about 400,000 and 500,000 respectively, compared to Moscow's approximately 9 million. Indeed, Ivanovo, because of its female-dominated textile industry, was known during the Soviet period as the "city of brides." The pace of life in Cheboksary and Ivanovo is slower than that in the capital. The provincial cities are observably poorer than Moscow, and relatively less affected by the influx of imported goods, conspicuous consumption, and the renaming of streets and city squares to erase and repudiate the Soviet communist past. The three cities are located at varying distances from both political reforms and contact with the West, with Moscow residents having the highest rate of contact with Westerners and Western ideas. By contrast, in Cheboksary, a foreigner is still regarded as something of a novelty. Ivanovo is significantly closer to Moscow; Ivanovites can travel to Moscow more frequently than can residents of Cheboksary. Additionally, the three regions suffer from different degrees of unemployment and industrial collapse: the lowest unemployment rate is found in Moscow province, and the highest in Ivanovo province, with the republic of Chuvashiia in between, but much closer to Ivanovo's level. Finally, the cities differ on an ethnic basis. Cheboksary is the capital of a republic populated largely by people of Chuvash nationality, with a minority Russian population. By contrast, Ivanovo and Moscow are Russian-dominated, although Moscow, as the capital of the former

Soviet Union, is ethnically quite diverse. Despite these important differences, the basic desire to improve women's status was a driving force behind organizing in all three areas.

Indigenous organizations, civil society, and the formation of Russian women's movement groups

What were the roots of the women's organizations in these three cities? On what basis were they founded, and what enabled them to come together so rapidly between the end of the 1980s and mid-1990s?

Social movements tend to form and grow on the basis of networks and existing civic associations, sometimes referred to as "indigenous organizations." It is through such organizations that social movement networks form, allowing the movement to expand by recruiting new adherents.

The role played by indigenous organizations is complicated in the Russian case because of the paucity of civic organizations that existed under Soviet rule. "Civil society," a realm located theoretically between the "state" and the private sphere of household, family, and friendships, was largely absent from Soviet and post-Soviet Russian society. Public participation in civic associations was restricted to participating in the "mass" organizations run by the Communist Party – these ranged from trade unions to peace committees to the Soviet Women's Committee – all monitored by and responsible to state functionaries. This absence of civil society has restricted networking and movement expansion along associational lines, and not only for the women's movement. People inclined toward nonstate activism, once it became permitted in the late 1980s, had limited arenas in which to conduct popular outreach, beyond the state-run organizations.

These state-run organizations did serve, after a fashion, as indigenous organizations which formed the basis for social movement networking. The Soviet Women's Committee (SWC), and the women's councils (*zhensovety*) under its auspices, acted as incubators for women's groups that later emerged as organizations no longer run by the state. For example, a women's political club was allowed to form within the SWC in 1990; one of its founders later went on to form her own organization, the Women's Alliance. Numerous women's councils, which existed in factories as well as territorially (at the district, city, and provincial level) also developed independent streaks, and transformed themselves into "informals" – independent, nonstate associations.[21]

---

[21] Elena Zabadykina, "Zhenskie organizatsii sankt-peterburga," *Vse liudi sestry*, no. 5, 1996, p. 9.

Some of the women's councils remained part of the SWC, but were nonetheless quite strong and active in their communities; the Ivanovo city *zhensovet* (now the City Union of Women) is only one example of such an organization.[22]

Other state- and party-run organizations, including the Komsomol (the Soviet youth organization) and the party structures themselves, also produced activists who, in the late Gorbachev era, were eager to apply their energies and organizing skills to the creation of "informals." State-run academic institutions also served as a source of activists for late Soviet-era social movements. In this somewhat counterintuitive sense, the Soviet legacy of monopolistic, centralized, state- and party-run institutions thus assisted in the creation of civil society during the transition period.

Analysis of women's organization formation in Moscow, Cheboksary, and Ivanovo reveals that, absent civic organizations through which to recruit, the women's groups formed mostly on the basis of friendship networks, acquaintanceship through the workplace (though not through trade unions) or work-related professional activity (attendance at conferences), as well as through participation in Soviet-era organizations related to the state or Communist Party. The latter was the mode most often found in Cheboksary and Ivanovo, particularly because several leading activists there had worked for party- and state-related structures. Across the three cities, approximately one-third of the organizations were formed on the basis of personal acquaintanceship, friendship, or attendance at the same educational institution. The leaders of another third of the organizations met as colleagues in the workplace, at professional meetings, or conferences. A handful became acquainted through work in women's councils, the Soviet Women's Committee, the Communist Party, or the Komsomol, and a few formed their organizations by running ads in a newspaper, or after meeting like-minded women at women's movement events. Several of the leaders interviewed pointed to the fact that their having come together with other women, with whom they would later form an organization, had been purely "accidental" or happenstance.

Although friendship and collegial ties created effective core activists in Russia's women's movement (as is often the case in social movements), it becomes evident, when considering the possibilities for the expansion of the women's movement into broader society, that such expansion would require attracting new adherents to already existing organizations

---

[22] On the history of the Ivanovo women's council (up to 1989), see Genia Browning, "The Zhensovety Revisited," in Mary Buckley, ed., *Perestroika and Soviet Women* (Cambridge: Cambridge University Press, 1992), pp. 97–117.

and networks. Here, the Soviet legacy of minimal civic institutions again becomes relevant. Many of the women's movement organizations retained very small numbers of activists and members; their core group remained the same as the original group of founders and, often, the organization itself did not exceed that core group. The continued absence of popular indigenous civic organizations, which could play a recruitment role similar to that of black churches during the US civil rights movement, makes networking and increasing the size of extant organizations difficult. Civic networks (e.g., the human rights movement, the environmental movement, and the independent labor movement) are relatively new to the Russian scene. They may serve as breeding grounds for women's movement adherents in the future, especially as the paths of activists from those organizations cross with those of feminist activists at training sessions and seminars designed for leaders of civic associations.[23]

The overall level of civic organization in society determines, to some degree, the potential paths and access points through which new participants can be mobilized. Russia's largest cities, like Moscow and St. Petersburg, provide the most opportunities for movement expansion, through parallel movements, local conferences, and contacts with other regional activists at national conferences. Considerably more rural areas like Chuvashiia, operating with a lesser degree of nonstate organization in general, present fewer opportunities for recruitment and, thus, their organizations may remain smaller.

Finally, social movement researchers have claimed that women's movement expansion (beyond those people who already consider women's rights to be highly important or salient to them personally) is facilitated by membership in civic associations and labor force participation. In the United States, these have proven to be an important means by which women who consider women's rights to be relatively "less important" nevertheless become involved in feminist activism (by donating money to women's movement organizations, for example).[24] In Russia, the expansion of the movement's participant base may prove difficult given the limited degree of popular membership in other civic associations (through which to recruit), and the decline (in recent years)

---

[23] Valentina Konstantinova, interview, July 9, 1995. Women may also find themselves attracted to the women's movement after encountering sexism within other social movements, as was the case for some women in the civil rights and New Left movements in the United States. See Sara Evans, *Personal Politics* (New York: Random House, 1980).

[24] Pat Dewey Dauphinais, Steven E. Barkan, and Steven F. Cohn, "Predictors of Rank-and-File Feminist Activism: Evidence from the 1983 General Social Survey," *Social Problems*, vol. 39, no. 4 (November 1992), pp. 332–44.

of women's labor force participation. For the present, however, the organizations constituting the Russian women's movement are not apparently concerned with expanding their numbers; they are more occupied with pursuing their goals and attempting to initiate social change on their chosen issues through methods that do not require mass membership and mobilization.

Types of women's organizations in Russia

What kinds of organizations now populate the growing Russian women's movement? What are their primary concerns? What issues do they focus on, and what are their goals?

Given the decline in women's economic status during the early 1990s, it comes as no surprise that a significant number of groups are concerned precisely with employment issues. These include women's job-training programs, often in conjunction with a local branch of the federal employment services, such as Ivanovo's Center for the Social Support of Women and Families, or Moscow's Center for the Social Support of Women (operating under the Union of Russia's Women). Such organizations frequently teach courses in embroidery, handicrafts, and sewing, or accounting, governess training, and, sometimes, business skills. This category also includes groups of businesswomen (new entrepreneurs) who mentor and provide support to one another, such as the Cheboksary-based Women's Initiative club, or Moscow's Dzhenklub (Businesswomen's Club). Other groups, including the Association of Women Entrepreneurs, seek to provide jobs for women by promoting and developing women's entrepreneurship.[25] This category also includes women in some of the industries hardest hit by the economic crisis, such as the defense industry, which lost major government contracts during the transition period and has been faced with high levels of female unemployment, especially in research institutes. The main group representing that subcategory is the association Conversion and Women.

Also present are a large number of mutual support groups for mothers in a variety of categories. These include groups for single mothers, mothers of many children (usually three or more), and mothers of disabled children. This category also includes charitable organizations intended to help the neediest people, among whom women and children constitute the majority. Belonging to this group are large organizations like the International Association of Russian Women-Mothers, who

[25] Tat'iana Maliutina, interview, April 25, 1995.

raise money to send sick children from across the former Soviet Union to Italy for healthcare and rest, and many *zhensovety*, some of which have reorganized on a private basis, like Women of Krasnaia Presnia, a former district women's council in Moscow. The latter organization distributes material aid (in the form of fabric, soap, and other household necessities), and holds celebratory events on holidays, from March 8th (International Women's Day) to Children's Defense Day, Blockade Defenders' Day, and Easter.[26] These organizations, like the Committee of Soldiers' Mothers (perhaps the most well-known women's organization in Russia, dedicated to ensuring the observance of human rights within the Russian army, helping young men leave the army, lobbying for alternative service, and speaking out against wars), are devoted not so much to altering women's status at the societal level as to supporting families and children.

Other types of support groups exist for professional women in various fields, including: SANTA (for women in law enforcement); Women with a University Education (RAUW); the Association of Women Journalists; and the Association of Women [Film and Theater] Directors. The leader of the latter group explained that her organization was needed for material support, helping to finance women directors' projects, and also for psychological support, "So women [in this field] won't feel like they're alone."[27] Lesbian support organizations now exist, such as MOLLI, the Moscow Organization of Lesbian Literature and Art.[28]

The last few years have seen the development of women's crisis services, including hotlines for victims of rape and domestic violence, in nearly every major Russian city (e.g., the "Sisters" Rape Crisis Center, and the Moscow Crisis Center for Women). Consciousness-raising organizations, such as the feminist co-counseling group, Feminist Alternative (FALTA), and Klub Garmoniia (Club Harmony), and monthly lecture groups that invite people to speak about their research on women, such as Klub F-1 (First Feminist Club), also operate in the capital.

Other women's groups are associated with political parties. These include Women for Social Democracy, whose goals include involving more women in political decisionmaking, and "uniting women on the basis of social-democratic values,"[29] and the hardline communist Congress of Soviet Women.[30]

---

[26] Nina Tiuliulina, interview, May 22, 1995.
[27] Elena Demeshina, interview, March 26, 1995.
[28] Interview, November 27, 1994.
[29] Interview, November 22, 1994.
[30] Natal'ia Belokopytova, interview, May 12, 1995.

Finally, a few women's groups (e.g., Equality and Peace), research centers (e.g., the Moscow Center for Gender Studies – MCGS), and network-organizations (the aforementioned Women's League, the Inform Center of the Independent Women's Forum, and the Union of Russia's Women) include specialists on women's issues; they lobby state officials and conduct advocacy work on women's issues, as well as providing information and networking opportunities to women's organizations across Russia by holding seminars and national conferences.

Conceptual frameworks for categorizing women's organizations

The spectrum of women's movement organizing in Russia is quite extensive. On what dimensions or axes can the groups best be analyzed? Some theorists of women's movement organizing make an analytical division between "practical" and "strategic" groups, where the former are occupied with addressing immediate needs, and the latter are focused directly on the long-term goals of undermining institutionalized discrimination and sexism (such organizations are usually described as "feminist").[31] This framework may be criticized on several levels. First, there seems to be an inherent bias toward privileging "strategic" groups as the ones that are necessarily most "feminist," a distinction that, especially outside the First World, seems artificial.[32] Secondly, many women's organizations cross the line between ostensibly "practical" and "strategic" goals. Certainly, this is true in contemporary Russia, particularly because of women's increasingly poor economic conditions. For instance, some organizations adopt multiple goals, hoping to assist women in the short term with job training (practical activities), and also trying to alter discriminatory hiring policies in the longer term, by lobbying (strategic activities). It is difficult to categorize such organizations along this binary spectrum. Thirdly, the distinction between short-term (practical) and long-term (strategic) methods of acting on women's behalf appears fundamentally to be false. Whatever the methods used – whether "practical," such as enrolling particular women

[31] Such a distinction, between "strategic" and "practical" groups in the Brazilian women's movement, is made by Sonia Alvarez. See her "Women's Movements and Gender Politics in the Brazilian Transition," in Jane Jaquette, ed., *The Women's Movement in Latin America* (Boston: Unwin Hyman, 1989), pp. 28–29. Alvarez bases her distinction on Maxine Molyneux's description of strategic and practical "gender interests." See Molyneux, "Mobilization Without Emancipation?: Women's Interests, the State, and Revolution in Nicaragua," *Feminist Studies*, vol. 11, no. 2 (Summer 1985), pp. 232–33.

[32] I am grateful to Myra Marx Ferree for her criticism of this dichotomy.

in an employment-retraining program, or "strategic," such as lobbying for enforcement of gender-neutral hiring practices – it seems that the underlying goal is the same: to prevent instances of discrimination, and to improve women's social status, both of which are ostensibly the work of "strategic" organizations.

Moreover, the leaders of Russia's self-help and support groups (which might be conceived of as "practical") recognize and name sex-based discrimination as a problem, suggesting that they share the goals and understandings of "strategic" groups. Nor do the "practical" groups avoid political channels as their means of seeking influence and social change. Finally, the fact that women leaders from groups of both categories overwhelmingly agree that women experience discrimination in contemporary Russian society suggests that their struggle is a strategic (or "feminist") one, whether or not they choose to adopt that label. In sum, perhaps particularly during political and economic transition periods, the practical and the strategic are conflated.

The distinction, however, is useful as a descriptive shorthand in the Russian case. Strategic groups include those organizations occupied with promoting (largely) liberal feminism and women's empowerment (for example, the advocacy organizations, women's research centers, and consciousness-raising groups), although the latter are not necessarily interested in political participation or lobbying. Their overt intention is to improve women's status and/or struggle against discrimination in the long term. The practical groups, by contrast, are those trying to take up the slack resulting from the collapse of the state welfare system by organizing, through cooperation, to combat women's immediate problems (this category includes business-training and employment centers, charities, single-mothers' groups, and so on). Throughout the text, I refer to "pragmatic" organizations as those that focus mostly on issues of women's and families' welfare during the economic transition period. This use of the terms is not meant to suggest a sharp analytical distinction between "strategic" and "practical," but rather is a means of denoting the overall issue-focus of the organizations.

For analytical purposes, the women's movement organizations in this text can best be categorized on the following set of dimensions:

1. Issue-focus: What issues is the organization primarily concerned about? What are its main goals and purposes?
2. Politicization: Does the organization seek to influence the state, either by getting resources from it or by affecting policies? Or does it not posit such a goal?
3. Is the organization identified with the state historically or not?

4. At what level (municipal, regional, interregional, national, international) does the organization operate?
5. When was the organization founded and/or registered?
6. What size is the organization? Who belongs to it?

In table 1, I have divided the organizations in my sample into six major categories – those occupied with advocacy; self-help and support; consciousness-raising; opposition to violence against women; cultural promotion; and publishing. Despite variation in their specific concerns, almost all of the women's movement organizations referred to in this text share the same underlying goal, namely, altering women's status, understood broadly. Some organizations work to change women's status temporarily or on an individual basis (those organizations that engage in activism on "pragmatic" issues, the self-help and mutual support groups, and the women's crisis centers and hotlines). Although some of the self-help and mutual support organizations may not challenge the social order explicitly, even those groups operating within limited parameters are changing women's status – one woman at a time. Other groups seek to change women's status over the long term, with an eye toward overtly critiquing the division of labor in society, gender roles, patriarchy, and so on (these include the organizations that engage in lobbying on issues of sex-based discrimination, the research organizations, and the consciousness-raising groups).[33]

From table 1, where a number of groups appear in more than one location, it is evident that many organizations set multiple goals. This suggests that there are more issues and problems that people seek to resolve or address than there are groups to handle them. It also suggests that groups have not become narrowly specialized (although specialization may develop later as the movement expands). While several relatively narrow interest groups have emerged, many organizations have adopted a range of goals, issues, and strategies, and are striving to improve women's status along a variety of lines simultaneously. Thirty percent of the organizations in the table cross several boundaries, including the Union of Russia's Women (URW) network, which engages in both political advocacy and charity work across the country.

Organizational desire to influence the state (or the degree of "politicization") provides another dimension along which to categorize these groups. The politicization issue supplies little variation. Only 25 percent of the organizations interviewed stated that they neither influence the

---

[33] Even the Congress of Soviet Women, a hardline communist group, sought to alter the status quo for women ("to defend women's rights"), although their organization's main concern was an ideological one ("to reestablish the Soviet Union on a socialist basis"): Natal'ia Belokopytova, interview, May 12, 1995.

Table 1. *Groups by type and specific issue-focus*

Specific focus	Names of groups (Moscow-based unless otherwise noted)
	Advocacy
Discrimination issues	Equality and Peace; Inform Center of the IWF; URW; Women's League; Women for Social Democracy; Dzhenklub; MCGS; Association "Women and Development"; Center for Issues of Women, Family, and Gender Studies, at the Youth Institute
Pragmatic welfare issues	Cheboksary city *zhensovet*; Chuvash republic *zhensovet*; City Union of Women (Ivanovo); Single-Parent Families Committee (Ivanovo); Klub Delovaia Zhenshchina (Ivanovo); Women's Liberal Fund; Congress of Soviet Women
	Self-help and support
Job training	URW; Center for Social Support of Women and Families (Ivanovo); Urals Association of Women
For professionals	*Arts*: Sofia; Tvorchestvo; MOLLI; Association of Women [Film and Theater] Directors. *Law enforcement*: SANTA. *Defense industry*: Conversion and Women. *Women with a university education*: Association of University Women; Association of University Women (Chuvash branch).
Entrepreneurship	Dzhenklub; Association of Women Entrepreneurs; Perepodgotovka; Women's Liberal Fund; Women's Alliance; Innovation Fund; Businesswomen's Club (Ivanovo); Klub Zhenskaia Initsiativa (Cheboksary); Urals Association of Women (Ekaterinburg); Confederation of Businesswomen of Russia (Ekaterinburg)
For women as mothers	Tolko Mamy; Committee of Single-Parent Families (Ivanovo), Committee of Multi-Child Families (Ivanovo)
For families and children	Committee of Soldiers' Mothers; Association of Russian Women Mothers; Preobrazhenie; Society "Women of Presnia"
Charity	Association of University Women (Chuvash branch); Cheboksary city *zhensovet*; Chuvash republic *zhensovet*; City Union of Women (Ivanovo); Committee of Single-Parent Families (Ivanovo); Committee Multi-Child Families (Ivanovo); Congress of Soviet Women; Women's Alliance; URW; Society "Women of Presnia"
For lesbians	MOLLI
Consulting and advice for women	Cheboksary city *zhensovet*; Chuvash republic *zhensovet*; City Union of Women (Ivanovo); Committee of Single-Parent Families (Ivanovo); Women's Liberal Fund; SANTA; Center for Women's Initiatives
	Consciousness-raising
Groups	Feminist Alternative; Klub Garmoniia
Lectures	Preobrazhenie; Klub F-1

Table 1 *(contd)*

Specific focus	Names of groups (Moscow-based unless otherwise noted)
Societal	Association of Women Journalists; Feminist Orientation Center; Association "Women and Development"; Dzhenklub
	Anti-violence against women
	"Sisters" Rape Crisis Center; Moscow Crisis Center for Women
	Culture
	Salam Bi (Cheboksary)
	Publishing
	Moscow Center for Gender Studies; Petersburg Center for Gender Issues; Inform Center of the IWF; Archive–Database–Library project; Preobrazhenie; Center for Women's Initiatives

state nor want to influence the state (such influence falls outside the scope of their organizational goals). Falling into this category are several self-help and mutual support organizations: the Ivanovo Center for Social Support of Women and Families, the Moscow-based Association of Women [Film and Theater] Directors, the Center for Women's Initiatives, the single-mothers' association Tolko Mamy (Only Moms), SANTA (for women in law enforcement), and the lesbian support group, MOLLI. Likewise, the anti-violence groups (e.g., the Moscow Crisis Center for Women and "Sisters" Rape Crisis Center) were not seeking influence over the state; they, like several of the consciousness-raising organizations (Klub Garmoniia, the Feminist Orientation Center) and the mutual support groups, were more interested in individual work with women than with policy change.

Viewed from the other side, however, 75 percent of the organizations interviewed (across the cities) posited influencing the state in some way as a goal. This shared emphasis on influencing the state (whether to alter policies, or to obtain resources such as office space or funding for job-training programs) may be due to the state's historical monopoly and top-down distribution of resources. The concentration of resources and control over their distribution by the state continues to a certain extent today, especially with regard to obtaining office space and the granting of privileges to nonprofit organizations.

On the third dimension, historical affiliation with the Soviet party-state, considerably more subjectivity enters the picture. The Union of Russia's Women (URW), having stemmed from the Soviet Women's

Committee, was thereby formerly linked to the Soviet party-state, as were the many *zhensovety* across the country. Currently, however, they are no longer "official" state bodies. Although the categories are no longer objectively descriptive, terms like "independent women's movement" have been appropriated by the groups in the IWF and Women's League, and modifiers like "official" and "nomenklatura" (elite–bureaucratic) are still applied to the state-derived groups like the URW and the *zhensovety*. Most of the women's movement organizations today have a large stake in not being perceived as "state" or coopted bodies, which makes the use of these terms contested and complex.

On the registration dimension, the organizations vary widely. A number of organizations remain unregistered for various reasons.[34] Some are based in academic institutes, and have not restructured themselves as independent nonprofit organizations. Others are denied registration because of homophobic discrimination (e.g., MOLLI). Some groups have no need of registration in order to conduct their activities (the consciousness-raising group Klub F-1, for example), or cannot afford the costs. For those organizations that are registered, registration includes the following categories: those that registered under the auspices of another organization previously registered (and thus could engage in transactions through that organization), labeled "within another organization"; those registered at the municipal level; at the regional level (either at the *oblast* (provincial) level or at the republic level, in the case of several groups in Chuvashiia, which is a constituent republic of the Russian Federation); the interregional level (a category created for organizations having an insufficient number of branches throughout Russia to qualify as a national or "all-Russian" organization); the national ("all-Russian") level; and the "international" level (organizations with branches abroad, or which are joint Russian–foreign organizations). Tables 4 and 5 in the appendix (pp. 273 and 275) provide specific information on organizations' dates of formation and/or registration, as well as registration level.

The size of the organizations in my sample varied widely, from a handful of members to several thousand across Russia. Table 6, in the appendix (p. 277), lists the organizations by the size of their memberships (individuals) and by city. A number of the organizations had collective as well as individual members. The collective members are in some cases women's businesses, enterprises, and other women's

---

[34] In my sample, of fifty organizations in four cities (Cheboksary, Ekaterinburg, Ivanovo, Moscow), thirty-nine were registered; and eight were unregistered. The status of the remaining three could not be ascertained.

organizations. The larger organizations are most often Russia-wide, or "interregional." As one would expect, the consciousness-raising groups are relatively small, as are the groups in Cheboksary and Ivanovo (compared to those based in Moscow, several of which are organizations with multiple branches in other cities). Some of the organizations (especially those based in academic institutes) do not have members as such; in those cases the staff members serve as the organization's activists and leaders.

In some instances, the label "membership organization" does not entirely capture the nature of the groups in question. Women's councils (zhensovety), for example, although they have members (and usually a core subset make up a presidium), do not seem to devote energy to recruiting many more members. Indeed, with exceptions, most of the smaller organizations (100 individual members or fewer) interviewed appeared to have attained a comfortable size; it seemed from interviews and participant observation that outreach to new members was not high on their organizational agenda. In general, the group leaders did not tend overall to maintain precise data about their organizations' membership; many informants guessed as to the size of the membership, or presented a range in which they believed the membership size fell. The very fact that leaders were not fastidious about keeping membership data only emphasizes the point that membership outreach was not, on average, a priority of these women's movement groups.

Activists

The leaders of these organizations constituted a diverse collection of women. By profession, the largest number of group leaders (twenty) were involved somehow in academia, either in research or teaching. The second biggest group (sixteen) comprised women whose main form of work (whether paid or unpaid) was leadership of their women's group (or work as part of its staff). Eight activists worked in radio, publishing, or journalism; four in the creative arts; five for parliamentary deputies or for analytical centers affiliated with the parliament; two were in law. One activist was an engineer, another worked for the Ministry of the Interior, and one had set up a business in the private sector. This distribution of occupations suggests that, on the whole, the activists were trained in highly skilled jobs that required a good deal of facility in self-expression.

The activists, many of whom were working full-time in addition to pursuing their activism, also had families and children. Of sixty-six activists for whom data was available on this question, 85 percent had at least one child.[35] The plurality of activists had only one child; this is not atypical for Russians living in large cities. Activists outside Moscow (in Cheboksary and Ivanovo) tended to have more children on average; Nina Temnikova, with ten children, was the soft-spoken leader of the Ivanovo Committee of Multi-Child Families. Ten activists had grand-children. The activists' children ranged in age from three to forty-two.

The majority (62 percent) of the activists interviewed were married (thirty-eight of sixty-one for whom I have answers to this question), though a significant number of them were divorced and living without a partner (16 percent), and six of those married were on second and third marriages (26 percent had been divorced at some point). Only five of the activists were single; six were widowed; and one was living with a female lover.

In age, the activists ranged from twenty-seven to sixty-five, but 58 percent fell between the ages of forty-one and fifty-five.[36] Only eight activists of sixty-six (12 percent) were aged thirty-five and under. The dedication of the activists in their thirties and forties, many of whom were juggling children, jobs, and activism, was impressive. The energy level of the activists over fifty (despite the rigors of daily life in Russia) was also striking. Several of them explained that it was only after their children had grown up that they were able to devote so much time and energy to activism; even so, some were criticized by their families for their movement activity.

The activists were also very well educated. Forty-one percent had graduate degrees, and all but one had obtained at least a college-level education. Such high levels of education on average exceed that of the female population considerably.[37] It is often the best-educated groups in society who are capable of and interested in expressing the needs of a population group, and who may have the spare time in which to do so. Moreover, it is precisely this group of women (the educated specialists) who, during the early years of the transition period, were suffering most from unemployment, and therefore may have been inspired to take action collectively against that phenomenon.

---

[35] Table 7 in the appendix (p. 279) provides more detail on the activists' number of children.

[36] A handful of activists were hesitant to reveal their ages; I approximated in a few cases. Statistics were calculated on the basis of activist age at time of interview (1994–95).

[37] As of a mini-census conducted in 1994, approximately 21 percent of women between the ages of twenty-five and forty-nine had attained a higher education; for women between fifty and fifty-four, it was 15.5 percent, for women between fifty-five and fifty-nine, 12.5 percent, and women between sixty and sixty-four, only 8.5 percent. See *Zhenshchiny Rossii: statisticheskii sbornik* (Moscow: Goskomstat Rossii, 1995), p. 77. Consult table 8 in the appendix (p. 279) for a breakdown of activists' education levels.

Group membership

Who, according to the activists, belongs to their organizations; what types of women constitute the membership?[38] Based on data from the leaders of women's groups, the rough average age of these organizations' membership was forty-one. This suggests that the leadership of these organizations is older on average than the membership; the average age of the sixty-three women's group leaders who reported their own ages was forty-eight. No significant difference in the age of membership across the case study cities appeared. Among the groups concerned primarily with support for women with children, the age of the mothers associated with the groups (at thirty to thirty-five) tended to be younger than that of other groups' membership on average.

Similarly, the leaders of the organizations reported having more education on average than their membership. The difference in education between leaders and members was not vast, however; around 80 percent of groups whose leaders had data on this question were composed of women with at least a higher education (half of these were organizations some of whose members also held advanced degrees), and only a handful of organizations' membership was reported as lacking a higher education on average. Again, the educated specialists were most prone to lead and to join women's organizations of all types. Given the formation of so many organizations through ties at work, and through friendship, it seems sensible that women of similar ages and educational backgrounds would cluster into these movement groups.

Organizational overlap and networking

There is a good deal of overlap between the membership (and even leadership) of these organizations.[39] Moscow activist Elena Ershova, indefatigable and outspoken at sixty years of age, perhaps topped the list:

I belong to many organizations: Women's League, as the co-chair; [I am] president of the Women's Center, Geia; a member of Women in Global Security (WINGS), and of Women in International Security; chair of the Russian division of the International Women's Forum – an organization of women

---

[38] Table 9, in the appendix (p. 279), lists data on age, education, and occupation gleaned from interviews about organizational membership.

[39] The Inform Center of the IWF, for example, comprised women who also led other organizations, including: Eleonora Ivanova, Conversion and Women; Marina Liborakina and Tat'iana Konysheva, the Feminist Orientation Center; Nina Gabrielian, Sof'ia and Preobrazhenie; and Tat'iana Klimenkova, Preobrazhenie and MCGS.

leaders, including Margaret Thatcher, Sandra O'Connor, and others; and a member of Klub F-1.[40]

In Cheboksary, Nina Petrova, long-standing activist and chair of the city *zhensovet*, was among the founders of the city's new Women's Initiative Club. In Ivanovo, Olga Khasbulatova (a learned historian of Russia's pre- and post-revolutionary women's movement), in addition to initiating the Ivanovo Center for the Social Support of Women and Families, was also a member of the Businesswomen's Club in Ivanovo, and part of the URW's administration in Moscow. Leaders of 41 percent of the organizations interviewed in Moscow belonged personally to other women's groups, and twenty-two activists in the three cities combined reported that their organizations belonged to at least one of the women's networks (the URW, the Women's League, and the IWF). Such crosscutting individual memberships (and organizational affiliations with multiple coalitions) within social movements are common phenomena in other countries as well, especially in smaller cities.

The leaders of Russia's women's organizations routinely appeared at women's movement events, whether or not their organization belonged to the network or group sponsoring the occasion (usually lectures, seminars, or conferences). Such events provided opportunities for networking, information exchange, and even consciousness-raising. The monthly lectures at Klub F-1 probably attracted the largest number of leaders of other organizations in Moscow.[41] Similarly, a seminar in Cheboksary, sponsored by the Chuvash branch of the Russian Association of University Women, attracted (by invitation) the leaders of the city and republic women's councils, and a founder of the new Women's Initiative Club.

Despite a seemingly extensive overlap of movement leaders at events, some clustering of activists did occur (i.e., events tended to draw a semi-predictable set of leaders, depending on the sponsoring organization), enabling us to draw tentative conclusions about network boundaries. Meetings of the Consortium (the Western-funded women's movement network in Moscow) tended to draw women from organizations attached to the Women's League, as well as to the IWF, and rarely drew those affiliated with the URW (although Tolko Mamy, a single-mothers

---

[40] Elena Ershova, interview, April 18, 1995.
[41] Attendees included Mariia Arbatova (leader of Klub Garmoniia); Liudmila Zavadskaia (deputy to the Duma, from the Women of Russia faction); the leader of Equality and Peace; Elena Ershova (co-chair of the Women's League); the researcher/activists from the Gender Center at the Institute of Ethnology and Anthropology; Elena Demeshina (the head of the Association of Women [Film and Theater] Directors); Nina Gabrielian (of Preobrazhenie and Sof'ia, and also one of the original founders of Klub F-1); and Tat'iana Zabelina (on the board of the "Sisters" Rape Crisis Center).

group existing under the umbrella of the URW, did send representatives to Consortium meetings from time to time). The Women's League bi-annual meeting drew (naturally) member-organizations of the Women's League, plus Tatiana Troinova of the Inform Center IWF, who was invited by one of the Women's League's co-chairs. Likewise, a five-year anniversary party celebrating the creation of the Moscow Center for Gender Studies (MCGS), one of the central founders of the IWF network, drew few women from the Women's League or URW spheres of influence. A roundtable event held in June 1995 (sponsored by the American Bar Association) to discuss a law under formation about violence in the family brought out several IWF-affiliated activists, but was attended by none of the Women's League or URW regulars; the situation was similar at a press conference held to announce the publication of a manual on creating women's crisis centers. Conversely, URW events – large conferences, mostly – tended to draw activists from the Women's League and IWF, as well as the URW-affiliated network of organizations. The URW-sponsored conferences frequently included participation by high-level government officials, which may explain some of their attractiveness to activists from other networks.

Regional differences between the movements in Moscow, Ivanovo, and Cheboksary

Despite regional differences, the movements in all three cities shared several attributes. The women's organizations, with few exceptions, were run on a volunteer basis. They were resource-poor, and nearly all of the leaders interviewed cited a lack of money and other material resources as the main problem for their organizations. Each city had at least one group politically advocating on women's behalf, and also sported a businesswomen's organization, although the one in Cheboksary appeared only in mid-1995. Women's organizations in all three cities sponsored semi-regular events, especially conferences on women's issues, although, again, this was a new development in Cheboksary. Activists' ages ranged widely within each city, with more variation on the ends of the spectrum in Moscow.

Despite Cheboksary's status as the capital of the ethnic republic of Chuvashiia, the movement in Cheboksary was not significantly divided over ethnicity: in three of the four women's groups, ethnic Chuvash and Russians worked together. The one purely Chuvash women's association was based on a choral group, and had formed to promote Chuvash culture and protect the environment. Despite its ethnic basis, the group seemed open to cooperation with the city women's council (run by an ethnic Russian); both groups invited each other's members to their events. The leadership of the movements in Ivanovo and Moscow was almost entirely ethnically Russian, with a smattering of Jewish,[42] Ukrainian, Armenian, Estonian, and various European ancestries, which had no visible or measurable bearing on group cohesion or on intergroup cooperation.

The most evident difference between the cities' movements was size and length of standing. The movements in the two smaller cities were considerably more unified than that in Moscow, but were tiny and far less diverse. While there were dozens of active women's groups operating in Moscow, there were fewer than a dozen in Ivanovo and Cheboksary combined. Of the three movements, Cheboksary's was in its earliest stages, with two women's groups inherited from the Soviet era (the city- and republic-level women's councils) registered in 1991, two new groups registered in 1994, and one in the process of registration (in mid-1995). Ivanovo's women's council was also registered in 1991; four more organizations registered between 1991 and 1994.[43] By contrast, women's groups in Moscow were active as early as 1987, and organizational formation peaked in 1992–93. This difference in the timing of movement emergence and growth is probably attributable to the speed at which glasnost traveled from Moscow out to increasingly smaller and more distant cities and towns, and also to exposure to Western influence. Such exposure was most likely in Moscow, far more limited in Ivanovo, and even less likely in Cheboksary.

Secondly, movement cohesion varied greatly between Moscow on the one hand and Cheboksary and Ivanovo on the other. According to Moscow interviewees, despite the presence of some overlapping group membership, fragmentation was a major problem for their women's movement. Moscow activists and organizations retained relatively long-standing mutual animosities and political differences over perceived affiliation with the Russian and/or Soviet state and Communist Party across its three main indigenous networks and within the foreign-constructed coalition, the Western-sponsored US–NIS Women's Consortium. Some Moscow organizations were recipients of funding from Western foundations and governments, which at times exacerbated conflicts while enabling the organizations to carry out effective projects that would otherwise have been outside their reach. For the most part,

---

[42] Jews are considered an ethnic group in the former Soviet Union. "Jewish" thus implies "nationality" as well as religion.

[43] A sixth organization, the Ivanovo city division of the Committee of Soldiers' Mothers, formed in response to the war in Chechnia, and operated under the aegis of the city women's council.

the Ivanovo and Cheboksary movements exhibited none of the fragmentation based on perceived affiliation with the state or Communist Party so evident in Moscow. Furthermore, relative to the groups in Moscow, those in Cheboksary and Ivanovo were resource-poor, and received no Western funding.[44] Western funding could not then serve to exacerbate already existing disagreements.

The movements also differed on the extent of access to political allies within the elite. Ivanovo's political opportunity structure in particular was favorable to women's movement "success," in that the chair of the main women's organization (the city women's council) also held a seat in the city legislature, and was able to bring women's group proposals to the attention of the legislature herself. Similarly, in Cheboksary, one of the city women's council's members was also a representative to the republic's parliament. Furthermore, the Chuvash republic is small enough that the charter conference of a new group – the Klub Zhenskaia Initsiativa (Club "Women's Initiative") – was attended by the president of the Chuvash republic himself, who made a charming and self-denigrating speech, apologizing for the fact that he was not wearing a locally produced suit.[45] While this is no indication of the group's potential access to policymakers, it seems encouraging that the republic president had enough interest in women's concerns to attend the conference. The political opportunity structure for Moscow's women's groups, which mostly seek to influence *national*-level policymakers, is considerably more limited. For a time, however, the Women of Russia faction served as an ally (at least partially) of the women's movement in the Russian Duma, and the movement has built working relationships with officials in the Ministry of Social Protection. These issues will be taken up in more detail in chapter 4.

Another important difference between the movements in these cities concerns the motives for organizing. Here, the variation stems largely from differences in the regions' economic situations and unemployment rates. The poverty of Ivanovo and Cheboksary served as the most significant motivation behind women's organizing. As a result of the economic crisis situation in Ivanovo in particular, women's organizations there were largely motivated by the impoverishment of the province's residents. This factor was least important in Moscow, where the

[44] The one exception I am aware of is the Chuvash branch of the Russian Association of University Women, which received a small Western grant to fund a women's leadership training seminar conducted by an American organizer from the American Association of University Women, in conjunction with Russian activists from Moscow and Zhukovskii, in May 1995.

[45] Nikolai Fedorov, speaking at the Charter Conference of Klub Zhenskaia Initsiativa, Cheboksary, May 30, 1995 (author's notes).

economic situation, though verging on the dreadful for women, was "healthy" enough to merit organizations devoted to consciousness-raising and other nonmaterial pursuits, as well as employment-training programs, mutual aid groups, and advocacy groups fighting for women's and children's economic rights.

The broad diversity of the organizations and activists comprising the Russian women's movement is striking. Some organizations encompass several thousand members, yet are nearly invisible within Russia. Others, with merely a handful of activists, are known across the country within the women's movement community, but are familiar to very few average people. The activists running the organizations have undertaken a massive job. Most often on a volunteer basis (or for low pay), they promote their organizations and their goals, with little media attention or economic support. Deeply concerned about the economic and political effects of the transition period on women, many of the activists focus on contacts with state officials in an attempt to influence legislation and/or policy in a nondiscriminatory direction. Others, particularly in the self-help and support category, concentrate on helping as many women as possible adjust to the new economic circumstances. Against an historical background of Soviet political rhetoric about women's equality, the activists all share the desire to facilitate women's "self-realization" and to help women live up to their potential. Amidst animosities and disagreements, the activists work to change Russian realities for women, during one of the most challenging transitions of the twentieth century.

Despite the movement's internal divisions, the activists involved in it perceive themselves as participants in a collective effort. As one Moscow activist put it, the women's movement consists of a conglomeration of women who (most often) belong to one of the three indigenous, Moscow-based women's movement networks, who are all "asserting women's interests, although those interests are understood in different ways."[46] The fact that the movement is not cohesive does not seem to detract from activists' sense of joint participation in a single movement.

The experience of the women's movement in Russia resonates with that of social movements elsewhere, in that it seeks to achieve a variety of cultural, political, and economic goals, while suffering from insufficient resources and internal divisions and conflicts between activists. Similarities to social movements outside Russia notwithstanding, however, the Russian women's movement exhibits several puzzling features. First, although female political leaders, researchers, and

[46] Elena Kochkina, interview, July 22, 1995.

activists frequently cite a plethora of violations of women's rights (from disproportionate female unemployment to violence against women), and there has been a great deal of movement activity on these issues, there have been no large national demonstrations or confrontational protests for women's rights. Secondly, there is little cooperation between groups in Moscow, even those that share similar goals and strategies. Finally, although all of the organizations are practically devoid of income, they lack membership-building strategies, and seem almost disinterested in attracting new members. These paradoxes and their ramifications for the study of social movements form the subject of the next chapter.

Scholars of contentious politics have argued that social movements are likely to fare best where "parliamentary politics, democratic institutions, and durable political competition" have already taken root.[1] In places where those conditions do not hold, such as the post-Soviet states, we can fully expect social movements to look and behave differently from their Western counterparts. But whatever their appearance and characteristics, all social movements – in any country – are engaged in attempts to serve essentially the same purpose: to work toward social change that will rectify a situation perceived as unjust. In other words, social movements strive to alter the status quo of the power distribution in society – whether at the level of material resources or the more intangible level of status and "identity." Most often, social movements, including the women's movement in Russia, entail struggle over a combination of these material and intangible interests.[2]

By the mid-1990s, the Russian women's movement was conducting that struggle under extremely strained conditions. Women's organizations were uniformly poor, run by volunteers on "enthusiasm," while the economic circumstances surrounding them became increasingly desperate. Women suffered most, as a group, from the deepening economic crisis. Russian women rapidly went from having one of the highest labor force participation rates worldwide – over 90 percent – to being the least employable workforce in Russia, making up approximately two-thirds of the unemployed in 1994.[3] Affordable daycare, once

[1] Doug McAdam, Charles Tilly, and Sidney Tarrow, "To Map Contentious Politics," *Mobilization*, vol. 1, no. 1 (March 1996), p. 22.
[2] Groups within the movement may elect to pursue such changes in women's status at the individual level, helping women improve their circumstances in a way that does not challenge the social order; others may have more far-reaching visions about altering women's status at the societal or even global level.
[3] The State Statistics Committee (Goskomstat) put women at 64 percent of Russia's registered unemployed in 1994. However, unemployment figures are widely disputed, and vary across Russia. For example, in July 1994, women made up 77 percent of Moscow's registered unemployed; in Saratov, according to unemployment office employees, as of 1993, 90 percent of those recently unemployed were women. See

widely available (if of low quality), became a rarity, as factories cut such "luxuries" out of their budgets. The Russian political system, meanwhile, was in a state of near constant convulsion. Society was rocked by violence, from the outbreak of wars on the Russian periphery to astronomical increases in crime rates, including rape and domestic violence.

Social movements often emerge during political and economic transitions. In that sense, the Russian women's movement is far from unique. Social movement theorists have repeatedly shown, first of all, that it is changes in the "structure of political opportunities" – including those accompanying transitions from authoritarian and totalitarian regimes – that encourage movements to emerge. Secondly, movements become possible as activists and participants are recruited through social networks and "indigenous organizations." And finally, before they dawn, social movements must also have achieved a critical mass of individuals who recognize that the discrimination or oppression they are experiencing is a systemic, or political, problem, not a personal one, and that the rectification of the injustice is possible. This process is diversely referred to as "framing," "cognitive liberation," and the "transformation of consciousness." Later, movement activists use framing again, to transmit their messages to society at large and mobilize the public, helping the movement expand. Together, these three concepts (political opportunities, organizations and networks, and framing) constitute the "political process model" of social movement emergence and development.[4]

The use of these concepts sheds analytical light on the emergence and development of the contemporary Russian women's movement. Shifting political opportunities, in the form of glasnost and perestroika, enabled the Russian women's movement – among others – to emerge at the end of the 1980s. Women's organizations formed along associational lines, and, in some cases, combined into several larger networks based on "indigenous" groupings and contacts at conferences. Activists underwent individual changes in their perception of discrimination against women; they later engaged in framing women's issues for societal and

---

Osnovnye pokazateli sotsial'no-ekonomicheskogo polozheniia i khoda ekonomicheskoi reformy v Rossiiskoi Federatsii v 1994 godu (Moscow: Goskomstat, 1995), p. 52, cited in Penny Morvant, "Bearing the 'Double Burden' in Russia," *Transition* (September 8, 1995), p. 7; Sarah Ashwin and Elain Bowers, "Do Russian Women Want to Work?," in Mary Buckley, ed., *Post-Soviet Women: From the Baltic to Central Asia* (Cambridge: Cambridge University Press, 1997), p. 35, n. 16; and "Russia: Neither Jobs Nor Justice. State Discrimination Against Women in Russia," *Human Rights Watch Women's Rights Project*, vol. 7, no. 5 (March 1995), p. 7.

[4] See for example, Doug McAdam, *Political Process and the Development of Black Insurgency, 1930–1970* (Chicago: University of Chicago Press, 1982), ch. 3.

political consumption. In these ways, Russian women's movement organizing is typical.

Naturally, however, social movement organizing in Russia, when observed through the lens of "indigenous organizations," differs considerably from that found in the essentially stable democracies whose scholars produced the political process model. For example, networking, though an integral part of movement-building in Russia, remains highly limited. Women's movement mobilization has taken place thus far almost entirely through women's organizations. And even within that community, networking is restricted: local women's groups in Moscow, working on similar projects, are often unaware of one another. Decades of totalitarian control left Russia lacking the associational networks common to civil societies, a fact which has greatly reduced the Russian women's movement's mobilization potential. The lack of associational networks has also complicated the formation of women's groups, and explains their frequently small size. None of the groups were formed out of community networks (such as schools or churches). By contrast, most Western social movements – including those in authoritarian regimes – emerged against the background of well-established civil societies, replete with a variety of associational forms and communications infrastructures which facilitate movement mobilization.[5]

By the mid-1990s, scholars concerned with social movements increasingly sought to evaluate theories of social movements in light of those movements' experiences in countries lacking an extensive history of democracy. On the basis of such research, theorists could discover whether the approaches used to describe conditions in Western European and North American social movements could be "safely imported" into other regions of the world not categorized as "capitalist democracies."[6] The contemporary Russian women's movement case suggests that several social movement theory approaches prove useful in pointing out the elements common to Western and post-Leninist social movements. Generally speaking, the emergence, development, and success of social movements in Russia, as elsewhere, depend on activists' opportunities for networking, outreach to the population with appealing issue frames, openings in the political opportunity structure, available financial resources, and so on. These tools of Western social movement

---

[5] Evidence of civil society under authoritarian regimes can be found in Sonia Alvarez, *Engendering Democracy in Brazil: Women's Movements in Transition Politics* (Princeton: Princeton University Press, 1990); Jane Jaquette, ed., *The Women's Movement in Latin America: Feminism and the Transition to Democracy* (Boston: Unwin Hyman, 1989); and Jo Fisher, *Mothers of the Disappeared* (Boston: South End Press, 1989).

[6] McAdam, et al., "To Map Contentious Politics," p. 29.

theory can be applied in the Russian case to demonstrate that the economic and political transitions in Russia were causal in the women's movement's emergence, and in shaping the way it continues to develop. Yet, despite certain commonalties between the factors affecting the emergence and development of women's movements in Russia and the West, the Russian women's movement distinguishes itself from Western social movements in several rather enigmatic ways.

Paradoxes of Russian women's movement organizing

The Russian women's movement differs substantially from those movements that are commonly the subject of social movement theory in the West. The effects of Russia's economic and political transitions, as well as its political history as a totalitarian regime, are revealed in three of the movement's more paradoxical characteristics.

First, though extremely resource-poor, many groups fail to engage in member outreach or domestic fundraising; in 1994 and 1995, few were attempting to attract new members to their organizations. Secondly, the Russian women's movement appears to be a nonmobilizational movement, holding few rallies and focusing entirely on nondisruptive means of creating change. Thirdly, despite resource poverty, the small size of movement organizations, and fundamental similarities in goals and tactics, the movement groups – in Moscow – exhibit precious little collaboration with one another, although outside Moscow collaboration across organizations was quite high.

Why is it that Russian women's movement organizations neglected outreach and domestic fundraising strategies, despite overwhelming resource poverty? Part of the reason is that Russia lacks a tradition of donation to and membership in nongovernmental organizations (NGOs). The totalitarian system that forbade political expression and organization independent of the state naturally lacked an infrastructure that would enable donation to NGOs. While the branch of social movement theory labeled "resource mobilization" addresses the fact that movements require a certain level of economic resources in order to mobilize successfully, it does not take into account the idea of a country like Russia, unaccustomed to the rudiments of support for NGOs, including checkbooks, direct mail, mailing lists, and so on.[7] Given such conditions, movement organizations' desire to focus on new member outreach is therefore much diminished; in fact, the lack of an economic

---

[7] See John D. McCarthy and Mayer N. Zald, "Resource Mobilization and Social Movements: A Partial Theory," *American Journal of Sociology*, vol. 82, no. 6 (1977), pp. 1217–20.

infrastructure supporting NGOs severely curtails Russian women's organizations' ability to expand their mobilizational base through member outreach. Furthermore, because there is no infrastructure for simple donation to NGOs, membership in an organization implies a far greater commitment than becoming a member of an NGO does in the United States, for example. In Russia, membership suggests direct participation and activism, which is certain to limit membership size.

Turning now to the second issue, why do Russian women's movement groups shun public protest and other more typical conflictual means of stimulating social change? Interviews with movement participants, as well as direct observation, confirmed that the Russian women's movement (in Moscow as well as in the provincial cities) was pervaded by an aversion to measures perceived as instability-provoking, including mass demonstrations or protests. There are two main reasons for this timidity regarding public conflict as a means of promoting social change. First, the movement arose at the end of a cycle of political protest in Russia, which reduces mobilization potential.[8] And, secondly, the movement emerged into a period of violent political conflicts in Russia. These included Yeltsin's shelling of parliament in October 1993, growing numbers of industrial strikes, and the outbreak of several nearby wars in the territory of the former Soviet Union. Protest is currently associated with revolution and revolt; in the mid-1990s, the desire for stability far outweighs the potential benefits envisioned by women's movement activists entertaining the idea of mass protest.[9]

Perhaps the most interesting of these questions is the third: what lies behind the differences between levels of cooperation among women's movement groups in the capital, and that in the provincial cities of Ivanovo and Cheboksary? There are three basic reasons for the lack of collaboration between women's groups in Moscow: (1) the perception of certain organizations as being affiliated with the "state" (a negatively charged association, in a post-totalitarian society), and a fear of enforced unity within a top-down organizational structure (also related to the history of totalitarian social organization); (2) the existence of

---

[8] Sidney Tarrow, *Struggle, Politics and Reform: Collective Action, Social Movements, and Cycles of Protest* (Occasional Paper No. 21, Western Societies Program, Center for International Studies, Ithaca, Cornell University, 1989), p. 50.

[9] One activist suggested that, under current economic conditions, demonstrators are seen as people who have been coopted and paid off by political forces; otherwise, they (like everyone else) would be working, trying to make money to feed their families. She pointed out that demonstrating would be particularly dangerous for the women's movement, because a number of women's groups receive US funding, and the charge of political cooptation might therefore easily stick: Tat'iana Konysheva, personal communication, May 1997. The issue of US and other Western funding is addressed extensively in chapter 7.

competing associational networks; and (3) the presence of international sources of funding for women's movement organizations. All three issues operate very differently in the provinces than they do in the capital.

First, in Moscow, there is an almost unrelenting animosity between new "independent" women's groups on the one hand, and the heir to the Soviet Women's Committee (the Union of Russia's Women) on the other, because of the latter's perceived identification with the Soviet party-state. This was not at issue in the provinces. Although the Soviet Women's Committee had multiple branches throughout Russia, its subdivisions (*zhensovety*, or "women's councils") functioning at the local level were not necessarily perceived as state-bureaucratic organs, but instead as potentially, and occasionally concretely, helpful organizations. Also, local women's councils were not associated closely with the privileged state apparat, unlike their parent organization, the Soviet Women's Committee, whose central headquarters was located in Moscow, and whose staff was perceived as being part of the elite, privileged class.

Secondly, whereas in Moscow there were multiple social networks through which women were mobilized into activism (some of which were based on or associated with state- and party-related organizations and some of which were not), in the provinces there tended to be only one: the local Communist Party, or its affiliated organizations, such as the Komsomol (Communist Youth League). In Ivanovo, for example, the city's activists had all worked in Communist Party-affiliated organizations, including the Komsomol organizations at their academic institutes, and, in several cases, had met each other through such work. There, these acquaintanceships and working relationships contributed to movement solidarity later on.

Furthermore, prior to the Soviet regime's collapse in 1991, there were no women's organizations in either Ivanovo or Cheboksary available to assert their brave independence of the state, in contrast to the state-run women's councils. In Moscow, however, there were a number of women's organizations that pre-dated the collapse of the Soviet state. Thus, there are two kinds of conflicts, both due to the collapse of the totalitarian regime, that prevent collaboration between women's organizations in Moscow. The first type of conflict arises between the feminist organizations that tended to spring from "independent" associations toward the end of the Soviet regime, and those that were descended from mobilizational networks identified with the Soviet state and Communist Party rule, such as the Union of Russia's Women. After the regime's collapse, the "independent" groups tended to vilify those groups descended from state-run organizations. In cities like Moscow where multiple and competing networks were present, movement fragmentation is therefore high, complicating coalition-building. The second type of conflict arises within the network of "independent" women's movement organizations, between those who were activists before the regime's collapse, and those who became involved in women's organizing later, when activism had become not only nondangerous, but even financially profitable (if only for a handful of women).

Finally, fractionalization of the movement in Moscow was further driven by the fact that numerous women's organizations there were engaged in semi-ferocious struggles over the acquisition of funding, the vast majority of which came from external foreign sources. Where reliance on a domestic membership base is impractical, competition for limited foreign funds escalates. Furthermore, because of the way that grant competitions tend to be structured, groups multiply as activists seek funding for their own individual projects. Where resources are so short, one might expect to find women's organizations bonding and collaborating, pooling funds in order to accomplish more. However, the opposite was true in Moscow as of the mid-1990s. Cooperation was not only limited, but conflicts over foreign funding were overt. In the provincial cities, however, distance from the West and from Western funding sources kept such competition to a minimum. Whereas social movement groups in any country may compete for funds, social movement theory has not adequately addressed the importance of foreign funding's impact on movement organizing. In fact, social movement theorists have, in general, underestimated or overlooked the role of international influences (ideas, funding, international agencies, and so on) on social movement organizing outside the industrialized West.

In order to make sense of the above-described peculiarities of Russian women's movement organizing, I introduce three concepts – *economic opportunity structure, political history,* and *international influences* – and rely on them in the chapters that follow. These concepts also address two significant gaps in social movement studies: international influences on social movements, and the shape of social movements in countries emerging from totalitarian regimes.

Economic opportunity structure

Just as they operate under a changing political opportunity structure that provides openings as well as challenges, social movements also emerge and develop within an economic opportunity structure. The economic opportunity structure has two levels. First is the occurrence of rapid, fundamental economic changes in society that may inspire or depress organizing. Increasing levels of women's unemployment, for instance, can spur the creation of women's mutual assistance groups or employment-training organizations, as occurred in the early 1990s in Russia, while poverty can also draw women away from activism and reduce the money available for donation to local organizations. Economic opportunity structure also includes local infrastructural conditions that facilitate or limit the possibilities for social movement organizing, such as communications costs, the relative cost of outreach techniques (such as direct mail), the ease with which funds can be transferred to an organization, the existence of a bank checking system (absent in Russia), reliable mail and telephone systems, and so on. Movements may vary in their capacity for resource mobilization, and in their level of familiarity with fundraising and a nonprofit sector in general, two elements missing from most Russian activists' experience.

Political history

Political as well as economic legacies can have significant effects on social movements. Political history refers to the way that the legacy of political institutions, cycles of protest, and the defining political events of a country's history affect social movements' development. For example, although the political institutions of a totalitarian regime may collapse (thereby altering the political opportunity structure and creating the possibility for autonomous organizations to form), the distrust and fear of the state sphere (and the people and organizations identified with it) engendered by that totalitarian history may remain. In the Russian women's movement case, this has affected the potential for coalition-building between formerly state-run women's organizations and new autonomous ones, even when they share the same goals. Similarly, a movement emerging at the end of a cycle of protest, and into a period of great political instability, may be limited in its opportunities and desire to engage in mass or conflictual collective action. The Russian women's movement's first years took place against a backdrop of extreme political instability, from the August 1991 coup overthrowing Soviet rule to the 1993 shelling of the Russian parliament and the eruption of war in Chechnia. The timing of the women's movement's emergence in relation to these defining historical events has pushed women activists to avoid forms of mobilization that could be construed as conflictual or instability-provoking. In essence, political history pervades social movements' experience, shaping – though not exclusively – the means they adopt to create social change, the organizational structures they choose, and internal movement dynamics. The political history of post-Leninist regimes has been little explored by social movement theorists, although area studies specialists are beginning to conduct rich analyses in this field.[10]

International influences

International influences (or the "international opportunity structure") refers to the ways in which events, individuals, and trends outside a given country can influence the emergence and development of a social movement within it. This concerns, for instance, the diffusion of ideas across national boundaries, creating movements in multiple countries that share goals and even tactics. Russian women's movement activists in many cases, for example, have been influenced by Western feminism, through direct exposure to feminist literature, travel to Western countries, and/or encounters with Western feminists visiting Russia. The international opportunity structure also includes the financing of indigenous movements by foreign governments and foundations, and the complex dynamics such funding can create.

The influence of the international environment on social movements has been a neglected subject in social movement theory.[11] Sociologist John Meyer, however, uses what he calls "world society" theory to explore the ways that the international environment assists in the diffusion of ideas across national borders – a phenomenon directly relevant to social movement development in the global information age.[12] Naturally, however, countries are "embedded" in global society to differing degrees (dependent on local or internal – rather than international or external – political conditions).[13] This suggests that local circumstances

[10] See Jane Dawson, *Eco-Nationalism: Anti-Nuclear Activism and National Identity in Russia, Lithuania, and Ukraine* (Durham, NC: Duke University Press, 1996); Kathleen E. Smith, *Remembering Stalin's Victims* (Ithaca: Cornell University Press, 1996); and M. Steven Fish, *Democracy from Scratch* (Princeton: Princeton University Press, 1995).

[11] There are exceptions. Anthony Oberschall has discussed the effects of the international environment of alliance systems. Also, some social movement research discusses crossnational "spin-off" movements, although little systematic empirical work has been done in this area. See Doug McAdam, "Conceptual Origins, Current Problems, Future Directions," in McAdam, John D. McCarthy, and Mayer M. Zald, eds., *Comparative Perspectives on Social Movements* (Cambridge: Cambridge University Press, 1996), pp. 33, 39.

[12] See, for example, John W. Meyer, "Rationalized Environments," in W. Richard Scott and Meyer, *Institutional Environments and Organizations* (Beverly Hills: Sage, 1994), pp. 29–30. See also David Strang and John W. Meyer, "Institutional Conditions for Diffusion," in the same volume, pp. 100–12.

[13] Nitza Berkovitch, "From Motherhood to Citizenship: The Worldwide Incorporation of Women into the Public Sphere in the Twentieth Century" (dissertation, Stanford University, 1995), p. 200.

play the deciding role in creating opportunities for change, and that those opportunities do not stem entirely from the international political and social system. These local conditions can radically and dramatically change, altering the access to transnational ideas. This occurred, for instance, at the end of the 1980s in Eastern Europe and the Soviet Union, where the Iron Curtain that had defiantly kept world society at bay for decades finally crumbled under Gorbachev's glasnost policy, allowing for the transnational diffusion of ideas into new territory.

There is no doubt that the international diffusion of ideas about women's roles and feminism has played a key role in shaping the contemporary Russian women's movement. The transnational diffusion of money, however, has been equally important – a process neglected both by world society theory and by social movement theorists to date. Given the economic crisis in Russia, it has been international sources of funding that have tended thus far to fill the gap, producing a situation where foreign foundations and even governments are able to finance social movement activity in Russia, simultaneously advancing a foreign agenda and attaching strings that can in part determine movement priorities and tactics. Other international factors affecting the Russian women's movement include: international lending agencies' economic policies, which indirectly motivated some Russian women's groups' formation; the use of an English-language vocabulary on women's issues by some Russian women's groups and the ramifications for framing issues for popular consumption; the role of international bureaucracies like the UN and ILO (International Labor Organization), whose policies legitimate Russian women's groups' demands to some extent in the eyes of Russian state officials; and, finally, the role of individual foreigners in creating coalitions within the Russian women's movement, as well as serving as mediators between some Russian women's groups and the state. It is not simply that the diffusion of ideas across national borders can play a significant role in movement emergence, but that a variety of international factors can continue to affect movement development, especially, perhaps, outside the advanced capitalist states.

Russia's dual political and economic transition away from a totalitarian polity and command economy, in combination with the legacy of its political history and various international influences, has had significant repercussions for the form of its contemporary women's movement. This book applies the above-described set of concepts derived from social movement theory as a framework with which to analyze and understand the nascent Russian women's movement of the early and mid-1990s – a social movement occurring outside the "contemporary core democracies"[14] that have been the focus of so much scholarship on social movements. Taken together, these concepts form a crosscultural model of social movement organizing and development that explores five interrelated opportunity structures: socio-cultural or attitudinal (i.e., framing), political, economic, political-historical, and international. This "multiple opportunity structure" model lends insight into the origins and evolution of the Russian women's movement, and also facilitates the crosscultural analysis of social movements worldwide.

[14] McAdam, et al., "To Map Contentious Politics," p. 28.

3   Feminism, femininity, and sexism:
     socio-cultural opportunities and obstacles
     to women's movement organizing

Q. Why did you decide to form a *women's* group?
A. Because I'm a woman. (Laughs.)
                              Interview with Nina Iakovchuk, May 5, 1995.

In order to emerge publicly, social movements need to gather a core group of people who perceive the existence of a shared, societal injustice, and who believe that a challenge to the existing order might hold some hope for improving the situation. Social movement activists, by definition, have begun such a transformation of consciousness. They regard the injustice or set of injustices experienced by a given societal group or class (of which they are often, but not always, a part) as a systemic problem. Furthermore, activists believe that overcoming the injustice is feasible; otherwise they would be unlikely to enter into social activism, which is usually low-paid or volunteer work, with few immediate rewards. The women's movement activists in Russia who began women's organizations of various types between 1987 and 1994 possessed a well-developed sense of women's oppression, a consciousness transformed from seeing women's problems as being individual or personal to seeing them as political or social – as shared injustices.

This chapter explores the process of transformation of consciousness and the obstacles that confront it in the Russian case. I consider the transformation of consciousness among women's movement activists, and also the potential for that transformation to spread more widely in Russian society. Without this transformation the movement cannot hope to achieve a mass status that might hasten cultural change.

Activists' transformation of consciousness

All social movement activists undergo a process of transformation of consciousness, by which they recognize and name discrimination against a societal group, often "framing" the injustices they face differently than does the society in which they live. To activists, the set of

54

common problems they experience is no longer seen as resulting from a personal failing, but is perceived instead as evidence of systemic oppression. This transformation of consciousness is crucial to the formation of activist groups and organizations. What are the sources of such cognitive change?

Ideas are shaped by experiences and by social discourse. Without an atmosphere of collective support, an individual's experience of discrimination may often be perceived as personal failure. In the presence of collective support, however, that experience may be labeled instead as a shared phenomenon. The authors of a short-lived Soviet dissident women's journal, for example, experienced discrimination within the dissident movement, dominated by men who laughed off women's particular concerns and oppression. One of the journal's editors, Anna Natalia Malakhovskaia, described the process of creating the journal (in 1979) as one that enabled the women involved to express their conviction that the "personal" was, in fact, not personal, but shared – indeed, political:

[In creating the journal] we revealed for ourselves and, we hoped, for other women around us that the reason for each woman's unhappiness lies not in her being unlucky, or unskilled, and not in her personal fate, but in some much broader, all-encompassing laws by which our world lives. We learned later that this same spirit lies behind other women's publications in many countries.[1]

Commonly, the transformation from viewing problems as individual failures to labeling them as systemic oppression occurs through a process of consciousness-raising (C-R), often in the format of discussions with friends and acquaintances. Though not nearly as widespread as C-R groups in the 1970s in the United States, such groups did exist in Russia, starting in the late 1980s.[2] Some of these were informal meetings where women raised topics like "What does it mean to be a woman?" – the theme of a discussion in 1991 among a group of young sociologists and psychologists who would later found the Feminist Orientation Center.[3] Other consciousness-transforming processes occurred during seminars designed to initiate conversations on similar themes, such as becoming conscious of discrimination, the topic of a seminar sponsored by the Petersburg Center for Gender Issues in July 1993.[4]

[1] Anna Natal'ia Malakhovskaia, in FemInf, no. 1, 1992, cited in Marina Liborakina, Obretenie sily: rossiiskii opyt (Moskva: CheRo, 1996), p. 91.
[2] On consciousness-raising groups in the United States, see Jo Freeman, ed., Women: A Feminist Perspective (Palo Alto, CA: Mayfield, 1975), pp. 451–55.
[3] Liborakina, Obretenie sily, p. 66.
[4] The seminar (Feminism – the Third Eye) is described in Liborakina, Obretenie sily, pp. 53–63, and in Vse liudi sestry, no. 1–2, a publication of the Petersburg Center.

Direct experience of a consciousness-raising group, though important for many of the early activists in Russia's women's movement, is not the only means of altering consciousness. Some activists believed they had been feminists since childhood, but had "discovered" it only later in life, when they encountered discrimination as adults. Olga Lipovskaia, for example, a feminist in St. Petersburg, was raised by her grandmother, a woman she described as strong and independent:

[Because of my grandmother] it never occurred to me that I was worse somehow, weaker, or less capable than a man. But when my adult life began, there was a discrepancy: I kept coming up against situations where people were evaluating me not as a person, as an individual, but as something secondary in relation to the main person – a man. I wasn't aware of it immediately, and didn't understand it at first, but then, sometime in 1980, I got hold of my first [Western] book on feminism . . . and I was happy to see that a lot of the things I was thinking about had already been considered, written about, and read by thousands of women (granted – only in the West).[5]

Lipovskaia's transformation of awareness was followed by her decision (in 1988) to establish a small-circulation journal, self-published and composed in large part of translations of Western feminist literature, called *Women's Reading* (*Zhenskoe chtenie*), to facilitate other women's cognitive liberation.

For many activists, Russia's movement toward the establishment of a market economy motivated a change in consciousness, a process that may also be occurring in the general population, spurred by increasing female unemployment. In 1993, when women made up over two-thirds of the unemployed, and only 23 percent of those reemployed, Alevtina Fedulova, the chair of the Union of Russia's Women, explained in a popular magazine that the transition toward a market economy was "throwing women out of social, political, and economic life . . . They are crowding us into the house, into the kitchen, to our 'natural' destiny. We cannot allow this." It was not only Fedulova's group consciousness that was evident from the article. The journalist authoring the article agreed, stating: "Probably not every woman would be able to answer the question, 'What is discrimination?' But almost every woman feels it herself."[6] Indeed, one activist working with an organization that helps to reorient women for new jobs believed that the increasingly open form of discrimination during Russia's transition period was enough to sponsor a transformation of consciousness among women, especially those over

---

[5] Ol'ga Lipovskaia, "Lichnost' v feminizme," *Zhenskoe dvizhenie v SSSR*, no. 1, November–December 1990, pp. 1, 5.
[6] Nadezhda Os'minina, "Rossiia – muzhskogo roda?," *Rabotnitsa*, May 1993, pp. 10–11.

thirty-five, who have had great difficulty finding employment under the new labor market conditions:

I think now, with the increased discrimination in the political and economic situations, that a basis for feminism will arise. Some employers are saying things like, "You must pledge not to get married, or not to have children for five years." That's the face of capitalism that for us is not acceptable [*priemlimyi*]. It calls up fear and anticapitalist sentiment. We've fallen into a situation where we [women] now feel ourselves discriminated against. I think it's totally shameful, in a civilized country, to limit hiring to people thirty-five and under. I see that it's superficial – when a general manager is twenty-three years old, he doesn't need some 47-year-old lady. But people should understand the negative character of that phenomenon.[7]

The changing economic situation and the stark appearance of unemployment, especially among educated women, brought discrimination into the open, fueling changes in consciousness for activists, and possibly for women in the population at large.

The sense of group consciousness among activists is far simpler to document than that sense in the broader population, since large-scale survey research has barely touched upon this question.[8] Activists evince a strong feeling of group consciousness as women, based on perceived discrimination and on a recognition that women's problems differ from men's. On this basis, activists chose to create women's organizations, rather than collaborate with other, male-dominated informal groups or political parties. With the advent of perestroika, women activists across the political spectrum began to organize in their own interests, separately from men. The leader of the hardline communist Congress of Soviet Women explained that they had created a women's organization because women's issues tended to be "overlooked by men."[9] A leader of Conversion and Women, a group advocating on behalf of women in military industries, explained that the group had been formed by women for women, "simply because the discrimination going on was clearly against women."[10]

However, in addition to organizing against discrimination directly, women's groups in Moscow in the mid-1990s continued to meet in part

---

[7] Marina Pavlova, interview, April 24, 1995.
[8] Survey data occasionally provides insights into the level of group consciousness. For example, in Russian surveys conducted in 1993, 15 percent of women surveyed claimed that women were "in a worse position and had fewer rights" at work than men. See Valentina Bodrova, "Povedenie rabotaiushchikh zhenshchin na rynke truda v perekhodnyi period," All-Russian Institute for the Study of Public Opinion (VTsIOM), 1993.
[9] Natal'ia Belokopytova, interview, May 12, 1995.
[10] Eleonora Ivanova, interview, February 6, 1995.

for the purpose of mutual support and consciousness-raising. Said the leader of the Association of Women [Film and Theater] Directors:

Part of our work is really psychological – so women won't feel like they're alone. The most important thing to understand is that your problem isn't just yours alone. We all go on precisely the same path, all of us overcome the same obstacles.[11]

Similarly, Elena Ershova, the leader of several groups including an organization that ran a leadership school for women, pointed to the benefits of women organizing separately from men:

Women think they're equal, but also have a deep feeling of second-class status. When we do things ourselves, we gain confidence. We cease to be afraid.[12]

The importance of consciousness-raising, creating a space where women could "reveal" their thoughts/selves (*proiavit' sebia*; *samora-skrytie*)[13] and challenge the idea that their experiences as women were unique to them as individuals, was thus combined in many organizations with activities challenging the gendered division of power in Soviet/Russian society.

It is important to recall that a person may perceive injustice as a shared, political phenomenon, yet doubt that any public actions to alter the situation would be effective or, especially in the case of a repressive regime, even feasible. That is, in order for social activism to occur beyond the informal C-R group level, people must believe that there is potential for social change. In the Russian case, such beliefs were long blocked by the presence of the repressive Soviet state, which assiduously suppressed dissidents, including those who raised issues of injustice toward women. Informal organizations (those not sanctified by the Soviet state and Communist Party) were forbidden. The potential for change opened up only with the advent of political freedoms under Gorbachev. Under the increasingly free political conditions, women activists realized that the new circumstances would enable them to safely begin to assert their demands to rectify injustices toward women at the societal level. An organizer with a Moscow-based lesbian group, for example, confirmed that perestroika had made public organizing on such previously taboo topics possible:

Q. Could this group have existed before perestroika?
A. We could have created it, but not openly. We couldn't have done it other than secretly.[14]

---

[11] Elena Demeshina, interview, March 26, 1995.
[12] Elena Ershova, interview, April 18, 1995.
[13] Interviews: for example, Elena Ershova, April 18, 1995; Marina Pavlova, April 24, 1995.
[14] Interview, November 27, 1994.

An activist with the Inform Center of the Independent Women's Forum (a women's advocacy organization) agreed that public organizing and group advocacy on women's behalf was feasible only after the establishment of new freedoms under Gorbachev: "We couldn't have existed before perestroika, except as a club. Perestroika was a great thing."[15] In addition to economic distress, perestroika thus also brought women the freedom to challenge overt labor-market discrimination and more long-term gender-based oppression in Soviet/Russian society. The combination of political and economic transition had created conditions for transformation of consciousness and public action alike.

Women's movement ideology: feminism

Q. What does the word feminism or feminist mean to you?
A. I don't know.
Q. Have you heard the word?
A. Of course.
Q. Any impressions of it?
A. No.

> Interview with a leader of the Committee of Multi-Child Families
> (Ivanovo), April 4, 1995

Whereas discrimination can be an impetus to organizing, in order for people to come together in collective action intended to counter that discrimination, they need some type of ideology to link them with one another, an ideology that frames their experience as a collective one, and motivates them to take action. In women's movements, this role is often played by "feminism," an ideology (or range of ideologies) that, at base, views women as an oppressed group, one that deserves equal rights and treatment.[16]

An examination of the frameworks used by Russian women's movement activists to describe feminism reveals, in broad terms, the ideologies that underlie these activists' transformation of consciousness, and that they use to sum up their beliefs and justify the actions they take on behalf of those beliefs. What did feminism mean to Russian women activists in the mid-1990s?

Interviews revealed that feminism lacked unanimous support among Russia's women's movement activists. Moreover, the definitions used by

---

[15] Tat'iana Troinova, interview, April 19, 1995.
[16] I recognize that there are a multiplicity of feminisms, and many definitions of the term. See, for example, Carol Anne Douglas, *Love and Politics: Radical Feminist and Lesbian Theories* (San Francisco: ism press, 1990).

women activists varied widely, even among those that considered themselves feminists. Many viewed feminism as a means to sisterhood, personal freedom, and consciousness.[17] Said Olga Voronina, feminist philosopher,

For me personally, [feminism is] something that, culturally speaking, helps one to live in this world and survive. Reading feminist literature gave me new resources to overcome the obstacles that lay in my path . . . When I had any free time at all, I read about feminism, explaining the socio-cultural reasons for my situation. It wasn't just me in that situation.[18]

Related to the feeling of freedom (often the freedom to choose, rather than be governed by societal stereotypes), many activists chose a "liberal" definition of feminism, which signified a commitment to equal rights and equal treatment. For example, one of the leaders of the Women's League network, Elena Ershova, labeled herself a "liberal feminist," saying, "I'm for freedom of choice and equal opportunities."[19] This sentiment was echoed by many activists:

Feminism is admitting a woman's right to be who she is; it means women's equality and her freedom – the freedom to run your own life, and to destroy women's perceived inferiority, her secondary status in relation to men.[20]

Feminism, in my view, is a movement for equal rights and equal opportunities for men and women in all areas of life. It's a movement for women to have the right to an equal chance with men in all spheres.[21]

Mixed opinions of feminism were also common, especially (but not exclusively) in Ivanovo and Cheboksary. Illustrative was the opinion of a former member of the Chuvash republic women's council, who identified feminism as "women's fight for their real rights." "But," she continued, "if the woman is equal to the man in a family, it doesn't lead to happiness."[22] A leader of the Moscow-based Women for Social Democracy echoed this ambiguity: "[Feminism] means an active women's position on all issues, struggling for equal rights and opportunities. We're 'for it' in that sense. But we don't want it to exceed reasonable bounds: we don't want it to be a struggle against men."[23]

Several activists maintained negative associations with the word feminism, with a significant subgroup identifying feminism or "feminist"

[17] Interviews: December 6, 1994; December 7, 1994; October 4, 1994.
[18] Ol'ga Voronina, interview, April 27, 1995.
[19] Elena Ershova, interview, April 18, 1995.
[20] Interview, December 6, 1994.
[21] Ol'ga Khasbulatova, interview, April 6, 1995.
[22] Zinaida Sutrukhova, interview, May 30, 1995.
[23] Interview, November 22, 1994.

with total female independence and a concomitant rejection of men. Declared the chair of the Ivanovo women's council:

I think [a feminist is] a woman who . . . wants to achieve a lot, to achieve it by herself, so that women would be admitted as having more opportunities, equality with men. The point is that she wants to achieve it *herself*, and doesn't need the help of men. And that's the mistake.[24]

The chair of a hardline communist women's organization in Moscow echoed this opinion:

Well, maybe it's because of propaganda, or something else, but here, we immediately think of bluestockings. The kind of woman who takes it all upon herself, absolutely independent. But we want to be female, we want the support of a husband, and we don't want to negate men's rights. It would be nice if men would free us from some of our work. In Russia, women are so burdened. We'd be *happy* if some of the burden would be shifted off to men. Of course we're in favor of women's independence. But we value men too![25]

A few activists reacted to their own notions of feminism with outright repulsion. Said the chair of Ivanovo's Committee of Single-Parent Families:

I'm not a feminist myself. Maybe I'm wrong, but to be a pure feminist – it's a sick person [*bolnoi chelovek*] . . . I think they're fanatics, who want to separate themselves from society [*otorvatsia ot obshchestva*]. We need to solve our problems together in society.[26]

Views of feminism as a negative, aggressive phenomenon were not immutable. After sitting through an extensive seminar on women and activism, a young leader of an ecological organization in a town near Cheboksary said that her original association with the word feminism had been "warrior-like." After the seminar, however, her opinion had changed to a more positive evaluation: "Now it seems that feminism is about women's struggle for equal rights. 'Person' doesn't just mean 'man' [*Chelovek eto ne tol'ko muzhchina*]."[27]

A number of activists made clear their rejection of "Western" or "radical" feminism in particular, which they often linked to female superiority, separatism, lesbianism, and a foolish derision of chivalry. Maia Kazmina, at sixty-five years of age, a lawyer and member of the Women's League, felt that her job was to struggle for women's equal rights, but that feminism, by contrast, was "women's struggle for super-iority," a struggle she rejected.[28] Similarly, for the leader of a Moscow-

---

[24] Natal'ia Kovaleva, interview, April 3, 1995.
[25] Natal'ia Belokopytova, interview, May 12, 1995.
[26] Larisa Nazarova, interview, April 4, 1995.
[27] Al'bina Endiuskina, interview, May 27, 1995.
[28] Maia Kaz'mina, interview, April 13, 1995.

based advocacy organization also supporting women's entrepreneurship (Dzhenklub), feminism signified

when a woman tries to prove that the male half of humanity is totally inferior in the mental and physical senses, and that women are better, so they should rule and be in power everywhere. I think it's an exaggeration. We aren't striving for opposition [*protivopostavlenie*]; that's not what we're interested in.[29]

The association of feminism with radical separatism was cause for dismay to several activists and female officials working to raise women's status in society. Olga Samarina, the director of the Ministry of Social Protection's Department on Family, Women, and Children's Issues, identified herself positively with a liberal feminism, the "struggle for equality in rights and the opportunity to realize them." However, she felt equally strongly that "radical" forms of feminism were negative. Not only did radical feminists refuse men's help in putting on their coats, according to Samarina, but they also rejected men altogether:

In Germany, I saw radical feminists who said there should be female reservations that men shouldn't be allowed on . . . Maybe I don't have the right to say this, but it smacks to me of fascism on the basis of sex . . . When they don't let a man take part in raising his own child, when they don't let men into the family at all . . . I think those women are unhappy; maybe they got involved with dishonorable [*neporiadochnye*] men, and had bad memories about them.[30]

An implicit and explicit identification of feminism (radical and non-radical) with lesbianism also informed several interviewees' responses to the term. One strongly feminist-identified activist declared her opposition to "radical feminism," defined as "radical lesbian centers who think that men and male chauvinism are at the root of discrimination." In contrast with such beliefs, she felt that cooperation rather than separatism was the proper path: "I think we should cooperate and have harmony with men and between the sexes."[31] Although this activist was aware of various types of feminism, and was thus able to identify as a feminist while rejecting "radical" feminism, most of the Russian population is not as well versed in the particulars. "Feminism is not liked," explained one activist. "It's identified with lesbianism."[32] Some activists recognize this fact and struggle against it. For example, Sasha Smirnova, a young activist from an organization called Women's Light (located in Tver, a city between Moscow and St. Petersburg), reported the following exchange: "When I told a friend that I was joining Women's

[29] Nina Iakovchuk, interview, May 5, 1995.
[30] Ol'ga Samarina, interview, March 24, 1995.
[31] Elena Ershova, interview, April 18, 1995.
[32] Interview, December 1, 1994.

Light, she couldn't believe it. She said, 'How can you be a feminist? You have a fiancé.'"[33]

The identification of Western feminism with antichivalry was noted by several activists as a reason to reject it. For the co-leaders of Russia's women's radio station (Radio Nadezhda), Western feminism was too extreme:

It's fine with us if men get up so we can take their seats on public transportation, especially if women are carrying these tremendous bags. Or hold doors open for us, as they did when we were in France.[34]

Radical feminism, Western feminism, and lesbianism, then, are for some activists equated with feminism per se, while for others feminism may be defined as more of a liberal feminism, safe, irreproachably advocating equal rights for women, but not entailing a radical restructuring of society, or a rejection of traditional gender roles and heterosexuality.

While liberal feminism generally presupposes an element of equal rights and equal treatment for men and women, some Russian activists based their sense of group consciousness on a different understanding of the relationship between men and women's natures, a "gynocentric" type of feminism that attributes different essential natures to men and women. For instance, some activists denigrate politics as an unproductive, destructive male "game," and celebrate female compassion as therefore a necessary addition to the political system. The idea that women should go into Russian politics in order to humanize it is encapsulated by a remark made by Eleonora Ivanova, supporting Galina Skorokhodova's campaign to enter the Russian parliament (both are leaders of the association Conversion and Women): "Morality is particularly characteristic of the female soul. And thus I'm fighting for as many women as possible to enter the Duma."[35] The value of increasing women's numbers in politics, then, is not only to give women an equal voice in high-level decisionmaking, but to alter the nature of that process, by injecting more of what Russians refer to as the female "principle" (nachalo). Said a Cheboksary activist, "Women are softer; they have their own role and mission. In politics, they should bear influence in peaceful, women's ways."[36] Thus, to a certain extent,

---

[33] Quoted in Janet Maughan, "Women's Work: Finding a Place in the New Russia," *Ford Foundation Report*, 1996, p. 20. Such homophobia has traditionally been used (in Russia and elsewhere) as a means to discourage women from identifying as feminists, and from becoming involved in activities that undermine patriarchal norms, such as joining a women's organization or taking part in a women's movement. See Suzanne Pharr, *Homophobia: A Weapon of Sexism* (Inverness, CA: Chardon Press, 1988).

[34] Tat'iana Zeleranskaia, interview, July 10, 1995.

[35] Eleonora Ivanova, "My ne mozhem oshibat'sia," *Vestnik*, no. 4, 1995, p. 25.

[36] Interview, May 31, 1995.

among Russian activists, women's group consciousness is based on the idea that women and men are inherently different, and not on a feminism that posits an essential similarity between the sexes.

Summing up, Russian women's movement activists had multiple opinions about feminism. Many embraced it as a liberating ideology; others endorsed a "liberal feminism" only half-heartedly; some rejected feminism altogether; others supported a more gynocentric feminism. On average, those activists having a more negative association with feminism tended to be about ten years older than those endorsing feminism as a positive phenomenon (average age fifty-two vs. forty-two). It is clear from the foregoing that mixed and negative attitudes toward feminism were common enough, even among movement activists, that a further analysis of the reasons and historical basis for such attitudes seems warranted if we are to understand the sources of these attitudes. Only then can we evaluate the potential for feminism as an ideology to expand beyond the circle of women's movement activists into the population, providing a platform on which to mobilize women toward a more widespread transformation of consciousness.

Attitudinal obstacles to feminism: the Soviet legacy

Activists' mixed attitudes toward feminism are connected to the Soviet legacy, which left a considerable and multifaceted prejudice against "feminists" and the liberal feminist rhetoric of "equality." This legacy operated in several ways, from propaganda on the part of the Soviet leadership intended to derogate feminism to indirect ways in which the regime's policies and pronouncements produced a reaction against so-called equality between the sexes.

The corruption of "feminism"

According to feminist historian Olga Khasbulatova, even before the 1917 revolution the Bolshevik leadership, through propagandistic efforts, intentionally portrayed feminism as an alien, bourgeois ideology, one that was frowned upon and seen as being counter to the goals of the proletarian revolution:

In our country, in our science, and in our consciousness, the word feminism had an ideological coloring. It meant "a fight against men." And, as such, it wasn't going to become popular – besides which, our ideologists of the women-workers' movement used the word feminism to counterpose the nonproletarian women's organizations with the proletarian ones. Therefore, our women's organizations, the liberal-democratic ones, sensing that, avoided calling themselves feminists. And you will practically never find the word feminist, not in a single speech, from any women's congress, from 1908, nor in the works of women leaders, saying that they're feminists. They avoided the word, and applied it only to the Western [women's] movement. But that division, that there were feminists "over there," but that we're not feminists, was a purely ideological one.[37]

The equation of feminism with "fighting against men," as seen above in some of the activists' statements, also had its root in the Bolsheviks' attempts to portray feminism as a divisive movement aimed to pit women against men, rather than proletarians against capitalists and bourgeois rulers. The overall effect of the propaganda was to make a feminist identity highly undesirable.[38] One activist stated that she considered herself a feminist, having spent her entire life fighting for women's rights, but that this identification had occurred despite the negative connotation of the word: "Feminism in Russia was a curse word, a term of abuse."[39] Another activist agreed: "Most of society views feminism as obscene, or indecent . . . Most people think it's either abnormal or laughable."[40] Tatiana Troinova, an activist affiliated with the Inform Center of the Independent Women's Forum, confirmed the latter idea, rooting her reluctance to verbally identify herself as a feminist in society's long-standing attitude toward the concept:

The young women in my organization are reading about feminism. They want to look at their position in society from that perspective, but they don't *call* themselves feminists. And neither do I: on the everyday level, among my friends, it gives rise to laughter.[41]

Negative propaganda from the Soviet state about feminism persisted well beyond the years of the revolution. Activist Elena Ershova explained that the Soviet mass media's selective portrayal of feminism during and after the 1970s (stressing separatism) had reinforced a definition of feminism so negative as to have created women activists "who say they're not feminists, [but] who in fact are":

Our mass media showed only the most radical part of the second wave of Western feminism, the "down with men" part, the rejection of men, and of the family. In Geia [one of the women's organizations with which she worked], we

---

[37] Ol'ga Khasbulatova, interview, April 6, 1995.
[38] It is not just in Russia that feminism is portrayed as "bourgeois" or Western; this occurs in many developing countries. See Amrita Basu, "Introduction," in Basu, ed., *The Challenge of Local Feminisms* (Boulder: Westview Press, 1995), pp. 6–7. Moreover, feminists are frowned upon and labeled as "man-haters" by many people throughout the world.
[39] Interview, October 28, 1994.
[40] Interview, October 31, 1994.
[41] Tat'iana Troinova, interview, April 19, 1995.

understand the term, but we don't want to use it: why upset the public? We like using "equal opportunities" and "freedom of choice" – it doesn't disturb anyone. It makes sense for practical purposes. Everyone understands it and even men can't object to it.[42]

The Soviet leadership's portrayals of feminism have thus warped the vocabulary and framework available to women's movement activists, when trying to discuss gender-based oppression and socio-economic or political inequality, making feminism, as such, almost unavailable as an ideology.[43]

Although large-scale public opinion research on the definition of "feminism" has not been conducted in Russia, the results of a small-scale survey carried out in a group of twenty-four "average" women – not activists – from the city of Ivanovo supported the thesis that using "feminism" as an outreach tool would not be a wise choice, at least in the short term, for the women's movement in today's Russia.[44] Of the women surveyed, in May and June 1995, nine provided no answer to the question, "What, in your opinion, does the term 'feminism' signify?" Another eight respondents answered with variations of "I don't know," "I don't understand the expression," and so on, bringing the total of women in the sample unfamiliar with the term to 71 percent. Four respondents gave answers suggesting a "negative" association with feminism, such as "masculine qualities in women" and "women's hegemony." Only three respondents presented answers reflecting feminism in its liberal sense, such as "women's struggle for equal conditions and for their rights" and "women's struggle for equal rights with men," bringing the total of respondents identifying something neutral or positive with "feminism" to 12.5 percent. Absent large-scale survey research, there is no way of knowing whether this small poll reflects popular opinions, but the sample does seem to reflect the same types of perceptions as the activist sample, except with an understandably much higher proportion of "don't know" answers.

---

[42] Elena Ershova, interview, April 18, 1995.

[43] Another critique of "feminism" in Russia, heard more rarely, is that the population rejects it as just another in a series of empty "isms" – like "communism," "Marxism–Leninism," and so on, to which the population has become "immune, as with any ideology." See Nadezhda Azhgikhina, speaking at a roundtable on Russian and Western feminism, reprinted as "Rossiiskii i zapadnyi feminizm: problemy dialoga," *Vy i my*, no. 10, Fall 1994, p. 18.

[44] I designed the survey, which was conducted by the staff of the Center for the Social Support of Women and Families (Ivanovo). The respondents were all receiving reeducation/job-training courses from the Center. Twenty-one of them indicated on the survey that they were unemployed; one said she was a housewife; one said she was "formally" working; and one survey was missing data on that question.

The corruption of "equality"

Although the Bolsheviks rejected "feminist" ideology as such, in their rhetoric they did adopt a framework of gender equality very progressive for its time. Upholding women's right to vote and striving for women's full political and economic participation created an impression among some people that feminism – understood as a struggle for women's political rights in the West – was irrelevant to Russia, where women had been granted full citizenship rights quite early on.[45] The struggle for women's suffrage in Russia, for example, was won a few months prior to the Bolshevik revolution in October 1917.

While proclaiming equal rights from above, generations of Soviet leaders also managed, as a byproduct of their economic and social policies, to reinforce a gendered division of labor (especially within the home), and thereby to give "equality" a bad name. Women's "equal rights," in the Soviet Union, amounted to women working full-time outside the home, as well as full-time inside it, a phenomenon known as the double burden. Men in the Soviet Union played minimal roles in childcare and domestic chores, leaving women with an seemingly endless and exhausting job maintaining the family, under less than ideal economic circumstances. Moreover, women's "equal" participation in the workforce in many cases meant women's labor was applied in the least skilled (and nonmechanized) occupations, at low pay and with low prestige.[46] Feminist philosopher Olga Voronina summed the situation up well:

the myth of emancipation as a means of masking discrimination and exploiting women led to a deformation of the very concept of emancipation, in women's consciousness. For the average Soviet woman, emancipation is what she already

---

[45] Marina Pavlova, interview, April 24, 1995.
[46] Many scholars have documented a variety of ways in which the idea of "equality" was corrupted in reality in Eastern Europe and the Soviet Union. See, for example, Gail Lapidus, *Women in Soviet Society: Equality, Development, and Social Change* (Berkeley: University of California Press, 1978); Barbara Jancar, *Women Under Communism* (Baltimore: Johns Hopkins Press, 1978); Alena Heitlinger, *Women and State Socialism: Sex Inequality in the Soviet Union and Czechoslovakia* (Montreal: McGill-Queen's University Press, 1979); Marilyn Rueschemeyer, ed., *Women in the Politics of Postcommunist Eastern Europe* (Armonk, NY: M. E. Sharpe, 1994); Sharon L. Wolchik and Alfred G. Meyer, eds., *Women, State, and Party in Eastern Europe* (Durham, NC: Duke University Press, 1985); Sharon Wolchik, "Women in Transition in the Czech and Slovak Republics: The First Three Years," *Journal of Women's History*, vol. 5, no. 3 (1994), pp. 100–07; and Nanette Funk and Magda Mueller, eds., *Gender Politics and Post-Communism: Reflections from Eastern Europe and the Former Soviet Union* (New York: Routledge, 1993).

has, that is, a lot of work, under the guise of equality with men. Of course, this doesn't suit her at all.[47]

In essence, the equal rights ideology of the Bolsheviks has prevented the contemporary women's movement from relying on the demand for "equality" as a rallying cry, because women identify equality with suffering.

The pursuit of "femininity"

Feminism shouldn't be about being stuck involuntarily on a tractor.

Laima Geidar, lesbian activist[48]

Related to the Soviet version of "equality" with men that entailed extremely burdensome work is the idea that "equality" exists in opposition to "femininity" – a value that many Soviet women held dear, perhaps because their lives under a closed, communist regime seemed almost to make it impossible to achieve. The stress on heavy industry, rather than consumer goods, produced a striking uniformity of clothing and consumer items, from hair dye to cosmetics, which, in turn, enforced a certain uniformity of appearance. In a moving essay, Slavenka Drakulic, a Yugoslavian writer, emphasized the importance of "femininity" to women in Eastern Europe as a means of achieving a sense of individualism, with which to counter the uniformity imposed by life under communism.[49] Despite the fact that women in the Eastern bloc drove tractors and worked in construction, the communist socio-economic system did prescribe widely divergent roles for men and women, as was visible in sex-role divisions of labor in the family, and in vertical and horizontal occupational segregation by sex. Drakulic's point, however, was that economic hardship and the lack of attention to consumer goods, including fashionable clothing and makeup (considered by the regime to be a bourgeois concern), made it difficult for women to differentiate themselves – from men, on the one hand, and as individuals on the other.[50] Similarly, Larisa Lisiutkina, a cultural studies specialist, affirmed that the totalitarian regime had "deformed and

---

[47] Ol'ga Voronina, "Zhenshchina i sotsializm: opyt feministskogo analiza," in M. T. Stepaniants, ed., *Feminizm: vostok, zapad, Rossiia* (Moscow: Nauka, 1993), p. 223.

[48] Laima Geidar, interview, July 17, 1995.

[49] Slavenka Drakulic, "Make-up and Other Crucial Questions," in her *How We Survived Communism and Even Laughed* (New York: Harper Perennial, 1993), pp. 21–32.

[50] One could question why women might have wanted to express their individuality through makeup and fashion to begin with. Are women's desires for individuality channeled into or limited to this particular form? And, if so, by what cultural norms?

humiliated" both men and women, and had "[denied] individual differences, including the differences between men and women."[51]

The desire to reclaim women's "femininity" is also related to some women's contemporary attraction to manifestations of chivalry. What might be regarded as patronizing in the West is seen by many women (activists included) instead as a reflection of well-earned respect for women in present-day Russia. For instance, Tatiana Zeleranskaia, the chief editor at Radio Nadezhda, explained that, when she was in France, men's tendency to hold doors open for women brought forth an unusual feeling for her:

When I was in France, I felt like a woman at each step, because any man, without even looking at me, regardless of how I look, or how old I am, would say, "Madame," and hold the door for me. Everywhere. But that's nice! You start to feel like a human being.[52]

The context of Soviet economic life and its perpetual inconveniences which burdened women tremendously continue to have a strong impact on women's perception of themselves in relation to men. In telling her story about men and doors in France, Zeleranskaia made it clear that it was not men's recognition of her physical attractiveness that had impressed her during her trip. In fact, she even pointed out that the men in France had opened doors for her "regardless" of how she looked – a point which suggests her awareness of women's objectification. In France, Zeleranskaia felt she had received respect not only for her "femininity," but, more importantly, for her humanity. Thus, for many women, the burdens of their lives under Soviet rule may make the advent of occasional manifestations of chivalry (holding doors, helping women into their coats, kissing women's hands, and so on) a welcome change. It is not seen as an objectification or patronization of women but, rather, almost as a recognition of their heroic efforts.

In sum, the pursuit of "femininity" clashes directly with the perception of feminism, as well as with the concept of equality. Russian women, for example, are becoming Mary Kay and Avon cosmetics representatives (saleswomen) in droves, which enables them to earn a steady income. In interviews with representatives, one journalist discovered that all of them valued the "self-reliance" that came with independent earnings, but were careful to disassociate themselves from "feminism," which implied a rejection of "femininity": "'This kind of independence has changed the way we live; it changes our relationship

---

[51] Interview with Larisa Lisiutkina, *Zhenskoe dvizhenie v SSSR*, no. 1, November–December 1990, p. 3; Larissa Lissyutkina, "Soviet Women at the Crossroads of Perestroika," in Funk and Mueller, *Gender Politics and Post-Communism*, p. 277.

[52] Tat'iana Zeleranskaia, interview, July 10, 1995.

with men,' said Tatyana Navrodskaia, a Mary Kay consultant. 'But it's not feminism. You can still remain feminine.'"[53]

Feminism-independence vs. family-dependence

A few activists with academic backgrounds explained their rejection of feminism, as well as the popular rejection of it, in terms of a reaction against indigenous Russian feminism, personified, it seemed, in Alexandra Kollontai, and other like-minded female communist revolutionaries in the early Soviet period. These indigenous feminists (at least, in the understanding of some women activists) defined women's freedom in opposition to the family. Explained an activist from Ekaterinburg:

I don't approve of Kollontai, who thought that "the family limits women's freedom." Russian feminism, earlier in this century, was more radical than feminism in the West. What mostly bothers me is that, according to Russian feminism, women should have rights, but not responsibilities. Not for the husband, not for the children. That's the Russian feminist tradition.[54]

After seventy years of a Soviet state that, if nothing else, lauded women for their roles as mothers, a role women could feel proud of, the tight link between women and the family is not something that women feel comfortable turning their backs on. Furthermore, in the context of a political regime that so thoroughly monopolized the public sphere, the private realm of household and family became highly valued for its relative autonomy. Some women's dislike of "feminism" – interpreted in part as involving an "escape" from domesticity – can be better understood from this perspective.[55]

The identification of women with the family also reinforces the idea that women's "motherhood function" is naturally given, and worthy of "protection" through restrictions on women's labor (the Soviet and Russian labor codes include a lengthy list of hazardous professions forbidden to women).[56] While feminists in the West may think such restrictions unfair, in Russia, a country where healthcare and maternity care are in precipitous decline, where maternal mortality rates are

[53] Alessandra Stanley, "New Face of Russian Capitalism," *New York Times*, August 14, 1996, pp. C1, C16.
[54] Svetlana Kornilova, interview, June 8, 1995.
[55] On this and other clashes between Western and Soviet perceptions of feminism, see Beth Holmgren, "Bug Inspectors and Beauty Queens: The Problems of Translating Feminism into Russian," in Ellen E. Berry, ed., *Postcommunism and the Body Politic* (New York: New York University Press, 1995), pp. 15–31. Similar sentiments have been documented in Eastern Europe. See, for instance, Joanna Goven, "Gender Politics in Hungary: Autonomy and Antifeminism," in Funk and Mueller, *Gender Politics and Post-Communism*, pp. 224–40.
[56] Interview, December 1, 1994.

climbing, and where increasing numbers of children are born with a variety of pathologies, protecting women's reproductive "rights" through labor restrictions may be the only way that women see to preserve their health and that of their children.

Similarly, the economic difficulty of Soviet life forced a dependence on men's help that made women's "independence" (believed to be an integral part of "feminism") not only unappealing to the average Soviet woman, but even impossible. Explained Marina Pavlova, head of the Center for Business Assistance to Women (a job-retraining organization):

[Feminism hasn't been an issue here because] our life was so hard. Our life demanded help from men; our family budgets were always two-salaries, the male and the female. There was no basis for American feminism here.[57]

A member of a single-mothers' association (Tolko Mamy) agreed, saying she did not consider herself a feminist because its connotation of independence was inconsistent with the conditions of her life:

I want to relax, to share my problems with someone else, not have to do everything alone. Being a feminist would mean wanting to be totally independent, to not be involved with a man . . . I'm a strong woman myself, and capable, but I'm tired of doing it all.[58]

That same exhaustion, however, in some women (in this case, an activist with one of Russia's original feminist consciousness-raising groups), gives rise to an embrace of feminism, and in some (rare) cases, an acknowledgment of male privilege in society:

I'm not a fan of struggling against men, but in our society in Russia, men too often use their rights and male privileges, and too often relate disdainfully and arrogantly to the women off whom they're living. They use women's energy in the most direct sense of the word. Even if they don't beat women, or steal their money, they all the same live off women. We all serve men, absolutely all of us. The most intelligent, the most sweet man you could find, all the same waits for you to clean his socks. In the best-case scenario, he'll go shopping, and carry the heavy bags. But all the same, my husband will say, "I went with *you* to the store, I helped *you*." It's so deep-seated in them.[59]

For the majority of women, though, feminism appears to endorse a total independence, as well as a rejection of the family; it is thus seen as undesirable and unrealistic.

---

[57] Marina Pavlova, interview, April 24, 1995.
[58] Informal conversation, February 4, 1995.
[59] Ol'ga Voronina, interview, April 27, 1995.

Equality of suffering: feminism as divisive in a post-totalitarian state

The self-identification of women as a group – an aggrieved group – is further complicated by the Soviet state's repressive legacy, one which affected men as well as women, although in different ways. In considering women's oppression, many women argue that men in Soviet society were oppressed as much as women. They therefore reject feminism – an ideology that appears to focus solely on women's oppression – as not truly reflecting Soviet or post-Soviet conditions. In other words, if women and men were both oppressed equally by the state, then feminism, which seems to divide women from men and sets women's interests apart from men's, is an inappropriate ideology. Valentina Melnikova, press secretary for the Committee of Soldiers' Mothers, explained that she had never considered herself a feminist because of the nature of the Soviet regime:

Feminism for me, is a movement for women's rights. But the thing is, that was never relevant for me, because in our country, *nobody had rights* . . . Why should we talk about women's rights, when everyone is without rights? We shouldn't make separations: we're just citizens . . . Maybe when basic rights are observed, when a citizen can be a citizen . . . then there can be some supplementary rights for women, some supplementary women's struggle . . . Nobody in this organization thinks that women are particularly oppressed.[60]

Nina Gabrielian, a writer and activist with a women's advocacy organization, as well as with a women writers and artists group, explained similarly the popular feeling among Russian women of having oppression in common with men, rather than being oppressed as a result of male domination of the state and the home:

Mentality here is really important. A few years ago, Tatiana Klimenkova [a feminist philosopher] went to [a local women writers' club] where there's no scent of feminism, to give a lecture on feminism, about how the world is androcentric, and so on. There was a backlash – the women said, "But we *pity* our men." This emotional reaction occurs because during the Soviet period both men and women were deprived of their rights. Sure, woman was the slave of a slave. But because of the way things were, with men also being oppressed by the state, women saw their men as comrades in misfortune [*tovarishch' po neschastiu*].[61]

Put differently, the presence of a common enemy – the communist state – in some cases suppresses the sense of women's oppression by patriarchy.

This response is found in noncommunist postauthoritarian regimes as well. Argentinean women, for instance, have also expressed the idea that

[60] Valentina Mel'nikova, interview, May 12, 1995.
[61] Nina Gabrielian, interview, March 19, 1995.

men and women were both oppressed by the state, and that feminism therefore did not apply. Said an activist with a organization of Mothers of the Disappeared:

I don't believe we're feminists. I believe that women in Argentina are oppressed, by the church and by our laws, and I consider that women are equal to men, but I believe that this country has a lot of problems that affect men and women.[62]

Even in nonauthoritarian societies, divisions other than gender-based ones may be the priority in any given community. Sociologist Raka Ray, for example, has argued that women organizing in Calcutta were reluctant to see men as a group with interests separate from and opposed to their own. This reluctance Ray believed to be a result of class being the primary rhetorical frame for societal divisions, because the region was politically dominated by a communist party.[63] In the post-Soviet case, it may not be social class, but *ruling* class that creates the relevant division, still producing a nongendered "us vs. them" struggle, with the population set in opposition to a corrupt and incompetent ruling class.

For these varied reasons, "feminism" appears to have too many negative connotations and associations to operate successfully as a frame with which to talk about women's oppression in post-Soviet Russian society. The absence of a shorthand frame, however, is not the only obstacle to the expansion of the women's movement, and to the transformation of consciousness in contemporary Russia.

Women's socio-cultural status during the transition: attitudes as obstacles to women's movement expansion

The multifaceted Soviet legacy of antifeminism is reinforced by contemporary, post-Soviet societal attitudes toward women. Although discrimination on the basis of sex has always existed in Soviet Russia, such discrimination became increasingly overt with the advent of glasnost (in the form of commercialism) and perestroika (in the form of labor discrimination). During the transition period, women's movement activists have contended not only with the derision of feminism, but with "newly" overt sexism, pornographic images of women, a patriarchal-nationalist upsurge that espouses the return of women to the home, and a renewed stress on women's "natural predestination." Women's movement expansion is hindered in part by the overt messages about

---

[62] Quoted in Jo Fisher, *Mothers of the Disappeared* (Boston: South End Press, 1989), p. 151.
[63] Raka Ray, paper presented at University of California, Santa Cruz/International Sociological Association conference on social movements, Santa Cruz, May 19, 1996.

women's proper roles expressed by public officials, in social structures, in daily interactions, and in the mainstream media (including journalistic treatment of "feminism" and the women's movement). Social attitudes and discourse about the proper role of women have a significant effect on the process of transformation of consciousness.

Public expression of sexism

Social attitudes toward women and women's roles in Russia are frequently essentialist in nature, and often openly sexist. In 1993, then Labor Minister Gennadii Melikian was quoted as saying, "There is no point in creating jobs for women, when there aren't enough jobs for men."[64] Because at that time women made up about two-thirds of Russia's unemployed, the remark seemed particularly insensitive.[65] The subtext of Melikian's argument was the widespread notion that women should be at home raising the children, rather than working outside the home for a salary. Such role stereotypes persist, despite the fact that, under current economic conditions, most families require two salaries in order to stay afloat. Also reflecting Russian politicians' differential evaluation of women's contribution and proper societal role was an incident that received attention from feminist groups in Moscow (and from no one else): in November 1994, Moscow mayor Yuri Luzhkov handed out presents to particularly impressive municipal employees – personal computers for the men and irons for the women.[66]

The labor market also reflects societal attitudes toward women's roles and employment opportunities. Job advertisements, for instance, openly exhibit discrimination on the basis of both sex and age, inviting applications exclusively from men in some cases. According to feminist journalist Nadezhda Azhgikhina, classified ads seeking male applicants to fill positions as accountants and lawyers in new private businesses are commonplace.[67] Moreover, "For hire" advertisements in Russian papers sometimes read more like personal ads than want ads: one can readily encounter advertisements that state "seeking attractive woman, with European features, under thirty-five, and without hangups." The latter phrase is even abbreviated, as b/k (bez kompleksov), and signifies either sex work, or that the woman in question should be willing to put

[64] Anastasia Posadskaia, "Demokratiia minus zhenshchina – ne demokratiia," Ogonek, no. 38, 1993, p. 9.
[65] Rossiiskii statisticheskii ezhegodnik (Moscow: Goskomstat, 1994), p. 459, cited in Penny Morvant, 'Bearing the Double Burden in Russia," Transition, September 8, 1995, p. 7.
[66] "Moskva zavalena vitaminnoi produktsiei," Vechernaia Moskva, November 23, 1994.
[67] See Nadezhda Azhgikhina, "A Movement is Born," Bulletin of Atomic Scientists, July/ August 1995, p. 49.

up with sexual demands by bosses, clients, and so on – an institutionalized form of sexual harassment. Women's roles in the private sector are
being restricted, reflecting a specific societal attitude about women's
proper place, especially in the business world.

Examples abound with which to illustrate social discrimination and the
reinforcement of sex-role stereotyping in Russian society during the
transition period. In 1994, for instance, a two-volume encyclopedia was
published, called *Encyclopedia for Boys* and *Encyclopedia for Girls*. Aside
from chapters on health and beauty, the girls' volume was exclusively
concerned with domestic labor, from taking spots out of clothes to
special ways to prevent bread from spoiling. The boys' volume, in sharp
contrast, contained chapters ranging from apartment repairs ("Your
home is your fortress") to hand-combat skills, to methods for starting
one's own business.[68] These encyclopedias were distributed in one of my
interviewees' daughter's first-grade class, and were widely available in
local bookstores. The girls' proper sphere was clearly delineated, beginning and ending within the home, whereas the boys' sphere extended
throughout the socio-economic arena. This stands in sharp contrast to
the Soviet regime's official rhetoric, which proclaimed that Soviet women
and men were equal in all ways, with similar responsibilities and identical
opportunities in the labor sphere, and even in contrast to the new
Russian constitution of 1993, which recognized that men and women
have equal rights and should have equal opportunities to realize them.

Returning to the kitchen

At the outset of perestroika an unofficial campaign was initiated to
"facilitate women's return to their natural predestination," a campaign
which intensified as the transition toward a market began, and which
reinforced the boundaries of Russian women's limited socio-cultural
status.[69] The "return to the kitchen" campaign was promoted in the
mainstream press, accompanied by warnings about the dangers wrought
by women's emancipation. Olga Voronina described the trend:

The pages of newspapers and journals were covered with articles on the
"women's" theme, though they only printed the opinions of fans of patriarchal
values. Even the *Domostroi* [a sixteenth-century Russian guide to household
management], in which, as is well known, beatings were considered the favored
means of educating one's wife and children, started being propagandized as a

---

[68] *Entsiklopediia dlia devochek* and *Entsiklopediia dlia mal'chikov* (St. Petersburg:
RESPEKS, 1994).
[69] For an overview of perestroika's impact on women, see Mary Buckley, ed., *Perestroika
and Soviet Women* (Cambridge: Cambridge University Press, 1992), and V. V.
Liubimova, ed., *Zhenshchiny v sovremennom mire* (Moscow: Nauka, 1989), part II.

monument to national culture. The point of the overwhelming mass of publications was one – everything was the fault of women and their emancipation. [Valentin] Rasputin [a well-known writer], for example, affirmed that "emancipation is a moral mutation, the moral degradation of the weaker sex." It was increasingly emphasized that today's women suffered from overemancipation and its costs.[70]

Marina Liborakina, an activist with several Moscow-based women's organizations, similarly argued that the "return to the kitchen" campaign took on a mass character, in the media, advertisements, television shows, and women's journals, accompanied by a "blaming mechanism" for women who resisted it – such women were doing harm to men. Liborakina writes, "In this context, a woman's desire to have a well-paid, skilled occupation is seen as egoism: not only does she want to work, she wants to steal this work away from her husband, her brother, her father." The preferred image for women was that of a happy wife and housekeeper, "creatively (!) actualizing herself by mastering a variety of pretty, shiny convenient [household] items."[71] The resemblance to the image of the ideal housewife of the post-World War II era in the United States described by Betty Friedan is striking.[72]

Feminist political scientist Svetlana Aivazova agreed that the private sphere was being resurrected in Russia, after decades of invasive state interference, alongside the myth of a "natural destiny" for both sexes, aimed at limiting women to the private sphere. Aivazova, however, believed the propagation of this myth would inspire women's movement activity and growth, because women, being more educated than men on average and accustomed to high levels of public and productive activity outside the home, would protest the new myth.[73] Indeed, as the transition continued, public opinion surveys suggested that women, even with young children, were increasingly less likely to want to "return to the home." Surveys in late 1992 showed that only 18 percent of women with young children would choose to be full-time housewives if their families could afford it, as opposed to 32 percent in 1991. In other words, despite the increase in the "return to the home" rhetoric, the numbers of women not wanting to work outside the home had dropped.[74]

[70] Voronina, "Zhenshchina i sotsializm," p. 206.

[71] Liborakina, *Obretenie sily*, pp. 50–51.

[72] See, for example, Betty Friedan, "The Way We Were – 1949," in Philip L. Fetzer, ed., *The Ethnic Moment: The Search for Equality in the American Experience* (Armonk, NY: M. E. Sharpe, 1997), pp. 53–67.

[73] Svetlana Aivazova, "Zametki na poliakh stat'i Ann Snitow 'Budushchee feminizma v stranakh byvshego vostochnogo bloka'," *Vy i my*, no. 10, Fall 1994, pp. 16–17.

[74] M. Baskakova, "Sotsial'naia zashchita zhenshchiny – materi v usloviakh transformatsii obshchestva," in V. A. Tishkov, ed., *Zhenshchina i svoboda* (Moscow: Nauka, 1994), p. 144.

The idea of separate spheres and roles for men and women was also reinforced during the transition period by representatives of the Russian Orthodox Church. Church adherents argued that accepting women into the priesthood was "a perversion of the norm, not the establishment of equality," and, while claiming to describe "reality," instead prescribed separate spheres of life and activity for women and men, based ostensibly on women's and men's essential natures:

Let's leave aside the . . . fact that in each man there's something female, and in each woman there's something male, and let's stick to the main thing: a man is more aggressive, more active, more curious, more risk-taking; his creativity is a constant search for innovation. Women create continuity, peace, reliability. Man creates, woman reproduces.[75]

A hegemonic discourse thus reinforced traditional sex roles, stressing women's primary role as reproducers of the nation. Although it is difficult to gauge cultural responses to this discourse, we might hypothesize that the effect of such rhetoric was to depress the likelihood that the women's movement's message about uprooting sex-role stereotypes would get a widespread and sympathetic hearing. It is, however, also possible that the blatantly patriarchal rhetoric itself may have inspired transformation of consciousness in some women.

The new commercialization of women's bodies

Complementary to the idea that women's sphere should not extend beyond the home was an upsurge, beginning under glasnost, of the commercialization and public objectification of women's bodies. The most visible means of objectification was printed pornography. This formerly forbidden fruit became a commonplace presence in the public realm. Pornographic materials were sold in underground street crossings (perekhody), dubbed porno-khody, and wallet-sized pictures of naked women were a staple on the dashboards of many taxicabs. One of the most incongruous sights in the new Russia, particularly in Moscow, was the presence of elderly women standing on busy sidewalks, doing a brisk business in the sale of plastic shopping bags, nearly all of which sported a partially naked, voluptuous woman against the background of a variety of Western corporate symbols. The transformation of women's bodies into consumer goods extended to television and printed advertisements, where women appear in seductive poses and seem to exist in order to serve men and please the (heterosexual) male eye. The proliferation of pornography in a country in which, for decades, laws forbade it was

[75] Iakov Korotov, "Liubov' ne ishchet svoego: ni muzhskogo, ni zhenskogo," Segodnia, March 18, 1995, p. 5.

regarded by some women as simply a phase, a natural reaction against (or liberation from) the asceticism of communism. Others reacted to the spread of pornography with outrage. The Petersburg Center for Gender Issues, for example, initiated a suit against the Russian version of *Playboy* magazine after it published a series of "misogynist" painted images of famous Russian women, including one of Catherine the Great topless, and another of mathematician Sofia Kovalevskaia masturbating.

Sexual objectification of women was also the message expressed in the veritable "epidemic" of beauty contests, which began in the late 1980s, and which glorified various body parts: "Miss Bust, Miss Legs, Miss Ass, and so forth."[76] Marina Liborakina pointed out that these contests became popular at the same time as free elections began for Russia's Supreme Soviet, and noted with irony that as women's representation in politics plummeted, these contests became their own version of "democracy for women."[77]

While pornographic and consumerist images of women did not create an obligatory new identity for women in Russia during the transition period, it seems plausible that the proliferation of these images did have an effect on women, and on women's self-image, not to mention on the ideas and stereotypes that both men and women develop about women's capacities and proper social roles, thereby potentially complicating outreach by the women's movement.

Negative portraits of feminism in the mainstream media

If sex roles during the transition are portrayed as increasingly immutable, and are transmitted through television and other media sources, this may obstruct the women's movement's expansion. Similarly, the media's attitude toward feminism may shape popular receptivity to ideas countering sex-stereotyping and the gendered division of labor. Mainstream media coverage of feminism, however, is rare and usually negative, a fact perhaps echoed in some of the definitions given by activists.

Typical of the negative portrayals of feminism in the Russian press are those articles labeling feminism as a Western phenomenon, an extremist "struggle against men." One such article was published in 1994 in the nationwide newspaper, *Izvestiia*. Its author, a female Russian journalist and sociologist teaching in Chicago, described feminists as women who attack men verbally for attempting to help them with heavy suitcases. She also related a conversation with a feminist friend, who put forth the

[76] Liborakina, *Obretenie sily*, p. 78.   [77] Ibid.

theory that social roles based on gender were the result of sex-role socialization, and that physical differences were "completely unimportant." The author dismissed this idea. She did, however, point out that "family relations" had been altered by feminism, such that men took an equal role in American homes, sharing the housework, "even cooking." And at the close of her article, the author validated the idea of "respect for women as equal partners," and felt that it should be resurrected in Russian society as well. But the overall tone of the article was patronizing toward American feminists, portrayed as extremists who believed it wrong for women to wear makeup in order to please men, and who supported Lorena Bobbitt (who believed that "the sexual needs of her lawful spouse were too burdensome for her").[78] Mention of the actual struggles of feminism, concern about the division of power in society, and men's domination of economic and political decisionmaking did not receive such close attention.

Yet the absence of mainstream media writings about feminism merits our attention more than the occasional negative portrayals of it. A content-analysis study conducted by the Association of Women Journalists, of three months' worth of the mainstream press in fall 1995 revealed that a meager 1 percent of *Izvestiia*'s articles concerned women.[79] It is difficult to uncover the reasons for such a paucity of articles on the topic, but editorial preference and the societal atmosphere may be causes. At a roundtable meeting sponsored by several women's movement groups in 1993, one of the editors of a mainstream women's journal was asked why they had not more actively published materials on feminism. The editor apparently replied that she had pushed very hard to get the journal to publish materials about feminism, but had been unsuccessful. Another participant at the roundtable asked, "And who, at your women's journal, is not letting you print those materials?" The editor thought for a moment and answered, "The very air itself doesn't allow it [da sam vozdukh ne daet]."[80]

Public opinion on emancipation

The lack of media coverage about women's issues and feminism means that the general public is unlikely to be exposed to ideas that contradict the above-described patriarchal images of women's proper societal roles,

---

[78] Ada Baskina, "Amerikanskie zhenshchiny usilivaiut bor'bu protiv muzhchin, a nashi sdaiut svoi pozitsii bez boia," *Izvestiia*, September 7, 1994.

[79] The study included: *Izvestiia, Segodnia, Moskovskii komsomolets, Argumenty i fakti*, and several women's magazines/papers: *Rabotnitsa, Krestianka*, and *Moskvichka*. The study was briefly described in Liborakina, *Obretenie sily*, pp. 80–81.

[80] The interaction was recounted by Nina Gabrielian: interview, March 19, 1995.

and the unappealing images of feminism and feminists that are widely accepted. It is thus not surprising that public opinion on the subject of emancipation reflects confusion and disaffection toward the concept.

Public opinion surveys reveal an ambiguous attitude toward women's liberation in general. According to a Russian news broadcast in 1995, a public opinion poll (of people "all ages and professions") asked respondents whether they were in favor of the "emancipation [emantsipatsiia] of women": 30 percent were in favor, 22 percent against, 24 percent found it difficult to say, and a full 24 percent did not know what "emancipation" meant. When the field was narrowed to Moscow and St. Petersburg, 32 percent of those questioned welcomed emancipation, and 32 percent opposed it. In rural areas, however, to which alternative sources of information about feminism would be unlikely to spread, although 36 percent welcomed emancipation, the majority of the village populations did not know what the term signified.[81]

Without a means of reaching the public, especially outside Russia's major cities, the women's movement might be limited to the circle of women who participate in movement events. To a certain extent, large-scale movement expansion may therefore be at the mercy of the mainstream media and its willingness to act as a tool of consciousness-raising, through its portrayals of the women's movement, "feminism," and women's oppression. The presence of relatively small-circulation feminist publications and more mainstream women's magazines, however, may mitigate this situation.

Changing socio-cultural attitudes toward feminism and feminist ideas

The portrayal of feminism in the media is not completely cut and dried – one occasionally encounters positive coverage of feminism, even in the mainstream media. Moreover, in recent years, feminist ideologies have emerged as part of the public discourse, largely due to the presence of a mainstream women's press, a small-circulation independent women's movement press, and efforts by women's movement activists to lobby the mainstream media and public officials. The mainstream women's media's occasional use of feminist frameworks and coverage of women's issues may promote a sense of group consciousness. As women read about others in similar situations, they may realize that their problems arise from social conditions, rather than from their own personal failures.

[81] RTR, *Vesti* (television news), March 5, 1995, 2 p.m.

Women's press coverage of feminism

Before glasnost, there was precious little coverage of feminism in the mainstream press. Most of the positive coverage began in women's newspapers emerging in the early 1990s, such as *Delovaia zhenshchina* (Businesswoman; a tabloid-size, sixteen-page monthly newspaper, founded in November 1990, with a circulation of approximately 100,000 by 1992), which folded after a few years, and *Novaia zhenshchina* (New Woman; founded in 1992, and defunct soon after), and in occasional supplements to mainstream papers, such as the newspaper *Federatsiia* (Federation), which published four special four-page supplements on women in 1993, called "Vera, Nadezhda, Liubov" (Faith, Hope, Love). These publications covered subjects previously largely ignored by the press, from feminism as a critique of the traditional division of labor between men and women to sexual harassment, domestic violence, and announcements about new women's organizations and their activities.[82] One article pointed out the irony of domestic violence being seen as a family affair, in which male violence is excused almost automatically, whereas, if an unknown man hits a woman on the street, it is considered assault, and the man is prosecuted to the full extent of the law.[83] In an attempt to further inform women of their rights, "Vera, Nadezhda, Liubov" published several UN conventions that Russia had signed, including the UN Convention on the Elimination of All Forms of Discrimination Against Women.

The Soviet/Russian mainstream women's press thus temporarily became a potentially superb source for altering the spectrum of discourse, and creating opportunities for change in social attitudes at the societal and individual level. In early 1991, the first issues of *Moskvichka* (now a weekly Moscow-based woman's newspaper with a circulation of 175,000; tabloid-size, usually sixteen pages, with more of a stress on human interest stories than on high politics), for instance, printed all kinds of statistics about women: about the percentage of female leadership in the national economy, the small percentage of women (compared to men) who raised their skill-level rankings during their first three years of work in a given place, and the high percentage of women whose work did not demand the skill and/or educational level they possessed. One

---

[82] On feminism, see Svetlana Aivazova, "'Novaia zhenshchina'?: pochemu by net?," *Novaia zhenshchina*, no. 1, 1992, p. 2. On sexual harassment, see Natal'ia Gaidarenko, "Ne boites' skazat' 'net!,'" in the same issue, p. 14.

[83] El'vira Novikova, "Zhenshchiny i nasilie," "Vera, Nadezhda, Liubov'," supplement to *Federatsiia*, no. 92, 1993, p. 3.

eye-catching article counted up the amount of work a housewife with a husband and two children does each year:

She washes 18,000 knives, forks, and spoons, 13,000 plates, and 3,000 pots and pans; carrying [these things] around amounts to lifting five tons per year. Statisticians counted the number of steps housewives take while carrying out domestic chores and going to stores, and it totaled over 2,000 kilometers per year.[84]

Presented in this light, it is clear that women's "domestic chores" count as *work*, even if they are not compensated monetarily. It is also clear that such chores, especially when not shared, contribute to the exhaustion that so many Russian women feel. Publishing these kinds of statistics helps women readers to realize they are not alone with their burdens. Women's groups can draw on those potential sentiments.

Similarly, an early issue of *Moskvichka* published an interview with St. Petersburg feminist Olga Lipovskaia, reprinted, interestingly enough, from the mainstream newspaper *Pravda*, in which Lipovskaia debunked the common perceptions of feminism, explaining that feminists were not man-haters, and that an all-female "utopia" would be the equivalent of totalitarianism. She also explained that feminism stood for equal rights for everyone: not just legal rights, but undermining stereotypes, and entailed viewing the traditional division of labor as being socially, not biologically, determined. At the end of the article, the editors of *Moskvichka* declared their intention to pursue a "thorough discussion of the subject."[85] They followed through with another Lipovskaia article, "Woman as an 'object of consumption,'" later that year.[86]

Coverage of feminism and women's issues within the mainstream women's press is mixed. The early issues of *Moskvichka* were certainly progressive, and continued to provide coverage of research on women's public opinion polls (in part because Galina Sillaste, the leader of a women's research organization, sits on *Moskvichka*'s editorial board). *Moskvichka* also served as the vehicle for the publication of the political bloc Women of Russia's bulletins, and, starting in June 1994, printed a regular column on women in the Duma (the lower house of the Russian legislature). Despite these efforts, the newspaper's message is not exclusively feminist. In the guise of articles, for instance, *Moskvichka* runs extensive advertisements for beauty salons. One of these relayed the story of a woman deserted by her husband for a younger woman, a tragedy remedied by a month's work by the salon, which turned her into

---

[84] "Slabyi pol?," *Moskvichka*, no. 1, 1991, p. 1.
[85] Ol'ga Lipovskaia, "Feminizm – slovo ne brannoe," *Moskvichka*, no. 2, 1991, p. 6.
[86] Ol'ga Lipovskaia, "Zhenshchina kak 'ob'ekt potrebleniia,'" *Moskvichka*, no. 8, 1991, p. 7.

a lady (*dama*) with a lovely figure, enlivened face, a modern haircut, "and a happy smile – she and her husband worked everything out. Now, to him, his wife is the most beautiful, the most desirable one."[87]

Similarly, *Sudarushka*[88] (a small-size weekly newspaper, with a circulation of 52,700), which occasionally covers women's movement groups and events, devotes much of its space to sewing patterns and "human interest" stories, and does not pay particular attention to "feminism." The Soviet-era monthly magazine, *Rabotnitsa* (Woman Worker), after creating columns on "the women's movement" and "speaking of feminism" in 1990, continuing until 1993, underwent a makeover, and emerged in 1994–95 (with a circulation of approximately 500,000) as an occasional source of information about women's movement groups, but without its former columns focusing specifically on the movement.

The transition period brought financial hardship to the women's press, and many publications (like *Delovaia zhenshchina* and *Novaia zhenshchina*) folded. In their place appeared glossy new women's magazines (including a Russian version of *Cosmopolitan*), and semi-trashy papers like *Zhenskie dela* (Women's Affairs; with a circulation of 450,000), each monthly issue of which pictured a bare-breasted woman on the cover, and the statement "A monthly newspaper for Her and for Him." Even *Zhenskie dela*, however, included the occasional antitraditional message. Amongst relationship advice ("Want to improve your sex appeal?" and "How to get yourself married") and beauty tips, one article in mid-1995 noted that, while "today's women's educational level and professional qualifications often exceed those of men," women rarely attain high professional positions, and men advance more easily in their careers. The social psychologist writing the article suggested that women should insist on a more fair division of responsibilities within the home, "including childrearing."[89] This blatant defiance of the traditional division of labor suggests that a feminist message about choice and socially determined sex roles is breaking through to the popular media.

The mainstream media and the feminist message

By the mid-1990s, in addition to having several "women's press" vehicles (granted, of varying quality and type) for occasional attention to

---

[87] "L. V. Samaia krasivaia, samaia zhelannaia," *Moskvichka*, no. 25, 1994, p. 3.

[88] "Sudarushka" is the diminutive form of "sudarynia," a pre-revolutionary term for "Madame."

[89] Lidiia Onishchenko, "Uchit'sia, pravo, ne greshno, dazhe esli v roli uchitelei vystupaiut muzhchiny," *Zhenskie dela*, no. 7, 1995, p. 4. For the "relationship advice," see p. 11 ("Mezhdu nami – devochkami") of that issue.

their ideas, the women's movement had developed fairly good contacts in the mainstream media, from Radio Nadezhda, a women-run radio station that includes coverage of women's movement organizations' activities, to *Ogonek* (a popular newsmagazine) and *Nezavisimaia gazeta* (a liberal newspaper), which began a bi-monthly women's page in late 1995, edited by Nadezhda Azhgikhina, a leader of the Association of Women Journalists. The newspaper *Moskovskaia pravda*, too, began a monthly "women's" page in 1995, with articles on rape, abortion and the need for contraceptives, the upcoming UN Worldwide Conference on Women, and the formation of a club for female directors of textile factories.[90] *Express-khronika* (a weekly four-page newspaper, with a circulation of 15,000, financed by the Eurasia Foundation and other Western sources) initiated a page on "the women's movement," edited by feminist activist Tatiana Lipovskaia, which provided digests of stories from the small-circulation independent women's movement press, and articles on women's movement groups, like the "Sisters" Rape Crisis Center for women in Moscow.[91]

Russian television has also adopted an occasional focus on women and feminism. Channel TV 6, for instance, has recently begun a talk show called *Ia Sama* (I Myself) with one chair occupied by Mariia Arbatova, a playwright and leader of Moscow's Klub Garmoniia, as mentioned in the introduction to this book. Arbatova sees the show as a venue that helps propagate a definition of "feminist" as someone who is "not a . . . lesbian, a spiteful man-hater, or a sexually unsatisfied lady from academic circles who makes her salary from Western grants by studying women's issues."[92] Even if the episodes provide little opportunity for feminist analysis, the very pronunciation of the word on Russian television on a regular basis may help to overcome some of the popular unfamiliarity with feminism.

In the meantime, feminists in Russia persist in using the term. Said a woman doing press relations for a feminist advocacy group in Moscow:

This work with the press is important because if people talk about and hear about the term "feminism," and if there's a concrete political program behind it, for example "to end the war in Chechnia," then it won't be a scary word, like "man-hating." It needs to be pronounced. It's men that profit from feminism being seen as hatred of men.[93]

Of the major Moscow newspapers, *Segodnia* devoted the most

[90] See *Moskovskaia pravda*, July 27, 1995, p. 8; June 29, 1995, p. 8; March 29, 1995, p. 8.
[91] See *Express-khronika*, June 23, 1995, p. 2.
[92] See interview with Mariia Arbatova, "Teper' ia pishu prozu," *Vy i my almanakh*, no. 1 (13), 1997, p. 25.
[93] Laima Geidar, interview, July 17, 1995.

coverage to the women's movement and feminism. This coverage was relatively balanced. In a short piece about a seminar at the Moscow Center for Gender Studies (MCGS), held in preparation for the UN Fourth Worldwide Conference on Women, a journalist defined "gender" for the readership, and described the purpose of MCGS as being to create a positive image of women, "which goes beyond stereotypes about women's natural predestination." The author devoted one-third of her article to a description of MOLLI, the Moscow-based lesbian organization, one of whose representatives appeared at the seminar. This may have been for sensationalist purposes, but the description of the organization was fair, and MOLLI's leader was quoted extensively, saying how insulting it was for lesbians to be seen as "perverts" and "mentally ill." The article defined gender as "one's social sex"; and "gender analysis" was defined as positing the differences between the sexes not as "natural givens" but rather as stemming from social, economic, and political conditions.[94] *Segodnia* later printed a lengthy article about the UN conference by Marina Liborakina, co-director of the Inform Center of the Independent Women's Forum, thereby giving voice to a feminist activist.[95]

Most impressively, in October 1994, *Segodnia* published a four-page insert (for their subscribers only, not for newsstand sales) on women in the twentieth century, providing statistics about women's status (on a variety of indicators from employment, education, and the use of contraceptive methods, to an index of women's status). Two pages were devoted to full-color maps, charting the levels of women's alcoholism and rate of tuberculosis infection, the percentage of women employed in strenuous physical labor, and the birth rate and abortion rate, across Russia's provinces. Another map illustrated the electoral success of the political bloc, Women of Russia, accompanied by an article entitled "The Political Chances for Feminism." This was an expensive project, and the fact that it did not appear on March 8th (International Women's Day), often the only day on which newspapers devote significant attention to women's issues, suggests that *Segodnia* took the project seriously.

Although mainstream media coverage of feminism remained quite sparse, the coverage that women's movement activists were able to generate had become increasingly balanced by the mid-1990s. To a certain extent, then, the mainstream media has helped to propagate positive impressions of feminism and of feminists, which might help to

---

[94] Elena Klimenko, "Sotsial'nyi pol rossiiskikh zhenshchin," *Segodnia*, December 20, 1994, p. 6.

[95] *Segodnia*, October 26, 1995.

counterbalance the widespread negative societal impressions of these concepts.

The independent women's movement press

While the market eradicated indigenous women's newspapers like *Delovaia zhenshchina*, foreign funding made possible the publication of several small-run feminist journals in the early 1990s, such as *Vy i my* (You and We; founded in 1990), *Vse liudi sestry* (All People Are Sisters; 1993), and the newsletter *Vestnik zhenskogo informatsionno-obrazovatelnogo proekta* (Bulletin of the Women's Informational-Educational Project; 1995). Other feminist publications operated on indigenous funding, or through other organizations; these included the journal *Preobrazhenie* (Transfiguration; 1993), *FemInf* (Feminist Informational Journal; 1992), and the newsletter *Zhenskoe dvizhenie v SSSR* (The Women's Movement in the USSR; 1990). This independent women's movement press covers feminism and the women's movement directly, but its publications are reproduced in such limited circulation that their impact in the broader population is nearly insignificant.[96]

These publications do, however, focus directly on feminism, and provide a wide variety of definitions for it which might appeal to the public, rather than the implicit definitions perpetuated by mainstream press articles. Feminist author Nina Gabrielian, for example, defined feminism as an ideology that did not blame individual men for women's oppression, but rather as one which pointed to a social structure that sustains gender hierarchy, to the detriment of both sexes:

Who discriminates against women? Men? No, women are discriminated against by social institutions, which manipulate *both* sexes, and by various political

[96] To provide some impression of the limited circulation of the women's movement press, *Vse liudi sestry*, for example, has had five issues since its inception, at about 1,000 copies per issue; the newsletter *Vestnik* put out four issues in 1995, with perhaps a few hundred printed; and *FemInf* was put out four times between 1992 and 1994, also with a few hundred copies. *Preobrazhenie* is a thick journal that has had three (yearly) issues, with a circulation of several thousand copies. *Vy i my*, a joint US–Soviet/Russian newsletter/journal, has had thirteen issues between 1990 and the beginning of 1997, and now has a circulation of 5,000 distributed across Russia by activists. Even with limited circulation, the impact of these predominantly internal movement publications can be very strong, helping core activists to cement group identity, to share activist experiences, organizing tips, and ideas, and to promote movement organizing in general. A moving letter written to the editor of *Vy i my* attested to the value of the journal to activists. The author wrote that she had used materials from the journal in her on-the-job training courses for women working at schools and childcare centers, and had found out about women's movement organizations across Russia only from reading the journal: "It was amazing: the Americans were helping us discover each other." See Liubov' Shmyleva, co-director of the Congress of Women from the Kola Peninsula (Murmansk), *Vy i my almanakh*, no. 1 (13), 1997, p. 7.

techniques, which impute particular role stereotypes, assigning women a subordinate status relative to men. Thus, any person who thinks that sex discrimination is inadmissible and immoral can consider themselves a feminist, and those who are in favor of it can call themselves antifeminists, and thereby count themselves among the "honorary" circles where you find anti-Semites, chauvinists, and racists.[97]

In the first issue of *Vse liudi sestry*, the journal of the Petersburg Center for Gender Issues, Natasha Popova, a feminist activist, explained feminism thus: "In general, feminism is when it doesn't occur to anyone to relate to me disparagingly simply because I am a woman."[98] Olga Lipovskaia in the same journal provided a definition of feminism related to freedom:

For me, feminism is a way of life and a way of thinking. It's a type of world in which neither I, nor my daughter, nor my sisters and friends would be afraid to walk down dark streets because someone might rape them. It's equality in family responsibilities, and equal responsibility for childrearing for the father and mother. It's freedom of choice for both women and men: to create, to earn money, to sit at home with the children, or go on a business trip. It's when a person is valued for their professional abilities, not for their sex, when they're being considered for a job, or in an election to political office . . . In that world, the one we feminists want, there will be no place for a husband and father's cruelty to a wife and children, for the cruelty of one race toward another, and there will be no division into the weaker and stronger sexes. In a word, feminism is an integral part of the general concept of democracy. The pity is that in my country there are few people who understand that.[99]

These explanations perhaps help to undermine the popular conception of feminism as an ideology advocating the double burden, and denouncing men and femininity. The publications in which pro-feminist definitions appear are, however, available to only a limited circle of people, many of whom are activists already sharing a positive impression of feminism. Most of the population still learns about feminism and the women's movement only from the mainstream press, which presents a mixed picture at best, and is largely silent about these issues most of the time.

Framing the women's movement in post-Soviet Russia

Feminism is much maligned in Russia. Yet, as the increasing coverage in the media suggests, women's issues are significant to activists, and also to many average people, who may lack a political analysis of sex-based

[97] Nina Gabrielian, cited in "Novosti kul'tury," *Vestnik*, no. 2–3, 1995, p. 20.
[98] Natasha Popova, "Nash feminizm," *Vse liudi sestry*, no. 1–2, 1993, p. 3.
[99] Ol'ga Lipovskaia, "Nash feminizm," *Vse liudi sestry*, no. 1–2, 1993, p. 4.

oppression. Before joining a social movement organization, activists have often framed the issues for themselves. Later framing processes are intentional and are undertaken by social movement organizations and activists, in the attempt to reach out to the population at large. But, while a set of words providing a shorthand political analysis, like "feminism" and "discrimination" do exist, they are often perceived as being foreign, bourgeois, and irrelevant to the Russian situation. Other words, like "gender," do not exist at all in the Russian language. How, then, can activists hope to do outreach to the broader population, to attract them to a social movement supporting women's rights?

Social movement theorists have demonstrated repeatedly that issue framing is an important factor in determining whether or not people will be attracted to any given cause.[100] Without a language available to express the fundamental ideas underlying the social movement, the development of a suitable frame will be difficult. Moreover, in order for a frame to be most useful, it ought to "resonate" with positively regarded values, concepts, and ideas from within the culture of a given country (or community). In the United States, for instance, many social justice movements rely on a "rights" framework, because the idea of "rights" is fairly well entrenched in US political culture.[101] For the reasons explored above, "feminism" is a poor framework for women activists in Russia to use as an outreach tool, because "equality" does not resonate well with the population. But it is difficult in Russian to pithily express the idea of discrimination on the basis of socially constructed sex stereotypes, and the limits they place on women and men alike, especially absent the use of the words "gender" and "feminism" as a shorthand. Perhaps for this reason, some activists stick with these terms, trying to reclaim them, and to reeducate their audiences simultaneously.

The public use of "feminism" as a framework with which to discuss women's status is of relatively recent origin. During the Brezhnev era, discrimination against women was not discussed, except in academic and policymaking circles, where notice was taken of falling birth rates, and women's difficulties combining their "duties" as mothers and workers outside the home. In response to what Russian nationalists decried as a "demographic crisis" in European Russia, much discussion of ways to facilitate that combination occurred, ranging from egalitarian to patriarchal approaches, where the egalitarian approach advocated

---

[100] See for example, David A. Snow and Robert D. Benford, "Ideology, Frame Resonance, and Participant Mobilization," in Bert Klandermans, Hanspeter Kriesi, and Sidney Tarrow, eds., *From Structure to Action: Social Movement Participation Across Cultures* (Greenwich, CT: JAI Press, 1988), pp. 197–217.

[101] Witness movements for "civil rights," "children's rights," "fathers' rights," and "animal rights."

challenging sex-role stereotypes in the labor sphere and at home, and involving men more extensively in childrearing, and the patriarchal approach favored returning women to the home.[102]

While academics may have discussed the egalitarian approach as far back as the Brezhnev era, according to Marina Liborakina, a "feminist" analysis of the issues did not begin to enter public consciousness until feminist works in Russian were published, in the late 1980s and early 1990s. These analyses were written by academics, some of whom later formed Russia's first feminist organizations. Until that time, "it was not acknowledged that the conflicts in women's self-realization were being reproduced not only by traditional culture, but also by state policy, which supports a patriarchal family arrangement," where women, with unpaid labor, support the entire economic system.[103]

Some years later, gender analysis is still a rarity in Russian social science and government analysis. In fact, the terminology itself is as unfamiliar as the practice. In a March 1996 appeal to the Duma, a group of women's organizations demanded the establishment of a "gender expertise" group to analyze all legislation in light of its potential effects on women, and to make sure that the legislation was in line with the Russian constitution's clause guaranteeing women and men equality of rights and freedoms, and the opportunity to exercise them. Aware that the legislators would no doubt be unfamiliar with the term "gender," the women's groups followed "gender expertise" with an explanatory phrase: "that is, expert analysis from the perspective of observing the equal rights and opportunities of women and men."[104]

To some extent, the women's movement has adopted the vocabulary provided by feminist researchers during the transition period, and now works on framing women's issues for popular consumption (for decisionmakers in particular), providing explanations of the "foreign" terminology when they deem it necessary.[105] The very foreignness of the word "gender," however, has brought criticism upon those who use it as a means of framing the issue of women's inferior status in Russia. Some Russian activists are criticized (by other activists) for appearing to master English expressions like "gender" and "feminism" purely in

---

[102] For a summary of four approaches to the "woman question" in the early perestroika period, see N. Zakharova, A. Posadskaia, and N. Rimashevskaia, "Kak my reshaem zhenskii vopros," *Kommunist*, no. 4, 1989, pp. 56–65. For an analysis of social scientists' and state officials' policy approaches toward the "woman question" in the USSR, see Lapidus, *Women in Soviet Society*, especially ch. 8.

[103] Liborakina, *Obretenie sily*, pp. 48–49.

[104] "Obrashchenie k deputatam VI gosudarstvennoi dumy," author's files.

[105] The Moscow Center for Gender Studies is widely acknowledged as having originally provided this vocabulary in their various analyses.

order to talk with their Western colleagues, instead of focusing on ways to communicate feminist ideas to their own countrypeople in a language comprehensible to all.[106] Indeed, without such a language, activist efforts to facilitate transformation of consciousness within the general population may meet with difficulty.

Alternative frames: if not feminism, then what?

Marina Liborakina, in her book about the Russian women's movement's attempt to overcome discrimination in the cultural sphere, argued that "Cultural changes are impossible without the creation of a new symbolic order – images embodying new values and experience solving problems, which arise among those people able to build their destinies in a new way."[107] Creating the new symbolic order, however, is a difficult task for a new social movement lacking consistent access to the national media, most of which propagates a message opposite to the one adopted by the social movement. In Russia, that task is complicated by the fact that "feminism" and, to a certain extent, "equality" have both been delegitimated as positive concepts in the Russian socio-cultural arena. Against this background, we can explore the alternate frames that Russian women's movement activists have used to express their messages to the population and to decisionmakers.

Equal rights and equal opportunities

Although concepts like "equality" and "feminism" were devalued, the "equal rights" ideology of the Bolsheviks did establish a framework and retains some currency among women's groups and activists, albeit in modified form. Without endorsing "equality," and without using "feminism" (since the term carries such a strong negative valence) or "sexism" (a foreign word – *seksizm* – unfamiliar to nearly the entire population), activists can call for plain old "equal rights and equal opportunities," thereby sounding fair without sounding radical.

But there are two problems with the "equal rights and equal opportunities" framework. The first of these is that the phrase may be too similar to "equality"; that is, the subtle distinction between *ravnye prava i ravnye vozmozhnosti* and *ravenstvo* could be lost on parts of the population. Thus, that framework may fail to truly depart from the problems with the "equality" framework detailed above.

---

[106] See "Rossiiskii i zapadnyi feminizm: problemy dialoga," *Vy i my*, no. 10, Fall 1994, esp. pp. 21–22.

[107] Liborakina, *Obretenie sily*, p. 34.

The second problem relates to the concrete meaning that activists attribute to the concept "equal rights and equal opportunities" when it comes to policymaking. For some activists, the term is vague, simply shorthand for the idea that stereotypes should not impinge upon women's and men's life choices. In other words, if a woman wants to stay home and take care of her children, she should not be compelled to work outside the home; likewise, if a woman wants to work full-time, her choice should be facilitated by available childcare facilities, and by men's willingness to share or take primary responsibility for child-rearing. But it does not imply "equality" in the sense of "eliminating all differences between men and women." For example, one of the women running Russia's women's radio station (Radio Nadezhda) said:

for us, feminism means equal rights and equal opportunities and equal responsibilities: real equality. Equal rights [*ravnopravie*] but not equality in everything [*ravenstvo*] – because women are physically weaker than men, although women are psychologically stronger . . . But physically, it's absurd that women work on the railroad. There are some jobs men should have. So for us, feminism is equal rights, opportunities, responsibilities, but in no way for us does it mean equality in everything.[108]

Similarly, another activist agreed that the women's movement should focus on creating equal rights, but not on treating women and men as though they were biologically equivalent, arguing, "Nature gave women the motherhood function, which has to be protected."[109]

But not all women's movement activists agree with the idea that women need to be "protected," especially when it comes to Russia's labor code. These activists are working to *eliminate* "protective legislation" from the labor code, in the name of equal rights and equal opportunities. The existing laws include a ban on women's employment in hundreds of occupations, a ban on work deemed dangerous to a woman's reproductive health, and a series of other limitations having to do with pregnancy and maternity.

To many women's movement activists, this "protective" legislation is problematic for several reasons. First, the protective aspect of the legislation is seen as patronizing. Rather than providing information about the risks and benefits of any given job, the government chooses to rule that women cannot make intelligent decisions about their occupations (but does not make a similar assumption about men, who are not restricted from any occupations). Secondly, the legislation is seen as extremely hypocritical, because millions of women were and continue to be employed in occupations labeled as "hazardous" and in heavy

[108] Tat'iana Zeleranskaia, interview, July 10, 1995.
[109] Interview, December 1, 1994.

manual labor. Thirdly, many high-paying jobs are found on the list of restricted occupations, and, often, the restrictions seem nonsensical (for example, women are not allowed to drive buses, but are permitted to work as tram drivers; they are not allowed to be pilots, but may work as flight attendants; and so on).

For activists lobbying state representatives, however, the most important problem with the protective legislation is related to its effects on women and the apparently long-term economic crisis in Russia occurring during the transition period. As long as protective legislation is in force, employers face hiring women who can be moved – by law – from hazardous and burdensome jobs if they become pregnant or have a child under age one and a half; who cannot be fired if they are pregnant or have a young child (under age three), unless the enterprise is being completely liquidated; who cannot be employed in overtime work if pregnant, or if they have a child between the ages of three and fourteen; who must be granted part-time work if pregnant, or if they have children under age fourteen; and who may not be sent on business trips, or work night shifts, overtime, or on holidays if they have a child under three years of age.[110] In a now competitive labor market, women who benefit from all of these restrictions and privileges make unattractive employees. Activists argue that the labor code should be altered to reflect the value of "parenthood," rather than "motherhood."

In practice, eliminating this "protective" legislation and making the benefits gender-neutral would amount to eliminating women's privileges in the labor force. But, as the activists see it, as long as those privileges are in place, women will have a more difficult time winning promotions, and those women not yet employed will have an increasingly hard time getting hired. But many women do not want to lose these privileges, thinking of their short-term rather than long-term ramifications. For example, asked about this issue, one woman with a single-mothers' organization said:

Why do I say I'm not a feminist, but an antifeminist? Maybe it sounds paradoxical, but I'd like some discrimination against me as a woman, taking into account that I have to raise my child![111]

Apparently, popular enthusiasm for "equal rights and equal opportunities" as a framework, as long as it is linked to an apparent denial of women's privileges in the labor sphere, is not likely to garner a lot of support for the women's movement.

---

[110] See the Labor Law Code (KZoT), Chapter XI: Women's Labor.
[111] Interview, January 22, 1995.

Democracy

In an attempt to appeal to the population at large and to decision-makers, numerous women's movement activists try to frame their desire to improve women's socio-economic and political status as being somehow essential to democracy and the democratic process. This framework was publicized when the First Independent Women's Forum (the first nationwide gathering of women's movement groups) opened in 1991 under a slogan that would be later repeated by movement activists across the entire Russian spectrum: "Democracy Without Women Is Not Democracy!"

The idea behind the "democracy" framework is that having more women in power equals more democracy, and that democracy is desirable for Russia. By extension, establishing a new political system while excluding women is "undemocratic" and, therefore, undesirable. Some activists link the "democracy" framework to both macropolitics and micropolitics. In this view, the need to eliminate totalitarianism, replacing it with "democratic" relationships, exists in the public sphere, as well as in the family, where there exists a hierarchy based on sex. Wrote Marina Liborakina, "A society in which the idea of totalitarian control, a hier-archical type of social relations, is reproduced on the gender level, cannot be democratic ... Feminism, which speaks for free choice and self-definition of the individual, is a cultural choice in favor of real democracy."[112] Democracy, egalitarian relationships, and feminism are thus put on the positive side, weighing in against the hierarchical totalitarian system. Clearly the democracy framework has a certain appeal to activists precisely because it is counterpoised to the repressive Leninist past.[113]

Democracy as a frame for women's rights issues in Russia, however, is of rather limited utility, because "democracy" itself has been a victim, by association, of the transition period. By the mid-1990s, "democracy," as implemented in Russia, had been equated at the popular level with corruption, inflation, privilege, crime, Western incursions (in the form of violent movies shown on television, harmful food products, external interference in the economy), and so on. The popular value placed on "democracy" in the abstract was low, as demonstrated by an opinion poll held in January 1996. When asked: "Which do you think is more important, 'order' or 'democracy,' only 9 percent of respondents chose

---

[112] Liborakina, *Obretenie sily*, p. 107.

[113] Sonia Alvarez found a similar framing of feminist issues in Brazil, linking the emancipation of women to "larger struggles for justice and democracy in Brazilian society." See her *Engendering Democracy in Brazil: Women's Movements in Transition Politics* (Princeton: Princeton University Press, 1990), p. 102.

the latter.[114] "Democracy" may therefore also be an ill-chosen framework under which to promote a struggle for improving women's status.

Human rights

Some feminist activists have turned to the international language of "human rights" as a way to talk about feminism and altering women's status (meaning rights and the opportunity to enjoy them), such that the gap between men's and women's socio-political standing would decrease. Under this straightforward framework, "women's rights are human rights." Many activists have adopted this idiom, in part because it seems unassailable on moral grounds and reflects the language used to discuss women's rights in documents adopted by the United Nations and other international organizations.

Some activists replace "feminism" directly with "human rights." One of the main advocacy organizations in Moscow, the Inform Center of the Independent Women's Forum asserted on the cover page of its newsletter that their organization "shares the idea that women's rights are an inalienable part of human rights, and supports all initiatives that arise within the framework of defending human rights."[115] Elvira Novikova, an activist and longtime researcher into women's issues in Russia and the USSR, similarly put her faith in "human rights" as the framework that had the best chances of succeeding, given the bias toward the rhetoric commonly adopted by women's movements:

In the United States, there are many diverse sentiments toward feminism, but it's gotten into the social consciousness somehow, as opposed to in Russia, where the patriarchy is still very strong. We don't even accept the words "feminism" and such. But if we talk about it in terms of human rights, then we have a chance.[116]

Activists have had some success using these terms in their interactions with Russian state officials. The "human rights" language has even been integrated into policy papers issued by the Russian government. A Ministry of Social Protection position paper on improving women's status, affirmed by Prime Minister Chernomyrdin's government in January 1996, for instance, announced that it was based on the fact that "women's rights are an inalienable part of general human rights."[117]

---

[114] Seventy-seven percent of respondents chose order. See Michael Kramer, "The People Choose," *Time*, May 27, 1996, pp. 49–57.

[115] "My schitaem . . .," *Vestnik*, no. 4, 1995, p. 1.

[116] El'vira Novikova, interview, February 17, 1995.

[117] "Kontseptsiia uluchsheniia polozheniia zhenshchin v Rossiiskoi Federatsii," confirmed by decree no. 6 of the Russian Federation Government, adopted January 8, 1996, author's files.

There is no doubt that women's movement activists influenced this language through their framing of the issues.

Patriarchal domination

Sometimes radical frames emerge in unexpected quarters. Despite all the accusations that feminists are man-haters and so forth, noticeably few Russian feminists venture at all close to blaming men (individually or collectively) for women's relatively low status in Russia's economic, political, and social gender hierarchies. Yet, the political bloc Women of Russia (WOR), labeled conservative and antifeminist by not a few women's movement activists, provided a very unusual frame for analyzing women's status in one of their 1995 campaign brochures. In it, WOR argued that women's failure to attain powerful political and economic decisionmaking positions was the result of intentional actions by men occupying such positions, guarding them against encroachment:

Among directors of major enterprises, women make up 9 percent. In all, among [economic] leaders, women make up not more than 10 percent, but among all workers, they're 51 percent. It is evident that male managers [*muzhchiny-upravlentsy*] consciously do not allow women – in whom the voters increasingly place their trust – into power.[118]

The fact that this political bloc of women, who at the time held a place in the Duma, would use such a relatively radical framework suggests that the frames for improving women's status are in flux, and that politicians, as well as activists, are searching for frames that will effectively resonate with their audiences.[119]

Conclusion

The foregoing analysis suggests that the framing options available to women activists in Russia are highly restricted. On the one hand, the rhetoric of gender equality was appropriated by the Bolsheviks, who used it to justify women's engagement in industrial production, without altering the domestic division of labor. "Equality," therefore, is identified with women's experience under Soviet rule, during which it signified an oppressive "double burden" of full time work, both within and outside the home. Meanwhile, the Soviet leadership used the term "discrimination" mainly to describe policies of race-based oppression in the West, and derogated "feminism" as a bourgeois phenomenon. Precisely because of this legacy, the chairwoman of the Committee on

[118] Zhenshchiny Rossii, *Informatsionnyi biulleten'*, no. 5, September 1995, p. 14, sidebar.
[119] WOR also used the "equal rights and equal opportunities" and "democracy" frames.

Women's Affairs in the USSR Council of Ministers, Tatiana Lukia-
nenko, commenting in 1991 on the women's movement's potential for
success, stated: "I think that we need to replace 'feminism' with some
other word, simply to avoid confusion."[120] Russian women activists
have thus been left searching for a language with which to express
"gender" interests – a word with no Russian equivalent. Although some
activists have nonetheless adopted English-language terms with which
to frame their issues, this alienates average women as well as policymakers.

The lack of a resonant frame makes the spread of feminist ideas
difficult in Russia. Indeed, theorists argue, the spread of social movement ideas requires new frames, cultural symbols, and "vocabularies."[121] These new ideas, however, must draw to some degree on "the
larger societal definitions of relationships, of rights, and of responsibilities to highlight what is wrong with the current social order, and to
suggest directions for change."[122] In contemporary Russia, it is precisely
these social definitions that have entered a state of flux. Under such
transitional circumstances, the women's movement may not yet have
found a means of expressing feminist ideas in a way that culturally
resonates with the population.

Indeed, women's movement groups in Russia that are currently
calling for "equal rights and equal opportunities" (which entails disman-
tling "protective legislation" for women) may be clashing with the
popular desire in today's Russia to "restore the social safety net." The
WOR political bloc, whose election platform in 1993 had called for such
a restoration, ultimately adopted the feminists' position of ending
protective legislation, and were not reelected in 1995. Thus, not only
transformation of consciousness and framing, but also the "cultural
resonance" of social movement demands, becomes a critical component
contributing to the success and development of social movements.[123]

The flux in societal definitions about relationships, rights, and respon-

---

[120] "Po materialam 'Kruglykh stolov,'" *Zheskoe dvizhenie v SSSR*, no. 3, April–June 1991, p. 1.

[121] See Lynn Hunt, *Politics, Culture and Class in the French Revolution* (Berkeley: University of California Press, 1984), cited in Hank Johnston and Bert Klandermans, eds., *Social Movements and Culture* (Minneapolis: University of Minnesota Press, 1995), pp. 13–14.

[122] Mayer N. Zald, "Culture, Ideology, and Strategic Framing," in Doug McAdam, John D. McCarthy, and Zald, eds., *Comparative Perspectives on Social Movements* (Cambridge: Cambridge University Press, 1996), p. 267.

[123] William Gamson and Andre Modigliani, "Media Discourse and Public Opinion on Nuclear Power: A Constructionist Approach," *American Journal of Sociology*, vol. 95, no. 1 (1989), p. 5, cited in Dieter Rucht, "German Unification, Democratization, and Social Movements: A Missed Opportunity?," *Mobilization*, vol. 1, no. 1 (March 1996), p. 50.

sibilities during Russia's transition period has also included an unfettering of public sex-based discrimination and sexism. The media has extensively propagated a new image of women, which reinforces traditional sex-role stereotypes: the post-Soviet woman is no longer the "new Soviet woman," capable of driving a tractor and raising a family simultaneously (whether or not she wanted to); her relationship to society has contracted. She is now supposed to focus on her sex appeal, her home, and her husband and children, rather than on combining private- and public-sphere roles. The new image of women also creates socio-cultural barriers to the women's movement message about undoing sex-based stereotypes. Thus, changes in the definitions of societal relationships can also create varying opportunities and obstacles to movement expansion via the transformation of consciousness.

Despite whatever obstacles exist in the path of a social movement, activists still generally attempt to uncover a resonant frame for their issues, in order to "mobilize people and resources within the wider society in order to influence [the] authoritative elite," often through the media, because activists usually lack established and routinized connections to the policy establishment.[124] In Russia, however, this part of the paradigm breaks down somewhat. The "authoritative elite," accustomed to decades of top-down decisionmaking, is not particularly interested in the opinions held by the wider society, unless they are striking *en masse* or being otherwise extremely disruptive, practices in which women in contemporary Russia have not yet engaged on their own behalf as a social group. Therefore, women's movement activists may believe that outreach to the population is less important than finding ways to express their issues in terms that policymakers can understand. For reasons further explored in the remaining chapters of the book, the movement tends to focus most on connections with the state, and least on rallying the public to their cause.

---

[124] John D. McCarthy, Jackie Smith, and Mayer N. Zald, "Accessing Public, Media, Electoral, and Governmental Agendas," in McAdam, McCarthy, and Zald, *Comparative Perspectives*, p. 291.

4 "Democracy without women is not democracy!": political opportunities and obstacles to women's movement organizing

> The political situation is the most important thing, even more important than the lack of money. Here, instead of politics, we have antipolitics. It's not clear what will happen. We live on a volcano. Today it's like this. But tomorrow, the Bolsheviks or the radicals could come to power, and everything will fall apart; nothing will happen.[1]
>
> Moscow activist, commenting on obstacles to women's movement organizing

The political transition period in Russia, starting in the late 1980s under Soviet rule and continuing into the mid-1990s, created a multidimensional set of opportunities for the emerging women's movement. Glasnost reduced censorship, and allowed for open discussions of previously unaddressed issues, including discrimination against women in the labor force, lack of women's representation in high political office, and domestic violence. Meanwhile, the shift from Communist Party rule to a more pluralistic regime increased the relative openness of the political system to autonomous social movements, including the women's movement, and moderated the state's repressive character. Indeed, within a few years of the introduction of glasnost and perestroika, large women's conferences were held, independent of state control, and dozens of women's groups had formed, building on women's transformation of consciousness. These organizations raised controversial issues and spoke out publicly in ways that had attracted harsh repression only a decade earlier.

Yet, from their emergence in the late 1980s, the independent women's groups wishing to influence state policy in a feminist direction faced an uphill battle. The branches of government, and all the major political factions were, and continued to be, dominated by men, operating within a climate of backlash against active roles for women outside the domestic sphere. Meanwhile, in exchange for loans, the state was acquiescing to international lending agencies' demands to dismantle the social safety net (including social welfare benefits for women) and

---

[1] Interview, November 27, 1994.

allowing increasing unemployment, which affected women disproportionately. The women's groups hoping to counter these trends under-
took efforts to utilize their newfound political freedoms to petition the
state for redress of their economic and political grievances.

Due to a changing mix of allies within sectors of the government,
independent women's groups advocating for change managed to achieve
somewhat sporadic contact with the state, and affect the course of
several significant policies during the transition period. However,
because of the entrenched cultural, economic, and political obstacles
that the movement faced, and because of its continued relative power-
lessness, after several years of effort, the movement had not succeeded
in reversing the overall downward trend in women's economic and
political fortunes.

In fact, by 1995, the Russian women's movement had made few
inroads into the structures of political power. The dramatic transformation of the Soviet and Russian political systems was not in and of itself a
guarantee of success for any of Russia's emergent social movements.

Political opportunity structure is a multidimensional concept enabling us to analyze some of the reasons for a social movement's
success or failure. According to a consensus definition compiled by
sociologist Doug McAdam, political opportunity structure includes
four dimensions:

1. The relative openness or closure of the institutionalized political
   system;
2. The stability or instability of that broad set of elite alignments that
   typically undergird a polity;
3. The presence or absence of elite allies; and
4. The state's capacity and propensity for repression.[2]

Analysis of the shifts in the political opportunity structure for any
given social movement reveals a multifaceted and changing relationship
between that movement and the state. Openings in the state may
facilitate social movement activity and expansion; likewise, pressure on
the state from social movements can give rise to further openness, or to
crackdowns and state retrenchment. Instability in elite alignments can
present social movement activists with opportunities to find new allies in
positions of power, although those alignments can also become too
unstable, making the state almost inaccessible to social movement
demands. Social movement allies in the state may appear, lending
support to the movement; this may be rewarded with grassroots political

---

[2] Doug McAdam, "Conceptual Origins, Current Problems, Future Directions," in
McAdam, John D. McCarthy, and Mayer M. Zald, eds., *Comparative Perspectives on
Social Movements* (Cambridge: Cambridge University Press, 1996), p. 27.

support for the allies in question. Close analysis of the political opportunity structure for a social movement reveals that allies may be located at different access points in the formal or institutionalized political system, and that the state is far from monolithic, its representatives far from uniform in their attitudes toward social movement activists and issues. In studying all four elements of the political opportunity structure, it becomes clear that the relationship between states and social movements is a reciprocal and dynamic one.

This chapter illustrates these four areas of change in the political opportunity structure for the Russian women's movement during Russia's transition period beginning in the late 1980s. First, I examine the decrease in state repression, arguing that the decline in state-sponsored persecution of independent social movement activists and activities made possible the very emergence of a public women's movement. Next, I explore changes in the degree of openness of the institutionalized political system, with emphasis on changes in the Soviet Women's Committee (a part of the Soviet institutionalized political system directly relevant to the nascent independent women's movement), and in the formal legislative institutions of the Soviet and Russian state. The chapter then turns to changes in women's political representation over the course of the transition period, and the appearance of allies in positions of power, as revealed by their discourse and actions. After considering the role of sex-based discrimination in restricting the women's movement's lobbying success, the chapter moves to an analysis of shifts in the elite alignments that underlay the Soviet and Russian political systems, focusing on how the elimination of the Communist Party's power monopoly undermined the stability of the polity. Although the ideological instability of the Soviet political system helped enable the creation of the public women's movement in the late 1980s, the several upheavals in Russia's political system since 1991 have made it difficult for that movement to build consistently on its own successes in making allies within the various sectors of the state.

Declining repression and increasing openness in the institutionalized political system: glasnost and perestroika

The political transition period in Soviet Russia was marked by an incredible expansion in the discourse on women's issues, as well as in women's organizing activity. Changes in the political opportunity structure made possible the public appearance and spread of hundreds of women's groups in the early 1990s. With the advent of glasnost and perestroika, state repression of independent social initiatives declined substantially. The transformation of the repressive propensity of the state is evident if we compare the treatment of women's organizations in the late 1980s and early 1990s with that experienced by the first independent women's organization that appeared in the pre-perestroika era: the Almanac group.

During the 1960s and 1970s, the presence of a growing dissident movement, which included women, was felt in the USSR. Just as some of the women in the US New Left began to feel frustrated with their secondary roles within that movement, Soviet women dissidents grew increasingly dissatisfied with the way they were treated and their concerns dismissed within the male-dominated dissident movement. In 1979, in Leningrad, a small group of women involved in the dissident movement decided to create their own underground journal. Like other dissident publications, the journal was *samizdat* – self-published – and reproduced secretly. The women called their journal "Almanac: Woman and Russia."[3] Its contents covered the details of grisly abortion procedures in the USSR, the conditions in maternity hospitals, and many other themes previously publicly ignored. The group and their journal did not go unnoticed by the KGB, and members of the collective were soon brought in for questioning. Meanwhile, three of the founders of the Almanac collective split off to form the Mariia club, uniting their feminism with a religious identity, and publishing their own *samizdat* journal. The KGB response to these challenges was swift. Within less than a year, the Almanac collective had been disbanded, and several members (of both groups) were exiled from the Soviet Union. The journals ceased publication after only a few issues.[4]

It was not until Gorbachev's policy of glasnost that the discourse on such issues expanded, and organizing independent of the Soviet state was permitted. At the end of the 1980s, along with a variety of organizations focused on ecology, labor, and national independence, a small number of women's groups emerged, mostly free from persecution. The number of groups mushroomed in the early 1990s, leveling off a few years later. They ranged from politically innocuous women's charity groups to advocacy groups demanding equal treatment of women in politics and in the labor force, and overtly lesbian groups organizing for rights and visibility. The range of the permissible grew so vast that a

[3] The first issue of the Almanac was translated and published in the West as *Almanach: For Women About Women, 10 December 1979* (London: Sheba Feminist Publishers, 1980).
[4] Alix Holt, "The First Soviet Feminists," in Barbara Holland, ed., *Soviet Sisterhood* (Bloomington: Indiana University Press, 1985), pp. 237–65.

women's support organization (SANTA) was permitted to form even within the Ministry of Internal Affairs (MVD), the Soviet administrative equivalent of the FBI, in November 1991. Objecting to the absence of women from leadership and well-paid positions within the MVD, the group was disliked by its organizers' male colleagues. Admitted one of SANTA's founders: "We were a headache for them."[5]

Although state-sponsored repression was clearly in remission, for some women activists forming feminist organizations was a process accompanied by fear. One of the women who founded a Moscow-based feminist organization in 1990 said that the experience of the Almanac group weighed heavily upon the participants in her new organization: "When we organized our group, we were afraid that the response would be like it was in 1979. The fear of the KGB was on our shoulders."[6]

Despite such fears, the increasing openness under Gorbachev was evident in the nearly unanimous agreement among activists interviewed in 1994–95 as to whether their organizations could have formed before 1985:

No. I think, before perestroika, inasmuch as nobody was allowed to organize anything on their own initiative, it wouldn't have been possible. Perestroika has given us one thing, and that's the opportunity to unite and create something of our own.[7]

No, there was a monopoly.[8]

No, of course not, definitely not, it would have been impossible. Nothing like that was allowed, no dissidence [inakomyslie].[9]

Perestroika, in addition to expanding the limits of the permissible, also initiated explicit legal changes in the political opportunity structure that further made possible the blossoming of women's groups. It became feasible to register social organizations, and thus to acquire organizational bank accounts. But the process was confusing. Tatiana Riabikina, leader of an organization for women in the arts (Tvorchestvo), reported that she tried in vain to register the organization without success in 1988: "We couldn't even get ourselves registered for the first year and a half. They sent us all around: it wasn't clear who was supposed to register us as a social organization."[10]

---

[5] Nonna Nikonova, interview, March 17, 1995.
[6] Interview, November 21, 1994.
[7] Elena Demeshina, interview, March 26, 1995.
[8] Tat'iana Riabikina, interview, April 26, 1995.
[9] Interview, November 21, 1994. Only two activists interviewed felt that such organizations had been simply unnecessary before perestroika, when women were still under the social welfare guardianship of the Soviet state: Larisa Volkova, interview, June 9, 1995 (Ekaterinburg), and Larisa Nazarova, interview, April 4, 1995 (Ivanovo).
[10] Tat'iana Riabikina, interview, April 26,1995.

In addition to creating legal opportunities for women's organizations independent of the state, Gorbachev's policies brought a thoroughgoing change to public discourse on women's issues. With the introduction of glasnost, a window of opportunity appeared for women in the Soviet Union to raise new issues of concern to them. Women's issues became increasingly visible, as survey research on women's issues was made accessible and public meetings were permitted. Said public opinion researcher and women's movement activist Galina Sillaste: "I published the first results from the major survey, 'Women and Democratization,' around [1990]. It was the first survey research in Russia specializing on women's public opinion. Before that, no one wanted to let us study women's opinion; it was said that it was identical to men's and there was no reason to separate the two."[11] Glasnost was also accompanied by an explosion of the women's press. Independent (as opposed to state-owned) women's newspapers and magazines appeared, as well as small-run feminist journals.

In short, glasnost provided an opportunity to put women's issues on the agenda in a more public and contested way. Soviet women took advantage of this in March 1991, at the First Independent Women's Forum, bringing together dozens of new women's groups from across the Soviet Union. There, the issue of violence against women was raised (for the first time on a national scale), and the fact that women were being left out of the so-called democratization process was emphasized.[12] These changes in discourse and political opportunities for organizing have their origin in the history of the Soviet women's movement groups that emerged when political opportunities began to shift in the mid-1980s.

Expanding opportunities and the formation of the first women's movement groups: society organizing itself

The rapidly changing political opportunities for feminist organizing in the Soviet Union's final years can be illustrated by tracing some of the original connections between the women who later formed the first women's organizations independent of the Soviet state.

In the mid-1980s, the discussion of women's issues began in earnest, amidst changes in the institutionalized political system. Seminars on women's issues were initiated by state and Communist Party-related organizations. These events provided an accidental forum in which

---

[11] Galina Sillaste, interview, March 28, 1995.
[12] "Itogovyi otchet o rabote 1ogo Nezavisimogo Zhenskogo Foruma," Dubna, Moscow, 1991.

feminist academics, previously isolated from each other, became acquainted, and began to form the first feminist groups of the perestroika period. Said Olga Voronina:

We met at a seminar that was conducted in the Academy of Social Sciences under the Central Committee of the CPSU [Communist Party of the Soviet Union], about the status of women. At that point, Gorbachev had spoken out about the renewal of the women's councils. The seminar was very boring – those ladies [tetki] who'd talked all their lives about the Soviet experience in solving the woman question. It was dull. But each of us took part in the discussion, and we noticed each other. We worked in different places. Natalia [Zakharova] was working for Natalia Rimashevskaia, Valya [Konstantinova] was at that Academy of Social Sciences, and I worked at the Institute of Philosophy. It was fall 1987.[13]

From such chance meetings among the like-minded sprang Russia's first feminist organizations. Voronina, Konstantinova, and Zakharova encountered each other repeatedly at seminars, and then began to meet as a group in their free time, to discuss feminism and ways to counter the reassertion of sexist stereotypes, in particular, the "return women to the home" campaign that was spreading in late 1980s Russia. In April 1988, Zakharova brought along a new co-worker, Anastasiia Posadskaia, who shared their passion for pursuing feminism in the Soviet Union. In early 1989, Posadskaia formulated a declaration which became the foundation for their tiny new organization: LOTOS – the League for Emancipation from Societal Stereotypes.[14] Among other things, the declaration called for enriching perestroika with an egalitarian ideology, undoing the sex-based stereotypes that pervaded the political and economic spheres, and creating a new ethos whereby women would play a worthy role in the workforce, and men would enjoy a worthy role within the family.[15] LOTOS members continued to speak out at academic events, where their critical remarks on women's status in the Soviet Union met with disapprobation:

We talked a lot at seminars about stereotypes, about sexism in language, about social problems . . .

Q. At that time, how was that perceived, how did people take it?

A. It was perceived very negatively, as a rule. And we were taken for radicals. And in several seminars, they already knew us and wouldn't let us speak, for instance, in the Academy of Social Sciences. They would invite us because of our status as academics, because we were published, and well known, but

---

[13] Ol'ga Voronina, interview, April 27, 1995.
[14] *Moskovskii tsentr gendernykh issledovanii: 1990–1995* (Moscow: Moskovskii Tsentr Gendernykh Issledovanii, 1995), pp. 28–35.
[15] Memorandum LOTOSA/ LOTOS – Liga za osvobozhdenie ot stereotipov.

when we started saying things they didn't want to hear they'd just interrupt us and not allow us to have the floor.[16]

In 1989, the Soviet Congress of People's Deputies approved the idea of preparing a state program on improving women's status, and protecting the family, maternity, and childhood. Natalia Rimashevskaia, director of the Institute of Socio-Economic Population Problems within the Russian Academy of Sciences, was given the task of collecting a group of researchers and formulating a position paper (*kontseptsiia*) on the subject. Under Rimashevskaia's direction, several of LOTOS's members took part in writing the position paper, called "The State Program to Improve the Status of Women, the Family, and the Protection of Motherhood and Childhood." The document focused on creating a new, more egalitarian policy, which considered emancipation a "bilateral" issue: freeing women to take a more extensive role outside the home, and men to play a greater role within the family.[17] Based on an "egalitarian" ideology of equal opportunities, the *kontseptsiia* argued that the "natural division of labor between men and women had a social character" and not a biological one.[18] The paper also introduced the notions of full-fledged fatherhood and gender-neutral childrearing roles. Moreover, according to the *kontseptsiia*, the system of childrearing-related welfare benefits should accrue to the family, and not to the mother.[19] In 1990, the position paper was presented to the Soviet government, and Rimashevskaia's institute was allotted five staff positions with which to form the Soviet Union's first women's studies research laboratory: the Moscow Center for Gender Studies (MCGS), with Posadskaia at its head, and the other LOTOS members on staff.[20] MCGS would soon become the center of the emerging women's movement.

Meanwhile, in 1990, a new feminist organization appeared: NeZhDI – the Independent Women's Democratic Initiative, the acronym of which in Russian spelled a clear message: "Don't Wait!" NeZhDI, with considerable overlap of LOTOS's membership, and an equally egalitarian ideology, aspired to be a network of independent women's groups and feminists arranged horizontally, rather than vertically, as the Soviet Women's Committee (SWC) and other Soviet organizations had been.

---

[16] Ol'ga Voronina, interview, April 27, 1995.

[17] Natal'ia Rimashevskaia, in *Moskovskii tsentr*, p. 6.

[18] "Kontseptsiia Gosudarstvennoi programmy uluchsheniia polozheniia zhenshchin, sem'i, okhrany materinstva i detstva" (Moscow: Institute for Socio-Economic Population Problems, 1992), p. 6.

[19] Elena Kochkina, interview, July 22, 1995.

[20] *Moskovskii tsentr*, p. 38. Zakharova did not join her former colleagues, having accepted a position in Vienna.

After its founding seminars, several other groups outside Moscow adopted the same name.[21]

Russia's tiny feminist organizations grew and networked, coming together in early 1991 for the First Independent Women's Forum. Among the organizers of the Forum were LOTOS, NeZhDI, MCGS, and several other feminist groups, including SAFO (the Free Association of Feminist Organizations), which played a central financial and organizational role.[22] Two hundred or so women attended the Forum, representing forty-eight women's organizations. In the words of one of its organizers, the Forum was evidence that a plethora of women's organizations and initiatives had arisen from below, rather than having been organized from above. The Forum operated under the slogan, "Democracy Without Women Is Not Democracy," and its final document attested to the multiple forms of discrimination against Soviet women, both under state socialism and during perestroika.

Although the First Independent Women's Forum took place several years into perestroika and glasnost, it did not proceed without incident and hints of the repressive state apparatus. On the eve of the Forum, the popular newspaper *Moskovskii komsomolets* published an announcement of the conference, portraying it as a gathering of "overexcited lesbians."[23] The ramifications were serious: the Dubna city authorities withdrew their permission to host the Forum (a decision later reversed); the number of attendees ended up being smaller than expected; and, when the Forum opened, uniformed police were present in the auditorium.[24]

The First Independent Women's Forum was followed by a Second Forum, again held in Dubna. The Second Independent Women's Forum opened in November 1992 under a different slogan – "From Problems to Strategy" – and with a new agenda: devising strategies for integrating women and women's issues into the economic and political systems developing in Russia and the former Soviet republics. Up to that point, women had been more or less excluded from the "democratization" process. In the words of Anastasiia Posadskaia, the director of the Moscow Center for Gender Studies, by 1992, the attempts of

[21] Valentina Konstantinova, in *Moskovskii tsentr*, pp. 9–11.
[22] Interview, November 21, 1994.
[23] Nadezhda Azhgikhina, "Healing the Soviet Legacy Towards Women," *Demokratizatsiya*, vol. 1, no. 3 (1993), p. 92. The impression that lesbianism was the motif of the Dubna conference remained. Interviewed in 1995, one activist in Ivanovo (who did not attend the conference) said: "I heard opinions about it, in the newspapers – that it was a feminist gathering and sexually preoccupied": Natal'ia Kovaleva, interview, April 3, 1995.
[24] See "Itogovyi otchet," p. 1.

perestroika to liberate the individual without liberating the sexes had been as unsuccessful as the earlier socialist efforts to emancipate women without emancipating the individual.[25]

Networking among Russia's women's movement activists became possible at the Dubna meetings. Links were made between activists interested in similar issues, and a women's information network was created to keep activists in touch with each other, and up to date on movement events. Furthermore, as the public discourse expanded, allowing for mass media coverage of independent women's movement events, knowledge of the Forums spread. Twenty-four of the women's movement activists interviewed in Moscow in 1994–95 had attended either one or both of the Forums, and thirty-eight out of forty had been aware of their occurrence.[26]

Meanwhile, *Rabotnitsa* (Woman Worker), a mainstream state-run women's magazine with the highest circulation of any magazine in the USSR, began regularly publishing articles (by staff journalists, as well as by self-identified feminists)[27] covering the independent women's movement, using the term "feminist" and debunking the myth that calling oneself a feminist was the equivalent of saying that one was a "man-hater."[28]

Thus, as public discourse and networking opportunities expanded, a growing circle of women became increasingly aware of the nascent women's movement and active within it.

The Soviet Women's Committee

Glasnost and perestroika not only enabled new women's organizations to appear, but also helped to transform the old ones, such as the Soviet Women's Committee (SWC). In the late 1980s, the SWC underwent a

[25] Opening speech at the Second Independent Women's Forum, Dubna, Russia, November 1992, author's notes.
[26] Such widespread familiarity with these founding women's movement events among activists in Moscow does not reflect the situation outside Russia's major cities. Indeed, while all the activists interviewed in Ivanovo had heard of the Forums, none had attended either one. Cheboksary activists, located even further from Moscow, had neither attended nor heard of the Forums, except for two women who worked for the women's councils (branches of the former Soviet Women's Committee), and were likely informed about the Forums through contacts with their parent organization in Moscow.
[27] Ol'ga Lipovskaia, a feminist from Leningrad, was asked to write an article for the magazine, published as "Chelovek 'vtorogo sorta'?," *Rabotnitsa*, no. 7, 1991, pp. 16–17.
[28] See, for example, "Demokratiia minus zhenshchina ne demokratiia!," *Rabotnitsa*, no. 7, 1991, p. 16.

shift best understood as a change in the institutionalized political system of the Soviet Union.

The SWC, like all other social organizations of the Soviet era, was subordinated to the Communist Party. Originally created in 1941 as an antifascist committee, after the war, it became simply a women's organization, and the sole legal representative of women's interests. The SWC's purpose was in part to convince foreign women's delegations of Soviet women's high economic and political status, and, later, to represent the Soviet Union at international women's conferences, which proliferated, especially after the establishment of the United Nations Decade for Women (1976–85).[29] SWC representatives stressed the fact that the vast majority of doctors, lawyers, and teachers were women, but did not mention the miserly salaries and low prestige of those professions within the Soviet economic hierarchy. This hypocrisy turned many women against the Soviet Women's Committee.

In the Khrushchev era, miniature women's councils (*zhensovety*), originally born in the 1920s, were revived and established all over the Soviet Union. The *zhensovety* played the role of "transmission belts," to engage women's support of Communist Party policies, and also took on service provision (distributing vacation vouchers, allotting spaces for children in summer camps, and so on), much like the Soviet trade unions. In 1986, Gorbachev voiced his objection to the "formal" nature of Soviet women's organizations, and declared the reinvigoration of the *zhensovety*, now to be under the umbrella of the SWC.[30] Neither the *zhensovety* nor the SWC, however, were at that point seen as being concerned with defending women's rights, or increasing women's involvement in political or economic decisionmaking. Despite that fact, some activists regard the revival of the *zhensovety*, even "pocketed" (*karmannye*) or controlled as they were, as having been significant, a symbolic movement toward a new phase in women's organizing.[31]

Despite its origins, during the late 1980s the SWC became one of the important sources of change in the political opportunity structure for Soviet feminists. With the advent of perestroika and glasnost, the Soviet Women's Committee, too, expanded its horizons and became a sort of "indigenous network," a hub for several of the activists who would later split from the state-run women's movement, and move on to start their own organizations. For example, feminist journalist Larisa Kuznetsova

[29] Elizabeth Waters and Anastasia Posadskaya, "Democracy Without Women Is No Democracy: Women's Struggles in Postcommunist Russia," in Amrita Basu, ed., *The Challenge of Local Feminisms* (Boulder: Westview Press, 1995), p. 358.

[30] Mary Buckley, *Women and Ideology in the Soviet Union* (Ann Arbor: University of Michigan Press, 1989), p. 210.

[31] Valentina Konstantinova, interview, July 9, 1995.

joined political scientist Tatiana Ivanova (then a member of the SWC) to form a "political club" under the aegis of the SWC, holding monthly meetings at the SWC's offices.[32] Ivanova later formed an entrepreneurial support organization called the Women's Alliance, in part on the basis of connections made at the SWC and the political club:

Some of us who were in the SWC knew each other; those who saw [the SWC] for the window-dressing that it was, even before perestroika. We wanted to do something concrete.[33]

Some of the state-run *zhensovety*, too, struck out on their own, and became independent women's organizations. The *zhensovet* of the Zhukovskii Aerohydrodynamics Institute was among these.[34] However, its relations with the SWC became rocky when, in 1989, the *zhensovet* voted to choose Kuznetsova as their representative to the USSR Congress of People's Deputies, to run on the SWC ticket. Because Kuznetsova was not a member of a *zhensovet*, her candidacy was rejected by the SWC. Two of the Zhukovskii women fired off a protest letter to a Moscow newspaper, saying that the limitation of potential candidates to members of *zhensovety* was tantamount to discrimination, but the SWC's plenum refused to allow Kuznetsova's candidacy.[35]

Despite such bureaucratic obstacles, under perestroika, the SWC became one of the institutions in Soviet society that opened – if temporarily – to the budding feminist movement. First of all, as the political climate in the Soviet Union thawed, and Gorbachev's "new thinking" toward the West evolved, the SWC became a place for independent feminists to meet foreigners, one of the important factors in the formation of the Russian women's movement.

Opportunities for contact with foreign women through the SWC multiplied quickly at the end of the 1980s. One of LOTOS's original members described the situation:

The SWC started holding various seminars, started inviting academic women from Russia to these seminars, and they started doing joint seminars with their foreign contacts. And they started very actively inviting us, including me, and Valya Konstantinova, and all of LOTOS. At first I didn't really understand what was going on, but almost every week I was there, speaking at some seminar or another. And then I understood that we were "exotic beasts" for them. It was perestroika, there was pluralism: "Look, we have communists, look, we have democrats, look, we have feminists! Real, live feminists! And we even let them

---

[32] I. Viktorova, "Ne pora li potesnit'sia?," *Rabotnitsa*, no. 2, 1991, p. 10.

[33] Tat'iana Ivanova, interview, May 16, 1995.

[34] For the history of its formation, see O. Bessolova and S. Harder, "Problems of Women – Problems of Society," *Social Sciences*, no. 1, 1995, pp. 170–82.

[35] E. Bozhkova and L. Fedorova, "Chem zhenshchiny khuzhe?," *Moskovskie novosti*, no. 3, January 15, 1989, p. 9.

talk!" And then, when the idea of pluralism stopped being so exciting, they pretty much forgot about us, somewhere around 1991, when the USSR came to an end, when Pukhova was taken out [as chair of the SWC], and they put in Fedulova.[36]

The SWC also began to send independent Soviet feminists abroad, sometimes with unpredictable results. Valentina Konstantinova, for example, was sent to Finland in 1988, on a delegation to meet with the women's branches of a number of Finnish political parties. Before the meeting, Konstantinova was asked, by a woman she assumed was accompanying the group as a representative of the KGB, what she was planning to speak about:

Well, when I said what I was planning to talk about . . . you can imagine . . . it was 1988! I was going to talk about discrimination in all spheres of life, about abortion, about the high maternal mortality rates, the lack of women in decisionmaking, and say that our women's movement was paralyzed. The woman, having listened, said to me, "I wouldn't advise you to give that speech, because I know that country very well, and it's not accepted, in their culture, to wash your dirty laundry in public." It was a direct threat. And I, of course, spoke, I said what I'd wanted to say, but I was worried . . . After the speech, there was such resonance, that the women Finns started to say that this was the first time they'd ever heard that we also had problems, that we were sisters. And when we were about to return home, we were told that the Finns had written a letter, that they wanted to work with the Committee! They hadn't collaborated with the SWC much before, probably because of its political orientation.[37]

Konstantinova also ran into trouble after going to Czechoslovakia on a similar delegation:

Before the trip [the SWC deputy on international work] called me in and said, "Tell them we're returning to Lenin." It was the fashion then, under Gorbachev, that we were returning to Lenin. And it was clear to them, of course, that I wasn't going to say something like that – it was an interesting game, but I don't play games like that . . . I, of course, made my speech – instead of returning to Lenin, I gave a totally feminist speech, which then sounded very revolutionary . . . And my speech created such a tumult, inasmuch as I came in the name of the Committee, but with a totally different position. At the reception people came up to me, sat at my table, and said that they agreed, that changes in the policy of the SWC were needed . . . I said that I had no relation to the SWC, and that it was my personal position. I've never been in a more absurd situation in my life. And, after that, there was rather a parting of the ways between me and the SWC.[38]

The Soviet political opportunity structure for the women's movement had changed, at least temporarily, as the institutionalized political

---

[36] Ol'ga Voronina, interview, April 27, 1995.
[37] Valentina Konstantinova, interview, July 9, 1995.
[38] Valentina Konstantinova, interview, July 9, 1995.

system designated to deal with women's issues opened up to independent voices.

It seems likely that the establishment of the UN Decade for Women inspired some of the SWC's transformation. The number of international women's conferences grew, and the committee understandably sought experts who could represent the Soviet Union's new face abroad. Simultaneously, the USSR came under pressure to collect data and produce reports on the status of women, as mandated by the UN Convention on the Elimination of All Forms of Discrimination Against Women (CEDAW), which the Soviet government ratified in the early 1980s, meaning that feminist experts had to be cultivated and tolerated, even if only up to a point. According to Zoia Khotkina (later on the staff at MCGS), once perestroika was initiated, the SWC needed women like her:

The SWC was a two-faced organization. Mostly, it existed for foreigners . . . They needed *us* because when progressive women came from the West, people like us were also progressive, and had lot of knowledge. Olga [Voronina] would talk about the women's movement; I would talk about the economic situation with them. We were allowed to speak the truth only to foreigners.[39]

Although there was later a closure again on the part of the SWC, that organization indirectly became critical in changing yet another aspect of the political opportunity structure, namely, women's political representation and the availability of political allies. When the Soviet state collapsed in 1991, the SWC collapsed along with it, leaving its successor organization, the Union of Russia's Women (URW) to inherit its legal rights and property. The SWC thus made a transition from being a monopolistic organization under the protective wing of the party in power to being an organization (the URW) with vague status, officially existing outside Russia's new political power structure. In 1993, the URW served as a founder of the parliamentary bloc Women of Russia (WOR), a potential ally of the women's movement within the Russian state that will be discussed in detail below.

Political reforms, the collapse of the Soviet Union, and, most likely, repeated exposure to independent feminists transformed the institutionalized political system that had been in part embodied in the SWC. By 1994, the URW and WOR were initiating and participating in conferences and holding meetings on a variety of women's issues formerly seen as both radical and irrelevant to Soviet society, such as violence against women, employment discrimination against women, and the paucity of women in political decisionmaking positions. In part, the preparations

---

[39] Zoia Khotkina, informal interview, spring 1995.

for the upcoming UN World Conference on Women (Beijing, 1995) helped spark this interest. But regardless of motivation, the changing and expanding views exhibited by the SWC during the early years of glasnost and perestroika (and later, by the URW) illustrate a clear change in political opportunity structure, an increasing openness within the Soviet Union's institutionalized political system.

This increasing openness was also visible in the Soviet Union's and Russia's formal legislative institutions, as they developed a "national mechanism for improving women's status" in the late Gorbachev/early Yeltsin era, and thereby provided women's movement activists with new access to policymakers.

Developing a national mechanism for improving women's status

Changes in the national mechanism for improving women's status (defined as governmental and legislative departments and committees on women) can provide a measure of institutional openness or closure to a women's movement. The bodies that constitute the national mechanism are thus part of the political opportunity structure. A brief discussion of the history of the Soviet/Russian national mechanism dealing with women's issues reveals an institutionalized political system, the openness of which began to increase under Gorbachev's rule.[40]

When Gorbachev came to power in 1985, protective legislation was the basis for state policy on women. Policy aimed to create conditions for women to "successfully combine" their dual roles as workers and mothers. As Elena Kochkina, a researcher at MCGS, put it: "Men were not viewed as having primary parenthood functions; they had sort of an 'assistant' role, as fathers."[41] Moreover, as another feminist from MCGS said: "at the end of the 1980s, it was still the USSR, the Communist Party, a strictly organized society, and there was no opportunity for an informal organization to affect the government."[42] The potential for a women's movement to influence the state's formal structures at that point was fundamentally limited.

The first major institutional change signaling increased attention to women's issues, and enabling women's groups to gain access to the state, occurred in 1989. Late that year, a new Committee on the Affairs of Women and the Protection of the Family, Motherhood, and

---

[40] Information in this section is derived from the Russian Federation National Report to the Fourth World Conference on the Status of Women: "Actions in the Interests of Equality, Development, and Peace," Moscow 1994, and from the materials compiled by Elena Kochkina, used to write that report.
[41] Elena Kochkina, interview, July 22, 1995.
[42] Ol'ga Voronina, interview, April 27, 1995.

Childhood was created within the USSR Supreme Soviet.[43] Its deputy chair, Marina Rakhmanova, gave an International Women's Day interview to the national newspaper *Trud* (Labor), stating that women's equality in Soviet society had been achieved through quotas, which led only to women's formal representation. The committee, she said, sought new bases and principles, as well as information to fill the gap on empirical statistics relating to women's employment, health, and so forth. Surveys, for example, had shown that only 20 percent of women would quit their paid jobs if their welfare would be guaranteed; the others wanted to combine paid labor with domestic work. The committee's position was to allow for this "freedom of choice." As a result of the committee's formation, several laws were passed that were intended to improve women's social status, including increasing the benefits paid to women with children. Furthermore, the deputy chair explained, maternity leave was no longer "purely" for mothers: it could be taken in part or entirely by the father, grandparents, or any relative taking care of the child. The establishment of this committee was thus a positive change in the political opportunity structure, providing a clear location for women's movement groups to lobby – had any groups of significant strength existed at that time – and also altering a series of laws.[44] Also in 1989, a department of the Council of Ministers was created, on the Affairs of Women and the Protection of the Family, Motherhood, and Childhood. Similarly, within the USSR's Ministry of Labor (State Labor Committee), the Administration on Family Affairs and the Protection of Motherhood and Childhood was established. The increased attention to women, even if linked to their assumed family roles, was unmistakable.

Replicating the developments at the USSR level, in July 1990, a Committee on the Affairs of Women and the Protection of the Family, Motherhood, and Childhood, headed by Ekaterina Lakhova, was created within the Russian Supreme Soviet. And, at that committee's behest, another committee, on Family and Demographic Policy, was created under the Russian Federation Council of Ministers. The collapse of the USSR, at the end of 1991, eliminated the committees associated with the Soviet political organs. The Russian Federation committees remained, and, as women's movement groups appeared, they began to lobby for influence within the government, primarily through the Russian Supreme Soviet.

---

[43] In March 1991, the committee was renamed the Supreme Soviet Committee on the Affairs of Women, the Family, and Demographic Policy.

[44] V. Naumov, "Ei pokrovitel'stvuet parlament," *Trud*, March 8, 1991, reprinted in *Zhenskoe dvizhenie v SSSR*, no. 2, January–March 1991, pp. 10–11.

The most significant instance of women's group influence on the Russian Supreme Soviet, illustrating the openness of the institutionalized political system, occurred when, in 1992, a Supreme Soviet committee vested with the task of developing a new code of family law drafted a bill that deeply offended and worried the women's activist community, including the Union of Russia's Women (URW), the Women's League, and the MCGS. The bill, on the "Protection of the Family, Motherhood, Fatherhood, and Childhood," would have made the family (and not the individual) the sole subject of rights: only a family could own an apartment, a plot of land, and so on. Each family member's income was to go into a collective family budget. This had ramifications beyond property ownership. Marina Gordeeva, a leader of the URW, commenting on the law in early 1993, judged its standards as "absurd." For instance, she lamented, "'The right to decide the issue of having a child belongs to both spouses.' How are we to interpret that? Does it mean that the husband can prevent the wife from having an abortion? Or, conversely, from having a child? We're going to fight the adoption of any such law."[45] The law also included provisions making it mandatory for women with children under fourteen to work an abbreviated 35-hour week, thereby reducing their pay. The law passed its first hearing in June 1992. But with the women's movement's energies directed toward defeating it – lobbying parliamentary deputies, publishing critiques of the legislation, and organizing a "barrage of approximately four hundred negative appraisals in the form of letters, faxes, and telegrams" – it failed its second reading.[46] The openings in Russia's formal political institutions had created channels through which women's movement activists were able to mobilize successfully, in order to block legislation that had previously seemed on track to passage.

In another instance of movement access to an increasingly open state system, after a 1992 conference which served as the founding conference for the Women's League, a gender expertise group was created under the Higher Economic Council of the Russian Supreme Soviet.[47] The group began addressing the Russian government's failure to uphold international legislation on women's rights:

In May 1993, on our initiative, hearings in the Supreme Soviet were organized, about Russia's progress toward fulfilling or, more precisely, *lack* of progress

---

[45] "Interv'iu," *Zhenskii Diskussionnyi Klub*, January 1993.
[46] Waters and Posadskaya, "Democracy Without Women Is No Democracy," pp. 368–70.
[47] Svetlana Polenina, "Zhenshchina i gosudarstvo: pravovoi aspekt," in V. A. Tishkov, ed., *Zhenshchina i svoboda* (Moscow: Nauka, 1994), p. 21.

toward fulfilling the UN Convention on Eliminating All Forms of Discrimination Against Women.[48]

In October 1993, the Russian Supreme Soviet was destroyed, along with the newly institutionalized gender expertise group. In December 1993, elections to a new legislature, the Federal Assembly, took place, although not until 1996 did progress take place toward trying to establish a gender expertise group associated with the new legislature. The Federal Assembly's lower house, the Duma, contributed to the national mechanism for improving women's status by creating a Committee on the Affairs of Women, the Family, and Youth, which, by 1995, had established a working relationship with several Moscow-based women's movement groups, a process to which I shall return below.

Against this background of declining repression and expanding opportunities within the institutionalized political system, women's movement groups sought out powerful allies within the polity – another aspect of political opportunity structure.

Allies and access points for the Russian women's movement

The emergence of elite allies is often a critical component of the political opportunity structure for a social movement. Allies can provide institutional support and an influential channel into the corridors of power. They can create a climate of openness on movement issues of importance, and give public voice to movement activists. In return, they may receive popular support from movement constituents and adherents. Operating in an overall political climate of hostility toward women taking an active role in decisionmaking, women's movement activists in Russia engaged in a search for elite allies, some of whom rendered limited support, but alliance with most of whom was ultimately frustrated by the electoral process and by institutional change.

Women's political representation

Where there's power, there are no women, and where there are women, there's no power.

Russian adage

Russia's political transition period has brought considerable fluctuations in the levels of women's representation in national politics, particularly in the legislative branch. Before perestroika began in the mid-1980s,

---

[48] Elena Ershova, interview, April 18, 1995.

women regularly attained one-third of the seats in the USSR's Supreme Soviet, as the result of quotas. However, the women selected tended to be token representatives of the "masses" of workers and peasants, rather than being powerful political individuals in their own right (while the male representatives were Communist Party leaders, cabinet ministers, renowned academic leaders, and so forth).[49] Moreover, real decision-making power had never been vested in the Supreme Soviet, but rather in the Central Committee of the Communist Party of the Soviet Union, where less than 5 percent of the deputies were women.

The elimination of the Communist Party's power monopoly, and the introduction of increasingly free elections, altered the political opportunity structure for women's movement and other social activists. In 1989, semi-free elections to the Soviet Congress of People's Deputies (CPD) were held, with a significant number of seats reserved for the Communist Party, trade unions, the Academy of Sciences, and other official organizations. These included the Soviet Women's Committee (SWC), at the time still under the aegis of the party. Women won 15.7 percent of the seats, largely due to the seventy-five seats reserved for the SWC: the Communist Party's deputy list included only 12 percent women, and none at all were elected from the Academy of Sciences, despite the fact that women comprised one-third of scientific workers at that time.[50] In 1990, when quotas for seats were lifted, the proportion of female deputies elected to the Russian Federation Congress of People's Deputies dropped to only 5.4 percent. The declining representation of women in parliaments elected in the final years of the Soviet state further decreased women's access to positions of political power. Moreover, one analysis of the Russian CPD's activity shows that female representatives played an "entirely insignificant" role in lawmaking, as evidenced by women deputies' failure to contribute amendments to the Russian constitution and produce other legislative outputs.[51]

After the collapse of the USSR in December 1991, and the later destruction of Russia's own parliament in October 1993, free elections to a new Federal Assembly were held in Russia in December 1993.

[49] El'vira Novikova, "Zhenshchiny v politicheskoi zhizni rossii," *Preobrazhenie*, no. 2, 1994, p. 17. A similar point is made by Gail Lapidus, *Women in Soviet Society: Equality, Development, and Social Change* (Berkeley: University of California Press, 1978), p. 207; also on women's "career paths" to political power, see Barbara Jancar, *Women Under Communism* (Baltimore: Johns Hopkins Press, 1978), esp. ch. 5.

[50] Ol'ga Khasbulatova, "Evoliutsiia rossiiskoi gosudarstvennoi politiki v otnoshenii zhenshchin: obzor istoricheskogo opyta (1861–1917, 1917–1991 gg.)," in V. B. Korniak, ed., *Integratsiia zhenshchin v protsess obshchestvennogo razvitiia* (Moscow: Luch, 1994), p. 84.

[51] V. A. Tishkov, "Zhenshchina v rossiiskoi politike i strukturakh vlasti," in Tishkov, *Zhenshchina i svoboda*, p. 11.

Women won nine (5 percent) of the seats in the legislature's upper house – the Federation Council – and sixty (13 percent) of the lower house, called the Duma. Women's presence in the Federal Assembly reached a total of 11.4 percent,[52] thus more than doubling the percentage of women that were in the Russian CPD. Approximately one-third of women's seats in the Duma were won by the women's bloc, Women of Russia (WOR), which organized very quickly in the two months preceding the elections. The rest of the women's seats were won from a few other parties, and from single-mandate districts.[53]

The 1993 elections reflected an ambiguous political opportunity structure. Although WOR won a surprising 8 percent of the total vote, the other parties that reached out to women did so in a limited and discouraging fashion:

In the December 1993 campaign, Galya Venediktova [with Women for Social Democracy] organized for women from the Independent Women's Forum to take part in the election campaign [through Yabloko, a liberal political party]. Asya [Posadskaia, of LOTOS and MCGS] and some others ran with Yabloko. But women ended up at the bottom of the party list, and didn't get into the Duma.[54]

Indeed, most of the parties placed their female candidates' names at the bottom of the party lists, excluding women from the first third of the spots, thereby practically guaranteeing that few if any women would get into the Duma from a party list. For example, the first woman on the Agrarian Party's list was found in the seventieth spot; on the Russia's Choice list, after Ella Pamfilova, a popular cabinet minister who occupied the third spot, the next woman appeared thirtieth.[55] According to one election observer, in 1993, the party lists available for twelve blocs (excluding WOR) had a total of only 7 percent women.[56] To the extent that the 1993 elections increased women's political representation in

---

[52] Novikova, "Zhenshchiny v politicheskoi zhizni rossii," p. 18.
[53] Twenty-six women won election from single-mandate districts. The other women elected to the Duma came from the following parties: Yabloko (two), Russia's Choice (two), Democratic Party of Russia (one), Communist Party of Russia (three), Liberal-Democratic Party (i.e., Zhirinovskii's party: five). The Agrarian Party and the Party of Russian Unity and Accord (PRES) brought no women into the Duma. See "K sovmestnomu zasedaniiu Komissii po voprosam zhenshchin, sem'i, i demografii pri Presidente Rossiiskoi Federatsii i fraktsii Gosudarstvennoi Dumy 'Zhenshchiny Rossii': informatsiia ob itogakh provedeniia izbiratel'noi kampanii 1993 goda," in the Moscow Women's Archive, "Materialy fraktsii 'ZhR' v Gosdume RF," f. 5, op. 1, d. 10.
[54] Interview, November 22, 1994.
[55] "Uspekh dvizheniia 'Zhenshchiny Rossii' sensatsiia nyneshnykh vyborov," *Zhenskii Diskussionnyi Klub*, October–December 1993, pp. 1–3, reprinting an article from *Izvestiia*, December 2, 1993.
[56] N. Shvedova, "Kak ia khotela byt' vydumchivym izbiratelem," author's files.

parliament, and thereby potentially improved the political opportunity structure for women, it was due to the success of WOR.

That success was ephemeral. In the elections of December 1995, WOR failed to clear the 5 percent barrier required for representation in parliament. Only three of the WOR bloc's members won single-mandate district seats in the new Duma. The number of women in the Duma then stood at forty-six: about 10 percent. The opening in the political opportunity structure (as reflected by legislative representation, anyway) was closing anew.

With the defeat of WOR in 1995, women's representation seemed to be in decline. Other parties' representation of women was meager, though some strong female representatives have emerged. Meanwhile, the Federation Council, which is acknowledged to be a seat of far greater power than is the Duma, though its activities attract rather less attention, has only one female representative. None of the administrative heads of Russia's territories, or mayors of Russia's major cities were women, until November 1996, when a woman was elected to head the little-known Koriak autonomous okrug of Kamchatka.[57]

Between 1989 and 1995, the emergence of Women of Russia constituted perhaps the best chance for the women's movement to gain a political ally in the legislative branch of government. It is to the experience of this unusually successful women's party that we now turn.

The Women of Russia political bloc

Better a woman wielding a rolling pin than a man with a machine gun
[*Luchshe baba so skalkoi, chem muzhik s avtomatom*].[58]

In October 1993, at Yeltsin's order, tanks fired on the White House – the home of the Russian parliament – intending to break the deadlock that had arisen between the executive and legislative branches of government. When the shooting stopped, new elections were planned on short notice, for December 1993. With only two months to prepare, political parties and electoral blocs scrambled to gather signatures and organize political campaigns.

Activists at the Union of Russia's Women (URW) gathered the charters and programs of Russia's extant political parties, and discovered that none had a clear policy on the issue of women's status. They then

---

[57] Carol Williams, "Awaiting Another Revolution," *Los Angeles Times*, December 4, 1996, pp. 1, 6.

[58] Statement made by a male supporter of WOR, as reported by El'vira Novikova, interview, February 17, 1995.

wrote letters to twenty-seven of Russia's political parties,[59] inquiring about their policies on women and their views on women's role in public life, in order to ascertain which to support in the election campaign. Disgusted by the dismal and superficial responses that they received (from only three parties),[60] the activists, spurred on by Ekaterina Lakhova (then adviser to Yeltsin, and chair of the Presidential Commission on Issues of Women, the Family, and Demography), pulled together a women's political bloc – Women of Russia (WOR) – composed largely (but not entirely) of women who were somewhat powerful in the women's sector of Soviet public activity, and a few who were members of independent women's organizations.

The bloc was able to form because of a technical change in Russia's political opportunity structure. Under the electoral law governing the Duma elections, social movements were allowed to put forth "party lists," as long as the movement was registered by the Ministry of Justice at the federal level, had a charter that included political activity within its constituent organizations' goals, and could collect 100,000 signatures in support.[61] Three organizations, the URW, the Union of Navy Women, and the Association of Women Entrepreneurs, all having federal status, joined and registered as a political bloc with the Ministry of Justice, thereby gaining the right to put forth candidates. These movement groups took advantage of the new access to the electoral process, shaping their activity to match the new political opportunity.[62]

With WOR's successful bid for parliamentary representation, the elections of December 1993 altered the political opportunity structure, giving the women's movement a potential ally in parliament, albeit a parliament that was institutionally quite weak relative to the presidency. Moreover, evidence at the outset suggested that the bloc was merely a reincarnation of the Soviet-era SWC, which, upon the Soviet state's collapse, had become the Union of Russia's Women (URW), chaired by the same woman who co-led the women's bloc, Alevtina Fedulova.

Indeed, representatives of the independent women's movement were highly suspicious of WOR, both during their election campaign and afterwards. Activists portrayed WOR's deputies as old-style Soviet

[59] Wendy Slater, "Female Representation in Russian Politics," *RFE/RL Research Report*, vol. 3, no. 22 (June 3, 1994), p. 28.
[60] Interview with Ekaterina Lakhova, "Zhenskie golosa v partiinom khore," *Rossiiskie vesti*, May 18, 1995.
[61] Signature collection was facilitated by the URW's network of women's councils, and many signatures were also collected from the wives of military men: Maia Kaz'mina, interview, April 13, 1995.
[62] McAdam, McCarthy, and Zald, "Introduction: Opportunities, Mobilizing Structures, and Framing Processes – Toward a Synthetic, Comparative Perspective on Social Movements," in McAdam, McCarthy, and Zald, *Comparative Perspectives*, p. 10.

bureaucrats. Many pointed to Fedulova's previous twenty-year long chairpersonship of the Young Pioneers organization (the Soviet state-run version of the Brownies and Cub Scouts), and her leadership work with the Soviet Peace Committee (like the SWC, an organization created and controlled by the Soviet Communist Party), before she joined the top ranks of the URW in 1992, as well as her brief tenure on the Central Committee of the Soviet Communist Party (1990–91). Indeed, when invited to join forces with WOR, one major network of women's organizations, the Independent Women's Forum (IWF) let the offer slide:

Lakhova asked the IWF to join WOR for the election campaign. We just didn't answer their request. The IWF isn't a political organization, and we didn't really want to unite with them.[63]

It was striking, however, that WOR's election platform included a phrase reminiscent of the slogan used by the 1991 Independent Women's Forum – "democracy without women is not democracy" – namely: "Without women, there's no democracy!"[64] Some feminists affiliated with the Independent Women's Forum expressed frustration at the borrowing of their slogan without WOR's having acknowledged the influence that the autonomous movement had had on their political analysis, and also felt that the slogan was merely an empty phrase in WOR's hands, especially because, as the campaign progressed, another slogan: "Women of Russia – For Russia" seemed to eclipse the earlier, more radical one.

Allies may be revealed through their actions, and through their discourse. A detailed look at the evolution of the WOR bloc during its two years in parliament provides a more objective assessment of its value to the women's movement in Russia as an ally. Much of the feminist organizations' suspicion of WOR was based on its campaign rhetoric. Indeed, some of WOR's election campaign materials (aside from their platform) failed to stress women's rights specifically, focusing more overtly on the restoration of guaranteed social welfare benefits (education, healthcare, childcare), and stressing human rights, a stable society, and peaceful solutions to conflict. Also included was a point advocating a ban on the propagation of violence and pornography. The word "women," however, did not appear on a 1993 leaflet listing the ten reasons to vote for WOR.[65] On the other hand, WOR candidates did talk with the press about women's disproportionate unemployment,

[63] Elena Kochkina, interview, July 22, 1995.
[64] "Predvybornaia platforma ob'edineniia 'Zhenshchiny Rossii.'"
[65] "Pochemu ia golosuiu za politicheskoe dvizhenie 'Zhenshchiny Rossii'?!," handbill, 1993.

about women's low levels of political representation, and about the closure of childcare centers.

Over the course of their tenure in the legislature, WOR adopted more overtly feminist overtones. Some WOR deputies, for example, called publicly for the establishment of equal rights and opportunities for women, such as WOR faction chair Ekaterina Lakhova, who, when meeting with Bill Clinton and the other faction chairs in May 1995, took the opportunity to speak about "women's equality."[66] WOR deputy Zhanna Lozinskaia also spoke out in print against male parliamentarians' tendency to "forget" about socially responsible policies, and against political discrimination, including the quota system of the Soviet period:

After 1917, women were actively drawn into social and economic life. They became pilots, engineers, construction workers, railway workers, factory workers. But over time, only these "equalized" women remained in the very most arduous and filthy occupations. But women were present in high political posts only to make the statistics look nice.[67]

Liudmila Zavadskaia, the most feminist-identified WOR deputy, and the one most respected by independent women's movement activists, even before the 1993 election, spoke out in favor of changing the Soviet labor law mandating "benefits" for women workers. According to her, these benefits had never "eliminated the very reasons for discrimination," but, in a market context, they had begun to harm women's chances of being hired. Sharing the opinion of feminist academics affiliated with MCGS and other women's groups, Zavadskaia also criticized the Soviet system of limits on women's occupations, which forbade women to work in certain jobs that would be ostensibly dangerous to their reproductive capacity and health: "But don't these conditions affect men? . . . Nobody says that to men. Only to women, because women are not seen as being equal partners."[68] It was Zavadskaia, as a member of the Constitutional Assembly that prepared the draft of the new Russian constitution (passed in 1993), who successfully insisted on including a clause about equal rights: "Men and women

---

[66] Mariia Esmont, "Bill Klinton primiril rossiiskikh politikov," *Segodnia*, May 12, 1995, p. 2.

[67] Grigorii Drugoveiko, "Esli by v dume ne bylo nas!," *Moskvichka*, no. 12, 1995. Many WOR deputies expressed essentialist viewpoints (on women's difference from men, and the benefits that could accrue to the political system from women deputies' natural interests and predispositions). Such viewpoints are widely expressed throughout Russia's women's movement as well as the population at large, though there is also a contingent of activists who support the more egalitarian view that women's nature is socially rather than essentially or inherently biologically constructed.

[68] Liudmila Zavadskaia, "Raznye liki diskriminatsii," *Literaturnaia gazeta*, October 13, 1993, p. 14.

have equal rights and freedoms, and equal opportunities to realize them" (Article 19).[69] WOR echoed Zavadskaia's opinions when the bloc unanimously adopted a political declaration of equal rights and opportunities, calling for the legislative implementation of the Russian constitution's clause on the subject, and for antidiscrimination legislation guaranteeing equal rights in the labor sphere.

WOR deputies' discourse took an even more radical turn in June 1995, at a conference sponsored by the URW, WOR, Lakhova's Presidential Commission on Issues of Women, the Family, and Demography, and other organizations. There, Lakhova condemned the absence of women from high political positions, and argued that the women's movement and the mass media should act to alter societal consciousness about women's proper social roles, and to undo the "patriarchal-conservative stereotypical attitudes toward women."[70] Fedulova echoed Lakhova's rhetoric, criticizing the masses' "patriarchal consciousness, according to which politics is not women's affair," and, going further, stating that Russian culture had maintained women in a doubly oppressed state: "A woman was subordinated, and dependent: first on her husband – on a man – and then on the patronizing guardianship of the state."[71] Lastly, WOR's 1995 campaign literature overtly mentioned their support for "equal rights and freedoms, and equal opportunities to carry them out, for women and men," a change from the 1993 flyer that had provided ten reasons to vote for WOR.[72]

WOR's overt identification with feminism per se was more hesitant. In 1994, Lakhova was quoted as saying, in an interview with a Helsinki newspaper (reproduced in WOR's Russian-language bulletin), "Men are calling us feminists. That word doesn't frighten me; we're just fighting for our rights."[73] However, in an informational brochure on WOR, published in advance of the 1995 election, the answer to the question "How does WOR relate to radical Western feminists?" was simply: "Radical feminists are . . . warriors against the male principle [nachalo], but Women of Russia is intent on collaborating with men, in the name of society's well-being. We stand for a policy of equal rights and opportunities for women and men."[74] This question-and-answer was given a

[69] See Zoia Khotkina, ed., Seksual'nye domogatel'stva na rabote (Moscow: ABA-CEELI, Zhenskii konsortsium, and MCGS, 1996), p. 31.
[70] The Second All-Russian Women's Conference report, from the speech of Ekaterina Lakhova, published as the newsletter of WOR, in Moskvichka, no. 22–23, 1995, p. 7.
[71] Ibid., p. 8.
[72] "Zhenshchiny Rossii za Vera v cheloveka, za Nadezhda na sem'iu, za Liubov' k Rossii," campaign leaflet, 1995. Though equal opportunities were mentioned, the focus remained on the resurrection of a social welfare system.
[73] Zhenshchiny Rossii, Informatsionnyi biulleten', no. 2, 1995, p. 33.
[74] Zhenshchiny Rossii, Informatsionnyi biulleten', no. 5, September 1995, p. 2.

prominent position on page two of the brochure, suggesting that WOR believed it important to distance themselves from feminism – specifically, the "radical Western" variety. Yet in an interview in mid-1995, Galina Klimantova, head of the Duma's Committee on the Affairs of Women, the Family, and Youth, reluctantly admitted to being a feminist:

Well, to put it briefly, I think that feminism is a movement of women – this is my point of view, it's a movement of women for upholding their rights, for equal rights with men. Not a "fight," as it is often phrased . . . absolutely not, why fight? We're partners, after all: life and the world consist of men and women; it's an absolutely insane idea, to fight against men. But to be alongside them, to attain equal partnership, that is how I see the feminist movement.

Q. Do you consider yourself a feminist?
A. (Sighs.) It's hard to say if I am a feminist. But that I love to work with women, and occupy myself with it professionally, yes, from that point of view, I'm probably a feminist.[75]

Aside from WOR's unenthusiastic adoption of an overtly "feminist" identity, if we compare their above-noted rhetoric with the positions taken by the independent feminists of LOTOS and MCGS, it seems clear that the rhetoric of independent women activists and WOR deputies drew closer over time. This change over time is also reflected in WOR deputies' positions on the desirability of using "equal rights and equal opportunities" as the foundation for state policy.

In an interview in early 1991, Ekaterina Lakhova, then chair of the Russian (RSFSR) Supreme Soviet Committee on the Affairs of Women and the Protection of the Family, Motherhood, and Childhood, was asked how she felt about the women's movement's capacity to contribute to the solution of Russian women's problems. Lakhova responded:

Recently, in the press, I was reading speeches by a group of feminists, who are fighting for equal rights between men and women. Here, it pays to point out that the feminist movement in the West isn't the same thing as what we have here. Here, we need to precisely stipulate what equal rights means. We've already had equal rights as concerns using a sledgehammer. And that didn't lead to anything good at all. I agree that equal rights on the political level are necessary. But in my opinion, the primary destiny of women is to keep having children, to reproduce the population.[76]

For Lakhova, equal rights carried a somewhat negative connotation. Yet Lakhova's attitude changed over time, in part because of her dialogue with MCGS researchers, like Anastasiia Posadskaia, who worked with her from fall 1992 until summer 1993.[77]

---

[75] Galina Klimantova, interview, May 15, 1995.
[76] "Nashe interv'iu," *Zhenskoe dvizhenie v SSSR* (later, *Zhenskii Diskussionnyi Klub*), no. 2, January–March 1991.
[77] Elena Kochkina, interview, July 22, 1995.

Indeed, between 1992 and 1995, the phrase "equal rights and equal opportunities" became a framework held in common by all the strands of the Russian women's movement. In 1992, for example, the URW held a conference called "Women of Russia: From Discrimination to a Society of Equal Opportunities." At the conference, the government was criticized for not recognizing discrimination on the basis of sex as a state issue. The political and economic crises, however, had made discrimination against women more obvious, in the disproportionate numbers of women unemployed, the declining numbers of women in parliament, and slow movement of women into the business sphere. Speakers at the conference also noted that there was no law about equal opportunities on the books, and that, moreover, the courts had no practice considering cases of sex-based discrimination.[78] Likewise, in 1993, the Independent Women's Forum organization released a statement before the December elections, in which they addressed "men and women . . . who, like us, believe that a modern society should be not only one of equal rights, but also a society of equal opportunities."[79]

Echoing the positions taken by women's movement groups, in the 1993 election campaign, WOR, with Lakhova and Fedulova at its head, put forth an election platform stating that they stood for a society in which "all men and women are guaranteed not only equal rights and freedoms, but also equal opportunities for their implementation; where the equal representation of women and men in all the organs of power and administration is guaranteed."[80] Further illustrating the change in her viewpoint, Lakhova was quoted during the campaign as saying that women were excluded from decisionmaking at all levels, and labeling this as "clear discrimination that should be liquidated."[81] And in June 1995, when Fedulova spoke at the Second All-Russian Women's Congress, she echoed the Independent Women's Forum's 1991 slogan and equal opportunities framework, saying: "After all, democracy exists equally for everyone – both for men and women. The very state is clearly arranged on the basis of sex, here – it's just men in power. We don't want to oppose them. We're for a policy of equal rights and opportunities."[82]

WOR's discourse thus developed in a relatively radical direction,

---

[78] "Zhenshchiny Rossii: ot diskriminatsii k obshchestvu ravnykh vozmozhnostei," *Zhenskii Diskussionnyi Klub*, October 1992, p. 2, citing *Izvestiia*, October 2, 1992.

[79] "Obrashchenie uchastnits Nezavisimogo Zhenskogo Foruma," printed in *FemInf*, no. 3, December 1993, p. 6.

[80] "Predvybornaia platforma ob'edineniia 'Zhenshchiny Rossii.'"

[81] "Ekaterina Lakhova: 'Diskriminatsiia zhenshchin dolzhna byt' likvidirovana,'" *Zhenskii Diskussionnyi Klub*, October–December 1993, p. 3.

[82] "Politika: slovo zhenskogo roda," *Sudarushka*, June 27, 1995, p. 4.

reaching a point where it closely corresponded, on many occasions, to that of the independent women's movement. But rhetoric is insufficient as a measure of political alliance. What concrete steps or actions did WOR take while in the Duma that could be regarded as support for the Russian women's movement?

Among WOR's most significant accomplishments was the formation of the Duma Committee on the Affairs of Women, the Family, and Youth, headed by WOR deputy Galina Klimantova. It is likely that the committee would not have been formed if not for WOR's insistence.[83] This committee made a point of meeting with representatives of the independent women's movement, and inviting activists to parliamentary hearings on issues that concerned women.[84] By June 1995, Klimantova had made an agreement with a network of women's movement organizations to meet with her and other WOR deputies on a monthly basis, to exchange ideas and hear proposals from these groups, which could then be addressed or adopted by WOR. It seemed that the groundwork had been laid for a real alliance. If WOR had remained in parliament, it is likely that the independent women's movement might have enjoyed greater influence in the Duma.

In addition to establishing the Duma's Committee on Women, Family, and Youth Affairs, while in the Duma WOR was able to lobby women's movement causes with the executive branch. The Duma committee maintained a close relationship with the Ministry of Social Protection's Department on the family, women, and children.[85] Deputies from WOR also managed to meet with Prime Minister Chernomyrdin, to discuss the socio-economic status of women, as well as expressing opposition to the decaying healthcare system, and to the armed forces' draft practices.[86] And Lakhova, even after election to the Duma, remained chair of the Presidential Commission on Issues of Women, the Family, and Demography.

WOR also acted as a conduit between the women's movement and state representatives by sponsoring several large women's congresses, and providing women's movement activists with opportunities to meet and pressure deputies as well as government officials. For example, WOR held a conference in November 1994: the First All-Russian Women's Congress: Labor, Employment, Unemployment, in Moscow. The resolution discussed (briefly) at the end of the congress was written

---

[83] Ekaterina Lakhova, "Ia ne prizyvaiu moskvichek vyiti s kastriuliami na stolichnye ploshchadi," *Moskvichka*, no. 25, 1994, pp. 6–7.
[84] Galina Klimantova, interview, May 15, 1995.
[85] Lakhova, "Ia ne prizyvaiu," pp. 6–7.
[86] "Vremia" (television news), February 21, 1995.

by two independent women's movement activists: Elena Ershova of the Women's League, and Svetlana Aivazova, co-leader of the Moscow-based women's lecture organization Klub F-1. Among other things, the resolution called for improving the national mechanism to implement the constitutional principle of equal rights and opportunities; developing a program to improve women's status; Russian ratification of the International Labor Organization (ILO) Convention 156, so as to help create equal opportunities in the labor sphere; governmental establishment of economic programs to foster women's employment; and media support for a discussion of changing male and female role stereotypes, to help formulate a more positive image of women in the press.[87]

Such calls for action are important, especially when made by parliamentary deputies. But the ability of WOR to influence legislation through concrete actions – an important ability for a social movement ally to have – was limited by their numbers. With fewer than two dozen deputies, WOR was hardly in a powerful position. Despite that disadvantage, WOR did play an important role in the Duma, influencing several pieces of legislation with ramifications for women. WOR deputies initiated and drafted bills revising the Family and Marriage Code (altering alimony regulations to reflect the new economic conditions), on housing privatization (to prevent parents from selling their housing and leaving children homeless), on benefits to families (such that welfare benefits would accrue to the family, and its members would all have equal opportunities to fulfill family obligations), and others, as well as organizing hearings on social policy, consumer goods, and youth policy. WOR deputies also played an important role in amending the budget to protect children's programs, an issue very important to the pragmatic wing of the women's movement.[88]

WOR deputies also took active part in developing and supporting the human rights commissioner law (finally passed and signed by Yeltsin in February 1997).[89] This creation of a human rights commissioner's office was viewed by the women's movement as a potential site for complaints about violations of women's rights due to discriminatory hiring and firing practices. The Women of Russia faction also lent significant support to the creation of a law on violence against women (the draft bill "On Ending Violence in the Family"), a high-priority

[87] "Resoliutsiia," distributed at the First All-Russian Women's Congress: Labor, Employment, Unemployment, Moscow, November 1994.
[88] For a list of bills initiated and drafted by WOR members and the Committee on the Affairs of Women, the Family, and Youth, see "Otchet o zakonotvorcheskoi deiatel' nosti deputatov fraktsii politicheskogo dvizheniia 'Zhenshchiny Rossii,' chlenov Komiteta po delam zhenshchin, sem'i i molodezhi."
[89] Lakhova, "Ia ne prizyvaiu," pp. 6–7.

issue for a number of women's movement organizations and activists. Based on these actions, WOR again seemed cast as an apparent ally of the independent women's movement.

Discourse and actions aside, the WOR faction unquestionably included a number of individual women's movement allies – women who were active members of Russia's independent women's organizations, as well as being WOR deputies. Irina Vybornova and Larisa Babukh, both original members of the Women's League, won positions in the 1993 parliament with WOR.[90] Also impressive is the record of Dzhenklub, a Moscow professional women's organization with powerful connections. Said Nina Iakovchuk, its president:

About half of the WOR faction are constant members of our club.

Q. Were they members of your club before they got into the Duma?
A. Of course, at the very beginning, the first meetings, they were among the founders.[91]

One of the co-founders of Klub F-1 bragged with good reason that a number of Duma deputies got their consciousness raised originally at the club's monthly meetings, which began in September 1992.[92] These deputies included several from the WOR faction, specifically Liudmila Zavadskaia, perhaps the most outspoken feminist on WOR's 1993 party list. Moreover, Svetlana Aivazova, political scientist and co-leader of the club, served as adviser to the WOR faction.

Concrete evidence aside, at base, alliance is a subjective concept. Highly important, then, in determining whether WOR was an ally of the women's movement are movement activists' attitudes on this issue. Feelings about WOR in the activist community were mixed. Some groups lauded WOR's efforts to pass a law on violence against women. Activists from pragmatically oriented groups supported WOR's legislative efforts on behalf of children, especially their program, "Children of Russia."[93]

Still, many activist women retained a negative attitude toward WOR. The leader of the Association of Women [Film and Theater] Directors was critical:

Q. Do you think that WOR defends women's interests?
A. No, not women's interests. The most obedient women are in there; the

---

[90] Elena Ershova, interview, April 18, 1995.
[91] Dzhenklub's connections in the late Gorbachev era (when the organization formed) went as far as Raisa Gorbacheva, who, after hearing about the organization, apparently contacted Iakovchuk by phone to offer her support: Nina Iakovchuk, interview, May 5, 1995.
[92] Interview, November 15, 1994.
[93] Nina Tiuliulina, interview, May 25, 1995.

nomenklatura has been obedient for decades. They're taught to be obedient ... I haven't seen a single initiative from WOR ... Maybe I don't understand something about politics, but it seems to me that they *have* no political positions, and therefore they have no influence ... From the outside, it looks like there was another nomenklatura quota being applied: there should be 10 percent women. And 10 percent were elected. And just as they did in the old days, they sit there quietly.[94]

Some activists felt that the media was to blame for failing to cover WOR's genuinely helpful legislative activity,[95] but many felt that WOR had truly failed to represent women's interests in general. Several interviewees exempted Zavadskaia from their critical evaluations of WOR as a whole, crediting her with WOR's emphasis on equal rights and opportunities.[96]

The alliance between WOR and the independent women's movement, shaky at best, was also short-lived. In 1995, the WOR bloc did not replicate its spectacular 8 percent, failing even to cross the 5 percent threshold for entrance into parliament. Only three of WOR's deputies (including Lakhova) reentered the Duma – all from single-mandate districts. Analysts afterwards believed that WOR had stuck too firmly to a centrist position, alienating potential adherents on both sides of the political spectrum. Moreover, some activists argued that WOR had failed to open its gates to the independent women's movement, a potential source of votes. WOR may also have failed for a more general reason: having promised to reestablish the social welfare network in Russia, WOR was unable to meet popular expectations. A disappointed populace then rejected them. In the words of the Cheboksary *zhensovet* leader: "Earlier we supported them. But they did nothing for us. They haven't passed a law on social protection."[97]

Without WOR, the independent women's movement may have lost ground in the Duma, especially as regards support from the Committee on the Affairs of Women, the Family, and Youth. Led by Communist Party deputy Alevtina Oparina in the aftermath of the December 1995 elections, the committee seems less amenable to the issues that motivated actions such as the law on violence against women. Oparina quickly relegated that law to the bottom of the priority list, from whence it has not yet emerged for its first reading in the Duma.[98] On the other hand, the Duma's Committee on Labor and Social Policy may be the

---

[94] Elena Demeshina, interview, March 26, 1995.
[95] Interview, December 6, 1994.
[96] Interviews, December 1, 1994; November 21, 1994; Tat'iana Riabikina, interview, April 26, 1995.
[97] Nina Petrova, interview, May 29, 1995.
[98] Martina Vandenberg, personal communication, June 5, 1996.

new site of alliance for the independent women's movement. The committee's deputy chair, Tatiana Iarygina, affiliated with the liberal party, Yabloko, helped to organize feminist organizations' participation in parliamentary hearings on the Labor Code in March 1996, providing an important opportunity for women's movement activists to voice their demands for a nondiscriminatory labor law.

Allies and access points in the executive branch

Although they are operating in a less financially stable atmosphere than that which existed during the Soviet period, Russia's ministries continue to play an important role in policymaking. Access to executive branch ministerial departments was therefore important to women's movement activists, who quickly discovered that some sectors of the bureaucracy were more open to dialogue than others.

If WOR was the women's movement's best potential ally in the legislative branch up until its defeat, then the Ministry of Social Protection was the movement's main supporter in the executive branch. Until her removal in 1996, Liudmila Beslepkina, the minister of social protection, served as an ally for the women's movement, at least indirectly. In an introduction to a 1994 book about integrating women into the process of societal development, Beslepkina argued that women's sociopolitical status was worsening, not improving, and that discrimination against women in Russia had become "rather noticeable." She overtly opposed the increasingly popular idea, propagated especially in the mass media, of "returning to the patriarchal past" and relegating women to the kitchen.[99]

Beslepkina's feminist discourse was in marked contrast to the attitudes exhibited by representatives of the Ministry of Labor. Indeed, interministerial clashes at women's conferences over the course of 1994–95 revealed both allies and opponents of the women's movement. A brief analysis of speeches made by Beslepkina and Valerii Ianvarev (deputy minister of labor) at a women's conference in September 1994, held at the URW offices in Moscow, and sponsored jointly by the World Bank and the URW, serves to illustrate the contrast.[100]

After a speech by Fedulova (chair of the URW, and WOR deputy), which painted a sad portrait of women under Russia's new economic conditions, and stressed the need for reducing women's unemployment,

---

[99] Liudmila Beslepkina, "Gosudarstvennaia politika v otnoshenii zhenshchin," in Korniak, *Integratsiia zhenshchin*, pp. 4, 6.
[100] The following material on the conference is based on author's notes.

Ianvarev took the floor. Ianvarev began his remarks by noting that it was the first time he'd been "surrounded by so many beautiful women at once." He also invoked a bureaucratic style reminiscent of the Soviet era, pointing out that the "correlation of labor function and maternity function is determined by the stage of development through which society is passing." Ianvarev's speech was almost schizophrenic, affirming that indeed discrimination was extant, and that two salaries were necessary for families to maintain their minimum living standard, but arguing simultaneously that women didn't mind losing their jobs. In support of his argument, the deputy labor minister suggested that, according to a survey of unemployed women, two-thirds did not think that they would find new jobs, but that it was not a catastrophe, rather, a positive phenomenon. This statement gave rise to a noisy stir in the auditorium, provoking Ianvarev to apologize, saying: "I didn't mean to offend the women." The Russian woman seated next to me frowned and whispered, "He has a male perspective."

Beslepkina spoke next, on the welfare of women and families during the transition period, making sure to counter the deputy labor minister's remarks. Unemployment, said Beslepkina, is hard for women, both psychologically and financially. She stressed the Russian economy's need for women's labor, and expressed her opposition to the idea that women should be exclusively the keepers of the domestic hearth. "Women don't want to exit the national economy: it's illiterate and tactless to say so," she lectured. The audience supported her.

The Labor Ministry had, at that time, proposed a new labor code, to replace the Soviet-era document. The new code was reviled by women's movement organizations for its discriminatory articles.[101] Article 117, for example, stated that fathers could receive certain benefits granted to mothers automatically (limitations on night work, work on holidays, and business trips, for example) only if they were raising a child without a mother. Article 105.3 referred to a list of occupations forbidden to women (but not to men). Also, a series of articles granted maternity benefits and leave rather than parental benefits and leave (thus making women's labor less desirable to employers who would have to grant the benefits only to female workers). All of these articles were seen as discriminatory, reinforcing extant sex roles, and detrimental to women's labor market competitiveness. At the September 1994 conference,

---

[101] For a critique of the new labor code, see Marina Liborakina, "Predlozheniia k proektu trudovogo kodeksa rossiiskoi federatsii," distributed and discussed at a meeting of the Women's Consortium in Moscow, December 5, 1994. The critique was written in the name of the Independent Women's Forum.

WOR deputy Zavadskaia critiqued the labor code, objecting to its "patriarchal ideology."[102]

The dynamic between Beslepkina and Ianvarev at the September 1994 conference reveals an interdepartmental struggle over women's treatment in Russian society, with the Ministry of Social Protection speaking out for equal treatment, and the Labor Ministry favoring women's exit from the paid workplace. Clearly, the Russian state was not monolithic on this issue. The Ministry of Social Protection therefore provided a better entrance point to policymaking structures than did the Ministry of Labor.

The Ministry of Social Protection, in fact, had well-established contacts with women's movement organizations, particularly through Olga Samarina, head of the ministry's Department on Family, Women, and Children's Issues. The department was formed in January 1992, and charged with coordinating a unified state policy on women, as well as involving NGOs in the policy implementation process.[103] Contact between the ministry and women's movement organizations began in earnest somewhat later, according to Samarina, in the context of preparing for the upcoming United Nations Worldwide Conference on Women, held in Beijing in 1995, and widely known as the "Beijing Conference."[104]

Such contact between Samarina's department and independent women's movement activists tended to take place at various movement conferences and seminars. For instance, at a movement seminar held in April 1995, bringing together women from forty-one regions of Russia, Samarina gave a speech about the existing state bodies and documents relating to women, and called for joint action with women's NGOs. This was regarded as an important result of the seminar.[105] Samarina not only spoke; she also engaged in an extended question-and-answer session with members of various women's movement groups.[106] These kinds of opportunities for contacts with state officials are rare but productive.

The other main source of contact between the Ministry of Social Protection and the independent women's movement was the National

---

[102] Ultimately, the Duma decided to reject the new labor code, and simply revise the old Soviet-era one.

[103] Ol'ga Samarina, "O natsional'nom mekhanizme po uluchsheniiu polozheniia zhenshchin Rossii," *Informatsionnyi vypusk*, April 1995, p. 2; Ol'ga Samarina, interview, March 24, 1995.

[104] Ol'ga Samarina, interview, March 24, 1995.

[105] Larisa Fedorova and Elizaveta Bozhkova, "Osmyslenie sobytii," *Vestnik*, no. 2–3, 1995, p. 3.

[106] Transcript of the ADL Serpukhov seminar, April 1995, pp. 10–17.

Council on Preparation for the Beijing Conference. The National Council provided the first regular opportunity for contact between women's organizations and state structures; until then, women's issues had been dispersed among the various ministries, where they were always addressed alongside "family" and "children's" issues, painting women primarily as family members, not as independent citizens.[107] According to Samarina, dozens of women's NGOs were invited to National Council meetings, where they could "take a real part in developing policy."[108] Few women's movement organizations had official representatives on the National Council. However, activists from women's NGOs were permitted to attend the meetings, and did so.[109]

Although the National Council provided an open atmosphere for contacts between state officials and movement activists before the Beijing conference, after the conference the council became more closed to women's movement groups. At the council's final meeting, on October 24, 1995, representatives of women's groups were excluded.[110] A new interdepartmental commission created to replace the National Council ostensibly had room for some women's movement representatives. But communication between the Ministry of Social Protection and women's organizations about the new commission was spotty. Announcing at a women's movement seminar that the interdepartmental commission was already in formation, Tatiana Riabicheva, the head of the ministry's Department for Ties with Women's Organizations, stated, to the surprise of the activists present:

We haven't had a single document from women's NGOs yet! We've got over forty applications from ministries and departments. Where's the Independent Women's Forum? Asya Posadskaia had a seat on the National Council on Preparation for Beijing, but I'm afraid you'll lose that spot.[111]

The activists objected that they had never been informed that they had to apply for positions on the new commission. The deadline was April 6, 1996 – a few weeks away. Moreover, only interregional and national level organizations would be allowed to apply for positions on the commission, thus excluding many locally based women's movement organizations. The governmental body that had been a regular source of

[107] Marina Liborakina, "Obretenie sily," *Vestnik*, no. 4, 1995, p. 5.
[108] Ol'ga Samarina, interview, March 24, 1995.
[109] Officially represented were: Shvetsova (Women's Initiative Fund, Women's League), Iakovchuk (Dzhenklub), Sillaste (Women and Development), Vasil'eva (Union of Women Writers), and Posadskaia (MCGS).
[110] Commentary following Elena Kochkina, "Will Echoes of Beijing be Heard in Russia?," *Woman Plus*, January 1996.
[111] Tat'iana Riabicheva speech, March 1996, at a seminar on "Social Lobbying," Vykhino, Moscow, March 18, 1996, author's notes.

contact with women's organizations remained open for only a few years; its replacement seemed less oriented toward contact with the women's movement. The political opportunity structure, as far as concerns these particular allies and access points, was changing unfavorably for the women's movement.

A more stable access point for the women's movement was the Presidential Commission on Issues of Women, the Family, and Demography, established in 1992 and headed by Ekaterina Lakhova (adviser to Yeltsin on these issues for two years prior to the commission's establishment and, later, head of the WOR faction). The commission was charged with developing position papers and programs about women's and family issues, distributing information to branches of the Russian federal and local government, and executing presidential decrees on the subjects falling under its purview. It addressed issues such as family planning, abortion (supporting legal, safe, and free abortion), women's unemployment, and domestic violence.[112] Anastasiia Posadskaia, feminist researcher and activist at MCGS, was a member of the commission. In addition to incorporating movement activists, in the wake of the Beijing Conference, the Lakhova commission organized discussions and evaluations of the conference, in which women's movement organizations participated actively, in November 1995. And in April 1996 the commission organized a conference on Security Viewed Through Women's Eyes, again with women's movement participation.[113]

Yeltsin himself may be viewed as somewhat of an ally of the women's movement, based on his support for the commission, and on several decrees he issued concerning women's status. The first of these was published to coincide with International Women's Day, March 8, 1993. The decree called for creating a unified state policy on improving women's status, in order to provide for "identical conditions for actual equality for women and men, in the political, social, economic and cultural life of the country, and freely chosen self-realization for women in all spheres of activity," in line with the UN Convention on Eliminating All Forms of Discrimination Against Women.[114] Despite the fact that it was never implemented, some activists felt that the decree had a substantial impact:

[112] N. Azhgikhina, interview with E. Lakhova, "Zhenshchiny dolzhny pomoch' sebe sami," *Vy i my*, no. 11, Spring 1995, pp. 10–12.
[113] Information from "Post-Beijing Monitoring Survey," MCGS and Geia International Women's Center.
[114] Ukaz Prezidenta Rossiiskoi Federatsii no. 337, "O pervoocherednykh zadachakh gosudarstvennoi politiki v otnoshenii zhenshchin."

Ideologically, it was very important, because that was the first time that a special policy, at the level of state policy, had been formulated during the transition period in Russia from the perspective of equal opportunity policy.[115]

In June 1996, Yeltsin issued a second decree, on Russia's national plan of action to improve the position of women by the year 2000.[116] While these decrees may suggest some degree of presidential support for creating equal opportunities for men and women, it seems more likely that they reflect the influence of Ekaterina Lakhova, and, in turn, the influence on her exerted by independent women's movement activists.

The presence of new allies in power positions (whether in government ministries, parliament, or consultative bodies such as Lakhova's commission), and their disappearance from the political scene, created improvements and reversals in the political opportunity structure for the women's movement at the national level, largely affecting the women's movement groups based in Moscow, and their degree of access to policymakers.

Local allies and access points: Cheboksary and Ivanovo

Outside Moscow, in Cheboksary and Ivanovo, the political opportunity structure for local activists was more open and far less complicated than that at the national level. To a significant extent, women's organizations were integrated into the local power structures, and able to achieve direct policy benefits for their constituents.

Although representation of women in Ivanovo's city council level was quite high (five women out of thirteen deputies, as of March 1994), there were no women represented in the regional Duma at all.[117] However, in Ivanovo, the chair of the local women's council, Natalia Kovaleva, was one of the five female members of the city council, and, from that position, she was able to translate the demands of the local women's movement into action:

My deputyship helps a great deal. We've examined the issue of social protection of youth, in connection with the increase in unemployment. It was my initiative, to adopt a law about the social protection of teenagers. And now, an oblast-level law is being passed about that. This summer, we'll have an article that's protected in the budget, that provides money for summer work for adolescents from families in need. We're also creating a department for the city as a whole, a sector for working with families. In April, we're working out a program for the

---

[115] Elena Kochkina, interview, July 22, 1995.
[116] Penny Morvant, "Yeltsin Orders Social Reform Program," *OMRI Daily Digest*, June 19, 1996.
[117] Natal'ia Kovaleva, interview, April 3, 1995.

family, what we can do for families, within the budget. It'll be a small program. And, starting in February, we're getting a welfare payment for children, from the regional budget. We'd talked about that at a round table.[118]

The leaders of local women's organizations in Ivanovo agreed about the value of Kovaleva's deputyship. The leader of Ivanovo's Committee of Single-Parent Families, for instance, confirmed that her meetings with Kovaleva were the main method of influencing local politics.[119] The local women's organizations had contacts in the city administration as well.[120]

In a display of national-level personal contacts unusual for the provinces, the president of Ivanovo's Businesswomen's Club, Margarita Razina, used her own connections with Lakhova and Beslepkina to great advantage, parrying them into support for her club's yearly textile fair. Olga Khasbulatova, a local feminist academic, had brought Razina Beslepkina's phone number when the latter had been head of the Ministry of Social Protection's new department on women. Razina called, and proposed the textile fair. Beslepkina approved of the idea, and, consequently, the Ministry of Social Protection became one of the yearly sponsors of the event, sending out invitations across Russia and the former Soviet republics. Lakhova had also been helpful to Razina from her position as chair of the presidential commission, which provided financial assistance to Razina's club, including a computer and photocopier, to help organize the yearly fair and create a database of participants.[121]

The women's organizations of Cheboksary, the capital of Chuvashiia, a region considerably more distant from Moscow than Ivanovo, had no such ties at the national level. The Chuvash parliament (the State Council of Chuvashiia), however, had greater female representation than the corresponding body in the Ivanovo region: as of May 1995, there were forty-seven deputies in the State Council, of whom nine were women.[122] Moreover, as was the case in Ivanovo, the chair of the city women's council, Nina Petrova, was a powerful, well-connected woman, with ties to the city administration (where she worked, in the committee on social protection and labor) and to the regional parliament. Her women's council had successfully lobbied the Chuvash State Council to reduce the price of childcare at state-run centers to only 20 percent of its newly inflated cost. The women's council was also invited by the local

---

[118] Natal'ia Kovaleva, interview, April 3, 1995.
[119] Larisa Nazarova, interview, April 4, 1995.
[120] Nina Temnikova, interview, April 4, 1995.
[121] Margarita Razina, interview, April 6, 1995.
[122] Zinaida Sutrukhova, interview, May 30, 1995.

government to comment on changes in welfare benefits policies.[123] As was the case in Ivanovo, the women's council of Cheboksary and its chairwoman were at the center of local movement organizing.

However, the political opportunity structure for Cheboksary's women's organizations was affected by an atmosphere of contact considerably different from that in Moscow and Ivanovo. The status of Chuvashiia as a constituent republic of Russia meant that a powerful but also local executive administration was accessible to the women's movement, the participants in which were in some cases also officials of the Chuvash government. For example, the president of the Chuvash republic (Nikolai Fedorov) attended the May 1995 founding conference of a new Businesswomen's Club (Klub Zhenskaia Initsiativa), which counted a number of female republic-level ministers among its founders, as well as factory directors. The women's council leader, Petrova, was also a member of the founding group.

At the charter conference of that organization, President Fedorov was invited to speak by Kreta Valitskaia, the female labor minister, and did so, praising the women ministers in his cabinet, and even suggesting that they put forth the names of more women as candidates to governmental positions in Chuvashiia. "But you'll do this very softly, without offending the men," added Fedorov. In his speech, Fedorov pledged his support for the new organization, which he hoped would help "raise women's potential," and help women feel that they were full participants in society, rather than being restricted to their homes during the problematic economic transition period. But Fedorov also noted that, although the powerful women in his republic were organizing a potentially very important club, gender roles were gender roles:

I have no doubt that you know that women are women, men are men, and women should remain women. There should be moderation in everything.[124]

Whether the representation and involvement of high-level administrators in two of Cheboksary's women's organizations reflects an open political opportunity structure (allies in power) or simply a bureaucratic style of organization remains to be seen. However, the women's organizations in Cheboksary – including those populated by state administrators – seemed very sincere in their dedication to improving women's status and trying to take measures to counter the economic collapse in the region that had been affecting women disproportionately.

---

[123] Nina Petrova, interview, May 29, 1995.
[124] Nikolai Fedorov, speaking at the Charter Conference of Klub Zhenskaia Initsiativa, Cheboksary, May 30, 1995, author's notes.

Sexism in the legislative and executive branches of the Russian government

The mere representation of women in legislative or executive political bodies provides no guarantee that they will endeavor to create policies favored by the women's movement. But even if the intention is there, as one could argue was the case at the national level with Women of Russia or other movement allies, women in politics encounter an entire range of obstacles that men in the Russian political arena do not confront, namely, sex-based discrimination.

Discriminatory and patronizing attitudes toward female deputies have been reported from both the Russian Federation's defunct Supreme Soviet, as well as the more recently established Duma. In an interview, Alevtina Fedulova, chair of the Union of Russia's Women, and leading member of WOR, claimed that the WOR deputies to the Duma "feel comfortable, so far," although she added:

as before, people can still be heard saying, "Give the girl the floor!," and in the corridors, men say to me, "Alevtina, no other woman gets talked about more than you do." We understand that it'll be difficult for us. After all, we're the first.[125]

Fedulova's sentiment was echoed by Lakhova, chair of the WOR faction, in an interview, where she stated directly that "Male deputies don't accept us as politicians on an equal basis [*kak ravnopravnykh politikov*]."[126]

According to eyewitnesses, attitudes toward women in the parliament have remained somewhat consistent since the times of Russia's Supreme Soviet. Asked in 1991 whether it was hard for women deputies to operate there, Lakhova acknowledged that women deputies felt a lack of respect:

We thought we would come in and quickly carry out our election platforms. But here, they look at us [*vosprinimaiut*] just as they do in the provinces. Men see us as women, but not as deputies. You're explaining something to him about infant mortality, and he says that it doesn't become you to talk about such serious things, that you have to be a woman.[127]

According to Galina Sillaste, public opinion researcher and women's movement activist, in sessions of the Supreme Soviet, the devaluation of women's role in Soviet society was visible, evidenced by the "disre-

---

[125] "Mneniia zhenshchin-politikov o politicheskoi situatsii v rossii," *Zhenskii Diskussionyi Klub*, Interlegal, January 1994 (citing articles in *Moskovskaia pravda* and *Moskovskii komsolets*).
[126] WOR, *Informatsionnyi biulleten'*, no. 2, 1995, p. 34.
[127] "Nashe interv'iu," *Zhenskoe dvizhenie v SSSR* (later, *Zhenskii Diskussionnyi Klub*), no. 2, January–March 1991.

spectful attitude toward women who speak from the podium."[128] Galina Starovoitova, deputy to Russia's Supreme Soviet, confirmed this. At a 1995 feminist conference in St. Petersburg, Starovoitova recalled an illustrative incident:

Once, when the well-known democrat, Bella Denisenko – a professor, the deputy Minister of Healthcare – took the floor to put the issue of medical insurance on the agenda, speaker [Ruslan] Khasbulatov interrupted her. And when the people in the hall demanded to let her finish talking, he turned the microphone back on and rudely said, "Well, what else did you want to say?" At that, Denisenko, upset, answered, "But you hit me below the belt, now I'll just gather my thoughts and conclude." Ruslan Khasbulatov reacted immediately, saying, "I've got nothing to do with what's below your belt." And he turned off the microphone again.[129]

In the Duma, populist-fascist politician Vladimir Zhirinovskii perhaps raised "disrespect" to new heights, when, in 1995, he punched deputy Evgenia Tishkovskaia in the face, later excusing his act by claiming that he had been "fending off her sexual advances."[130]

Women activists have also met with disrespect when addressing state officials. In one particularly memorable instance, activist Tatiana Konysheva attempted to find out how familiar the legal institutions in Moscow were with the UN Convention on the Elimination of All Forms of Discrimination Against Women (CEDAW), to which Russia is signatory. Konysheva went to Moscow's Main Administration of the Ministry of Internal Affairs (MVD), and the People's Court (among other places), and encountered an alarming degree of sexism:

At the Main Administration of the MVD, I asked whom I should talk to about this issue. The woman didn't know where to direct me . . . [At their press service], when I started to talk with the journalists about the Convention, they said, "You know, we love women." I told them that the Swedish government had adopted a decision that men in families had to take one month off out of the twelve months allowed for parental leave. They answered by saying, "But we don't like Swedish women; they're not sexy." That was my experience at the MVD.[131]

At the court, Konysheva talked to a male judge, who dismissed the UN

---

[128] Galina Sillaste, "Any State Is Strengthened by Women's Prudence," *Moskvichka*, no. 2, 1991, p. 3.

[129] Galina Starovoitova, "Kakovo byt' zhenshchine-politiku v rossii segodnia" (stenogramma vystupleniia), in *Feministstkaia teoriia i praktika: vostok–zapad. Konferentsiia 9.6–12.6.95*, ed. Iuliia Zhukova, et al. (St. Petersburg: Peterburgskii Tsentr Gendernykh Problem, 1996), p. 36. Starovoitova, a long-standing pro-democracy activist, was assassinated in St. Petersburg on November 20, 1998.

[130] Alessandra Stanley, "Russia's Gross National Legislature," *New York Times*, January 19, 1997, Week-in-Review, p. 3.

[131] "Opyt vzaimodeistviia (skoree so znakom minus)," *Strategii vzaimodeistviia*, October 1995, pp. 4–5.

Convention as being far removed from anyone's interests, particularly given the low levels of appreciation for laws in general. When Konysheva asked him about the available statistics on violence against women (one of the points in the convention), his response was much more unexpected: "How many men have you had over the course of your life?"[132]

For political opportunities to expand, and for women's movement allies or activists to make headway with the state, at the very least, a certain degree of respect is required, particularly if the allies and activists themselves lack significant political or economic clout. It is far from clear that such respect has been achieved. Sexism creates barriers to the expansion of the political opportunity structure for women's movements, in much the same way that racism restricts the political opportunities of civil rights activists (in the United States and elsewhere), even if political allies and access points are available.

Instability of elite alignments undergirding the polity

Political instability, in particular, the collapse of the Soviet state and the weakness of the new Russian state, further complicates the political opportunity structure for the women's movement during the transition period. The rapid succession of political-institutional changes, the relative novelty of lobbying as a tactic, and the state's limited capacity for policy implementation all restrict the movement's developmental opportunities.

Institutional instability

The rapidly changing political opportunity structure had a retarding effect on women's movement groups' successes. Not only were allies found and then lost, with the 1993 and 1995 elections, but the institutional change in Russia's parliament between 1990 and 1993 also had a disruptive effect. The Moscow-based group, Conversion and Women (supporting women who lost their jobs in the defense industry), for example, was forced to start afresh making contacts in the Duma, after the destruction of the Supreme Soviet by Yeltsin in October 1993:

We had contacts established in the Supreme Soviet. I talked at the Higher Economics Council, twice, in 1993, in March, and in May, at the Supreme Soviet: they'd agreed to finance our project on reeducating highly qualified women to become world-class level managers. Because only men were being trained in that sort of thing. It wouldn't have been hard for me to gather the women; our only weak point was knowledge of foreign languages; after all, the

132 Ibid.

defense industry had been very closed off. The program was to begin in November. But then the October events occurred, and everything came to naught. Now, in the Duma, we have to start over from the beginning. We're only just now starting to get somewhere in the Duma. It's a hard process, trying to find an entry into the corridors of power.[133]

The extraordinary number of shifts in the political system confronting the women's movement (and other social movements) in post-Soviet Russia – the disbanding of the USSR, the establishment of a Russian Supreme Soviet, its destruction in October 1993, the creation of a women's party and its ascension to the new Russian parliament in December 1993, followed by new elections in 1995, and the failure of the women's party – made for a perpetual search not only for new allies, but also a constant struggle to master each new system. While gradual and even relatively sudden changes in political opportunity structures (such as elections) have surely created openings for social movements in Western countries, in Russia, the continuous systemic political instability during the transition period entailed far more fundamental and extreme changes than those usually categorized under the rubric of political opportunity structure in the West. The very instability of political institutions at the national level was a retardant rather than a spur to women's movement organizations' success.

The collapse of the centralized Soviet state has conditioned the women's movement's interaction with the new Russian state and its often ineffective political institutions. Following on the heels of the Soviet regime, the new Russian political system has inherited some of the exclusionary and antiparticipatory characteristics of its predecessor, but little of its power to enact policies and laws. When considering the specific relationship of social movements to the Russian successor state, the newness of lobbying (complicated by restricted public access to information) and the weakness of the Russian state's capacity for policy implementation are both important in this regard.

Lobbying without information

The Russian legislative system, like its predecessor, is not geared toward lobbying by large membership organizations, which, in more established democratic systems, often function to mobilize thousands of potential voters for a given candidate, should that candidate take a certain policy position. Instead, influence by large social organizations in Russia tends to take place through the executive branch rather than the legislature. For example, when striking coal miners demand payment of back

[133] Eleonora Ivanova, interview, February 6, 1995.

wages, they win their money ultimately by presidential decree, not by pressing their Duma legislators to pass a more stringent salary-payment law. As a result, organization building is not a priority for women's groups hoping to influence legislators. Aside from the employment-training organizations, few of the groups interviewed for this study had an overt new-member "outreach" strategy. In short, women's groups – even those interested in affecting laws and policies – are not focused on increasing their membership, perceiving that they have no need to mobilize large numbers of people in order to influence politicians.

When Russian women's movement organizations do engage in lobbying, they encounter a new and highly imperfect system. The rules regulating lobbying are vague; only in mid-1995 was a law "On Regulating Lobbying Activity in the Federal Organs of State Power" even discussed. In an "explanatory note" referring to the draft law and explaining its utility, the chair of the Duma committee responsible for it, V. Zorkaltsev, wrote: "Unfortunately, the mechanism of interaction between groups of citizens and those in power today is hidden behind the scenes, and is corrupt and chaotic."[134] This conditions groups' abilities to meet with lobbying success.

One reason for the chaos may be that the new Russian political system has inherited some of the secretive methods of its Soviet predecessor. This makes the acquisition of information difficult for social movement groups, whether it concerns drafts of new legislation or deputies' positions on legislative issues. Whereas personal contacts are the key to lobbying in all representative systems, the importance of such contacts with legislators should not be underestimated, especially in a relatively closed political system that holds few political allies for women's groups. Liudmila Zavadskaia, former deputy in the Women of Russia bloc, advised women's organizations that seek to influence legislation to do so directly, by encouraging their activists to become professionals – especially lawyers – and getting into the Duma's working groups, where laws are written. To her, this seemed a more practical method of influencing legislation than one where activists mobilize public pressure to lobby parliamentary representatives after the law has been written and is on the Duma's floor for a vote.[135]

Zavadskaia's advice may seem elitist, but it is profoundly sensible given the Russian political system and its degree of openness to social

[134] V. Zorkal'tsev, "Poiasnitel'naia zapiska k proektu federal'nogo zakona 'O regulirovanii lobbistskoi deiatel'nosti v federal'nykh organakh gosudarstvennoi vlasti,'" distributed at a seminar on "Social Lobbying," sponsored by the Inform Center of the IWF, held in Moscow at Vykhino, March 16–19, 1996.

[135] Liudmila Zavadskaia, speaking at a MacArthur Foundation seminar on the status of women in post-Soviet society, March 21, 1996.

organizations. Women's groups often have trouble acquiring draft legislation texts under review in the Duma. Marina Liborakina, one of the leaders of an advocacy organization, the Inform Center, noted that, "The legislative committees are not in the habit of sharing. We have to work very hard to get information."[136] Personal contacts with people in the Duma's legislative working groups can be the only way to access information about laws in development. For example, when a law on family violence was being developed by a Duma working group, one of the working group's members, Galina Sillaste (herself head of a women's NGO) spoke at a seminar sponsored by the American Bar Association in Moscow, describing the law to the women's movement activists present. Without Sillaste's willingness to share her insider information, the detailed content of the law would most likely have remained unavailable to the women activists attending the seminar, several of whom were specialists on domestic violence (from their work at crisis hotlines, legal defense organizations, and so forth). Sillaste encouraged the seminar participants to call her if they had ideas or comments on the bill's contents, and not to "wait for the first draft" to appear.[137] It seems increasingly clear why a Duma deputy might suggest that women's organizations' shortest path to influence would be to enter the working groups themselves.

Lobbying activity is further complicated by the lack of access to state-held information in general, another holdover of Soviet origin. Liborakina gave several examples:

Women's organizations are poorly informed, and information is inaccessible. Information is inaccessible about state programs referring to "family, women and children," as well as those that don't refer to them, including our international obligations and treaties. And information is inaccessible about credits, including credits from the World Bank, and about the obligations our government incurs as a result of those credits, because the World Bank credits obligate the reduction of expenditures on social welfare. But we can't get information about these international and internal obligations. As concerns the legislative branch, the basic mystery for us is that we periodically give them various proposals, but there's no certainty that they'll be looked at, or that we'll get an answer. That's how it's been with our article-by-article commentaries on the new Labor Code. And in the executive branch, there are no mechanisms that would guarantee our participation in the development or implementation of state programs.[138]

[136] Janet Maughan, "Women's Work: Finding a Place in the New Russia," *Ford Foundation Report*, Spring 1996, p. 20.
[137] ABA Seminar on the Law on Family Violence, Moscow, June 24, 1995, author's notes.
[138] Marina Liborakina, "Kak zhenshchinam podarili utiugi ili nekotorye soobrazheniia po kontseptsii vzaimodeistviia," *Strategii vzaimodeistviia*, October 1995, p. 10.

Although Russia's new popularly elected political legislature is more "democratically" founded than the rubber-stamp legislature of Soviet times, the closed character of the institution remains. Specifically, the lack of vital information about state treaties, legislative plans, and legislative calendars makes it difficult, if not impossible, to mobilize women on a larger scale in support of (or against) particular bills and policies. This contributes to movement activists' dependence on elite "patrons" who parcel out information only when it appears prudent for them to do so.

Weak state – weak society

Even when women's groups create temporary channels of access to the state and achieve policies consistent with their goals, their efforts can be fruitless because of the Russian state's inability to implement its policies and laws, an element of political opportunity structure more relevant in emerging democracies and other newly established political regimes than in stable democracies. Although it may be perceived as willing to engage in a certain amount of political repression or violence (pursuing war in Chechnia, for example), when it comes to running the country the Russian government is perceived as weak, in that its laws and decrees are disobeyed on a regular basis. The leader of WOR, Ekaterina Lakhova, for instance, expressed her disappointment with the way laws and policies were implemented in Russia, particularly those concerning women and the family: "There are special laws that concern the family directly. For instance, the law on welfare benefits to families with children. There's a decree by the Russian president about it. But the December [1993] decree isn't being carried out. Seven months have passed, and it's not being implemented."[139] Ten months later, Lakhova remained unsatisfied with the Russian state's ability to enforce its own laws, saying in May 1995: "I think we'll be able to talk about democracy when the laws operate in our country, when human rights won't just be declarative in our Basic Law, but also carried out in practice."[140] It is not only laws on women that fail to be implemented. Across Russia, wages are held in arrears for months at a time, despite state declarations making the detention of salary illegal.

Yeltsin himself has joined the chorus of Russian citizens and officials bemoaning the inconsistent implementation of laws and decrees. In June 1996, Yeltsin signed a new decree, mandating penalties for bureau-

---

[139] Lakhova, "Ia ne prizivaiu," p. 7.
[140] Ekaterina Lakhova, "Zhenskie golosa v partiinom khore," *Rossiiskie vesti*, May 18, 1995.

crats who fail to implement presidential decrees. Yet, the new decree only emphasizes Yeltsin's inability to guarantee that laws will operate once passed, and symbolizes his concern "about the general collapse in the state's ability to carry out its functions."[141]

While women's groups do engage in lobbying with some amount of success, the weakness of the state has discouraged women's movement organizations from building large constituencies in order to attract the attention of parliamentary representatives. Indeed, mass lobbying activity and social movement action designed to effect social change through legislation and policy assumes a political system in which rule of law is well entrenched. Political scientist M. Steven Fish reached a similar conclusion about civil society in Russia more generally:

> the decay of state power during the second half of the Gorbachev period, while creating some space for the emergence of independent societal power, may paradoxically have slowed the development of autonomous political organizations. A state that lacks effective administrative capacities and the authority to enforce universalization of the law – and the Russian state currently lacks both – may actually inhibit the growth and maturation of civil society.[142]

This point may be summarized by reversing Tocqueville's description of state–society relations in America: in the Russian case, a weak state is found together with a *weak* society, not a strong one. A state with limited capacity for policy implementation restricts the political opportunity structure for a social movement. Even if access and allies are available, legislated or decreed changes in the social distribution of justice may not come to fruition, because of the problem of state capacity.

Conclusion

Focusing on political opportunity structure enables us to conclude that, while state repression against independent social movement organizing has unquestionably declined, state capacity, too, has been eroded, leaving the women's movement in the unenviable position of having a largely unfettered voice, but little impact. In part, this is the result of Russia's executive-centered political system. Thus far, the women's movement has taken advantage of that system, using activists' ties to Lakhova, in her capacity as chair of the Presidential Commission on Issues of Women, the Family, and Demography. Such a political system,

---

[141] Robert Orttung, " . . . And Signs Decree on Implementing His Decrees," *OMRI Daily Digest*, June 7, 1996.
[142] M. Steven Fish, *Democracy from Scratch* (Princeton: Princeton University Press, 1995), p. 217.

however, leaves activists subject to the whims of the president, and discourages the building of a mass movement. Moreover, activists confront the fact that, despite Yeltsin's "strong presidency," his power of implementation is insecure, and his decrees are often not carried out. Yeltsin's failing health makes the situation still more unpredictable.

Analysis of the political opportunity structure for the women's movement during the transition period shows that the Russian state, whatever its implementation capacity, is far from monolithic, and that the presence of elite allies can alter a movement's opportunities considerably. The emergence of the Women of Russia (WOR) political bloc, and even the limited support from the Ministry of Social Protection and the National Council, under Beslepkina, created opportunities for activists to increase their influence on political decisionmakers. The failure of WOR in the December 1995 elections, and Beslepkina's removal from the ministry in 1996, however, illustrate the fragility of political alliances. Also, many state institutions remain hostile to the notion of women's advancement, and their representatives maintain that women's role should be limited to that of homemaker until the economic crisis has passed. And while the instability of the Soviet political system ultimately enabled the creation of the women's movement in the late 1980s, the multiple upheavals in Russia's political system since 1991 have made it difficult for that movement to build consistently on its own successes in making allies within the women-friendly sectors of the state.

In sum, the current political opportunity structure for Russia's women's movement has been thoroughly transformed from that of the pre-Gorbachev era Soviet Union. The most fundamental change may have been the legalization of NGOs, many of which have adopted some responsibility for defending citizens' material interests – perhaps a first step in building a civil society. The actual power held by these organizations, however, is quite limited. Indeed, as Russia's women's movement activists strive to improve women's position in society, they have encountered political as well as economic opportunities and obstacles, and it is to the latter of these that we turn in the next chapter.

5 "Unemployment has a woman's face . . .": economic opportunities and obstacles to women's movement organizing

Unemployment has a woman's face, but power has a man's.[1]

The changing political opportunity structure in Russia at the end of the 1980s, and continuing into the 1990s, allowed for the emergence of numerous women's organizations, ranging from advocacy groups, consciousness-raising groups, and women's research centers, to support groups for women in various professions. Many of these groups had a politicized orientation. They recognized that women's second-class status in Russia was socially determined, and tried to raise awareness of that fact, holding various seminars, meetings, and conferences; publishing critical articles in the press; initiating women's publications; making contact with state officials; and so on.

Meanwhile, as the 1990s began, new women's groups developed, intending to ameliorate the effects on women of Russia's economic crisis and devastating cuts in social services. The activities of these organizations spanned a broad spectrum, from charity events to women's job-training programs, from occupational health and safety inspections in factories to support for single mothers and women attempting to enter the business world.

But the economic transition did more than spur the creation of new women's groups. It also set a backdrop of hardship against which all independent organizations had to struggle to survive. In short, Russia's economic transition created both opportunities and obstacles for the emerging women's movement and its development.

There are two aspects of economic influences on social movements: those financial resource-related issues relevant to individual social movement organizations, and the economic conditions present in the broader society that create constraints and/or opportunities for the emergence and development of the movement as a whole. This chapter examines the effects of the new economic situation on the Russian women's

[1] El'vira Novikova, cited in *Vestnik*, no. 2–3, 1995, Appendix, p. 2.

movement, at both the macro- and micro-levels, a pair of factors I label jointly as "economic opportunity structure." At the macrosocietal level, the transition provided a certain opportunity or impetus for women's group formation, for women who are not feminist-identified to come together with shared problems, and potentially for feminist consciousness to grow. Simultaneously, at the micro- (or organizational) level, the economic transition created roadblocks to the development of women's movement organizations, such as financial hardship and constraints on national networking. Such limitations have been exacerbated by the historical absence of a nongovernmental (NGO) sector under the Soviet regime, a factor that differentiates post-Soviet social movement organizing from that in the Western countries about which most social movement theory has been written.

The role of economic change in the formation of women's movements

In a certain sense, the economic collapse in Russia served to foster the expansion of the women's movement, particularly of the pragmatic wing, which arose explicitly to address women's economic dislocation. First of all, the vast reduction in welfare benefits imposed by the Russian state (described in detail below) *de facto* targeted women. Sociologist Charles Tilly has argued that immediate threats to specific groups, such as unemployment or the reduction of benefits, are most likely to trigger "defensive" mobilizations and collective actions.[2] The development of self-help organizations, training programs, and charitable initiatives (to women and families, for example) can be viewed in this light.

Some theorists draw a different type of connection between women's movement formation and economic change, specifically, between middle-class women's entry into the labor force and the rise of women's collective consciousness, presaging the emergence of a women's movement. For example, it has been suggested that, when middle-class women in the United States joined the paid labor force in the 1960s, upon entering "male" occupations they found themselves in competition for resources with other workers – namely, men – thereby setting the stage for a new wave of the women's liberation movement at the end of that decade.[3] This particular relationship does not hold under Russian conditions; in the service of industrialization, Soviet women were brought into the labor force early on, and in a multitude of jobs,

---

[2] Charles Tilly, *From Mobilization to Revolution* (Reading: Addison-Wesley, 1978), p. 73.
[3] Steven M. Buechler, *Women's Movements in the United States* (New Brunswick, NJ: Rutgers University Press, 1990), p. 25.

with no sign of an emergent independent women's movement for decades to come. It may be that the Soviet state's guarantee of full employment mitigated women's collective consciousness-raising by reducing the competition for resources. Moreover, Stalinist controls prohibiting independent societal organizing served as a major impediment to the formation of a women's movement in the pre-perestroika years.

A related hypothesis, however, may lend greater insight into the relationship between changing economic conditions and women's movement growth in Russia. Some theorists contend that, in the United States, middle-class women changed the way they perceived themselves upon entering the workforce in the 1960s and 1970s, viewing themselves as workers, not as mothers, and thereby gaining "new standards for social comparison." This comparison might have "generated the belief that the category 'women' was treated unjustly, and this belief was an impetus to political activism."[4] Soviet women, by contrast, were compelled to see themselves simultaneously as both workers and mothers, and women's entry into the labor force *en masse* in the 1930s was not marked by a change in feminist consciousness in the same sense (although it was marked by a drop in birth rates). However, with the advent of unemployment associated with the transition toward a market economy, Russian women found themselves in stiff competition with men for job opportunities, and many women, having become unemployed, experienced direct sex-based discrimination when they sought new jobs. This could become a source of transformed consciousness, and has already led to activism.

Women's economic status in Russia

Women's economic status underwent a severe decline in the former Soviet bloc, beginning in 1989.[5] From women's perspective, the process of transition to the Russian version of a market (labeled by one woman activist as "caveman capitalism") has been accompanied by several disruptive and negative trends.

---

[4] Bert Klandermans, "The Social Construction of Protest and Multiorganizational Fields," in Aldon D. Morris and Carol McClurg Mueller, eds., *Frontiers in Social Movement Theory* (New Haven: Yale University Press, 1992), p. 89.

[5] See, for example, Valentine Moghadam, ed., *Democratic Reform and the Position of Women in Transitional Economies* (Oxford: Oxford University Press, 1994); Barbara Einhorn, *Cinderella Goes to Market* (London: Verso Press, 1993); and Nanette Funk and Magda Mueller, eds., *Gender Politics and Post-Communism: Reflections from Eastern Europe and the Former Soviet Union* (New York: Routledge, 1993).

Table 2. *Economically based causal chains leading to the emergence of women's movements in the West and in Russia*

West	Women's mass *entry* into the labor force	⟶	Competition with men and discrimination against women in the labor market/ labor force	⟶ Women's movement organizing
USSR:		Women's mass entry into labor force under Stalinist conditions	⟶ No women's movement	
Russia	Women's *exit* from labor force under introduction of market forces	⟶	Competition with men and discrimination against women in the labor market/labor force	⟶ Women's movement organizing

Women's unemployment

The first of these trends is rising unemployment. According to International Labor Organization methodology, the unemployment rate in Russia stood at 7.7 percent in June 1995. This figure, however, excludes "hidden" unemployment, a situation increasingly common in Russia, where workers remain on the rolls at a given factory, but receive only a small fraction of their salary, and are not in fact employed in productive labor, often due to the factory's lack of raw materials or encroaching bankruptcy. The Russian Labor Ministry maintains that, if both open and "hidden" unemployment were taken into account, the 1995 unemployment rate would be closer to 10 or 12 percent of the working-age population.[6]

Under the Soviet regime, the specter of unemployment was essentially unknown; the Soviet constitution declared a "right to work," and enforced this "right" with severe penalties for those who found themselves jobless. Unemployment has become a household word, particularly for women, who make up the vast majority of Russia's registered unemployed. By 1993, popular magazines such as *Rabotnitsa* (Woman Worker) were declaring that unemployment had a "female

[6] El'mar Murtazaev, "Tempy rosta bezrabotitsy v Rossii zamedlilis'," *Segodnia*, June 30, 1995, p. 3.

face." As of January 1994, Federal Employment Service figures showed that 68 percent of the registered unemployed were women.[7] Also, women found themselves disproportionately unemployed among the educated strata, making up 78.2 percent of the unemployed with a higher education in 1993.[8]

The growth of unemployment has come as a shock to women in Russia, who, under Soviet rule, had maintained an extremely high labor force participation rate (around 90 percent). The new trend toward pushing women out of the labor force is particularly hard for single mothers, who head 13 percent of Russian families; their salaries are the sole source of family income. In 1995, 55 percent of Russian single mothers were living below the poverty line.[9] In part, this is a result of female unemployment: women over age thirty-five with young children are increasingly hard pressed to find work.

There are two fundamental reasons for the disproportionately high number of women among the unemployed. First, one can point to a well-entrenched system of vertical and horizontal occupational segregation by sex. Russian women predominate in several of the industrial branches hardest hit by the changes in the economic system and the collapse of the USSR, including light industry, especially textiles.

A second reason for women's unemployment has deeper roots in Russia, but has been exacerbated by the privatization process. Now responsible for the profitability of their enterprises, employers prefer not to hire women, knowing that women hold full responsibility for taking care of the family, including sick children and aging parents. Also, women are the main beneficiaries of parental leave policies, and the sole recipients of other associated privileges that the Soviet regime granted specifically to women workers with children. These facts and policies encourage the commonly held assumption among employers that women constitute a less desirable and less productive workforce, since their family "responsibilities" encroach on their work time. Thus, women face the double-edged sword of the "double burden" – fully expected to take care of the family, yet discriminated against in the labor market for this very reason. Deprived of state subsidies under the new market-driven conditions, enterprise directors see no benefit to hiring or retaining women as part of their labor force, since they assume that

---

[7] From materials of the All-Russian Women's Congress: Labor, Employment, Unemployment, Moscow, November 29, 1994.

[8] L. S. Rzhanitsyna, "Zaniatost' i dokhody zhenshchin," in V. B. Korniak, ed., *Integratsiia zhenshchin v protsess obshchestvennogo razvitiia* (Moscow: Luch, 1994), p. 282.

[9] Marina Skazina, "Rossiiskim zhenshchinam pomozhet Tereza," *Segodnia*, January 10, 1995.

women with children will continue to take advantage of their legal right to work fewer hours.[10]

On top of officially registered unemployment, Russian women in certain industries also suffer from hidden unemployment. Galina Viatkina, a professor at a textile institute in Ivanovo, explained how hidden unemployment is a means of statistically disguising mass unemployment:

The various regional administration funds give money to factories, with which to hang onto their employees. Official statistics say that everything is just fine. These employees get a little more [money] than the people who are officially unemployed.[11]

Eleonora Ivanova, an activist with Conversion and Women, an organization representing women in the defense industry, further elucidated the subtleties of hidden unemployment:

Hidden unemployment is useful for everyone – except those who suffer from it. Because if they fire you, the enterprise is supposed to pay you, reeducate you . . . but they have no money for that. It's more profitable for them to hang onto you, with this minimal level of pay.[12]

Whether hidden or registered, unemployment's effect on women has not gone unnoticed at the policy level. In fact, when rising levels of female unemployment first began to attract attention in Russia, government officials argued that women, tired of their double burden, were grateful to be leaving the workforce, happy to give up on the working world that had provided many of them with difficult, nonprestigious, and uninteresting paid labor, and content to don aprons and slippers, becoming housewives at long last. However, one Russian sociologist studying the psychological adaptation of unemployed women, found that, while at first many women felt relief at leaving the labor force, after a short period of time they changed their minds and actively sought work, both to decrease their material dependence and as a source of stimulation beyond domestic chores and childcare. Moreover, their socialization included an assumption that women should all work outside the home. But although most of these women were over age thirty-five, with higher educational degrees, and some history of labor force participation, they comprised a social group from which most firms and enterprises had unfortunately become reluctant to hire.[13]

---

[10] Einhorn, *Cinderella Goes to Market*, p. 130.
[11] Galina Viatkina, interview, April 3, 1995.
[12] Eleonora Ivanova, interview, February 6, 1995.
[13] Elena Zdravomyslova, "Zhenshchiny bez raboty," *Vse liudi sestry*, no. 3, 1994, pp. 38–39.

For some social groups, unemployment has been more of a constant threat than a new development. One of the leaders of a Moscow-based lesbian support organization, MOLLI, commented, "For lesbians, it's not much of a difference from the past. The situation remains as it was. Now people are a little more afraid that they'll lose their jobs, especially if someone suspects them of being a lesbian – then you can lose your job even faster."[14]

Reductions in social welfare benefits

Another factor contributing to women's declining economic status during the transition period is the reduction of social welfare benefits established during the Soviet era. Since the start of the economic transition, the social welfare infrastructure undergirding mothers' paid employment has been severely cut. In a society where fathers rarely take a large role in childcare, women have been left stunned by the rapid decline in availability of institutional childcare, inexpensive children's summer camps, and other benefits that melted away with the collapse of the Soviet social welfare system. By 1994, as more and more single-parent families slipped below the poverty line, government officials began to refer to the feminization of poverty.

In general, the market-oriented reforms beginning in 1990 had a major impact on women's economic freedom and social status, by reducing social welfare programs and female employment rates. In part, this is due to foreign structural adjustment financing. When factories receive Western loan money, they are required to turn their social services (medical facilities, daycare centers, and so on) over to the local city administration. This effectively means that the services cease to exist, because the municipal budgets are incapable of supporting them. At a seminar on lobbying tactics, Moscow activist Elena Ershova commented on the situation with dismay: "Our government agreed to this, and now quietly ignores the results."[15] The effect on women with children is evident: the reforms deprived women of the Soviet-era guarantees that were designed to facilitate combining childrearing with full-time labor outside the home, albeit in the interests of the state's productive and reproductive goals.

The tremendous drop in the provision of public childcare in particular has affected women's status adversely. In the past several years, factories

---

[14] Interview, November 27, 1994.
[15] Elena Ershova, speaking at the Inform Center seminar on "Social Lobbying," Vykhino, Moscow, March 18, 1996.

have closed their childcare centers at unprecedented rates: in 1993, 5,000 childcare centers were closed, while others were privatized, placing them out of financial reach for many families. By mid-1994, despite laws contravening the conversion of childcare centers to commercial usage, the trend continued. Whereas in 1988, 70 percent of children had places in childcare centers, by 1994 it was down to 56 percent, with 370,000 children on waiting lists. Other children, as Women of Russia parliamentary deputy Ekaterina Lakhova stated, "are not even in line, inasmuch as the cost of putting a child in daycare significantly exceeds the minimum salary." Lakhova noted that Ministry of Economics officials had been indifferent to this trend since 1992, dismissing her objections and saying, "when we're through with the economic crisis, then we'll get to the kids."[16] The effect of this combination has been to push women back to the home, said a representative of the Ivanovo Center for Social Support of Women and Families:

For women, in the near future, taking care of children is going to be a major problem, because they can't count on the state-sponsored children's care centers, which are closing down. Now, when in the West, you're moving toward some expansion in this area, we're already shutting them down, turning backward. And also, it'll happen that we'll lose our option to choose: women will have to sit at home with the children.[17]

The closure of daycare centers, combined with female layoffs, creates a situation where women are encouraged and even forced to abandon paid employment.

This trend toward moving women out of the labor sphere received official sanction as early as 1987, when Gorbachev, in his book *Perestroika: New Thinking for Our Country and the World*,[18] sent a mixed message about women's proper role in society. On the one hand, Gorbachev called for concerted efforts to promote women to leadership positions in politics and economics. On the other, he wrote of the need to establish conditions that would facilitate returning Soviet women to their "purely womanly mission" – in other words, the private sphere of household and family.

Women's groups protested against this trend. For instance, the Union of Russia's Women sent a letter to heads of local administrations throughout various areas of Russia, urging that the "antisocial" policy of turning daycare centers over to private hands be stopped.[19] It is not

---

[16] See Ekaterina Lakhova, "Vcherashnie shchi liubite?: zakhodite zavtra," *Izvestiia*, April 19, 1995, p. 4.

[17] Ol'ga Khasbulatova, interview, April 6, 1995.

[18] Mikhail S. Gorbachev, *Perestroika: New Thinking for Our Country and the World* (New York: Harper and Row, 1987), pp. 116–17.

[19] Vladimir Chertkov, "Neuzheli ee udel – kukhnia?," *Sudarushka*, March 7, 1995, p. 3.

clear whether their action had any notable effect. Similarly, subsidized baby-food production has collapsed dramatically since the early 1990s. By 1994, the amount of baby food produced domestically was only 15 to 20 percent of the production levels in 1990, forcing families to increase their expenditures on imported baby food.[20] The Women of Russia bloc did manage to appropriate 580 billion rubles in the 1995 state budget to finance a program called Children of Russia (Deti Rossii), passed in August 1994, which covers production of children's food, family planning, measures to protect children from the Chernobyl region, children from the Far North, orphans, and disabled children.[21] However, despite protected budget status, the program was inadequately implemented.

In 1993, academics began to address the "antidemocratic" effects of the capitalistic economic reforms on women's status. Pointing to the elimination of some social welfare guarantees from the new constitution, they argued that the government had abdicated its responsibility to help women combine labor outside the home with their domestic chores and motherhood "duties." They reasoned that the goals of private entrepreneurship were in direct contradiction to those of working women: an entrepreneur had no reason to "waste resources on social programs designed to create conditions for women to combine their professional and public activities with their maternal and familial duties," such as childcare centers, pregnancy leaves, and so on. In the words of one academic, T. N. Sidorova, "Motherhood is now considered a woman's private affair."[22] Moreover, there was concern about women's decreasing opportunity to partake in political activity and administration, under circumstances (such as the lack of childcare facilities) that excluded women increasingly from the labor force and public life for years at a time. Sidorova suggested that such exclusion of women from paid labor would only provide "fuel" for the opponents of democracy, who oppose allowing mere "cooks" into politics.[23] The declining numbers of women represented in Russia's decisionmaking bodies may in part bear witness to the realism of her concern.

[20] Irina Rosenberg, "Detskoe pitanie v bor'be za federal'nyi biudzhet," *Segodnia*, February 28, 1995, p. 13.

[21] Viktor Khamraev, "Ekaterina Lakhova uverena, chto Rossiia vyzhivet 'bez vsiakoi postoronnei pomoshchi,'" *Segodnia*, June 2, 1995, p. 2.

[22] T. N. Sidorova, "Zhenskii vopros i demokratii," in V. A. Tishkov, ed., *Zhenshchiny i svoboda* (Moscow: Nauka, 1994), p. 55.

[23] Ibid., p. 54. Sidorova's reference is to Lenin's statement that, under communism, any cook (in Russian, a female noun, *kukharka*) would be able to run the country.

Economic discrimination as state policy

Women's economic status in Russia has been affected by other discriminatory tendencies as well, including several that are implicitly and explicitly sanctioned by the state. Indeed, economic discrimination against women in Russia is hardly new. For decades, women were tracked into branches of industry featuring low pay and low prestige. In August 1994, the wages in industrial branches with predominantly male labor forces ranged from 190 percent (electrical energy production) to 361 percent (gas) of the average Russian salary, while those in "women's" branches ranged from 49 percent (textiles) to 127 percent (food industry) of the average.[24] Despite having an overall higher level of education than men, working women are clustered in lower skill categories. Women rarely attain the level of managers or industrial executives.

Like most other countries, Russia has not avoided a gender-based earnings gap. According to a Public Opinion Foundation poll conducted in March 1996, discrimination against women is visible indirectly through major differences in wages. In their poll of 8,869 employed people in urban areas with higher or secondary education, women made up 87 percent of the group whose monthly income was under 100,000 rubles ($21).[25] And, while before perestroika women's average pay was 70 percent of men's, by 1994 it was only 40 percent of men's wages.[26]

Another increasingly visible form of discrimination against women in the labor force is sexual harassment. This has become a problem for young women in particular, evidenced in part by analysis of young women's employment opportunities. According to federal employment services data, 70 percent of girls graduating from high schools and institutes (*VUZy*) register for unemployment.[27] Researcher Zoia Khotkina estimates that it is precisely these young women who take out "seeking work" ads in Russian newspapers, and notes the very high frequency of ads that state "excluding intimate relations." The ads are taken as additional evidence for widespread sexual harassment (and rape) at work. One interviewee shared her experience on this subject, acquired while she was employed at a privately owned Moscow cafe:

I was working in a bandit-run, money-laundering cafe . . . In the cafe, they tried to force me to sleep with them. They call women "telka": a young cow, one that

24 Goskomstat figures, cited in *Kontseptsiia zhenskoi zaniatosti* (Moscow: Institut Ekonomiki RAN, 1994), Appendix 3.
25 "Study: Bulk of Low Earners are Women," *Moscow Times*, March 8, 1996.
26 Nadezhda Azhgikhina, "Zhenskie dela," *Ogonek*, no. 50–51 (1994).
27 Zoia Khotkina, ed., *Seksual'nye domogatel'stva na rabote* (Moscow: ABA-CEELI, Zhenskii konsortsium, and MCGS, 1996), p. 15.

gives birth, provides milk, and then is killed for meat. An object to be used, that's all. When I was working there, they put out an ad: cafe seeking a salesgirl. A girl of about eighteen came to the cafe: she was pretty, naive, nicely dressed, with her little employment book [*trudovaia knizhka*]. The forty-year-old boss took her off in his car and raped her – then he said she wasn't appropriate for the job.[28]

Such incidents are not isolated. One Moscow-based organization, set up to protect women from sexual harassment on the job, compiled an extensive list of private enterprises "where employers regularly abuse or harass their employees." The fund's director confirmed that "a number of women in Moscow informed him that they were raped by potential or current employers."[29] Although there are provisions in Russian law for prosecuting on the basis of sexual harassment (namely, Article 118 of the Criminal Code: Coercing a Woman to Enter into Sexual Relations), these provisions are invoked so rarely that, when in 1994 "the first known sexual harassment case in Russia" took place, the prosecuting attorneys were unable to find a precedent.[30]

In addition to governmental negligence in enforcing such antidiscrimination law, the Russian government itself supports several forms of *de jure* discrimination. For example, the Russian government has inherited from the Soviet system a governmental policy of direct economic discrimination, whereby 460 of 6,000 professions listed on government books are simply closed to women.[31] Further evidence of the Russian state's economic discrimination against women is seen in the fact that state enterprises reacted to the onset of economic crisis and unemployment by dismissing women. According to a Human Rights Watch report from 1995, in "a number of recorded cases where government enterprises conducted mass dismissals, they fired significantly more women than men."[32] One explanation for women's dismissals is the Soviet occupational stratification that placed women disproportionately in "superfluous jobs [which are] disappearing as the economy is restructured."[33]

Another explanation is that Russian employers overtly seek to hire men, and thus reject female job applicants on the basis of sex and the

[28] Laima Geidar, interview, July 17, 1995.
[29] Human Rights Watch, "Neither Jobs Nor Justice: State Discrimination Against Women in Russia," March 1995, p. 18, citing Dmitry Babich, "Workplace Harassment," *Moscow Times*, July 5, 1994.
[30] See Human Rights Watch, "Neither Jobs Nor Justice," p. 19.
[31] Galina Sillaste, speaking at Russian parliamentary hearings, "Women and Labor Law," Moscow, March 5, 1996 (transcript, p. 28). These include underground work, work involving poisonous chemicals, tractor driving, and many others.
[32] Human Rights Watch, "Neither Jobs Nor Justice," p. 7, citing Zoia Khotkina, "Gender Aspects of Unemployment," unpublished paper.
[33] Human Rights Watch, "Neither Jobs Nor Justice," p. 8.

presence of children. Human Rights Watch's visits to unemployment offices in Russia's major cities confirmed such discrimination, even in the state sector: "announcements posted on the walls described positions available, salaries and qualifications for jobs that blatantly included the specification that only men need apply."[34] Moreover, state-sponsored employment-retraining programs often track women into low-wage, unskilled labor, regardless of a woman's previous education and training.[35] The majority of unemployed women have a higher or middle specialized education, yet the employment offered to them at state-run employment offices is, as a rule, in "worker's" occupations.[36]

It is easy to imagine that such discriminatory practices and declining status would inspire either outraged activism or despairing apathy in parts of the female population. However, it is not only women's economic status that can motivate or depress activism, but the economic status of the family as well, which has been declining since early 1992. Until 1991, household incomes in the post-war period in the USSR had been on the slow incline. The collapse in real income occurred in January 1992, when prices were liberalized, "without sufficient compensatory measures." By 1993, according to official state statistics, 30 percent of the population was earning less than the subsistence minimum.[37] In 1995, Ministry of Social Protection statistics showed that 30 percent of families were still living at or below the poverty line. Furthermore, many people who were employed were not receiving their wages. This unresolved situation of wage arrears has created frustrating and impoverishing conditions. Said one woman working at the Ministry of Social Protection:

In factories a lot of people simply aren't being paid. My husband hasn't been paid since January. But his 150,000 [rubles] is considered part of the family budget. Although it's not there! . . . And when the monthly unemployment benefit is 39,000 and the monthly metro pass [in Moscow] costs 60,000. . .[38]

Given these conditions, there are surely grounds for mass, grievance-based protest and organizing among women in particular. Yet neither in Moscow nor in Ivanovo and Cheboksary (where women's economic status has declined even further) has this occurred. The discussion will return to the issue of women's response to their declining status after a

---

[34] Ibid., p. 15.
[35] Such training courses focus on sewing, hair styling, secretarial skills, and governess-training: ibid., pp. 15–16.
[36] "Materialy k parlamentskim slushaniiam, 'Zhenshchiny i trudovoe pravo,'" materials handed out at Parliamentary hearings on the Labor Code, March 4, 1996.
[37] V. A. Terekhina, ed., *O polozhenii semei v Rossiiskoi Federatsii* (Moscow: Iuridicheskaia Literatura, 1994), p. 21.
[38] Ol'ga Samarina, interview, March 24, 1995.

brief detour into women's economic conditions in the two provincial case study cities.

Women's economic status in Ivanovo and Cheboksary

Compared to Moscow, the regions surrounding Ivanovo and Cheboksary suffer considerably more from industrial decline.

In Ivanovo, unemployment and the crisis conditions in the textile industry have particularly severe implications for women. Due to lack of raw materials, many of Ivanovo's textile factories remain at a standstill for months at a time. No longer automatically provided to the factories by state orders, cotton must now be purchased at world market prices, and appears only sporadically. In effect, Ivanovo's enterprise directors had little opportunity to adapt to market conditions, and lack the capacity to make deals with now independent foreign countries like those in formerly Soviet Central Asia that had provided cotton in years past.[39] This has decimated employment opportunities in the region, with an adverse impact on family living standards. Moreover, conditions for employed women are admittedly discriminatory. There is a 30 to 40 percent difference between average male and female salaries. Even more disturbing is the fact that while women are 70 percent of those workers training to increase their qualifications, nearly all of those who achieve promotion are men. Also, because of industrial conditions in the region, childcare centers in Ivanovo are threatened. Said the deputy head of the social psychology department at Ivanovo State University: "The enterprises themselves are hardly breathing; they can't support children's preschools."[40]

Both women and men are unemployed in the Ivanovo region in very high numbers. As of January 1995, women constituted about 40 percent of the unemployed, far lower than the national average. This relatively high rate of male unemployment was rooted in the fact that it was not only the textile factories that had been forced to close, but also the local machine-building plants (which predominantly employed men). The purely symbolic unemployment benefits at that time were approximately 20,500 rubles, enough to buy a kilo of butter, while the minimum subsistence wage was 110,000.[41] And despite these conditions, only 13 percent of Ivanovo's unemployed received retraining in 1994.[42] Indeed,

---

[39] Galina Viatkina, interview, April 3, 1995.
[40] Roal'd Borisovich Gitel'makher, interview, April 5, 1995.
[41] Galina Viatkina, interview, April 3, 1995.
[42] Data from Regional Employment Center (Oblastnoi Tsentr Zaniatosti Naselenia), 1994.

jobs were scarce. Between January and September 1994, in the Ivanovo region, for every available position, up to seventy-five people were officially seeking employment (the average in Russia was 4.1 at that time).[43]

Cheboksary, like Ivanovo, is situated in a depressed region, dominated by light industry, with some electrotechnical industry and a large tractor-building factory. In Cheboksary's textile industry, over 90 percent of those employed are female. Women's salaries, in the Chuvash republic are, on average, 20 to 30 percent lower than men's. Twice as many women as men work in unskilled jobs, and one woman in five works under conditions that violate occupational safety and health standards.[44] Given the economic plight of these cities, the prospects for improving women's employment conditions in the near future seem low.

Women's organized responses to the economic crisis and sex-based discrimination

How have women responded to these privations and violations of rights in the economic sphere?

Labor unrest and strikes

Although strikes are unusual as a tactic among women's movements, we might expect to see strike activity as a form of women's organizing in Russia, based on the degree of economic deprivation, and because of women's concentration in certain industries particularly hard hit by Russia's economic reforms, such as textiles.

Yet, despite women's failing economic situation, there has been little specifically female strike activity. Teachers' strikes have occurred sporadically for several years, but despite a largely female workforce, the teachers do not strike "as women" per se.

Indeed, while Russian women have organized to retrain the unemployed, and to try to pass legislation ensuring equal treatment in the labor market, there has been little mass protest mobilization by women in any economic sector. Labor solidarity is limited, and fear of organized protest runs high. Privatization, accompanied by women's unemployment, produces a rather demobilizing situation in factories and firms,

---

[43] "Zaniatost' zhenshchin v usloviiakh perekhoda k rynochnoi ekonomike," tables and p. 3, distributed at the First All-Russian Women's Conference: Labor, Employment, Unemployment, November 29–30, 1994.

[44] Data from *Sovetskaia Chuvashiia*, January 1, 1995, and the Chuvash Republic Statistics Committee. I am grateful to Vera Shuverova for preparing this information.

where women even fear to make collective demands. Women also hesitate to protest against workplace discrimination, because they can easily be fired. Moreover, the legal system is little respected and "chronically" underfunded, and has rarely enforced antidiscrimination laws.[45] Laws forbidding sex-based discrimination in hiring and firing decisions are thus ineffective.[46] One activist-academic from Ivanovo put it this way:

> One shouldn't expect a great wave of women's organization in the factories, making demands. They'll just be told, "Be our guest, the factory gates are open. You don't like it here? No one's holding you." Women are afraid of creating oppositional structures, in the work collective, when they're constantly afraid of losing their jobs. They're hugely dependent . . . You don't have that happening in Moscow either, women's organizations in factories. Groups are forming on other bases. Women entrepreneurs can unite: they're all independent. Women just can't defend their rights now.[47]

The role of trade unions in defending women's economic rights

Whereas one might expect trade unions to adopt the cause of women's unemployment or sex-based discrimination, and thereby attract a significant following (especially in female labor-intensive industries like textiles), this has not been the case. Formerly controlled by the Soviet state, trade unions have been weakened dramatically by the privatization process. In most cases, the trade unions are helpless to stop plant closings. And in the face of mass unemployment, the trade unions have little recourse. Illustrative of the negligible power retained by trade unions is a phrase from the charter for Conversion and Women, formed to protect women in the defense industry: "among our goals is to defend women's rights in the defense industry, under conditions of mass unemployment, and also assist women in maintaining their scientific-technical potential, in finding employment, and in adapting to the changing conditions of life."[48] Whereas in other contexts trade unions might have been the natural choice for such tasks, in Russia they were inadequate for the job.

Trade union ineffectiveness has left a vacuum of power. Current labor conditions have been described as a "dictatorship of managers,"[49]

---

[45] See Laura Belin, "Duma Appeals on Funding for Judiciary," *OMRI Daily Report*, October 24, 1996.

[46] Article 170 of the Labor Code (KZoT) forbids discrimination in hiring or firing on the basis of maternity and/or pregnancy.

[47] Ol'ga Khasbulatova, interview, April 6, 1995.

[48] Eleonora Ivanova, "Chtoby ne bylo padcherits reform," *Ogonek*, June 1994.

[49] Natal'ia Mirovitskaia, "Women and the Post-Socialist Reversion to Patriarchy," *Surviving Together*, Summer 1993, p. 46.

replacing the Soviet-style dictatorship of the proletariat, which at least brought with it a certain degree of trade union power (even if only to distribute rewards for plan fulfillment). Moreover, today's trade unions are the beneficiary of very little trust on the part of Russians. According to a 1995 public opinion poll, only 8 percent of Russians trust trade unions, 22 percent don't entirely trust them, and a full 37 percent do not trust them at all.[50] Part of this mistrust may reflect the legacy of total control of the trade unions by the Communist Party before the perestroika period.

Historically, the trade unions were never energetic defenders of women's rights, but even the limited roles that trade unions did play in that area have now been officially scaled back. Although the post-World War II period brought the creation of special commissions within the trade unions to address social welfare issues for women (such as child-care and everyday concerns – food, vacation vouchers, and so on), and although these issues were raised in the trade union press, "the trade union committees did not take on the role of pressure groups on the power structures."[51] Indeed, one woman who worked as a researcher on women's issues within the central trade union organization during the Soviet period claimed that the trade unions were completely disinterested in stopping workplace violence and discrimination against women.[52] Echoing this claim, Russia's National Report to the UN in advance of the Fourth Worldwide Conference on Women (1995) stated that until 1992 the Soviet trade union organization had commissions on issues concerning women's labor and daily life at all levels, but that, by 1994, such commissions were rare; women's issues were ostensibly being addressed within other commissions.[53] The upshot of this change was simply that trade unions, since the early 1990s, have paid increasingly less attention to women workers.

In some cases, factory-based women's councils have replaced the trade unions, according to the Cheboksary city women's council leader Nina Petrova.[54] Similarly, in the city of Voronezh, a women's council activist at one factory claimed that the women's council was consulted whenever a woman was about to be fired: "And just let some manager

---

[50] The remainder of respondents were unsure. See Leonid Sedov, "Boris El'tsin pal zhertvoi Borisa El'tsina," *Segodnia*, April 8, 1995, p. 3.

[51] Ol'ga Khasbulatova, "Evoliutsiia rossiiskoi gosudarstvennoi politiki v otnoshenii zhenshchin: obzor istoricheskogo opyta (1861–1917, 1917–1991 gg.)," in Korniak, *Integratsiia zhenshchin*, p. 86.

[52] El'vira Novikova, in "Obraz zhenshchiny v sredstvakh massovoi informatsii, *Zhenskii Diskussionnyi Klub*, March 1992.

[53] Russian Federation National Report for the UN's Fourth Worldwide Conference on Women's Status (Moscow, 1994), p. 11.

[54] Nina Petrova, interview, May 29, 1995.

try to fire a single mother, or a mother with multiple children – we won't let it happen."[55] In Ivanovo, however, one academic at a textile institute argued that the factory-level women's councils were of little use to women whose rights had been violated: "At the women's council, all you can do is cry on someone's shoulder." She agreed, however, that the trade unions were equally helpless when faced with "bankruptcy, the lack of cotton, and so on . . . these are the reasons that the majority of people are being fired."[56] And, evidently, both trade unions and women's councils have been "powerless" to combat the non-payment of wages.[57]

It is widely acknowledged in Cheboksary that the trade unions, once "strong" because they had money and access to goods and services, are no longer so, nor do they have the power to defend women's rights.[58] A university professor and activist in Ivanovo agreed:

The trade unions aren't any help now. There's no one to back them up. In order to be able to defend someone, you have to be materially independent. The trade unions have no material base today that could make them feel capable of influencing something. Just shouting during demonstrations doesn't change anything. No one will support them materially; there isn't a whole lot of active support from the people either. The role of the trade unions at this point is insignificant.[59]

Natalia Kovaleva, chair of the Ivanovo city women's council, concurred, laughing when asked whether the trade unions were capable of defending women's rights:

I don't think they do much defending. The trade unions are just trying to survive. There are some trade unions that do defend . . . But a lot of them are also afraid of management; they're afraid of being fired. Many people are leaving the trade unions because they don't see any defense. Some are powerful, though; some still manage to get spaces at Pioneer camp [summer camp] for the children.[60]

One activist was even more direct, when asked if the trade unions were capable of defending women's interests:

It's a provocative question. My personal opinion is as follows. Until perestroika, I worked in the trade union. And we defended *management's* interests. Defending individual workers was not welcomed. I think the trade union should defend the rights of workers, but the trade unions are not interested in taking on such tough problems. Some trade unions, in some factories, do defend the

[55] Women's council activist, cited in Nina Fedorova, "Chtob ne propast' po odinochke," *Rabotnitsa*, March 1993.
[56] Galina Viatkina, interview, April 3, 1995.
[57] Fedorova, "Chtob ne propast' po odinochke."
[58] Iraida Stekol'shikova, interview, May 29, 1995.
[59] Ol'ga Khasbulatova, interview, April 6, 1995.
[60] Natal'ia Kovaleva, interview, April 3, 1995.

workers. But the trade unions don't stop women and people in general from being fired. The ones that are fired can't really turn to the trade union for help, because the trade union can't really help now.[61]

Without effective trade unions, and faced with powerless factory women's councils, women who sought a collective solution to the decline in their economic status as a group had little choice but to initiate their own, independent women's organizations. It is to the process of pragmatically based organizational emergence that we now turn.

The economic "opportunities" driving the formation of new women's groups

Activists' answers to questions about why their organizations formed revealed that many had been motivated by their observations of women's deteriorating economic status. Women from just under half of the fifty groups interviewed stated that their organization's purpose was at least in part to combat women's unemployment or other effects of the economic crisis. Many of these were pragmatically oriented organizations, trying to find the resources to do what the state could no longer accomplish, as the economic decline spiraled out of control. By 1992, women were starting to seek their own solutions to the growing problems, "not counting on much state support."[62] Attempts to ameliorate women's conditions included the formation of employment-training programs, self-help groups, professional support groups, and businesswomen's organizations.

Women's group formation in the provincial cities on the basis of economic concerns

Economic motivations for group formation in the early 1990s were strongest in Ivanovo, a city in the throes of severe industrial depression. There, the formation of four out of five women's organizations whose representatives I interviewed was driven by economic goals, and the fifth, a businesswomen's club, though it had not formed directly because of economic pressures, was engaged in charitable activities for the unemployed and impoverished. Ivanovo's Center for Social Support of Women and Families, for example, which provided retraining courses for unemployed women, began at the initiative of Olga Khasbulatova,

---

[61] Interview, name withheld.
[62] Nadezhda Azhgikhina, "Zhenskaia bezrabotitsa v postsovetskoi Rossii," *Posev*, no. 5, 1994, p. 32.

an academic specialist on the pre-revolutionary Russian women's movement.[63] The Committee of Single-Parent Families (a split from the
Committee of Multi-Child Families, and in fact, mostly a committee of
single mothers) also formed because of the deteriorating economic
situation in Ivanovo:

In 1993, the political and material situations in the country became more acute.
Unemployment appeared. It became hard for women, and they needed to turn
somewhere. They didn't know where. The enterprises and factories weren't up
to helping them. It was psychologically hard to adapt to the situation. Before, a
woman's child had been in daycare, she'd had a job, maybe not very highly paid,
but she could live normally. And now, she's being fired from work, the daycare
centers have become [expensive], or are being closed down. So women decided
to unite in the face of this.[64]

Although Ivanovo's city women's council predated the economic
crisis, it was the appearance of major economic troubles that inspired
the women in it to register their organization:

In 1991 when the [Communist] Party committees were dismissed, we decided
that we needed to preserve the women's councils. Because the problems
appearing were very serious ones. We saw right away that unemployment had a
woman's face. And because in this city, we have a lot of families where both the
man and the woman work in factories. And when the textile industry is in such a
difficult situation today, the entire family is in a difficult situation. So we didn't
want the women's councils to cease to exist.

At that time, in February 1991, we held a conference, in the city women's
union. And there, we from the city women's council decided that we'd change
our name to the Union of Women. We saw that if we didn't unite in a more
general way, we'd end up all dispersed, isolated. In June 1991, we registered
with the regional Department of Justice. We have our own bank account in the
city.[65]

The women's councils of Cheboksary and the Chuvash republic also
predate the economic transition, but since its advent, have focused
heavily on assisting women's adaptation to the economic transition,
conducting unemployment counseling and engaging in charitable activities. Also, Cheboksary's newest organization (as of 1995) formed
directly in response to the economic crisis in their region. A businesswomen's "initiative" club, its formation was spurred by the Chuvash
republic's labor minister (a woman), who was joined by various female
factory and private firm directors, as well as ministers and other
state administrators, with the goal of combating unemployment and
cooperating to maximize women's business activity under market

[63] Marina Mints, interview, April 6, 1995.
[64] Larisa Nazarova, interview, April 4, 1995.
[65] Natal'ia Kovaleva, interview, April 3, 1995.

conditions.[66] The executive director of Cheboksary's recently formed branch of the Russian Association of University Women also claimed that her organization aimed to help solve Russia's economic problems, and to engage in charity for women in need of assistance.[67] Only one of Cheboksary's five women's groups – an ethnic Chuvash women's cultural organization – expressed no direct concern with the effects of the economic transformation.

Moscow groups' formation on the basis of economic concerns

A number of Moscow-based women's organizations, too, formed in response to the economic downturn in the early 1990s. One organization, Conversion and Women, formed in the aftermath of a seminar held to discuss women's problems in the defense industry during the transition to a market economy. The seminar organizer and founder of the group explained the motives behind the organization's formation:

When state orders started being reduced, the [defense industry] enterprises started losing money, and had to either fire their employees or retain them on a very low salary: that was summer 1992. In January 1992, the price liberalization had begun. In summer 1992, our pay was frozen; we got just enough to make ends meet. Literally, I had enough money for bread, milk, and *kefir* [a yogurt-like beverage]. And that's it. So, hard times led to the seminar and the organization being founded. We wanted a program of conversion with a social welfare program, with special attention to *women* and conversion. Because we felt it: the first strike in conversion was against women. Women were fired first; women's salaries were fixed, didn't go up; the men got requalification training and reeducation first – and the surveys we conducted proved this.[68]

The Union of Russia's Women (URW), heir to the Soviet Women's Committee (SWC), also formed due to the increasing economic dislocation accompanying perestroika. One woman who had remained as a staff member for the URW after the SWC disbanded explained the way that the SWC adjusted its vision and purpose when economic restructuring began:

We knew, with the advent of perestroika, and the openness about all of women's problems, that it would lead to unemployment, especially for women, by the end of the 1980s, when they were talking about turning enterprises into joint stock companies, private property, destatization, and so on. We saw that it would bring major misfortunes to women. At that time, the SWC had already begun to reorient its focus from the international arena to domestic affairs. We developed programs to address the problems of women within the country. But

[66] Charter for the Chuvashiian Republic Club, "Women's Initiative," Cheboksary, 1995, author's archive.
[67] Ol'ga Bubina, interview, May 31, 1995.
[68] Eleonora Ivanova, interview, February 6, 1995.

then the republics spun off, and in Russia we saw that there was no major organization for women that could cope with women's issues and problems. So, in 1990, it was decided to unite the extant women's councils, and create a single system or social program, to work with women in Russia. And thus in 1990, the URW was formed, as a component part of the SWC; . . . until that time, Russia hadn't had its own women's organization [the SWC having had republic-level subdivisions in all the Soviet republics except Russia]. The URW formed in order to work within Russia. And when the Soviet Union's structures collapsed, and when the republic women's organizations went their separate ways, the only thing left was the URW.[69]

A wide variety of women's organizations began their efforts in response to the threat of female unemployment in particular. One of the main responses has been the initiation of employment-training or retraining programs for women. For example, the URW and its regional subdivisions provide retraining and counseling programs for women at risk of unemployment (and for those already unemployed).[70] Unemployment was also the motivation behind the formation of the Association of Women [Film and Theater] Directors, according to its leader, Elena Demeshina:

Unemployment was the main reason why we decided to join together . . . For people in the arts, it's very difficult [as state funding for the arts has withered]. Earlier there was a system. Maybe it was oppressive. But people knew they could achieve something. There used to be trade unions. Granted, they were perverse [izvrashennyi] Soviet institutions, but they did defend people's rights, and it was impossible to just kick a person out into the street if you didn't like them. Now that system no longer exists. And its disappearance affected women a great deal. In any area of production, nobody needs a woman with a child.[71]

Unemployment also transformed the goals of one Moscow-based women's support association called Tvorchestvo, described in the introduction to this volume. Formerly an organization for women in the creative professions (writers, composers, and so on), as the economic transition "progressed," its goals turned more to providing courses and consultations for women on handicrafts and sewing (including the repair of old clothes). Said the organization's director, "Forty percent of the women who come to the courses are unemployed, or fear losing their jobs, especially at the scientific-research institutes."[72]

Increasing unemployment also brought women together into activism, as they recognized the mass nature of the phenomenon, and the fact that it seemed to be shared primarily by women. The leader of the Russian Confederation of Businesswomen (based in Ekaterinburg) attributed

[69] Interview, February 2, 1995.
[70] Interview, February 2, 1995.
[71] Elena Demeshina, interview, March 26, 1995.
[72] Tat'iana Riabikina, interview, April 26, 1995.

the increased interest in her organization to the fact that "a lot of women became aware that they could lose their jobs [something highly unlikely until the early 1990s], and joined the Confederation [for psychological support]. It's harder to fire a confident woman."[73] Another woman from Ekaterinburg also noted that unemployment had been a motivating force, drawing women together in an organization supporting women's entrepreneurship (the Urals Association of Women): "It's one of the things that moved us to unite; we had to solve the problem together."[74] No longer able to count on the state for support, unemployment made women realize they had to "count on themselves."[75]

While many women's organizations formed as a direct result of the dramatic increase in women's unemployment, many groups have felt the effects of women's unemployment, even if they did not originally form in order to address that issue. The republic- and city-level women's councils in Cheboksary, for example, both responded to increasing levels of women's unemployment by more actively raising the issue with the local administration, pushing for the establishment of retraining courses for women, and for tax breaks to enterprises creating new workplaces for women.[76] The domestic violence hotline at the Moscow Crisis Center for Women has noted an increase in calls from women who have lost their jobs, are sitting at home, and simply "want someone to talk with."[77]

Associations of women entrepreneurs have also been affected in a variety of ways by rising unemployment. Nina Iakovchuk, of Dzhenklub (a Moscow-based advocacy organization also supporting women's entrepreneurship), stated that women's unemployment was a frequent theme of the organization's lobbying attempts and seminars, and pointed to the pitiable fact of high unemployment rates among women with graduate degrees and high skill levels.[78] Likewise affected by women's rising unemployment, the businesswomen's club in Ivanovo organizes a yearly textile fair, providing half of the space on a charitable basis to unemployed women who can then occupy booths and sell their handmade wares.[79] And Tatiana Maliutina of the national Association of Women Entrepreneurs stated that her organization's goal was to reduce unemployment "through enterprises, through education, pre-

---

[73] Svetlana Kornilova, interview, June 8, 1995.
[74] Larisa Volkova, interview, July 9, 1995.
[75] Interview, October 15, 1994.
[76] Nina Petrova, Iraida Stekol'shikova, interviews, May 29, 1995.
[77] Interview, October 4, 1994.
[78] Nina Iakovchuk, interview, May 5, 1995.
[79] Margarita Razina, interview, April 6, 1995.

paring women, giving them psychological support. We want to fight unemployment by offering work."[80]

Alongside increasing unemployment, Russia's economic transition has provided both women and men with the opportunity to open small businesses and enter the private sector. Indeed, for women over age thirty-five, whose prospects of being hired at either a state-run or private firm are now considered quite low, attempting to open a business may seem an attractive option. Yet few women take this route; women have had notorious difficulty acquiring start-up capital, credit, and loans. Furthermore, not having held high governmental positions under Soviet rule, only a small number of women were in a position to take advantage of the opportunity to transfer state property into private hands once the transition began (a process that has become known as "nomenklatura privatization"). Also, by the time women began entering the sphere of entrepreneurship, in late 1991 and early 1992, most of the country's resources had already been parceled out, and credit had become "impossible."[81] Further discouraging women from entrepreneurial activity is the potential danger of attracting racketeers, and the massive time commitment which many women could not balance with their domestic obligations.[82] Meanwhile, fictitious (or false-front) businesses are occasionally registered under women's names, although the owners are, in fact, men.

Women's response to the economic crisis, and to their own declining economic status, has been expressed in a variety of organizational forms. In this way, the economic transition created a major opportunity for women to collaborate, and both to recognize and to try to solve some of their shared problems. Many of these "pragmatic" women's organizations were formed by women who self-identified as feminists; others were not, although their leaders later came in contact with feminist-identified women and their organizations at conferences and other movement events. The economic transition, then, promoted women's movement organizing, and helped lay the groundwork for further consciousness-raising. But the economic transition toward a market

---

[80] Tat'iana Maliutina, interview, April 25, 1995.

[81] "Women's Entrepreneurship in Russia," from *Zhenshchiny v mirotvorchestve i sozidanii*, Association of Women Entrepreneurs, p. 2, author's archive.

[82] For more detailed discussions of women's entrepreneurship in Russia, see Sue Bridger, Rebecca Kay, and Kathryn Pinnick, eds., *No More Heroines?: Russia, Women and the Market* (London: Routledge, 1996), esp. ch. 6. On gender and entrepreneurial culture in 1990s Russia, see Marta Bruno, "Women and the Culture of Entrepreneurship," in Mary Buckley, ed., *Post-Soviet Women: From the Baltic to Central Asia* (Cambridge: Cambridge University Press, 1997), pp. 56–74.

economy has created obstacles to women's movement growth in Russia, as well as opportunities.

Resource mobilization and the economic obstacles to movement growth

Although Russia's economic crisis provoked a good deal of women's organizing, the economic conditions under which that organizing has occurred have been very constraining, creating a difficult situation for women's groups' self-perpetuation, mobilization, and national-campaign building.

Of all the organizational problems mentioned by activists, none was more widespread than deficits of financial and material resources. Many of the group leaders interviewed complained of a lack of stable financing. In fact, all of the activists who responded affirmatively to a question about whether their organization had any problems mentioned financial and material woes, ranging from a lack of monetary means to carry out their programs to a lack of office space, technology, and staff. Only rarely did women's organizations actually have office space (although most of the women's councils did, as did some of the foreign-funded groups, the Committee of Soldiers' Mothers, and several of the businesswomen's groups and employment-training programs); many organizations worked out of a leader's apartment, and met by arrangement for events at libraries, academic institutes, or other public spaces, including foreign foundation offices. Acquiring office space in Moscow was particularly difficult because of the inability of NGOs to cope with the astronomical rental costs. Several Moscow groups were housed at the expense of another organization, whether an institute or a larger NGO. The press secretary of the Committee of Soldiers' Mothers (CSM), for example, put it this way:

Everything comes down to money. As long as we have this space in the Center for Human Rights, we exist. If something happens, then where would we go? How would we operate? Of course, we started out in people's kitchens, in their homes, in the street, in the metro. But now the volume is such that it couldn't be done in a kitchen. So the first issue is housing. The second is finances.[83]

The Moscow-based Innovation Fund of Women's Employment and Assistance to Entrepreneurship experienced the nightmare envisioned by the CSM's press secretary: the organization that had housed them first reduced their space, and then forced them out; they now operate out of the leader's apartment. In some ways, a meeting place is the first

---

[83] Valentina Mel'nikova, interview, May 12, 1995.

necessity to movement-building or coalition-formation and, more often than not, it is lacking. The absence of places to meet makes it difficult to mobilize. Said one activist:

Another obstacle is that a network should exist not only on email, but to gather somewhere, to meet, but that costs a lot. We're still at the very beginning. So there are some primitive things that need to be done. There's no *place* for people to meet.[84]

Few groups had their own telephone numbers; usually the contact phone was that of the organization's leader. And, in 1995, the cost of telephone calls (and faxes) was rapidly becoming prohibitive. Bringing together members of an organization having branches in multiple cities was next to impossible without large chunks of foreign funding, since airline and even rail tickets became very expensive with the decline in state subsidies, not to mention the costs of hotels, food, and meeting halls. Similarly, holding an interregional seminar had become extremely difficult. Galina Sillaste described the problem of networking as "colossal: everyone is supposed to be able to travel on their own personal funds, and no one can pay."[85]

The women's organizations as a rule had no paid staff, with exceptions including a few groups whose leadership was financed by foreign grants. Typically, there were no funds available to purchase technology (such as faxes, photocopy machines, or computers), and none devoted to publishing (because of the skyrocketing costs of paper and printing), though numerous organizations did mention their desire to have such technology available for publishing purposes. Marina Pavlova, for instance, advertised her organization's employment-training program by typing all her advertisements on a typewriter.[86]

Most of the organizations' leaders worked at other (paid) full-time jobs (in some cases, multiple jobs), and funded any group activities out of their own pockets, although the activists' personal resources were limited. Those activists with access to office equipment were in a privileged position vis à vis other activists when competing for foreign grants (a process that often requires receiving a faxed application form from Moscow or abroad, and so on).

Exacerbating the lack of material and technical resources is Russia's dilapidated communications infrastructure. The telephone lines are unreliable; faxes tend to arrive garbled, and intercity phone connections can be at times almost impossible to achieve. As the head of the Association of Women Entrepreneurs put it:

[84] Tat'iana Klimenkova, February 3, 1995.
[85] Galina Sillaste, interview, March 28, 1995.
[86] Marina Pavlova, interview, April 24, 1995.

Even if you have a fax, you can't send things . . . [and we] have these miracles with the postal service: when we sent the invitations to the conference in July, in November we found out that the postal service didn't ever send them! We were half in shock.[87]

One activist working on issues of women and violence similarly cited material obstacles to communication as the main obstacle to networking in Russia: "It's hard even to phone other cities. There aren't any faxes. Even expenditures on mail and photocopying are high. We lack technical equipment. How can you create a network under these conditions, when you can't even reliably send letters?"[88]

The networking opportunities for women's groups are therefore severely limited. With insufficient funding for meetings, telephone calls, and other common forms of intergroup communication, the potential for a national movement (or even a strong national organization) is extremely small. Even regular information exchange between cities comes up against financial constraints. With no affordable or accessible means to link women's organizations, networking is reduced to the rare occasions upon which women attend national conferences or interregional seminars. Within cities, of course, these problems are much reduced.

Despite these material problems, little effort is made by women's movement groups to increase their membership through outreach, as a means by which to expand their funding base through potential dues collection. The main reason for this is that most of these organizations do not in fact collect dues or other membership fees. Although many groups in Moscow exist on the basis of sponsorship by foreign organizations and foundation grants, those that do not often reject the idea of membership dues as a source of organizational financing, something which might be regarded as peculiar by leaders of Western social movement organizations. In fact, of the fifty women's organizations interviewed for this study, only one claimed to receive "substantive" dues from its members: the Ivanovo-based Businesswomen's Club.[89] Three others mentioned collecting minimal or symbolic dues; one claimed that dues were collected irregularly (putting out the word to members in advance of organization events that required financing). One woman, the head of an umbrella organization of women's small businesses, stated that, although dues were requested (from the better-off organizational members), she often accepted dues as "intellectual product" – or in kind – where a member agreed to conduct a useful seminar for the

---

[87] Tat'iana Maliutina, interview, April 25, 1995.
[88] Interview, December 1, 1994.
[89] Margarita Razina, interview, April 6, 1995.

organization.[90] Some employment-training programs charged minimal fees for their courses; the members of one feminist consciousness-raising group, described in the introduction to this volume, paid a small fee each week to compensate various instructors who taught classes for the group.[91]

Why was dues collection such a rarity for these organizations? Interviews provided several answers. Three respondents stated that their organizations (the Women's Alliance, Tvorchestvo, and SANTA) had given up on dues collection because their members had too little money. By contrast, two respondents stated they were planning soon to institute a dues or formal membership system (Moscow's Dzhenklub and the hardline communist Congress of Soviet Women). But the majority of respondents from women's groups simply stated that their organization had never collected dues and did not plan to do so. These ranged from politically active advocacy organizations (the Women's League, the Inform Center of the Independent Women's Forum) to self-help groups (Ivanovo's Committee of Single-Parent Families) and professional women's support groups (the Association of Women [Film and Theater] Directors). Asked if dues were collected, the head of the latter organization answered: "No, we don't collect dues because our colleagues live so poorly. We could collect, say, 1,000 rubles apiece, but what's the point?"[92] Her organization was searching for sponsors for an upcoming film festival, supported in past years by the Russian Ministry of Culture. Other organizations took the sponsorship route as well.

Although some groups operated on the basis of sponsorship and donations, a number of activists expressed reluctance to seek sponsors external to the group. Some believed that sponsors would come only with strings attached, or that people would try to use or claim the organization for their own purposes. Said the leader of the Women's Alliance:

We had this sort of problem: men started coming to us to offer us money. And then we understood that these sponsors wanted something in return. So we refused [because they wanted] to use our organization for their own goals.[93]

This is apparently not only an issue for women's groups, but for Russian NGOs in general. According to a 1994 article in *Ogonek*, a popular magazine, the main reason why NGOs are reluctant to accept or seek

---

[90] Interview, November 16, 1994.
[91] Mariia Arbatova, interview, April 16, 1995.
[92] Elena Demeshina, interview, March 26, 1995. At that time, 1000 rubles was worth about twenty cents.
[93] Tat'iana Ivanova, interview, May 16, 1995.

sponsorship (or even charitable donations) lies in the history of Soviet "charity" organizations:

The practices of the so-called charitable organizations of the late Soviet period – like the Children's Fund or the Peace Fund – gave rise to an understandable mistrust. Today, many people assume that charity here is just a method of money laundering, or an attempt to find a cover [krysha] for some kind of illegal business or the solution of personal or individual problems.[94]

The long-standing lack of a law governing charitable donations has contributed to this distrust. Another related issue is the objects of corporate sponsorship. In Russia, as of 1994, the most likely objects of charity (from banks) were: children, religious organizations, medical facilities, cultural enterprises, disabled people, educational institutes, the poor, veterans, pensioners, sports facilities, and private individuals.[95] Women's issues are not widely recognized in Russia as an object for private, charitable donations.

The economic downturn in Russia has also adversely affected women's organizations' ability to survive and make themselves known. Recent years have witnessed the closure of several Russian women's organizations (such as the Center for Women's Initiatives) and newspapers (e.g., Delovaia zhenshchina and Novaia zhenshchina). Only one organization interviewed put out a newsletter for its members (the bimonthly Vestnik, starting in April 1995, for the groups belonging to the Independent Women's Forum network). There are several more substantial women's journals stemming from independent women's groups, although most of these are published on a highly irregular basis (once or twice per year). Additionally, the women's political bloc (Women of Russia) published several bulletins while in parliament, and a four-page newsletter (within the Moscow newspaper Moskvichka). A few organizations had put out a one-time informational bulletin or leaflet about the work of their groups. Most respondents, when asked about newsletters, mentioned that they had wanted to produce a newsletter, but that the costs were prohibitive. Probably typical of most women's organizations having branches in more than one city, Women for Social Democracy lacks a newsletter; thus its affiliates communicate "by writing letters."[96] The paucity of women's movement group publications greatly complicates communication and networking at the national level. Given these constraints, to some extent, the small-circulation women's press has operated as an informational link between widely dispersed women's organizations and activists, informing them about events, new laws,

---

94 Lena Yang, "'I togda pridut nastoiashchie novye russkie,'" Ogonek, no. 50–51, 1994, p. 6.
95 Ibid.   96 Interview, November 22, 1994.

conferences, and issues, and even publishing the contact information for groups in different cities.

Resource shortages and a poorly developed economic infrastructure that is not conducive to grassroots organizing or fundraising have led some women's groups to seek external Western funding. Although when the political arena began to expand under glasnost a space was created for women's organizing, the economic sphere has not similarly grown to embrace women's organizations. Nor have resources from the state in support of women's organizations been forthcoming. In various ways, then, the economic opportunity structure for the Russian women's movement's development is quite constrained and, to some extent, determined by forces external to Russia.

Economic ramifications for women's movement growth

What are the overall ramifications of Russia's economic crisis for the women's movement's growth and expansion, according to activists? When asked whether or not the women's movement would grow, several respondents linked their answers to economic conditions. A few were pessimistic, believing the conditions of daily life too oppressive to expect any room for increased organizing. Said one activist with Women for Social Democracy, "We'd like it to grow. But life has become so hard that so much of women's energy is going toward just trying to stay afloat . . . for a lot of women, it's just survival that matters."[97] The leader of the Women's Alliance, also a professor of women's studies in Moscow, answered the question by pointing to the demobilization of young women, wrought by the change in economic conditions, and the push to return women to the domestic sphere:

I don't see much potential for that. Women are isolated economically. They've been chased into a corner. Women are closed up behind the four walls of their kitchen . . . I try to raise women's respect for themselves, at least. My female students ask, "What kind of future do I have?" I ask them what they want in the future. They say they want to find rich men to support them. These are political scientists! And they want to be kept! "And if I don't find a rich man, what am I supposed to do? I came here from Volgograd, where my mother worked as a doctor, but was fired recently. And I'm not going to find work there as a political scientist! So I need to find a rich man, a sponsor of sorts." It's prostitution, fully legal prostitution.[98]

Likewise, Elvira Novikova, a longtime activist with academic interests in

---

[97] Interview, November 22, 1994.
[98] Tat'iana Ivanova, interview, May 16, 1995.

women's organizing, had a negative opinion about women's movement prospects in Russia:

I wouldn't want to play Cassandra, the prophet. But I think that the situation is so bad, the gap between the powers that be and society is expanding so much, the understanding that nothing at all depends on you, although they call it democracy . . . These days no one tells you, "You're nobody, a cog in the wheel." But that's what you are, in fact . . . After all, what's the point of the women's movement? It's an important element of civil society. You asked me about the Center of Women's Initiatives [her former organization]. And three years have passed, and as many initiatives as there are, there are as many initiatives which shut down. People lose interest: they see that there are no results. Life is not getting better, people are just getting older. And if you look at the younger generation: they're running away from politics entirely. So my prognosis is that the generation of our granddaughters will be less educated than we are, because the proportion of women in the institutions of higher education is decreasing; they'll be less socially active than we are. The situation is truly very bad . . . Earlier, we counted on the party, on the trade union, on something. And now, there's nothing to rely on at all. There's no channel through which to transfer women's interests from below.[99]

In general, the conditions of daily life for women create enormous time constraints for those who want to engage in political activism. One activist with a single-mothers' group pointed to this issue:

I don't really believe these articles like the one about some woman gynecologist who opened her own business and who has three children. Someone else must be looking after the kids. And it takes time to get to work and back, and go to the stores. True, there are things to buy now, but the prices are so high that you still end up spending time to find the store with the best prices.[100]

Some activists believed that a certain amount of demobilization had taken place in the past, precisely because of increasingly strained economic conditions. In 1993, one feminist activist observed a sharp decline in women's activism, "purely because of the difficulties of life." This was changing, however. Interviewed in late 1994, she felt that women's organizing potential was

appearing anew . . . 1990–92 was the peak of activity. [That period was followed] by a complete withdrawal from the women's movement: it's the lack of money, people have their own affairs to deal with; work, not enough energy. Now [in late 1994] more women are getting into it. In our group, new forces are coming in and the old ones are returning.[101]

Most respondents, in fact, seemed to feel more inspiration than despair about the women's movement's chances for growth, based on the economic conditions in Russia. One woman thought that economic

[99] El'vira Novikova, interview, February 17, 1995.
[100] Interview, January 22, 1995.
[101] Interview, November 21, 1994.

deterioration would promote political organizing, as light industry and other branches predominantly employing women were repeatedly shunted aside by the state.[102] The self-help groups, too, would flourish, since the state did not appear to be "doing anything to help."[103] One leader of a support group for multi-child families claimed that the high levels of discrimination against women were enough to provoke organizing, as women see that "men are hired first, men's salaries are higher, and the management posts are mostly occupied by men."[104] Similarly, as women were fired, one academic suggested, it would provide an impetus to organization.[105] Women would become active, especially women with higher education, as they found themselves without positions and prestige. "Everything's been taken away from them," suggested one feminist activist, "they're getting angry already. Maybe four years ago, it wasn't that way; maybe they thought, 'Indeed, it'd be better to head back to the home.' But not any more."[106] In a less dramatic sense, women's unemployment has swollen the ranks of many women's organizations, even if for purely pragmatic reasons, as unemployed women flock to join business clubs and retraining groups.[107] And other activists have pointed out that the economic crisis has motivated increasing numbers of women to "speak out in favor of a more social orientation to state policy: the need to put people before reforms."[108]

Conclusion

The economic arena, like the political arena, is subject to changes that affect the potential for and the shape of social movement organizing. As the economy in Russia changes, it provides varying levels of opportunity for social movements' emergence and development.

At the macroeconomic level, Russia's economic crisis conditions in the 1990s have presented an interesting set of possibilities for women's organizing. On the one hand, some activists see the worsening economic situation as fuel for a change in consciousness, increased perception of injustice and collective identity, and therefore heightened and expanding organizing. Indeed, the economic transition period has served to inspire the formation of many women's groups. On the other hand, however, the depressive and demobilizing effects of the economic crisis have led

---

[102] Margarita Razina, interview, April 6, 1995.
[103] Interview, December 1, 1994.
[104] Nina Temnikova, interview, April 4, 1995.
[105] Interview, September 19, 1994.
[106] Tat'iana Klimenkova, interview, February 3, 1995.
[107] Martina Vandenberg, interview, April 20, 1995.
[108] Interview, October 28, 1994.

to a situation where many activists (as well as nonactivists) work multiple jobs and are left with limited leisure time in which to organize, write, hold meetings, and so on, especially given the prevailing household division of labor. At the macrosocietal level, then, the economic opportunity structure for the Russian women's movement is at best ambiguous.

Meanwhile, economic constraints at the organizational level are clearly present and severe in the Russian women's movement case. Given the limited resources currently available to women's groups, we can expect that they will continue to confront serious financial obstacles to intercity networking and the expansion of their program work. Resource mobilization, in the concrete financial sense, presents a very real obstacle to movement development.

The third element of the economic opportunity structure is more subtle: economic infrastructure and its historical roots. While the logic behind resource mobilization might suggest that a "rational" organization would, if poor, seek to develop its constituency and thereby expand its funding and/or membership base, Russian women's movement organizations have not made outreach and domestic fundraising a priority. Russia's history of state monopoly over the public sphere has left today's movement organizations lacking an outreach and fundraising tradition, on the one hand, and lacking an economic infrastructure for NGOs on the other. Under the Soviet regime, mass public organizations like the Soviet Women's Committee and local women's councils were state-funded. Even the source (and, for a time, major supporter) of the feminist-identified wing of the Russian women's movement, the Moscow Center for Gender Studies (MCGS), had its origin in an institute of the state-funded Academy of Sciences. The economic transition toward a market economy left MCGS – and, to some extent, the academic feminist wing of the movement – a victim of the collapse of state funding for the sciences, particularly the humanities and social sciences; it is now largely supported by foreign foundation grants.

Likewise, the lack of an economic infrastructure for NGOs (including direct mail, checkbooks, a reliable postal service, and so on) limits the utility of a membership-expansion strategy, and thereby alters the priorities of Russian women's organizations. Large membership advocacy organizations are still impractical in Russia. Limited resources and infrastructural gaps make direct mail contributions impossible, and put the publication of newsletters out of financial reach. These factors help to keep Russia's women's organizations small in size. Without dues and newsletters, a large advocacy organization could not operate, but a small one can. Under these conditions, the issue of economic sponsorship becomes significant. Many groups rely on grants and donations by foreign foundations and sister organizations. The ramifications of foreign funding for a social movement are addressed below in chapter 7.

In part, the case of the Russian women's movement illustrates how the economic infrastructure of the past can affect present-day economic opportunities. The next chapter focuses in more detail on the past, taking a closer look at how Russia's political history affects the organizational dynamics of the women's movement, and at the obstacles to cohesion and mass mobilization that the movement faces.

6 Remembrance of things past: the impact of political history on women's movement organizing

The functioning of social movements in Russia is not a norm of cultural and political life.[1]

Decades of Soviet rule have shaped the opportunities available to the Russian women's movement in important ways. In the economic realm, because all social organizations under the Soviet regime had been controlled and supported by the state, women's groups emerging in recent years have lacked an economic infrastructure that could support grassroots organizing and fundraising. The general absence of civil society under Soviet rule has similarly constrained the contemporary women's movement's ability to network and expand along associational lines. As one scholar writing about movement organizing in Eastern Europe succinctly observed, "block recruitment of viable communities and associations does not operate when there are no blocks to recruit."[2] The Soviet socio-cultural legacy has also created obstacles to women's movement mobilization; these are embodied in a well-entrenched set of social attitudes about women's roles and rights, shaped by the Bolsheviks' antifeminist ideology. In the political sphere, the history of Soviet rule preceding the transition period has had a significant impact on the dynamics between women's movement groups, and on their organizational structures and tactics. Political history, the construct I use to describe the process through which this impact occurs, forms the subject of this chapter.

Political history can be divided into three elements: the history and legacy of political institutions in a given country; the cycles of protest that have arisen in that country; and the "defining political events" of

---

[1] Marina Regentova and Natal'ia Abubikirova, no title, unpublished typescript, 1995, p. 26.
[2] See Anthony Oberschall, "Opportunities and Framing in the Eastern European Revolts of 1989," in Doug McAdam, John D. McCarthy, and Mayer M. Zald, eds., *Comparative Perspectives on Social Movements* (Cambridge: Cambridge University Press, 1996), p. 103.

that country's history. The first element, political-institutional history, involves analyzing previous political institutions and the legacies that may remain in their wake at the time of a social movement's emergence. The Soviet state's long-term monopolization of the public sphere, for instance, is reflected in post-Soviet social movements' interorganizational dynamics. Women's groups exhibit mistrust of the state, and of organizations and individuals they believe are identified with it. Also, some women's organizations are split along newcomer vs. oldtimer lines. This line of division is particularly salient because of the danger inherent in operating under the totalitarian regime, a condition which changed rapidly under Gorbachev. Monopolization of the public sphere under Soviet rule also contributed to social atomization, and fostered a "limited good" or zero-sum mentality.[3] These legacies of Soviet rule have had a cumulative and dampening effect on the women's movement's ability to cohere and form coalitions. The Soviet legacy has also had an impact on post-Soviet movement groups' organizational structures, inculcating an avoidance of hierarchy.

The second aspect of political history concerns the location of a given social movement in relation to a broader cycle of protest occurring in society. Location in the cycle of protest has ramifications for a social movement's mobilization potential, and for the tactics of protest and challenge in which it may engage. The Russian women's movement arose and began to grow in 1991, just as a cycle of social protest was ending in Russia and the former Soviet Union. Its location at the end of the protest cycle may have made the use of mass mobilization techniques unlikely.

The third aspect of political history refers to the "defining events" of a country's history, and to the moment when a social movement emerges in relation to those events. In other words, it is not only the location of a social movement within a protest cycle, but also its location in the flow of history that may have an impact on its form. The Russian women's movement's first years occurred against the background of extreme political instability and violence, from the August 1991 coup that effectively led to the overthrow of Soviet rule to the October 1993 shelling of the Russian legislature and the eruption of wars in several post-Soviet states. These events have colored the women's movement's choice of tactics, and have pushed women activists to engage in forms of collective action that could not be portrayed as provoking political instability.

---

[3] See Ken Jowitt, "Political Culture in Leninist Regimes," in his *New World Disorder: The Leninist Extinction* (Berkeley: University of California Press, 1992), pp. 77–78.

Political history's effects on the relationships between organizations, on organizational structure, and on collective action repertoire combine to produce a social movement that seeks social and political change while placing almost no priority on mass mobilization. This fact makes the women's movement in Russia unusual among social movements, and gives us important insights into the ways that post-Soviet Russian society is organizing itself.

Social movement theory and political history

Political scientists Gabriel Almond and Sidney Verba, in a study of variations in political culture, use the term "political history" – which includes political institutions and regime type, as well as defining historical events – to explain the differences between five countries' political cultures. They define political culture as "attitudes toward the political system and its various parts, and attitudes toward the role of the self in the system."[4] Political history, and the political culture that it shapes, varies from country to country and clearly has implications for social movements. Almond and Verba contrast the "civic" culture of the United States to Italy's "alienated" political culture, one perhaps similar in ways to that in contemporary Russia. They attribute the difference to political history:

> The picture of Italian political culture that has emerged from our data is one of relatively unrelieved political alienation and of social isolation and distrust . . . If we consider Italian political history, these tendencies are not surprising. Before unification, Italy had experienced centuries of fragmentation and external tyranny in which allegiant subject and citizen orientations could not develop. In the brief century of their national history, Italians have learned to associate nationalism with humiliation, and constitutionalism and democracy with ineffectiveness.[5]

Almond and Verba compare this to the participant political culture of the United States, which "emerged in the West as a result of a gradual political development – relatively crisis free, untroubled, and unforced."[6] Such differences in political history are essential to the comparative study of social movements. After all, social movements are shaped not only by the political and economic systems in which they operate, but also by the political histories operating in the background.

---

[4] Gabriel Almond and Sidney Verba, *The Civic Culture* (Beverly Hills: Sage Publications, 1989), p. 12.
[5] Ibid., p. 308.   [6] Ibid., p. 368.

The legacy of totalitarianism and its impact on coalition-building

The goals of many contemporary Russian women's groups are similar. A majority of activists questioned were concerned about women's status, in connection with – and across – a variety of issues: women's unemployment and economic discrimination against women; the collapse of the social welfare system; violence against women; and the need to preserve women's intellectual potential and assure women a role in state decisionmaking. But despite some fundamental agreement that women in Russia find themselves in an unequal status position in relation to men, there is little visible cooperation across the Russian women's movement networks in Moscow that seek to affect national policy. In fact, many activists complained of a pervasive lack of solidarity among women's organizations. Much of the reason is rooted in the political history that permeates these groups, dividing people along a variety of lines.

Several activists in Moscow voiced frustration with the Russian women's movement's apparent inability to unite across its main indigenous networks – the Women's League, the Union of Russia's Women (URW), and the Independent Women's Forum (IWF). Tatiana Zeleranskaia, of Russia's women-operated Radio Nadezhda, spoke up in favor of Russian women uniting on common ground:

In general, we support this idea: let there be many women's movements. We're in favor of that. But we're opposed to them fighting among themselves, and getting involved in male-type politicking. Women ought [to unite], despite the variety of the movements, and there are lots and lots of women's organizations now: it's not just the Union of Russia's Women, there's Women with a University Education, Women Entrepreneurs, women in the creative professions, and so on . . . they should all find enough reason to unite on some common platform . . . That's what should be happening. But they haven't united.[7]

Eleonora Ivanova, of Conversion and Women, a group that belongs to both the IWF and the Women's League, also spoke of the need for the networks to unite in order to act more effectively:

We're trying to unite them all: a coalition is better for accomplishing goals. Our women's movement isn't ripe, or maybe there are just different interests in different regions, so there's no actual need for unification, but there are various issues we could unite on, to achieve certain goals. And after we achieve them, please, go right ahead and split back up into your individual organizations. And

---

[7] Tat'iana Zeleranskaia, interview, July 10, 1995.

then new coalitions can be formed around different issues. It strikes me that that's the only way to get something positive accomplished.[8]

The desire to unite exists, but seems difficult to achieve in practice.

There are many reasons that social movement groups in any country decline to cooperate with one another. Some may disagree over substantive ideological issues, over priorities, or over tactics. Yet it is difficult to argue that the women's movement networks, in the Moscow case, differ in these areas. All of the main networks within the politically active national women's movement are integrated to some degree into politics; all have active members who have run for office (thus, it is not a question of dividing over "autonomy" vs. working within the state system); all are essentially women-only (thus it is not a question of whether or not to organize separately from men); all contain members who identify themselves as "feminists." Nor do they explicitly disagree over strategies for promoting social change that would benefit women. What, then, keeps these women's networks from collaborating more closely?

Suspicion and the state

One salient obstacle to uniting the Moscow groups with each other stems from their existence in a post-totalitarian state, and the related struggles over group and personal identity that arise in connection with their political and personal histories. Many women's groups and individual activists accuse each other of having worked with communists in the past, of being former communists, being affiliated with the "nomenklatura," with the Soviet regime, or with the present-day Russian government – in essence, of being somehow tainted by association with the state or the bureaucracy in any of its past or present forms. Political scientist Ken Jowitt has identified a distrust of the state – and as a byproduct, in this case, also a distrust of those formerly identified with the state – as an element of Leninist political culture, fostered by the totalitarian state's monopolization of the public sphere, and the coercion that the state used to maintain its monopoly.[9] Political culture is slow to change;[10] the reluctance to cooperate with formerly state-affiliated activists or organizations is entrenched and inertial.

While a certain amount of mutual backstabbing, accusations, and rumor-mongering is typical of any social movement in any country, the

---

[8] Eleonora Ivanova, interview, February 6, 1995.
[9] Jowitt, "Political Culture in Leninist Regimes," p. 69.
[10] Harry Eckstein, "A Culturalist Theory of Political Change," *American Political Science Review*, vol. 82, no. 3 (September 1988), pp. 789–804.

suspicions and accusations prevalent in the Russian case are tinged with a particularly Soviet experience. One activist with the Association of Women Journalists explained that networking within the women's movement was complicated by "the reaction to the Soviet period: everyone is suspicious of everyone else; cooperation is low. And it's not only a problem for the women's movement."[11] Trust and suspicion seem to turn on the following issues: perceived identity with respect to the Soviet past, perceived affiliation with the Soviet or Russian state bureaucracy, and activists' length of time in the women's movement, a factor made relevant by Russia's political history.

Although some activists made accusations about others' loyalties vis à vis the Soviet and Russian state, more common were such statements about other organizations or networks within the women's movement. The terms used by activists to describe other women's groups were often loaded, centering around issues of identity in relation to the Soviet past and the state. For instance, in categorizing the politically active, organized sector of the women's movement, activist Laima Geidar divided it into two parts, "the official and the unofficial":

The official organizations are the *zhensovety*, the Union of Russia's Women . . . The unofficial organizations are those formed in the wake of the First and Second Independent Women's Forums. These include various Gender [research] Centers, . . . the Inform Center project, the Feminist Orientation Center, and others, in other cities.[12]

Elena Demeshina, with the Association of Women [Film and Theater] Directors, made a similar distinction:

The women's movement is split into those who were from the Soviet period, the official ones, that our women deputies belonged to: the "Women of Russia" are the ones who were high up in the Komsomol, or the Soviet Women's Committee, which was a totally official organization, or the Pioneers: a lot of women worked there.[13]

In fact, various respondents made such claims about the identities of many of the best-known organizations in the Russian women's movement, including the Union of Russia's Women, the Women's League, and the Moscow Center for Gender Studies (historically affiliated with the IWF), regardless of their members' actual histories:

Q. What do you think of the Women's League?
A. They're the same old party functionaries. What was there has remained: they've repainted themselves [*perekrasivshiesia*].[14]

---

[11] Interview, October 15, 1994.
[12] Laima Geidar, interview, July 17, 1995.
[13] Elena Demeshina, interview, March 26, 1995.
[14] Interview, name withheld.

Q. What kind of relations does the Union of Russia's Women have in general with the Gender Center [MCGS]?

A. The Gender Center – it's part of the state structures. It's not a social organization. It's a department of the Ministry of Labor, being part of the Institute for Socio-economic Population Studies. We have normal relations with all the ministries.[15]

Q. What relations does your organization [Association of Women (Film and Theater) Directors] have with the Union of Russia's Women?

A. The Union of Russia's Women . . . well, our contacts with them haven't worked out, to this point, because they have a purely nomenklatura approach – although we're prepared to work with them.[16]

The point is not that any or all of these portraits or attributions are valid, but rather that the activists' perceptions betray a clear division between old, "official," untrustworthy organizations, on the one hand, and new, "unofficial" ones on the other. Under post-Soviet conditions, the notion of "independence" from the state may have little descriptive value, but still carries emotional content, and is very much contested by activists.

The Union of Russia's Women (URW) bears the brunt of the accusations made about state bureaucratic affiliation. As the Soviet Women's Committee's legal inheritor, the URW benefits materially, but the inheritance comes with a perceived state affiliation, as well as a top-down organizational structure. Although a staff member interviewed at the URW stated that it was truly a different organization from the SWC, having different goals,[17] the perception that it was closely tied to the Soviet state – and is closely tied to the Russian state – remains. The URW is arguably the most powerful women's organization in Russia, with the best office space (an entire building in central Moscow, inherited from the SWC), and the most widespread network of women's groups across the country (the former zhensovety), although many of these are inactive and had served mainly as window dressing. Despite these facts, or perhaps because of them, the URW has not, to date, engaged in much cooperation with other women's organization-networks in Moscow. The URW did not, for instance, sign onto an open letter to the Duma composed by members of a new coalition of Independent Women's Associations in early 1996, although they were informed about it.[18]

The perception of the URW as a state-related organization detracts

---

[15] Interview, February 2, 1995. The interviewee did not seem to be aware that as of April 1994 the MCGS had been officially registered as a nonprofit, nongovernmental organization.

[16] Elena Demeshina, interview, March, 26, 1995.

[17] Interview, February 2, 1995.

[18] Personal communication, Elena Kochkina, June 2, 1996.

from its opportunities for collaboration with other women's groups. This is due in part to the URW's historical ties to the SWC. Activist Tatiana Ivanova, who formerly worked for the SWC, readily acknowledged that the SWC had not been a major defender of women's rights, or even a place available to women:

the Soviet Women's Committee never defended women's rights anyway. It just represented the [Communist] Party viewpoint abroad. They never let anyone into the building even. There was a guard who stood at the door, didn't let in any of the needy, or any refugees. Their style and their staff are all the same as it was – [Communist] Party-affiliated [pri-partiinye].[19]

The perception of the URW as the SWC's inheritor persists. Anna Potemkina, a Moscow activist, stated that "the URW is more or less [fakticheski] a state structure."[20] Its chairwoman, Alevtina Fedulova, is widely viewed as a "lady of the nomenklatura [nomenklaturnaia dama],"[21] because of her high-level ties to a number of Soviet-era state-run organizations. Few feel that the URW has left its past behind, and one interviewee (who had been associated with the SWC and worked inside the URW's administration) felt that, by putting Fedulova in charge of the URW in 1992, the organization had simply "changed the sign outside the door [vyveska]."[22] Elvira Novikova, who also had been a member of the SWC said of the URW: "I don't really know what they're doing, I admit it. I think there's still a bureaucratic spirit there, it's remained. The old people there are still there; old in age, and in their thinking . . . they're trying to accomplish something there, but it's hard for me to say."[23] Other activists were equally mystified by the URW: "I don't know what the URW is up to nowadays, besides occupying that nice building. We don't hear about their activities anywhere."[24]

Many women activists feel angry that because of its history as the party-affiliated SWC, the URW seems to maintain special ties to the state, and a monopoly on representing "Russian women." One woman, from the "Independent Women's Initiative" of Voronezh stated at a women's movement seminar: "The Union of Russia's Women stands like a deaf wall between [our independent organizations] and the government. We have the right to demand its end."[25]

Other activists, however, sometimes in rather unexpected quarters,

---

[19] Tat'iana Ivanova, interview, May 16, 1995.
[20] Anna Potemkina, interview, March 17, 1995.
[21] Interview, December 6, 1994.
[22] Interview, June 25, 1995.
[23] El'vira Novikova, interview, February 17, 1995.
[24] Larisa Podgorbunskaia, interview, May 4, 1995.
[25] Seminar on "Social Lobbying" sponsored by the Inform Center, held in Vykhino, Moscow, March 16, 1996, author's notes.

registered positive feelings toward the URW. One activist with a con-sciousness-raising organization, the Feminist Alternative, praised the URW for having taken several newspapers to court for running sexist job advertisements:

They were the first to raise the issue of discrimination against women in the press, in job announcements . . . they went to court, and won, they took it to the end . . . At long last, it wasn't just words, but action. The women's movement has gotten bogged down in conversations, but it's already time to start acting. Concrete work like that is good: there's something to show for it. Our organization hasn't ever done anything like that, like going to court; maybe that's out of fear, helplessness. The SWC had experience with such [state] structures; they were all *in* those structures, so they felt stronger, they weren't afraid. It's very useful.[26]

Another activist, despite past quarrels between her organization and the URW, pointed to that organization's "good work with the unem-ployed."[27] Others praised the organization for retaining a strong staff infrastructure and the mass structure of the SWC, with several active local divisions, such as the city women's council in Ivanovo.[28]

Concrete instances of cooperation between the URW and other major women's networks in Moscow have occurred. One representative of the Women's League, for instance, stated that they work "fairly closely" with the URW, that they invite each other to meetings and conferences.[29] And in summer 1995, the URW was among several women's group networks in Moscow to participate in judging a funding competition sponsored by several foreign foundations, for travel to the UN Fourth Worldwide Conference on Women, in Beijing. Some integration of the URW into other women's movement communities has thus taken place.

Reliable information (about the past or the present) is not readily accessible in Russian society; it is therefore terribly hard to judge the validity of many respondents' claims about each others' organizations. Each organization can be expected to paint itself in the most "indepen-dent" possible light – especially in front of a foreign researcher. In any case, the accusations about groups being "party" and "nonparty" or "state" and "nonstate," whether true or not, do serve as one

---

[26] Interview, November 21, 1994. The URW brought their suit to the Court Chamber on Information Disputes because several newspapers had violated the Russian constitu-tion's clause about men's and women's equal rights and freedoms by publishing advertisements for lawyers' and accountants' positions that were only open to men: Vladimir Chertkov, "Neuzheli ee udel – kukhnia?," *Sudarushka*, no. 7, March 1995, p. 3, interview with Marina Gordeeva, responsible secretary of the URW.

[27] Tat'iana Riabikina, interview, April 26, 1995.

[28] Interviews, June 25, 1995; December 7, 1994; Elena Ershova, interview, April 18, 1995.

[29] Interview, early October, 1994.

explanation for why, under conditions when women as a group are being discriminated against, they do not unite as a group to fight back. Staking a claim on organizational identity – and needing to contrast one's organization's merits with the foibles of another, such as affiliation with the state bureaucracy, present or past – thus serves as one of the obstacles to cooperation and coalition-building within the Russian women's movement.

Political scientist M. Steven Fish, studying the activity of six Russian democratic political organizations from 1990 to 1994, found a similar cause for disunity between those formerly associated with the old regime and those who were not. Even groups having nearly identical goals chose not to unite, often because uniting would have meant a blurring of identity boundaries for their groups, an identity which turned in some cases on past affiliation or nonaffiliation with the Communist Party. In fact, one of Fish's interviewees described members of a group he felt were "former communists," by saying "in the eyes of some people, they appear repainted,"[30] precisely the same term that one woman quoted earlier used to describe other activists she perceived as being formerly identified with the state nomenklatura.

While fragmentation and mutual mistrust in post-Soviet social movements may in part reflect the "legacy of Communist Party rule,"[31] the Soviet–communist past can in some cases have the opposite – unifying – effect. Whereas in Moscow the perception that individual activists and organizations had been linked to the Soviet–communist past contributed on balance to distrust and fragmentation within the movement, in Ivanovo, a much smaller, provincial city, the situation was reversed. In Ivanovo, one reason for the high levels of organizational unity and movement cohesion (and as a result, an impressive degree of cooperation with local government bodies) seemed to be that essentially all of the main women's group activists in the city were former activists in Communist Party-affiliated organizations. Most often, they had been leaders in the Komsomol at their educational institutions, and had worked together for years.[32] This contrasts sharply with the rocky history shared by diverse women's groups in Moscow. There, women's

---

[30] M. Steven Fish, *Democracy from Scratch* (Princeton: Princeton University Press, 1995), p. 91.

[31] Ibid., p. 111.

[32] Ol'ga Khasbulatova (Center for Social Support of Women and Families), Margarita Razina (Businesswomen's Club), and Natal'ia Kovaleva (Ivanovo city *zhensovet*, now City Union of Women) knew each other from Komsomol work: see Ol'ga Khasbula-tova, interview, April 6, 1995. Kovaleva and Razina had also worked in the party structures. Larisa Nazarova (Committee of Single-Parent Families) and Nina Temni-kova (Committee of Multi-Child Families) also said they had been leaders in the Komsomol at their institutes.

organizations formed out of multiple networks, including the party structures, producing women activists whose roots lay on both sides of the state–society divide. In Ivanovo, however, there appeared to have been a single mobilizing structure through which networking took place, namely the Communist Party and its affiliated organizations.

Thus, although Communist Party affiliation can serve as a point of contestation, that particular aspect of the Soviet political legacy can also have positive effects – under certain conditions. It is precisely the people who have a history of working in the Komsomol and/or the Communist Party (at least in a provincial city like Ivanovo) who now have the skills to organize nonparty social movement organizations. In that sense, the Communist Party and other state-affiliated organizations (e.g., the Komsomol, the Soviet Women's Committee) may have acted as incubators for some of today's women's movement group leaders. In a roundabout way, some aspects of the Soviet legacy may have assisted civil society formation, rather than having been exclusively detrimental to it. But on the whole, the communist legacy has had divisive results for today's women's movement.

Oldtimers and newcomers

A further emergent line of division, particularly visible within one branch of the Russian women's movement – the Independent Women's Forum (IWF) network – is a division between the originators of the movement, who feel that they took all the risks under the repressive Soviet regime, and the "newcomers" to the movement, perceived as having benefited from the originators' efforts. In an unpublished article, Marina Regentova and Natalia Abubikirova, two of the early activists in the Russian feminist women's movement (their organization, SAFO – later called FALTA, the Feminist Alternative – was founded in 1990), describe this division in terms of the progression of a dramatic play:

Act One: The Idealists are on stage. They are acting under a situation of open hostility and counteraction from society, and have no chance of getting any financial support. The idealists are full of energy, hope, ideas, and the desire to change the world. Often, they are romantic and unselfish, and do not expect any kind of benefits in the event of achieving their goals. They attract and unite people . . . They do not notice the scene changing.

Act Two: The Pragmatists are on stage. This is the time when the idealists' efforts are beginning to bear fruit. The actual possibility of reward appears, including monetary reward. Hanging back for some time in the shadows, the pragmatists unnoticeably, but purposefully establish and strengthen their power positions.

Act Three: The scenery changes. For the idealists, a period of deep disappointment begins. For the pragmatists, it's the opposite: a time of ascent.

The play has a few happy endings. One of them is that the idealists exit, in order to start everything anew. The other is when the idealists become pragmatists. And in both cases, in the background, there's a flow of new pragmatists, yet another stage of the movement's development.[33]

Later in their article, Regentova and Abubikirova discuss the history of the Inform Center of the Independent Women's Forum, and its outgrowth from the IWF. The IWF began as two conferences, held in March 1991 and November 1992, called respectively the First and Second Independent Women's Forums. The groups attending the Second Forum posed the idea of creating an umbrella organization, a network of groups. The Forum never registered officially, but in 1994 a group of women – some of whom had been involved with the Forums from the beginning, and some of whom became involved only with the Second Forum – founded the Inform Center of the Independent Women's Forum, with the aid of a grant from the Ford Foundation, and registered it officially. Several activists thought it unfair for the Inform Center to use the name "Independent Women's Forum" when registering the Inform Center officially, because it had not been elected "representative" of the entire Independent Women's Forum network, and voiced their objections in public. By referring to the Inform Center's history in their article, Regentova and Abubikirova's implication (though not stated directly) is that pragmatists now control an organization that was founded with the efforts of idealists, who are excluded from it.

The split in the Independent Women's Forum described in Regentova and Abubikirova's article and the reasons for it were corroborated in several interviews as being a split between the "founders" and the "inheritors" of the late Soviet feminist legacy. An American activist in Moscow explained the infighting as follows:

The grandmothers [*babushki*] of the Forum were Rita Beliakovskaia, Marina Regentova, Natasha Abubikirova, Olga Lipovskaia, [and others]: they put together the First Independent Women's Forum, and now they feel betrayed . . . They put in the hard work when it was dangerous to be a feminist, and now they feel excluded from the palace that's been built on their foundations.[34]

Olga Lipovskaia, director of the Petersburg Center for Gender Issues, confirmed this, also focusing on the Inform Center:

The Second Forum was not authentic like the first one was . . . The Independent Women's Forum as such was never registered; they registered the

[33] Regentova and Abubikirova, no title, pp. 10–11.
[34] Martina Vandenberg, interview (conducted in English), April 20, 1995.

Inform Center IWF instead, to get the [Ford Foundation] grant. The Second Forum – the Inform Center – excluded the organizers of the First Forum from the profits, while using their program ideas in the grant-writing process.[35]

For those who participated in feminist organizing under the repressive Soviet regime, their early activism seems to have set up a line of division, as well as suspicion of the motives of newer entrants into the women's movement. Testifying to the salience and emotional resonance of having been a participant in the feminist movement under the repressive regime, one organizer of the First Independent Women's Forum said:

And when we opened [the Forum], it was March 1991, it was the CPSU, it was the KGB, there were representatives of the KGB there among us, and it was scary . . . I was scared. And why not! I didn't think I'd be sent to prison, but I could have been fired.[36]

That some of the organizers of the First Forum feel that the newer activists in the feminist movement have taken advantage of the risks undergone by the earlier activists is clear. Perhaps spurred by these feelings, some activists voiced resentment toward newcomers to the movement. Said another of the organizers of the First Forum:

The First Forum was Voronina, Filippova, Lipovskaia, Konstantinova, Klimen-kova, Posadskaia, Khotkina. There were the people who were in SAFO [Free Association of Feminist Organizations], and we had some kind of unity [edinstvo]. Now it's a different atmosphere, with different relations. A lot of ambitions have appeared, power has been attracted.[37]

Speaking about ill feelings between some groups in the women's movement, Eleonora Ivanova, of Conversion and Women, talked about what it felt like to have been a later entrant into the Independent Women's Forum branch of the Russian women's movement:

We [Conversion and Women] weren't at the First Forum; maybe they think we're upstarts or pretenders to the throne [vyskochki]. We showed up only at the Second Forum, and [they think] we're making a claim on something, to leadership [na chto-to pretenduem]. We weren't making a claim to anything, we just wanted to help the Forum to register. I'd already been through that process, and we wanted to help them to speed it up.[38]

[35] Ol'ga Lipovskaia, interview, July 5, 1995.
[36] Interview, name withheld.
[37] Interview, November 21, 1994. According to the booklet of materials published after the First Independent Women's Forum ("Itogovyi otchet o rabote 1ogo Nezavisimogo Zhenskogo Foruma"), its organizing committee consisted of nineteen people: Natal'ia Abubikirova, Irina Alexandrova, Natal'ia Filippova, Ol'ga Kazachenko, Zoia Khotkina, Tat'iana Klimenkova, Valentina Konstantinova, Elena Kochkina, Nadezhda Krylova, Natal'ia Lebedeva, Ol'ga Lipovskaia, Elena Mezentseva, Anastasiia Posadskaia, Marina Regentova, Genrietta Savina, Liudmila Sherova, Vera Stromova, Valeriia Tukmanova, Ol'ga Voronina.
[38] Eleonora Ivanova, interview, February 6, 1995.

While veterans of any social movement may begrudge sharing the stage with newcomers and rising stars, and may believe that the newcomers have a different set of values (too radical, or not radical enough), in the Russian case, early activism ran a risk of repression simply irrelevant to later activism. This line of division serves as an obstacle to coalition-building, even within the feminist-identified branch of the Russian women's movement, where differences over ideology or degree of radicalism are not a primary fault line, although, as we shall see below, those disagreements are relevant between branches of the movement. The Soviet state's overwhelming and repressive presence, and then relatively sudden disappearance, created a line of division between women's movement activists, whereby early activists, who began their work under the repressive regime, could ask newer activists now enjoying even a certain measure of financial reward for their activism: "Where were *you* when we were fighting for the freedom you enjoy today?" This split is due to the Soviet Union's totalitarian political history, which made organizing civic associations impossible, nearly until the state's collapse. It would not be salient in a country that had not undergone such a radical transformation in the degree of political repression against social interest groups.

Ideological differences: traditionalists vs. feminists

The Russian women's movement on the whole does include ideological lines of division such as "traditionalist" vs. "feminist," where "traditionalist" implies some acceptance of women's stereotypical gender roles and occupations. When used by activists to characterize rival networks, however, these distinctions, like those about state affiliation, seem to be more a reflection of political-historical divisions than of present objective reality. Nina Gabrielian, for instance, an activist with the women's club, Preobrazhenie (Transfiguration), which participates in several networks (the Independent Women's Forum and the Women's League), described the "network within the Independent Women's Forum" as being "more feminist," in contrast to URW, which she saw as "more traditionally oriented."[39] Olga Voronina, a researcher at the Moscow Center for Gender Studies, agreed, suggesting that the URW "retained their very traditional orientation," and that, whereas some women in the presidium of the Soviet Women's Committee had been inclined to egalitarian ideas, "mostly it was women with a traditional character, for whom the word 'feminism' brought forth a negative reaction."[40] However, a highly

[39] Nina Gabrielian, interview, March 19, 1995.
[40] Ol'ga Voronina, interview, April 27, 1995.

placed staff member of the URW, who had also worked there when it was still the SWC, believed the opposite to be the case, stating: "We consider ourselves a feminist organization."[41] Furthermore, some of the rhetoric employed by the women's political bloc, Women of Russia (which was based in large part on the URW), is nearly indistinguishable from that of the Independent Women's Forum. The labels seem to reflect long-standing conflicts based on perceived affiliation with the state, rather than describing actual ideological differences.

Ambition as a post-Soviet phenomenon

The Soviet legacy has contributed to dividing the women's movement's politically active networks in Moscow, by setting up a state vs. nonstate dichotomy, linked to a distrust of the state that accompanies Leninist regimes and that may outlast them. Many women activists, however, also attribute the divisiveness within the Moscow-based women's movement to ambition – especially among those women's groups whose goals include influencing state laws and policies. When asked about obstacles to networking, "ambition" or "ambitions for status" was one of the most oft-cited explanations. One activist said, "Some groups just want to be the most important in the movement . . . in our movement there's a lack of women's solidarity."[42] Another pointed to the same phenomenon: "In Moscow, especially, some people are very ambitious . . . people want to be leaders."[43] Svetlana Kornilova, an activist with an Ekaterinburg-based women's group, said that the obstacle to networking was simple:

There's no desire for networking. Each one thinks it's better than the others, and is jealous about the other organizations that arise. "Why did *you* form, when *we* already exist?," they say.[44]

Feminist activist and scholar Valentina Konstantinova similarly attributes the weakness of coalition-building in Russia in part to "personal ambitions."[45]

Whereas ambition is clearly a crosscultural phenomenon, it is also – in the view of numerous respondents – a phenomenon related to the Soviet legacy. Manifestations of ambition have prompted some to refer to a Soviet mentality, derived from a Soviet upbringing and a lack of

---

[41] Interview, February 2, 1995.
[42] Tat'iana Ivanova, interview, May 16, 1995.
[43] Eleonora Ivanova, interview, February 6, 1995.
[44] Svetlana Kornilova, interview, June 8, 1995.
[45] See Valentina Konstantinova, "Women's Political Coalitions in Russia (1990–1994)," in Anna Rotkirch and Elina Haavio-Mannila, eds., *Women's Voices in Russia Today* (Brookfield, VT: Dartmouth Publishing, 1996), pp. 236–37.

experience with political pluralism. Activist Tatiana Riabikina explained the fractious nature of the women's movement thus: "It's because we lived for so long under a monopoly: one party, one trade union, one women's group."[46] Another activist with a women's club (which had split a few years earlier) attributed the fierce competition between women's groups to socialization under the Soviet regime:

Now, there's competition, as well as cooperation, which is unpleasant for me to talk about. There's a certain mentality which is still deeply rooted in our society, and it takes an unpleasant form. The old Soviet mindset [Sovkovyi mentalitet] hinders cooperation. We don't have any within our group, but it exists among groups.[47]

Irina Kovaleva, general director of Russia's women's radio station, answered a question about the obstacles to cooperation among women's groups with reference to the same psychological issue:

I think that we need to change the mentality and consciousness of the women in our country, which we're trying to do, with our radio station. Women in this country have a lot of ambition, they have a Soviet [Sovkovaia] ideology, wherein the main thing is forgotten, for the sake of the personal, the private, the individual [radi chastnogo]. The struggle to attain a position takes precedence over the things that should be most important for women.[48]

Another activist agreed:

The squabbles within organizations: it's all due to the mentality of the Soviet person. The Soviet upbringing [Sovetskoe vospitanie] was a method for managing people: the more isolated people are, the easier it is to control them, to turn them against each other. Life is a struggle, for a piece of bread, for power, etc. It's a subconscious process.[49]

It is somewhat ironic that the Soviet regime sought to instill a devotion to a collective social consciousness dedicated to building communism and the like, but instead (in these respondents' opinions) produced individualists who put their own status and advantage ahead of everything else. This state of affairs coincides with Ken Jowitt's claim that Leninist regimes can in fact reinforce cultural patterns that they intend to eliminate, in this case, the notion of "limited good," a zero-sum perception of the world, which resonates with these respondents' assertions.[50] In this view, power, like any other resource, is not to be shared, but rather controlled and hoarded. Several interviewees accused other

---

[46] Tat'iana Riabikina, interview, April 26, 1995.
[47] Interview, November 19, 1994. As a translation, "Soviet" does not fully capture the essence of the adjective "Sovkovyi/Sovkovaia." Sovkovyi stems from the noun "sovok" – dustpan – and is thus an ironic pun on "Sovetskyi [Soviet]". In this context it is used to mean "the average Soviet person who thinks and acts in Soviet ways."
[48] Irina Kovaleva, interview, July 10, 1995.
[49] Laima Geidar, interview, July 17, 1995.
[50] See Jowitt, "Political Culture in Leninist Regimes," pp. 77–78.

activists and organizations of hoarding their Western contacts, and pointed out that, under the new "market" conditions, information had become a "good" and was thus in limited supply (if one organization acquired information on how to obtain Western resources, that information would be best kept quiet, lest other organizations apply and thus reduce the available funds). Such a "limited good" perspective makes sense in a shortage economy. Jowitt's argument, however, would suggest that this is not so much a new phenomenon as a continuation of the political culture reinforced by totalitarianism, where "connections" are hoarded.

Lending credence to the notion that ambition and "limited good" perspectives are political cultural phenomena affecting today's social movements, there is evidence suggesting that fractionalization on that basis in post-Soviet Russia is not peculiar to the women's movement. The lack of unity across organizations with similar goals is also found in the legal profession (*advocatura*) – witness the nine bar associations in the Moscow area alone as of 1995.[51] Fragmentation has also been evident among Russia's "democratic" or "liberal" political parties. Although fragmentation based on ambition is no stranger to politics or social movements worldwide, it appears to be exacerbated by the Soviet legacy.

The novelty of organizational pluralism

Russia's political history, under which the state monopolized the public arena, thereby ruling out nonstate organizations, suggests another complementary explanation for the severity of fragmentation within Russian social and political movements. According to Regentova and Abubikirova, dynamics endemic to the women's movement include "conflict avoidance and a lack of experience in solving conflicts," as well as the absence of time in which to have accumulated "experience of informal [i.e., nongovernmental] activity."[52] In other words, activists have no experience upon which to draw to help resolve conflicts within their organizations, or to aid them in forming coalitions. Similarly, Valentina

---

[51] Pamela Jordan, "Russian Advocates in a Post-Soviet World: The Struggle for Professional Identity and Efforts to Redefine Legal Services" (dissertation, University of Toronto, 1996).

[52] Regentova and Abubikirova, no title, pp. 10, 27, 26. William Gamson, in a study of "challenging groups" in the United States between 1800 and 1945, supports Abubikirova and Regentova's experience, finding that "groups that lack mechanisms for dealing with internal division become crippled by factionalism and succumb when they might have succeeded." See William Gamson, *The Strategy of Social Protest*, 2nd edn. (Belmont, CA: Wadsworth, 1990), pp. 101–02.

Konstantinova described Russia's new social movements as lacking "experience in organizational work,"[53] presumably because the organizational work under the Soviet regime had been monopolized by party-affiliated organizations. Likewise, lesbian-feminist activist Laima Geidar described the women's movement as being in its "adolescence [*podrostkovyi etap*],"[54] explaining in part why there was so little consolidation within the movement, and implying that there had simply not been enough time to gain experience in overcoming some of the obstacles to coalition-building.

Atomization

Still another factor contributing to the lack of networking and coalition-building between Russian women's groups is the totalitarian legacy of "atomization" – the Soviet regime's conscious attempt to break all ties between people outside the family and the collective, that is, to eliminate civil society. The most significant manifestation of atomization within the women's movement is isolation. In response to questions about what hindered networking, the term "isolated [*razobsheny*]" came up frequently as a description of women's organizations.[55]

Isolation of women's groups and activists from each other, even within major cities, not to mention across the country, is a very real factor in preventing coalition-building. During interviews, I asked respondents if they were familiar with other women's organizations in Moscow working on similar projects or issues. In several cases, respondents were surprised to learn from me about the existence of other women's groups engaged in similar work. Moreover, in a few cases, women's group leaders in Moscow were almost entirely ignorant of all the other women's groups operating in the capital. One reason for this is a virtual information blackout in the mass media about women's group activity, in part a reflection of underdeveloped media outreach strategies by women's movement activists.

One example may suffice to illustrate the extent to which the major networks of the women's movement – even in Moscow – remain isolated and segregated from each other. In May 1995, the URW provided a meeting space for a roundtable organized by Martina Vandenberg, the American coordinator of the US–NIS Women's Consortium, to discuss the upcoming UN Fourth Worldwide Conference on Women in Beijing.

[53] Valentina Konstantinova, "No Longer Totalitarianism, But Not Yet Democracy," in Anastasia Posadskaya, ed., *Women in Russia* (London: Verso, 1994), p. 60.
[54] Laima Geidar, interview, July 17, 1995.
[55] Interviews, October 15, 1994; December 6, 1994.

Natalia Berezhnaia, leader of a women's rights organization called Equality and Peace, and also a member of the URW's administration, ran the meeting. Representatives of the Women's League and the Independent Women's Forum (IWF) attended the meeting (probably because they were invited by Vandenberg). Despite cordial interaction between network representatives at the meeting, the gap between the various networks was clear, especially when one representative of the URW present made a plea for civility within the NGO delegation to Beijing, suggesting that there were potentially explosive differences brewing beneath the surface. But most striking was the extent of unfamiliarity with each others' organizations. Tatiana Troinova, of the Inform Center of the Independent Women's Forum, and the ADL (Archive–Database–Library) project, said that she could compose a descriptive list of all the women's NGOs attending the Beijing conference from Russia, but that she would need basic information on the organizations in the Women's League, as well as information about the URW in order to do so. Troinova's lack of information seemed to be more the rule than the exception. Soviet atomization persists.

Thus, while networking and coalition-building may be financially constrained, there are additional reasons for the limited collaboration across Moscow's women's movement networks. These are attributable to the institutional legacy of totalitarianism, including struggles over identity and the labeling of groups in relation to the Soviet past, a lack of experience with pluralism and coalition-building, a competitive sense of ambition in a shortage society, and societal atomization.

Fear of hierarchy

The Soviet political legacy affects organizational structure, as well as intergroup relations, most often manifesting itself as a fear of hierarchy. Several activists mentioned hierarchy as one of the "nondemocratic" phenomena that they found distasteful in various women's movement organizations, and even rejected cooperation with organizations that they perceived as having a hierarchical structure. Sometimes hierarchy is imposed by Western foundations donating to Russian women's organizations, a fact which has given rise to additional fear and avoidance of the hierarchical model on the part of some activists, although it is seen as a reasonable demand for accountability on the part of donors. On the other hand, having had little experience with nonhierarchical organization, some activists simply find themselves at a loss to try and create new forms of organization. In describing the experience of the Inform Center of the Independent Women's Forum, Marina Liborakina, the co-director, said, "We wanted to do things cooperatively, but we didn't know how. All our experience had been in hierarchical organizations."[56]

Since its inception, the Russian women's movement has shown reluctance to engage in hierarchical organization. After the First Independent Women's Forum (March 1991), the participants had hoped to arrange a way to exchange information between the groups and individuals that had attended, and thus founded a network of independent women's organizations. The idea of formalizing the network as a hierarchical organization was defeated; according to two participants, "There was no desire to form yet another traditional structure, headed by a center, and with 'primary' organizations 'in the local areas,' awaiting orders about what had to be done and why."[57] At the close of the Second Independent Women's Forum (November 1992), it was decided that, although the time had come to "transform the Forum into an international women's social organization," that organization would be "free of a strict hierarchical structure."[58]

With the passage of time, however, some activists began to feel that the lack of institutionalization was detracting from the movement's effectiveness. Feminist philosopher Tatiana Klimenkova, speaking in December 1993, suggested that the activists' "fear of institutionalization" had begun to work to the movement's detriment: "The fact that the [Independent Women's] Forum hasn't been registered, to date, in the institutional sense, doesn't so much signify our independence and our resistance as much as it signifies our atomization. Not having registered, we are in danger of losing our resources. Of course, no one needs just another organization existing only on paper; a new type of organization is what's needed."[59] She explained that the new type of organization would be logically counterposed to the work of a "typical administrative apparatus that acts by introducing programs from the top down, by using political power."[60] More recently, another woman active in organizing the First Independent Women's Forum pointed out that battles over administrative structure had undermined activists' ability to unite into an effective organization after the Second Forum:

[56] Janet Maughan, "Women's Work: Finding a Place in the New Russia," *Ford Foundation Report*, Spring 1996, p. 17.

[57] Regentova and Abubikirova, no title, p. 8. This terminology (e.g., "primary [party] organizations") refers to the Communist Party's structure.

[58] *From Problems to Strategy: Materials of the Second Independent Women's Forum, Dubna, 27–29 November 1992* (Moscow/Hilversum: Center for Gender Studies/Ariadne Europe Fund, 1993), p. 55.

[59] Tat'iana Klimenkova, "Lichnoe – eto politicheskoe," *FemInf*, no. 3, December 1993, p. 2.

[60] Ibid., p. 3.

[The Second Forum didn't unite into an umbrella organization for] various reasons, in part because they didn't agree about the principles of organization, and the administration of it, that's what's terrible. Because another of the consequences of the totalitarian regime is that when anyone starts to talk about administration, everyone goes into shock. But without administration, it turns into anarchy.[61]

The desire for nonhierarchical, collective leadership-oriented organizations has been documented in the late and post-Soviet democratic political movement as well, along with some of the problems caused by collective organizational structures. In a blanket statement about independent associations at the close of the Soviet period, Fish described their "hyperdemocracy" as follows:

The new parties, trade unions, and umbrella organizations shunned hierarchy in favor of broad collective leadership. Lines of authority and responsibility were typically very poorly defined, often producing organizational paralysis and a leadership style that may be termed collective irresponsibility.[62]

A woman activist spoke in similar terms about the double bind for today's feminist organizations when people fail to take responsibility:

there's an attempt and desire, in the administration [upravlenie] [of women's groups] to avoid the patriarchal model and adopt a feminist one. So, when people don't do their work, you can't punish them, like a male director would, by depriving them of salary or something. But this is an issue for feminist groups . . . If your group is focused on individual self-development, then, go ahead, develop yourself, and good luck to you [na zdarove]! But if you want to do some kind of an action? And you say, Masha, can you make some calls, and Masha explains that she's depressed, etc., etc., you can't threaten to deprive her of her salary . . . because we're feminist, and democratic.[63]

Although antihierarchical organizational structures are not uncommon in women's movements in countries lacking totalitarian political legacies, the fact that this tendency is found in several post-Soviet social movements suggests that it is not simply a "women's" movement phenomenon, as does the fact that activists in these movements attribute their preferences for nonhierarchical organizational structure directly to their country's political history.[64]

It has been difficult for sectors of the Russian women's movement to

---

[61] Interview, name withheld.
[62] Fish, *Democracy from Scratch*, pp. 56–57.
[63] Nina Gabrielian, interview, March 19, 1995. Another significant problem is over-commitment. Many activists are affiliated with more than one women's organization, where they work on a volunteer basis, in addition to holding down sometimes multiple jobs.
[64] See Jane Dawson, *Eco-Nationalism: Anti-Nuclear Activism and National Identity in Russia, Lithuania, and Ukraine* (Durham, NC: Duke University Press, 1996); Kathleen E. Smith, *Remembering Stalin's Victims* (Ithaca: Cornell University Press, 1996), and Fish, *Democracy from Scratch*.

overcome the aversion to hierarchy instilled in the population by decades of top-down Soviet rule. While there is no normative value in hierarchical over collective organizational structures, it is true that pressure against creating a hierarchical organization has thus far prevented the Russian women's movement from coordinating its activities at a national level, and has also contributed to organizational fragmentation.

Umbrella organizations: unity without hierarchy?

Given the factors obstructing cooperation between organizations, what do activists think about the potential for coalition-building across the distinct networks of the Moscow-based women's movement? When activists were asked specifically about coalition-formation and for their opinions on the utility of an umbrella organization under which to unite the Russian women's movement, their responses split. Some activists wished for more united action within the women's movement, while others associated the notion of an umbrella organization with the old Soviet version of a mass organization – the Soviet Women's Committee in particular – in which the real interests of women found precious little expression.

Several activists favored the idea of establishing an umbrella organization under which to unite Russian women's groups. One of the founding members of Moscow's Klub F-1 liked the concept of an umbrella organization because it would permit groups to unite, while allowing each organization to "retain its individuality."[65] Several activists said that an umbrella organization would be valuable because it could coordinate activities among groups with mutual interests.[66] An activist with Equality and Peace (a women's advocacy organization) stated that, while the women's movement was not ripe for an umbrella organization, such a thing would be useful:

Working together would be valuable. Now, it's as though each finger of the hand is doing something, but there's no fist, and therefore, women's voice goes unheard [*Vot kak – kazhdyi palets v ruke chto-to delaet, a kulaka-to net, poetomy golos zhenshchin ne slishen*].[67]

An activist with the Independent Women's Forum agreed that the time had not yet come for women's organizations to unite, although she was "deeply convinced that we should work in a coalition of organizations . . . but I don't see the resources or the ability for that at the present

---

[65] Interview, November 2, 1994.
[66] Interview, November 21, 1994; Tat'iana Riabikina, interview, April 26, 1995.
[67] Interview, December 28, 1994.

time."[68] Other activists agreed that an umbrella organization to unite the Russian women's movement would be a positive innovation, but was simply not viable. A researcher with the Gender Studies Center at the Institute for Ethnology and Anthropology pointed out that, in the Russian situation, "there wouldn't be one umbrella, but thirty-three of them!"[69]

When asked to consider the benefits of an umbrella organization, some respondents pointed directly to their memory of the Soviet Women's Committee as a negative example:

It would depend on who was in it. There was one once, the Soviet Women's Committee. People should form their own organizations. Groups can collaborate, why not? It's great. But why do we need to centralize it all again?[70]

Experience shows that nothing other than the interests of a monopoly arise out of that. It was enough to have the Soviet Women's Committee, which subsumed all the interests of other organizations, personifying them only in itself. And now the URW is becoming that type of organization . . . And for many organizations and leaders of the women's movement, that provides a very lasting and negative example of what can happen if organizations are compelled to unite. People feel like we've had enough of that, we already experienced that, and we don't want it anymore.[71]

Because of the history of compulsory uniting-from-above, some activists felt that a coalition or umbrella organization should be used only to "solve a particular problem," such as the war in Chechnia (mentioned by several respondents in this context). "I feel cautious about just uniting for the sake of unity," said Svetlana Kornilova, of the Ekaterinburg-based Confederation of Businesswomen of Russia.[72] One activist, upon being invited to join the Women's League (a self-labeled confederation) was similarly hesitant: "I was frightened by the thought of the former [women's] committees, so I thought, I don't want to."[73] Elena Ershova, co-chair of the Women's League, expressed reluctance toward the idea of an all-encompassing umbrella organization: "I'm not opposed to it in principle. But we're historically tired of being united in that way: we were forced to. Now people want to show themselves separately."[74]

By contrast, in Ivanovo, respondents tended to think the question of uniting the women's movement under an umbrella organization was

---

[68] Interview, November 18, 1994.
[69] Interview, December 6, 1994.
[70] Interview, November 20, 1994.
[71] Galina Sillaste, interview, March 28, 1995.
[72] Svetlana Kornilova, interview, June 8, 1995.
[73] Interview, November 16, 1994.
[74] Elena Ershova, interview, April 18, 1995.

moot, since it was already essentially united – at least in their city, where the local women's council, a subdivision of the former SWC, acted as an umbrella for several local women's groups. Said Natalia Kovaleva, chair of the Ivanovo city women's council, "If you look at our city, I think you can see that there are advantages to that."[75] Representatives of organizations under the women's council's umbrella did not disagree. Nina Temnikova, for example, of the Committee of Multi-Child Families, responded by saying, "Here, I think it's already united, even with the city administration."[76] Margarita Razina, from Ivanovo's Businesswomen's Club (Klub Delovaia Zhenshchina), a women's organization independent of the women's council but on good terms with it, was only slightly ambivalent about the benefits to the Russian women's movement's uniting under one roof:

It's hard to say. I'm in favor of diversity in the women's movement. But probably, some socio-economic-political current of the women's movement should unite . . . It's not possible to influence state policy in isolation. Uniting and speaking out on one issue or another could be done through the URW, or through [the political bloc] Women of Russia. There can be some other uniting principle. But on the cardinal issues of the socio-economic and political position of women, there should be some unity – just for practical purposes. The textile industry is so split up that they can't even get cotton into Russia. But the Agrarians have influence, because they formed a party, they united.[77]

It is interesting that, in Ivanovo, people pointed precisely to the URW and its local branch as being potentially beneficial umbrella organizations, whereas in Moscow a number of the respondents who opposed the idea of unification tended to identify it with the URW and its predecessor, the SWC. Why should that be the case? After all, if the legacy of distrusting the state (and of state-related organizations) affected the entirety of Soviet society, should not Ivanovo's women activists share the opinions of women activists in Moscow on that subject, and eschew a collaborative relationship with the women's council?

There are several reasons why this is not the case. First of all, in Ivanovo, the local branch of the URW (the women's council) rather than being a "deaf wall" between women's organizations and the government, acted instead as a conduit between women's organizations and the local government: its chairwoman held a seat in the city duma, and from that position had actually been able to gain some concrete benefits for Ivanovo's women and their families. She, for example,

---

[75] Natal'ia Kovaleva, interview, April 3, 1995.
[76] Nina Temnikova, interview, April 4, 1995.
[77] Margarita Razina, interview, April 6, 1995.

obtained city budget funding for a "Mothers' Week" event. Another member of the women's council also served as the city administrator for social issues, and, from that position, arranged free public transportation for school-age children from multi-child families.[78] Thus, the local Ivanovo women's council may well have been seen as a helpful entity, rather than as the incarnation of elitism and privilege, the way the SWC (and later, the URW) was viewed in Moscow.[79] Secondly, residing in resplendent headquarters, monopolizing (to a point) contacts with foreign delegations, and, in essence, being visibly affiliated with the state power structures and elite class of the Soviet regime, the SWC and, by inheritance, the URW incurred the resentment and distrust of many Moscow women's group activists. The Ivanovo branch of that organization failed to incur resentment on that scale, probably because it had neither the resources nor the power and connections of its parent organization in Moscow, and was thus not strongly identified by local activists with the controlling and monopolistic state.

Coalitions as a sacrifice of hard-won independence

Another reaction against the Soviet period may be the fear that by joining a larger organization or uniting in some way with other groups, women's organizations would somehow relinquish the pluralism that they have benefited from in recent years. Galina Sillaste suggested that organizations shirk unification with other groups out of a desire to retain their independence.[80] Marina Pavlova, with the Center for Business Assistance to Women: Perepodgotovka, agreed:

Women know that it's easier to work together, but first each group wants to work alone. I understand that very well, because it was the same for me at the beginning. I wanted to be independent. Then, later, you understand that you need to network, to find support.[81]

Several umbrella organizations have developed in Moscow, but they operate more like amorphous networks than coalitions, which are typically established within social movements in order to conduct joint events or campaigns. One such network, the URW, as of June 1995, included 115 member organizations in eighty-nine Russian regions: women's councils, unions, associations, committees, and clubs – in fact,

---

[78] Natal'ia Kovaleva, interview, April 3, 1995.
[79] Not everyone found the local women's council helpful. In 1996, political scientist James Richter interviewed a single mother who had turned to that organization for assistance, and met instead with a rebuke and very little material aid: James Richter, personal communication, March 1998.
[80] Galina Sillaste, interview, March 28, 1995.
[81] Marina Pavlova, interview, April 24, 1995.

"any women's organization supporting the charter and programs can join the URW."[82] Yet when asked for a list of the organizations the URW had under its umbrella, a staff member said that no such list existed.[83] This would appear to make unified action on the "coalition's" behalf rather difficult. A second network, the Women's League, has over forty member organizations, but rarely signs on to any document, or provides expert opinions on a given law as the Women's League per se.[84] Although the co-chairs of the League may sign on to documents in the name of their own organizations, these organizations individually (by definition) are smaller than they are collectively, as the Women's League. Thus the potential impact of the Women's League, in a lobbying situation, might be more impressive to legislators or state administrators if it operated as a coalition (other than when attending their bi-annual meetings) rather than as separate organizations.

The third women's organization network is the Independent Women's Forum, which, as we have seen, has a contested membership, and includes organizations from all over Russia. It does not act officially as a coalition, and is not registered, although the Inform Center of the IWF (which is registered, and is designed to serve the network of organizations within the IWF, while being itself an organization within the IWF) did bring together representatives of several women's organizations in joint programs under its aegis.[85] Finally, the US–NIS Women's Consortium, a varied group bringing in representatives of groups in the Women's League, the IWF, and others, represents the only example of a post-Soviet women's organization coalition that cuts across the various indigenous networks of the women's movement in Moscow. But it is an unusual type of coalition – one designed and funded from abroad. From its inception in December 1994 until the end of its original grant from USAID in May 1996, the Consortium was held together by its American coordinator, Martina Vandenberg, and would never have existed if not for the grant, designed explicitly to bring together representatives of the different branches of the Russian women's movement. Rather than being an indigenous coalition, it is thus somewhat of an artificial creation.

---

[82] See Zhenshchiny Rossii, Bulletin no. 4, in *Moskvichka*, no. 22–23 (June 1995), p. 9.

[83] Interview, February 2, 1995.

[84] Elena Ershova, interview, April 18, 1995.

[85] As of 1995, among these were: Nina Gabrielian (Preobrazhenie and Sof'ia); Eleonora Ivanova (Conversion and Women); Natal'ia Khodyreva (St. Petersburg Psychological Center for Women); Tat'iana Klimenkova (Preobrazhenie and MCGS); Marina Liborakina and Tat'iana Konysheva (Feminist Orientation Center); Tat'iana Troinova (ADL). See "Informatsionnyi tsentr nezavisimogo zhenskogo foruma, Informatsionno-Obrazovatelnyi Proekt, 1994–1996" (brochure). Tat'iana Troinova has since left the Inform Center.

The Russian women's movement's coalition situation may be changing. In mid-1996, the Consortium received another block of funding from USAID, and replaced its American coordinator with a Russian: Elena Ershova, of the Women's League. It will be interesting to see if the Consortium retains its internetwork character without the presence of a neutral American, intentionally bringing representatives together from the various networks. Also, as of December 1995, a new indigenous coalition organization had formed: the Association of Independent Women's Associations (Assotsiatsiia Nezavisimykh Zhenskikh Ob″edinenii).[86] Including the Women's League as well as organizations from the IWF, the association has already acted as a coalition, by sending an open letter on women's status in Russia to the Duma, signed by over fifty organizations. Its next planned act (as of March 1996) was to send an open letter to all the presidential candidates. The outcome of this association's actions may determine whether or not the Moscow women's movement adopts the use of coalitions that cut across the various branches of the women's movement as their preferred organizational form when attempting to influence state policy.

The Soviet political-institutional legacy affects interpersonal and intergroup relations, as well as organizational structure, having ramifications for coalition-building and perhaps for organizational effectiveness. But in addition to these effects, Russian political history also has an impact on the women's movement's strategy and tactics, as well as on the ways that women's organizations view and choose to interact with the state. It is to these aspects of Russia's political history – specifically, the location of the women's movement within a broader cycle of protest – that we now turn.

Political history and a nonmobilizational women's movement

Social movements are usually characterized by protest actions and constituency mobilizations. The Russian women's movement is not a complete exception to this rule, but it is rather atypical. A Westerner's classic image of social movement activity might include large rallies, with posters, banners, chanted slogans, and so forth, and possibly civil disobedience. Such mobilizations are aimed at influencing legislators and executives to change laws and policies, rectifying perceived injustice, alerting the public to an issue, altering public opinion, and attracting

---

[86] Rebekka Kei, "Sozdana Assotsiatsiia nezavisimykh initsiativ," *Nezavisimaia gazeta*, January 18, 1996, p. 6.

adherents. Women's movements are no exception. From authoritarian regimes in Latin America, to the United States and Western Europe, women's movements have engaged in mass public protest, sometimes even violently.[87]

By contrast, the Russian women's movement to date has not engaged in similar large-scale actions, or in much dramatic small-scale civil disobedience. Why do Russian women's movement organizations not mobilize in the mass fashion typical of many social movements?

The exceptions: Soldiers' Mothers, Communists, and Women in Black

A few Russian women's organizations do engage in protests and demonstrations. The Congress of Soviet Women (CSW) – a hardline communist women's group founded in 1993 and affiliated with the left-wing party Working Russia – was one of only two of the thirty-seven Moscow-based organizations interviewed to state that their organization had engaged in demonstrations as a tactic.[88] On May Day 1995, for example, the CSW participated in a large, communist-sponsored rally at the base of Lenin's massive statue at Kaluzhskaia Square in Moscow. The other was the Committee of Soldiers' Mothers (CSM), which began to engage in demonstration tactics early on:

Our first group gathered in spring 1989, because their boys were taken from their institutes [of higher education] into the army. That was Mariia [Kirbassova], and 300 people or so. They went into the streets. It was probably the first unsanctioned demonstration in Moscow. It was on the Holiday of the Moscow Komsomol. They marched from Park Kultury to Red Square.[89]

The Committee of Soldiers' Mothers continued to engage in protest activity, picketing in Manezhnaia Square in 1990 to demand an end to "slave labor" in the army's construction battalions.[90] More recently,

---

[87] On violence in the early British women's movement, see Christine Bolt, *The Women's Movements in the United States and Britain from the 1790s to the 1920s* (Amherst: University of Massachusetts Press, 1993), pp. 188–90. On mass demonstrations in Latin America, see Sonia Alvarez, *Engendering Democracy in Brazil: Women's Movements in Transition Politics* (Princeton: Princeton University Press, 1990), and Jane S. Jaquette, ed., *The Women's Movement in Latin America: Feminism and the Transition to Democracy* (Boston: Unwin Hyman, 1989). On autonomous women's movements in Germany and Italy, see George Katsiaficas, *The Subversion of Politics: European Autonomous Movements and the Decolonization of Everyday Life* (Atlantic Islands, NJ: Humanities Press, 1997).

[88] Natal'ia Belokopytova, interview, May 12, 1995.

[89] Valentina Mel'nikova, interview, May 12, 1995.

[90] Valentina Mel'nikova, "Soldiers' Mothers Committee of Russia," *Monthly Information Newsletter* (Moscow Research Center for Human Rights), no. 3, December 1994.

hundreds of women traveled to Chechnia to physically take their sons home, and the CSM organized an official protest march ("For Life and Compassion") from Moscow to Chechnia starting on March 8, 1995 – International Women's Day – to recover Russian soldiers taken prisoner. They also participated in small weekly pickets at the back entrance to the Russian State Duma, and held occasional rallies in Moscow, including one on February 11, 1995, in Pushkin Square, with about 500 people. There, Valentina Melnikova, press secretary of the CSM, invited mothers to "wake up, open your eyes," and asked them not to give their sons over to the army. She, along with all the other speakers, called for an end to the war in Chechnia, saying, "we're not parliamentarians, we're mothers," and suggested that, although women alone lacked the power to end the war, they should do whatever they could in the interests of peace.

Aside from the Congress of Soviet Women and the Committee of Soldiers' Mothers, there has been little in the way of demonstrations, even among feminist-identified organizations. This may be changing, however. The International Women's Day rally described in the introduction to this volume, sponsored by Women in Black,[91] the "Sisters" Rape Crisis Center, and other women's groups (mostly those affiliated with the Independent Women's Forum), is one example of what may become a standard demonstration format. Except for the high percentage of foreigners participating, the demonstration was not dissimilar to a local women's movement event in the United States, such as a Take Back the Night march.

While other protests have doubtless occurred within the Russian women's movement, I was based in Moscow for nearly a year, and heard about very few. Large cities are usually the site selected for major demonstrations – and the women's movement held none in Moscow during that time. But even in my travels to other cities, where one might expect smaller local protests, not one of the women interviewed mentioned that there had been any demonstrations held by women's groups. Collective protest in the form of large public gatherings simply does not seem to be a significant part of the Russian women's movement. If mass collective action and protest is not a significant organizational form for the Russian women's movement, why might that be the case?

---

[91] Women in Black was founded in Jerusalem in 1988. Their protests consist of groups of women dressed in black, standing silently in public places, holding placards supporting the nonviolent resolution of conflict. Chapters of Women in Black exist in many countries, but it is not officially an international organization. See Gila Svirsky, "A Capsule History of Women in Black," *Objector*, Spring 1997, p. 13.

Collective action repertoire

Most of the collective activity directed at political and social change in the women's movement takes place in the form of conferences and seminars, as well as policy analysis and commentary on laws by women's groups and networks. Part of this is a function of atomization. Due to networking and transportation constraints, groups and individuals working in any given area of women's rights may be unaware of each other, or may see each other only rarely. Conferences and seminars for the Russian women's movement thus serve as sites of information exchange and as strategy planning meetings. They are a constant feature of the Russian social movement landscape. Between September 1994 and August 1995, there were at least twenty conferences and seminars in Moscow sponsored by women's movement groups (often with foreign funding), and many others outside the capital.[92] This does not include regular women's group meetings, some of which are also similar to seminars, featuring lectures and presentations.

How can we explain the Russian women's movement's preference for conferences, seminars, and policy analysis, as a collective means of provoking social change, over more traditional forms of collective action? And what role does Soviet and Russian political history play in conditioning that choice?

Sociologist Charles Tilly has suggested that a given population's repertoire of collective action is shaped in part by patterns of repression

---

[92] A partial list: International Conference, "Women of Russia: Issues of Labor and Employment" at the URW, September 21, 1994; Women to Women International, September 30, 1994, at the Academy of Management; "All-Russian Women's Congress: Employment, Labor, and Unemployment," November 29–30, 1994; First All-Russian Women's Conference (sponsored by the Ministry of Social Protection), December 16, 1994; academic roundtable including a discussion of domestic violence, called "Violence and National Security," March 21, 1995, at the Academy of Management; "Woman and Society," conference sponsored by MOLLI, April 14–16, 1995; "Gender/Culture: Shifting Paradigms" conference sponsored by the "Women's Liberal Initiative fund, May 18–20, 1995; a series of three Archive–Database–Library (ADL) conferences on preparation for the Beijing Conference (December 1994, April 1995, August 1995); Consortium seminar at the URW, "Preparation for the IV World Conference on Women's Status and the NGO Forum-95," May 11, 1995; conference on "Sexual Importunity and Domestic Violence," organized by the Consortium and the American Bar Association in May–June 1995; Second All-Russian Women's Congress: "Women in Politics and Policy for Women," June 6, 1995; American Bar Association Seminar on the Law on Family Violence, June 24, 1995; Ivanovo: "Social Transformation and the Status of Women in Russia," March 1995; a series of political/ organizational training seminars by Sarah Harder (AAUW) and Prolog: Volodarka (January 1995), Novocherkassk (March 1995), Cheboksary (May 1995), Ekaterinburg (June 1995).

in the polity and previous collective action experience.[93] This is surely the case for Russian women, who have known only a brief history of independent organization and collective action. Russian women activists, for these and other reasons, may not regard large-scale collective action as a sensible means of pursuing their goals. Their collective action repertoire regulates the activities in which women's movement organizations engage.

Where do social movements acquire a collective action repertoire? One significant source is work in previous social movements where mobilizational and organizational experience could have been gained. Although in the United States many women brought organizational skills from their work in the civil rights and New Left movements with them into the women's movement of the late 1960s and early 1970s,[94] there is little reason to believe that a similar process occurred on a wide scale in Russia. There is scant evidence that the women's movement in Russia has been able to benefit significantly from the social movements that preceded it, such as the independent labor movement, the democratic political movement, or the national independence movements of the late 1980s. None of the activists interviewed said that they had come to be involved in women's organizations through involvement in another previous social movement, although Natalia Belokopytova (of the Congress of Soviet Women) was on the executive committee of the hardline communist party Working Russia, which would have been a source of organizational experience for her.[95]

Social movement leaders' backgrounds provide an important source of collective action techniques, even absent previous participation in social movements. Social movement theorists have suggested that, while the political opportunities in a given country at a given time may condition the timing and shape of social movements, the "mobilizing structures" from which the movement emerges also have an effect on the movement's organizational forms.[96] In other words, movement

---

[93] Charles Tilly, *From Mobilization to Revolution* (Reading: Addison-Wesley, 1978), p. 156.

[94] Sara Evans, *Personal Politics* (New York: Random House, 1980).

[95] There are other exceptions: among activists that I met (but did not interview), at least two had previous experience in other movements. Tamara Alaiba, a leader of Ekaterinburg's Urals Women's Association got her start in the democratic movement, within the Republican Party of Russia (RPR), as an organizer in Ekaterinburg (then Sverdlovsk) and also as a "leading member" of the RPR's national coordinating council. (See Fish, *Democracy From Scratch*, p. 168.) Similarly, Natal'ia Saptsina was involved in the Workers' Union of the Kuzbass (an independent trade union in Kemerovo), before joining the organizing committee of the Second Independent Women's Forum in 1992, and becoming deputy chair of Russia's Social Democratic Party.

[96] Doug McAdam, John D. McCarthy, and Mayer N. Zald, "Introduction: Opportunities,

leaders may use organizing techniques familiar to them because of their previous experience and the skills available to them as a social group.[97] For example, the US civil rights movement's emergence largely from the mobilizing structure of black churches governed some of its "specific organizational features . . . from reliance on the mass meeting as a mobilizing device, to the disproportionate number of ministers in the ranks of early movement leaders."[98]

In the Russian case, research institutes were the primary mobilizing structures for the contemporary women's movement. A large number of today's women's movement organization leaders worked and networked with each other at institutes including the Institute of Philosophy, the Institute for the Study of USA and Canada, and the Institute for Socio-Economic Population Studies (and later, the Moscow Center for Gender Studies within it).[99] Certainly, the movement exhibits a disproportionate number of academics in its leadership: one-third of the sixty-three activists interviewed were working or had worked as academics and/or researchers; twenty-two had a *kandidat-nauk* degree (between an M.A. and a Ph.D.) and four had a *doktor-nauk* degree (the equivalent of a tenured professorship). The academic background of the Russian women's movement's leaders has a distinct impact on the movement's organizational features, namely the enthusiasm for seminars and conferences, and the desire of organizations to conduct gender-based policy analysis (*gendernaia expertiza*). As was the case with ministers and the civil rights movement, the Russian women's movement leadership may encourage forms of collective action with which they feel most comfortable, which in this case are academic types of actions, rather than mass public ones.

But this is insufficient as an explanation. After all, a variety of late and post-Soviet social movements *did* engage in mass political protest, as glasnost spread. Nationalists, democrats, coal miners, and environmentalists all held public protests, defying the decades-long ban on collective action. Furthermore, the academic backgrounds of Russian's women

---

Mobilizing Structures, and Framing Processes – Toward a Synthetic, Comparative Perspective on Social Movements," in McAdam, McCarthy, and Zald, *Comparative Perspectives*, p. 11.

[97] Mayer N. Zald, "Culture, Ideology, and Strategic Framing," in McAdam, McCarthy, and Zald, *Comparative Perspectives*, p. 267.

[98] McAdam, McCarthy, and Zald, "Introduction," p. 11.

[99] Institute of the USA and Canada: Elena Ershova (Women's League); Irina Karaganova (Women's Liberal Fund); Zhenya Israelian ("Sisters" Rape Crisis Center). Institute of Philosophy: Tat'iana Klimenkova (Preobrazhenie); Ol'ga Voronina (LOTOS). Academy of Social Science: Valentina Konstantinova (LOTOS); Institute for Socio-Economic Population Studies: Anastasia Posadskaia, Natal'ia Zakharova (LOTOS). This is only a partial list.

activists does not rule out protest tactics. Political scientist Jane Dawson claims that all the cases of antinuclear movements arising in Russia in the late Soviet period were initiated precisely by small groups of intellectual elites.[100] Furthermore, surveys have shown that, as of December 1992, the Russian intelligentsia engaged in more protest than any other occupational group, and were the most likely of these groups to participate in public organizations.[101]

Cycles of protest

What explanation, then, can be brought to bear to help us grasp the lack of public protest on women's issues in Russia, particularly in light of rising unemployment rates and economic discrimination, and reports of increasing violence against women?

Political scientists and sociologists have devoted increasing attention to the notion of "cycles of protest" as a factor in explaining social movements' likelihood of success. A cycle of protest is characterized by rapidly spreading mobilizations among diverse societal groups. According to Sidney Tarrow, the position that a social movement occupies in the course of a protest cycle may have ramifications for its success:

Groups that emerge on the crest of a wave of protest may profit from the general atmosphere of discontent created by the efforts of others during earlier phases of the cycle, while similar groups that appear late in the cycle – when demobilization has already begun and a backlash set in – are more likely to fail.[102]

The multi-issue, mass mobilizations that distinguished the late Gorbachev era have been characterized as a cycle of protest. As is the case in many such cycles, protests by coal miners were among the first to surface.[103] These were accompanied by nationalist mobilizations in the Soviet republics, democratic (anticommunist) mobilizations, anti-Stalinist protests, and environmental movement demonstrations. The peak of that cycle of protest is generally fixed in 1990.

Mark Beissinger, using a database of protest mobilizations (both by frequency and number of participants), has shown that the protest cycle in the Soviet case was clearly in decline by the time that the Russian women's movement emerged out of previously non-networked women's

---

[100] Dawson, *Eco-Nationalism*, pp. 29, 105.
[101] Donna Bahry and Lucan Way, "Citizen Activism in the Russian Transition," *Post-Soviet Affairs*, vol. 10, no. 4 (1994), pp. 330–66 (graph, p. 337).
[102] Sidney Tarrow, *Struggle, Politics, and Reform: Collective Action, Social Movements, and Cycles of Protest* (Occasional Paper No. 21, Western Societies Program, Center for International Studies, Ithaca, Cornell University, 1989), p. 50.
[103] Sidney Tarrow, *Power in Movement* (Cambridge: Cambridge University Press, 1994), p. 155.

groups in spring 1991. His analysis of mobilizations shows that the number of people participating in demonstrations peaked in late 1988–early 1989, then declined. In early 1991, a brief remobilization took place, with another one around the August 1991 coup. By July 1992, the population had apparently lost interest in demonstrations as a tactic, and they became harder to mobilize, despite elite efforts. Also, after March 1991, when the independent women's movement was holding its first conference (the First Independent Women's Forum), a dip in the number of demonstrations began, reflecting a developing elite pact to use the tactics of social peace, rather than disruption. After March 1992, the number of demonstrations dropped off considerably.[104] By the end of 1992, when the Russian women's movement had grown further and organized its second national conference of independent women's organizations, the protest cycle was at an end. The opportunity for the women's movement to ride the coattails of previous Russian mobilizations, according to Tarrow's model, were essentially nil.

A social movement's position in the protest cycle may also have ramifications for its tactical choices. Specifically, a movement's selection of tactics can reflect the end of a protest cycle and the consolidation of a new – and perhaps more just – order. In an article on the decline of urban protest movements in Chile after the establishment of a "fragile democracy," one author cited activists who rejected the previous tactics of mass mobilization used against the authoritarian regime out of respect for the newly established order. Having suffered under dictatorship, the Chilean activists feared "return to authoritarian rule and discouraged mobilization that could endanger democratic stability."[105] Having survived the Soviet regime, Russian women activists may seek social peace, the end of protest, and the adoption of nonconflictual means of engaging with the state.

Similarly discouraging as regards the potential for mass mobilization within the Russian women's movement is the fact that, when cycles of protest end, they "usually awaken a backlash against disorder."[106] Tarrow, for instance, describes how the French population became quickly disenchanted with the student protests of May 1968, given the students' "highly disruptive" tactics, "recalling the most conflictual

---

[104] Mark Beissinger, "Event Analysis in Transitional Societies: Protest Mobilization in the Former Soviet Union," in Dieter Rucht, Ruud Koopmans, and Friedhelm Neidhardt, eds., *Acts of Dissent: New Developments in the Study of Protest* (Berlin: Sigma Press, 1998), pp. 284–316.

[105] Patricia L. Hipsher, "Democratization and the Decline of Urban Social Movements in Chile and Spain," *Comparative Politics*, vol. 28, no. 3 (April 1996), pp. 285, 292.

[106] Tarrow, *Struggle, Politics, and Reform*, p. 44.

moments of French history."[107] Demands for order following the cycle of protest in Russia in the early 1990s would only have been reinforced by the traumatic political events that followed the Soviet Union's collapse.

The location of a movement within a larger cycle of protest may be crucial to understanding its tactical choices. But the location of a social movement within a county's political-historical timeline can also be important. What defining political events may affect a social movement's mobilizational choices and collective action repertoire?

In interviews, several activists expressed a fear of anything approaching riots, revolts, or revolutions. The fear factor is understandable. First of all, protests were rare during the Soviet period, but harshly repressed. In 1962, workers at the Electric Locomotive Works in the city of Novocherkassk (in southern Russia) struck to protest salary cuts and price increases. Troops fired on a crowd of peaceful demonstrators demanding the release of imprisoned strike leaders, killing twenty-four people. Seven of the strike leaders were later executed.[108] This was the largest worker uprising between the 1920s and 1989, when Soviet coal miners began strikes that mobilized over half a million people.[109]

While some activists may fear personal physical repression, others may simply identify mass protest with the tumultuous and violent political conflicts that have overtaken Russia since 1991. Although women's movement activists may remain unaware of the Novocherkassk events, all of them lived through the period including the August 1991 coup attempt, the breakup of the Soviet Union, the October 1993 shelling of parliament, and the breakout of multiple wars across the former Soviet republics. At this point, a high value is placed on stability. This fits neatly with Tarrow's suggestion that cycles of protest may be followed by demands for order.

Finally, given their historical experience, Russians may believe mass political protest to be the precursor to revolution. The image of women in particular protesting in public may even be associated with the February revolution, which began as a bread riot (mostly by female textile workers) in Petrograd on International Women's Day, 1917.[110]

Tarrow has suggested that each society has a shared history of collective action "forms," a repertoire that movements are "drawn" to employ. Although Russia's history of protest between the 1920s and the

---

[107] Tarrow, *Power in Movement*, p. 181.

[108] For a vivid account of the events, see David Remnick, *Lenin's Tomb* (New York: Random House, 1993), pp. 414–17.

[109] On strikes during the Soviet period, see Walter D. Connor, *The Accidental Proletariat* (Princeton: Princeton University Press, 1991), chs. 6 and 7.

[110] Fannina Halle, *Woman in Soviet Russia* (New York: Viking Press, 1935), pp. 90–91.

1980s is limited, those forms do exist and include mass demonstrations. The point, however, is that, rather than being drawn to that repertoire, Russians may feel that the use of those forms is not justified, given their past results. Rather than producing reform in the past, the use of that collective action repertoire may be viewed as having led to the disintegration of the Soviet Union and further economic and political upheavals.[111]

The idea that mass demonstrations can become dangerous, instability-provoking, or even revolutionary may keep large public protests out of the collective action repertoire of Russian women activists for some time, especially coming on the heels of the cycle of protest and the instability and violence that has followed it. There is also a sense that demonstrations and other public protests are "just politics," a waste of time, and an unprofessional course of action.

Some combination of these feelings was present among women activists, particularly those in Ivanovo, where a number of interviewees talked spontaneously about their dislike of demonstrations as a method of furthering their goals and interests. When asked about the differences between Moscow's and Ivanovo's women's movements, Olga Khasbulatova, an academic studying the history of the Russian women's movement, and a leader of Ivanovo's Center for Social Support of Women and Families, said:

We're not inclined to demonstrations and meetings. We're a more politically passive population. Despite the low level of living standards, our people aren't going into the streets. Sure, it didn't turn out the way people expected, but, why should people demonstrate against what and whom they voted for?[112]

Natalia Kovaleva, the chairwoman of the Ivanovo city women's council talked about her personal experience helping to suppress a small revolt among women at a local factory:

As the chair of the women's council, I don't want women going out into the streets with pots and pans, and yelling. You don't get anything done that way. A women's revolt isn't necessary. It should all be done in a civilized fashion. I meet with the head of the [city] administration frequently, and I tell him [that] a women's revolt is the most frightening thing. I experienced it once. Being the chair of the Union of Women, when all these processes, like staff reductions, began I was called by one factory and told, "Women have gathered here, come over." We went in with the [Communist] Party secretary. And the women said to him, "What are you doing here, get out of here." They kicked him out. It was a mob of engineering-technical workers. Slowly, we resolved the issues, made an agreement. But it was frightening.[113]

[111] Tarrow, *Power in Movement*, p. 19.
[112] Ol'ga Khasbulatova, interview, April 6, 1995.
[113] Natal'ia Kovaleva, interview, April 3, 1995.

Larisa Nazarova, chair of Ivanovo's Committee of Single-Parent Families, also pointed out that demonstrations were not her preferred method of action:

We send our city duma our proposals . . . But we don't gather demonstrations or anything; we don't shout in the streets. That's useless and a waste of time. We work out our issues with the higher organs of power in a peaceful way, making concrete proposals. I think that's correct. These spontaneous demonstrations don't get you anywhere.[114]

Similarly, in describing her organization's activities, such as yearly textile fairs, fashion shows, and design seminars, Margarita Razina of the Ivanovo Businesswomen's Club, stated:

These concrete events have established our authoritativeness, our image, as a serious group, which doesn't get involved in politics, which doesn't provoke or attend demonstrations or meetings, or speak out in favor of, or against anyone. All we do is engage in concrete affairs: that's our policy. To get something done.[115]

Several Moscow interviewees also mentioned women's revolts as being an undesirable option. Maia Kazmina, a member of the Women's League (and deputy director of the Moscow Union of Lawyers), when asked how women could best hope to address their socio-economic problems, emphasized the value of going through legislative channels, rather than using collective protest:

Only through legislation. You can have demonstrations and such, but the best way is through legislation, and through work in the executive-administrative organs, of course. It would be great if there were more women in those organs, as mayors and so forth. They might look differently at the issues.[116]

Elena Ershova of the Women's League expressed a similar opinion:

[There are] two ways: the constructive and the destructive. The constructive way: through the creation of a women's movement, groups, coalitions, advocacy, and lobbying. The destructive one: a revolt [bunt], like in 1917. Now it's so important to give women the opportunity to develop their potential, to help women go into business, start new lives. If we don't want a women's revolution with empty pots, we have to help them start new lives. Anpilov [leader of the hardline communist Working Russia party] is trying to mobilize women for the destructive path.[117]

Not surprisingly, these sentiments were echoed by an ally of the women's movement in a position of power: Ekaterina Lakhova, at the time, head of the Women of Russia faction in the State Duma, and adviser to the president on women's affairs. Lakhova was quoted in a

[114] Larisa Nazarova, interview, April 4, 1995.
[115] Margarita Razina, interview, April 6, 1995.
[116] Maia Kaz'mina, interview, April 13, 1995.
[117] Elena Ershova, interview, April 18, 1995.

Moscow women's newspaper as saying she wished Moscow women would take a more active part in reforming society. However, she stressed:

This doesn't mean that I'm calling upon Moscow's women to go out into the capital city's squares with pots [s kastriuliami]. It can be done differently, in a professional way [po-delovomu].[118]

In sum, for those activists and officials who want to *change* aspects of the socio-political system, rather than *overthrow* it, mass demonstrations and the amount of energy required in order to mobilize them may be perceived as a poor strategic choice given the cycle of protest and the movement's location in Russia's recent and conflictual political history.

Survey data on public mobilization

The evidence garnered from interviews and observation about women's movement activists' preference for certain types of tactics over others is borne out by public opinion poll data on the subject. GALSI, a women's public opinion polling organization run by Galina Sillaste, conducted a "survey of experts" at the First All-Russian Women's Congress: Labor, Employment, Unemployment, held in Moscow in late November 1994. Among the questions asked of the participants was one about the "efficiency [*deistvennost'*]" of various ways to counter discrimination against women in the labor sphere, by all accounts an issue of acute relevance. A scale was created on the basis of the answers:

In first place, in the opinion of 58 percent of the experts, is "unity in the actions of women's organizations in the struggle against unemployment." Experts prefer nonaggressive, evolutionary activities, such as: women's participation in the examination [*ekspertiza*] of draft legislative and other acts (52 percent), in professional lobbying in the Federal Assembly (51 percent); going to court (42 percent), to the mass media (36 percent), and to organs of administrative and representative power (13 percent); carrying out antidiscriminatory programs by women deputies (21 percent). Only 7.4 percent of experts chose "organizing meetings, demonstrations, and pickets in defense of women's employment and against social discrimination against women," which thus occupied the last – ninth – place on the efficiency scale.[119]

This may well be one of the reasons why the public mobilization of women – within the women's movement, anyway – is unlikely: the

[118] M. Posokhova, interview with E. Lakhova, "Ia ne prizivaiu moskvichek voiti s kastriuliami na stolichnye ploshchadi," *Moskvichka*, no. 25, 1994, p. 7.
[119] Galina Sillaste, "Evoliutsiia sotsial'nykh pozitsii zhenshchin v meniaiushchemsia Rossiiskom obshchestve," *Sotsis*, no. 4, 1995, pp. 64–65. The survey was paid for by the Presidential Commission on Issues of Women, the Family, and Demography, under the president of the Russian Federation (headed by Lakhova).

women leaders (the experts present at the conference) do not favor it, probably for the reasons elaborated earlier. It is important to note, however, that of the 221 respondents (93 percent of which were female), 42 percent represented women's nongovernmental organizations (NGOs), but 41 percent were representatives of state structures. Without a further breakdown of the answers, it is impossible to know whether the answers of representatives of the state structures and women's NGOs differed significantly. However, it is probably safe to assume that representatives of the state structures would be more amenable to intrasystem means than to extrasystem, potentially conflictual means such as demonstrations.

In mid-1995, I conducted a survey which included a question asking what types of political activity the respondent plans to take part in (voting, convincing friends and family to vote if a candidate reflects your views, going to rallies and meetings, working on an election campaign, and running for office). Four groups of women were surveyed: Moscow activists, Ivanovo activists, participants in a Moscow women's consciousness-raising group (Klub Garmoniia), and a group of unemployed women attending retraining classes in Ivanovo. The vast majority (69 percent) of those surveyed stated that they had no plans to attend rallies or meetings. The only respondents to answer the question about rallying in the affirmative were eight Moscow activists. The respondents planning to rally were affiliated with a variety of organizational types, some explicitly feminist, and other explicitly not so. Those expecting to demonstrate represent a range of age groups, from twenty-seven to fifty-five. This data, though a small sample, supports the information found by Sillaste's poll; only a small minority include demonstrating in their personal plans to enact social change.

How then can the demonstrations that *have* occurred with the participation of women's groups be explained? It seems likely that the mass-meeting activity of the pro-communist Congress of Soviet Women is a well-entrenched tactic inherited from the Soviet era and carried on by the Working Russia party, which would hardly frown on the idea of provoking renewed instability in Russia. It is harder to explain the demonstration tactics of the Committee of Soldiers' Mothers. It may be that, confronted with the death (or imminent death) of their sons, the Soldiers' Mothers feel a sense of desperation enabling them to overcome any fear of negative repercussions. More relevant, however, may be the fact that the CSM began its activities at the peak of the protest cycle, not at its end, as did most of the other women's organizations in Moscow. In explaining small protest actions like the march and vigil held on International Women's Day 1996, we can perhaps point to some degree

Table 3. *"Do you plan to take part in rallies and meetings* [mitingi i sobraniia]?"

	Yes (percentage)	No (percentage)	Undecided (percentage)	
Moscow activists	21	49	30	100% (n = 37)
Ivanovo activists	0	100	0	100% (n = 5)
Klub Garmoniia participants	0	89	11	100% (n = 9)
Unemployed women (Ivanovo)	0	87	13	100% (n = 23)

of Western influence, and to the fact that, while such demonstrations are public, and do express discontent with the status quo, they do so in a small-scale and nonthreatening manner, consistent with preserving and increasing social peace. On the whole, however, mass mobilization seems only a peripheral part of the Russian women's movement's collective action repertoire at present.

Conclusion

The women's movement in contemporary Russia is still a relative new-comer to the political stage. It is possible that the movement opts for small-scale actions rather than mobilization simply because it is new. But this is not a compelling argument. After all, Western social move-ments – including the US women's movement that emerged from the New Left, and the US gay rights movement that blossomed in 1969 – did not wait long before holding large public protests, which served in part to attract attention from the public and from decisionmakers, and helped inspire interest in and attention to movement causes.[120]

The impact of Russian political history on the women's movement's

---

[120] Katsiaficas dates the contemporary US women's movement's emergence to the late 1960s. Autonomous groups formed in 1967, and rapidly acquired a national focus. A national convention was held at the end of 1968. By August 1970, over 10,000 women had been mobilized to march down Fifth Avenue in New York City, while more modest-sized demonstrations were held across the country. Compared with the Russian women's movement's experience, this is a rapid transition from autonomous organization to national, mass mobilization. See George Katsiaficas, *The Imagination of the New Left: A Global Analysis of 1968* (Boston: South End Press, 1987), pp. 76–77, 148–50.

internal dynamics and organization, as well as on its interaction with the state, is a significant part of the opportunity structure in which that movement operates. The political history of institutions (totalitarian or participatory), of civil society's development (networked or atomized), and of cycles of protest and defining historical events have a significant effect on social movements, including on their propensity for mass mobilization.

None of this is to say that the situation in Russia's women's movement cannot and will not change. Even by holding small public actions like the women's demonstration against violence held on March 8, 1996, women's groups are showing the extent to which they are struggling successfully for change within a polity shaped by decades of totalitarian control. Also, the fact that women's groups are starting to engage the print and electronic media in discourse about feminism and women's issues is indicative of a trend toward attempting to shape public opinion, which could complement the tendency to focus on insular contacts with policymakers.

Finally, the fact that Russian women's groups do not engage in much protesting yet refer to themselves as being part of a social movement reminds us that we have to understand their movement in the context of a different political history. At base, social movements are conglomerations of people and organizations striving to create social change and redistribute power: whether on the cultural, economic, or political level – or on any and all three. The political history that pervades social movements' experience shapes the means they adopt to create that social change, the structures they choose, the dynamics internal to the movement, and the political system in which they operate. Decisions made by social movement leaders reflect a political-historical opportunity structure as well as current political and economic ones. Yet social movements are also embedded in an international context that creates obstacles and opportunities of its own.

7   International influences on the Russian women's movement

> This struggle for Western friends, for contacts, for influence, for the possibility to travel to the West, it has a very strong effect. But I think we'll live through it.[1]

As we saw in chapter 4, the UN Decade for Women (1976–85) allowed for expanded contacts with the West, and its echoes even played a small part in changing the political opportunity structure for Russian women with feminist viewpoints. This is only one aspect of the larger role played by the West, and by international organizations, in the Russian women's movement. New contacts with foreign women and their organizations, access to Western feminist literature, the opportunity to travel to the West, the availability of Western funding for Russian women's organizations (in the 1990s), a plethora of Western-sponsored training sessions and seminars for women, international conferences on women's issues, and the growing knowledge of international laws and standards regarding discrimination against women – all exerted influence on the development and dynamics of the Russian women's movement. Perhaps most importantly, in its struggle to frame issues of discrimination, the Russian women's movement has adopted the language of international documents, such as International Labor Organization (ILO) and UN resolutions, and has succeeded to some degree in framing women's issues in Russia as international issues, which grants the women's groups and their demands a certain amount of leverage in their interactions with the Russian government. Had society's near absence of contact with the West persisted, it would have produced a completely different contemporary women's movement in Russia, had one emerged at all.

By no means did Russia lack a women's movement until contacts with the West were expanded in the perestroika and glasnost period. Indeed, the Russian women's movement at the turn of the last century was a

---

[1] Interview, name withheld.

strong and viable one.[2] Its history, however, is only just beginning to receive attention in Russia, along with attention to early Russian feminists and their work. But when the movement resurfaced in the late 1980s, it found itself in an entirely new context, part of a world in which women's movements had already been established in many countries, but not in its own.

There is growing interest in the study of international influences on social movements. Scholars writing on women's movements, for example, have long pointed to the ongoing tensions between "global" and "local" feminisms, and to the perceived "cultural imperialism" of Western feminists.[3] Others studying the international aspect of social movement development have investigated the role of global communication in the spread of ideas and tactics[4] and the phenomenon of crossnational "spinoff" movements.[5] The role of "transnational advocacy networks" has also been the subject of study in recent years, as the boundaries between civil societies across the globe decay.[6]

Yet the transnational sharing of ideas may be joined or supplemented by the transnational flow of funding. The international "diffusion" of ideas as well as funding has been central to the Russian women's movement. Social movement theorists focusing on resource mobilization suggest that movements can become activated only when sufficient financial means to organize and propagandize have been accumulated. In the Russian case, those resources have come in part from Western organizations, including the US government, through the US Agency for International Development (USAID), and several private foundations. What resource mobilization theory does not discuss, however, is the strings that may be attached to funding, and what the ramifications of accepting funding from foreign governmental and organizational sources may be for a social movement. Along with providing crucial support for movement organizations, foreign-based aid can have unintended side effects, exacerbating divisiveness between groups, and can also play an influential role in setting movement priorities and tactics.

This chapter illustrates the importance of Western aid and influence

[2] See Richard Stites, *The Women's Liberation Movement in Russia* (Princeton: Princeton University Press, 1978).
[3] See, for instance, Chandra Mohanty, ed., *Third World Women and the Politics of Feminism* (Bloomington: Indiana University Press, 1991).
[4] See George Katsiaficas, *The Imagination of the New Left: A Global Analysis of 1968* (Boston: South End Press, 1987).
[5] See Doug McAdam, "Conceptual Origins, Current Problems, Future Directions," in McAdam, John D. McCarthy, and Mayer M. Zald, eds., *Comparative Perspectives on Social Movements* (Cambridge: Cambridge University Press, 1996), p. 33.
[6] Margaret Keck and Kathryn Sikkink, *Activists Beyond Borders: Transnational Advocacy Networks in International Politics* (Ithaca: Cornell University Press, 1998).

to the contemporary Russian women's movement and the ways in which that aid and influence have served to promote and challenge the movement, as it grows and develops. As we shall see, the Russian women's movement is embedded in an international environment which shapes the varied domestic opportunity structures addressed in previous chapters. In short, international influences alter the movement's political and economic opportunities, and even affect activists' choice of the words they use to discuss and frame their issues.

Western influence on the movement's origins

Women in Russia have taken a variety of paths to their activism, and have chosen to form women's organizations for many reasons. In interviews, one of the most oft-repeated paths to involvement in the women's movement was contact with the West, whether through reading Western feminist literature, meeting foreigners, or traveling abroad. Nearly half of the Moscow activists responding to questions about their paths to activism and the formation of their organizations mentioned some connection to the West. None of the respondents in Ivanovo and Cheboksary mentioned such influences as being causal to their drive to become activists, probably because access to Western literature and foreigners would have been far more limited in those cities (and in the provinces in general) than in Moscow. Aside from Western influences, activists in all three cities mentioned several forces leading them to activism, including: sensing the "need" to improve women's status, or to "help women"; discrimination they observed or experienced; encouragement from friends; hearing lectures on the women's movement or on feminism; and, in a few cases, having been forced to change their dissertation topic to focus on women.

Numerous women activists, particularly those with advanced degrees, mentioned that their exposure to Western feminist literature had been important to their activism and to the way they thought about women's status in Russian society. Olga Voronina, at the Moscow Center for Gender Studies (MCGS), for example, was drawn to Betty Friedan's analysis of women's social status while writing her dissertation on the sociology of the family in the late 1970s:

I didn't want to write a dissertation on Soviet family sociology, because I knew it would all be false and uninteresting, so I decided to write about American family sociology. And when I went to the library, I naturally began to run across feminist literature. And the first book I read was Betty Friedan's *Feminine Mystique*, which made an extraordinarily deep impression on me, with its expressiveness. I know there are faults with it, but for its time it was unbelievable. I fell into that literature, and understood that I knew nothing about myself as a woman, or about what it means to be a woman in this society, and it became really interesting to me. I wrote my dissertation and defended it with great pleasure.[7]

Valentina Konstantinova, like Voronina, an activist and academic at MCGS, explained how Western feminist literature inspired her to write about women's issues, long before MCGS was formed, and when information about Western women's movements was still kept under wraps:

I wanted to study women's issues; I'm not sure why, maybe out of personal experience, and after all there were these dual standards for women all the time . . . So, at first I decided to study women, but had rejected the communist approach, the Marxist–Leninist approach to solving the woman question. And in general, all the topics were so boring, when I looked at the dissertations on women, it was like, "The International Women's Democratic Federation in the Struggle for Peace," or "The Socialist International and the Woman Question," or "The Participation of Women in the Great Patriotic War," "The Increased Political Activity of Women in Central Asia, Tadzhikistan," etc. I had terrible yearnings . . . But then I started somehow to look at more of these journals. See, I was looking at literature from England and the USA, in English. [I was working at the Higher Party School, under the Central Committee of the CPSU], and the English Communist Party journal, "Marxism Today," was in the section of the library for special access only [spetskhran]. That journal printed some articles, and the feminist wing of the British Communist Party was relatively strong, and my interest began to be roused.[8]

Two women who helped found another academic gender studies center, in the Institute of Ethnology and Anthropology, also pointed to the link between Western information and how they became interested in studying women's issues in the USSR:

That's the question of questions, in this country, where that theme wasn't visible. We'd studied foreign materials our whole lives, mostly from America. And, in accordance with our scientific interests, and our internal women's interests, and perhaps by intellectual inclination, we chose this issue, out of all the others we'd worked on. Then we understood that we didn't have our *own* material . . . And when we started studying it, people didn't understand us at all. When we said we wanted to study an issue, not a region, people didn't understand us; people here worked on regions, like North America, by countries. And that's when we [formed the Center] . . . we ended up with a group of nine.[9]

If individual exposure to Western feminist literature spurred a certain amount of radicalization, in some cases, meeting foreigners spurred

---

[7] Ol'ga Voronina, interview, April 27, 1995.
[8] Valentina Konstantinova, interview, July 9, 1995.
[9] Interview, December 6, 1994.

actual involvement in women's organizations. One of the leaders of a women's rights advocacy organization, Equality and Peace, described the organization's founding as having been inspired by her work with the UN, in Europe, and her contact with representatives of a major international women's organization, the Women's International League for Peace and Freedom.[10] Larisa Podgorbunskaia, head of the International Association of Russian Women-Mothers, also emphasized the role played by a foreign women's group in the development of her organization:

Yeltsin went to Italy in 1992. The president of the academy [where I was working] also went to Italy . . . And Italian families were asking to take Russian children as guests, to Italy. They asked for orphans, children from the Chernobyl region, etc. And our embassy there introduced us to women from an Italian organization called "Women-Housewives." They're one of the patrons of our association. Despite the name, many of the women who run the movement "Women-Housewives" are not in fact housewives: they are journalists, have responsible posts, even in parliament; one has a high post in the chamber of commerce . . . We invited these Italian women to Moscow . . . The Italian women started sending us humanitarian aid, and we gave it out to orphanages here. And then we got the idea (plus, they asked us) to organize an international organization, because it would be easier to collaborate. So we became a part of the Italian organization.[11]

One of the early leaders of the Russian Association of University Women (RAUW) also pointed to the central role played by an international parent organization – the International Federation of University Women (IFUW) – in the her organization's formation:

I was invited to Geneva, [to participate in a conference] about the results of nuclear explosions in Nevada and Semipalatinsk. Women came up to me after my lecture, gave me the charter from the IFUW. At that time, there was only the Soviet Women's Committee, and no one could have imagined creating others . . . We registered officially in April 1992; before that, there were negotiations with the IFUW: ours is a branch of that organization.[12]

Meeting Western women had changed her expectations about the possibility of organizing, ultimately leading her to get involved in creating an independent women's group.

The Feminist Orientation Center, a group with very different roots from Equality and Peace, the Russian Women-Mothers, and the RAUW, began in 1990 as a type of consciousness-raising group among several women working at the School of Cultural Policy, an educational

---

[10] Interview, October 28, 1994.
[11] Larisa Podgorbunskaia, interview, May 4, 1995.
[12] Interview, November 20, 1994.

consulting organization, and then acquired more of an outward focus, as the result of joint work with foreigners:

We talked about our life histories; I know now that it was like consciousness-raising. Then a friend of ours came over from Helsinki, and wrote a book on female sex-socialization. We liked it. We started working with a group of Finnish women. Our first project was the "History of the Body" project. We did seminars with the Finns, and wrote about them in the new issue of *Preobrazhenie* [a feminist journal], an article on menstruation. So, we started our research collective, and realized we could do research for others . . . Then we started doing social/public activity [*obshchestvennaia deiatel'nost'*], not just research. In 1993, we registered with the Ministry of Justice, at the Moscow level, as a social organization, and started conducting training sessions.[13]

In several instances, Russian women's groups began as a direct result of contact with Westerners, or because of a desire for that contact. This motivated the formation of the Women's League, according to Elena Ershova:

As with all movements, it began in a rather ad hoc way. At the end of 1991, I was in the USA, and met women from Women's World Banking. I made a lot of new contacts in the women's movement. And then, sitting here in my living room with several colleagues, we talked about how we'd lose our contacts, and decided to hold a conference, so as to maintain the contacts and realize them.[14]

The conference was held in Moscow, in September 1992, with four representatives of Women's World Banking taking part. One of the Women's League's organizational members, the Center for Business Assistance to Women: Perepodgotovka, run by Marina Pavlova, also began with a communion of interests between Western and Russian initiative groups:

At that very time, there were some French women interested in our work. We worked with them; they helped us: they were interested in professional orientation (orienting each person to their own skills, inclinations, and to the job *they* want to do). We worked with the French organization called "Return to Work" (Retravailler). Their methods are oriented toward women. They found the money for it. We went to France for two months to learn their methods. In 1993, we changed our name to Perepodgotovka, and started spread the method of returning to work, based on the French methodology. We now have four Russians who went and were educated in France. We four can also now train *multiplikatory*: those who train trainers, as well as teaching women directly.[15]

About one-third of the total number of activists interviewed mentioned having traveled abroad, usually to the West, although the number may be higher. In some cases, such travel expanded women's horizons,

---

[13] Interview, December 7, 1994.
[14] Elena Ershova, interview, April 18, 1995.
[15] Marina Pavlova, interview, April 24, 1995.

and led to a desire to organize. Two of the founders of Moscow's feminist lecture and discussion group, Klub F-1, explained that they had been inspired to start the club while in Paris, attending an international seminar on feminism:

In 1992 at the seminar in Paris, that's when the feeling arose that we had to do something, more quickly. I knew a lot of people who were studying this theme – historians, political scientists – without a feminist perspective, and thought, we have to combine them.[16]

In some cases, travel abroad provoked changes in consciousness about lesbian rights, a subject which until quite recently was almost entirely invisible. Said one activist with an advocacy organization, the Inform Center of the Independent Women's Forum,

I had problems with lesbians at first. I'd never encountered that. They only surfaced with perestroika. At a congress in Prague, in 1992, I met some lesbians. It was shocking. I thought about it a lot, and I've decided, it's from god. And if someone asks me, how do you relate to lesbians, now, I'd say, How do you relate to your own right hand? It's natural.[17]

One of the leaders of MOLLI, the Moscow Organization of Lesbian Literature and Art, described a similar process:

During the recent trip to Atlanta [for a training session], with fifty-five women from all over the CIS [Commonwealth of Independent States], all the women got to hear about MOLLI, some for the first time. At first, the ones from Georgia and Armenia had a negative reaction. They were suspicious. But they came around . . . Asya [Posadskaia] and others said the women's movement had turned a bit "blue [*pogolubela*, slang for homosexual]" after we all returned. It's a good thing.[18]

In sum, contact with the West, whether through academic literature, meetings with foreigners, or actual exposure to the culture and organizing activities of Western women, has had a significant effect on the Russian women's movement, especially in Moscow. Some women started organizations because they were inspired by experiences abroad, or by what they had read, as the new possibility of pluralism opened up for them at home. Others came across new ideas, such as discrimination, and were forced to consider issues to which they might otherwise have remained unexposed. Some activists were inspired to expand the reach of their groups, to form new organizations, and to create branches of international organizations, after contact with foreigners. Both Voronina and Konstantinova, two of the founders of LOTOS, who later worked for the Moscow Center for Gender Studies, pointed to the

[16] Interview, November 2, 1994.
[17] Tat'iana Troinova, interview, April 19, 1995.
[18] Interview, November 27, 1994.

importance of Western feminist literature in their thinking and their work. Exposure to the West had an effect not only on feminist-identified groups: the Association of Women-Mothers and the Perepodgotovka Center for Business Assistance to Women do not self-identify as feminist, yet each of their leaders noted the key role of Westerners or travel to the West in their organizing experience. Certainly, in the realm of ideas, exposure to the Western women's movement played a significant role in the origins of contemporary Russian feminist groups, but for the women's groups that fall outside that category it was no less important.

Foreign lending agencies' influence

While ideational exposure to the Western world and its women's organizations has had an important impact on the formation and development of the Russian women's movement, Western influence has also had far more concrete consequences. For example, the International Monetary Fund (IMF) and World Bank's influence on Russia's economic reforms, mostly by insisting on the separation of the industrial and social welfare spheres, cutting social welfare benefits, and implementing industrial restructuring, has created some external stimuli for women's organizing. Women suffer most as a result of industrial restructuring and the unemployment it produces: in 1993, 34 percent of women and 22 percent of men gave "liquidation of the enterprise" as their "reason for becoming unemployed among workers with job experience," whereas 43 percent of men and 32 percent of women said they became unemployed "voluntarily."[19] Thus, the demands of Western – or international – lending agencies provide (albeit indirectly) part of the stimulus for the formation of women's self-help associations, as well as for reeducation and employment-training programs.

Foreign aid as a source of income for women's movement groups

Impoverishment at the hands of international lending agencies, however, has a flip side: foreign aid. At present, foreign granting organizations provide one of the main funding sources for Russian women's groups. Although foreign government and foundation money for women's movement groups provides a rather shaky ground for future organizing (since state foreign aid budgets can be cut, and

[19] Liam Halligan, "Unemployment by Gender," LSE and Working Centre for Economic Reform, Government of the Russian Federation, data from the Russian Federal Unemployment Service, 1993.

foundations can reassess their priorities), the fact remains that Western granting organizations are one of the only sources of funding in a society where charitable contributions from the rich have not been institutionalized as a societal norm, and fundraising is still unpopular. Similarly, the lack of financing or technical assistance from the Russian state leads women's groups to seek Western resources to fund their activities and programs. This occurs on a rather wide scale.

Activist interviews revealed that, as of mid-1995, few organizations were receiving any type of domestic funding, other than occasional "in kind" donations, such as office space. While four of the nine operative women's groups interviewed in Ivanovo and Cheboksary had received some kind of domestic funding, such funding sources in Moscow were infrequent. Of thirty-seven Moscow-based organizations, ten mentioned some kind of local funding, often in exchange for training programs (in such cases, the funds came from the federal employment services). Other sources of local funding included donations from: individuals (including group members); Russian companies (Aeroflot, for example, provided discount tickets to the Russian Women-Mothers group that sends children to Italy for rest and recuperation); other Russian women's groups; banks (three instances); and, in once case, a local bread factory. Of those ten, however, four also noted foreign sponsorship. In interviews, representatives of fifteen Moscow-based organizations noted a foreign grant of some kind, or assistance from foreigners ("friends") and foreign organizations.[20] By the end of 1995, at least four more organizations in my sample had received foreign grants indirectly from USAID. In total, foreign funding was noted by just over half of the Moscow groups interviewed for this study. Although Western funding did not create the movement in Moscow, it provides significant and valuable sponsorship.[21]

Western funding of women's organizations in Russia takes diverse forms. Western sources fund: newsletters, journals, and books;

---

[20] These include: Aid to Artisans, the Canadian Embassy, Caritas, Ford Foundation, Frauen Anstiftung (a German feminist fund), IREX/Eurasia, MacArthur Foundation, Soros Foundation, and Women's World Banking.

[21] According to program officer Chris Kedzie, between 1994 and 1996, the Ford Foundation granted $250,000 to the Inform Center; $200,000 to the US–NIS Consortium; $75,000 to the Moscow Center for Gender Studies, which held a summer school for the purpose of developing a gender studies curriculum; and $50,000 to Ecojuris-WLED (Women Lawyers for the Environment and Development). The Eurasia Foundation, which was created by the US State Department and funded through USAID, awarded grants totaling approximately $900,000, directed toward working with Russian women and women's organizations (including business-training seminars for women, and program support for women's NGOs) between May 1993 and May 1996.

conferences, seminars, and training sessions; email networks; and technological support (fax and photocopy machines, etc.). They also give direct grants to women's groups for diverse projects, including travel to international conferences.

Women's movement organizations in Russia publish precious few newsletters and journals, mostly for reasons of financial constraint. Those that are published, however, serve as essential information conduits across the network of women's organizations in Russia. Of the extant small-run independent women's movement newsletters and journals – *Vy i my* (You and We), *Zhenshchina plius* (Woman Plus), *FemInf* (Feminist Informational Journal), *Vestnik* (Bulletin), *Vse liudi sestry* (All People Are Sisters), and *Preobrazhenie* (Transfiguration) – all but *FemInf* and *Preobrazhenie* are funded by Western sources.[22] Foreigners have also paid for the publication of information documenting the major events of the Russian women's movement: the Concluding Document of the First Independent Women's Forum (March 1991) and a directory of participants and book of materials from the Second Independent Women's Forum (November 1992) were financed by contributions from American supporters and the Dutch women's group, Ariadna, respectively. Western money also provided for the publication of several important books in 1996, including a Russian version of *Our Bodies, Ourselves* – the only Russian-language text on women's health, written from an empowering, feminist perspective. Progress publishers produced the book, with funding from an American (Katrina vanden Heuvel), and it was distributed throughout Russia, by the USAID-funded US–NIS Consortium of Women's Organizations, based in Moscow. Also, the first Russian-language text treating the issue of sexual harassment in Russia, based on the materials from a 1995 seminar held in Moscow, called *Sexual Harassment at Work* (*Seksual'nye presledovaniia na rabote*), was published with funding from the American Bar Association, the Consortium, and USAID, in an edition of 1,100 copies.[23] Laden with data almost impossible to find in the public domain, on harassment and

---

22 *Vy i my* is a US–Russian journal with information about US and Russian women's movement activities, financed by Colette Shulman and Katrina vanden Heuvel (through fundraising efforts; later, distribution was covered in part by a MacArthur Foundation grant); *Zhenshchina plius* is a publication of ZhIF (Women's Innovation Fund East–West), funded by Frauen Anstiftung; *Vestnik* is the newsletter of the Inform Center of the Independent Women's Forum, financed by the Ford Foundation; *Vse liudi sestry* is the journal of the Petersburg Center for Gender Issues, financed by Frauen Anstiftung. These are all small-run publications.

23 Two Moscow-based women's groups, the ADL (Archive–Database–Library) and the Feminist Orientation Center, both of which have foreign funding, paid for transcribing the seminar tapes. See Zoia Khotkina, ed., *Seksual'nye domogatel'stva na rabote* (Moscow: ABA-CEELI, Zhenskii konsortium, and MCGS, 1996), p. 12.

violence against women, the book provides a resource for people working on these issues in isolation from each other. Foreign funding, in such cases, makes available a great deal of information that would otherwise be restricted to a mere handful of people. Many activists, however, felt that Western foundations paid too little attention to funding publications. Olga Voronina put it this way:

One of the main problems of the Russian women's movement is a total lack of literature. In the West, it was simultaneous: the appearance of books, pamphlets, articles, distributing them to the women's movement. We don't have that. We don't have our own books; there's nothing to begin with. We've wanted to start a publishing project in the MCGS [Moscow Center for Gender Studies], but the Western foundations aren't supportive of that, of translating Western feminist works. Training groups, seminars – absolutely. But I think we've already overfed ourselves on [ob'elis'] these seminars. They're local. A book has a more widespread resonance.[24]

Given the centrality of literature to movement growth, the fact that the West is one of the only sources of funding for feminist publications (however slight) suggests that, without Western funding, movement chances for expansion would be slim indeed.

Despite the growing desire within the Russian women's movement for foreign funding of books (translations as well as publication of Russian texts), a far greater share of Western money goes toward funding seminars, training sessions, and conferences. Some of these are jointly operated; others are run by Russian women's groups alone. There is a fair amount of debate over the utility of Western-sponsored training seminars, most of which fall into categories spanning a predictable spectrum: "Leadership Training," "Fundraising," "NGO Management," "Lobbying," "Coalition-Building," "Planning a Socio-Political Agenda," and so on. The National Democratic Institute and International Republican Institute (both funded by the US government) sponsor such events on a regular basis. Western women's groups like the League of Women Voters also acquire funding in order to hold joint seminars with Russian partners. Other women's groups apply for Western funding to sponsor their own conferences; one three-day conference in 1995, held by an association of women in Russia's ailing military industry (Conversion: Myths and Realities), brought together funding from a variety of such sources. Similarly, MOLLI (Moscow Organization of Lesbian Literature and Art) held a conference in April 1995 called Women and Society, sponsored by a grant from the USAID-funded Consortium.

Starting with the First and Second Independent Women's Forums,

[24] Ol'ga Voronina, interview, April 27, 1995.

networking at conferences has been one of the only opportunities for Russian women activists to encounter each other, exchange information about their projects, and engage in joint project formation. Foreign grants enable conference organizers to bring activists in from cities located a considerable distance from Moscow. Absent that funding, such activists remain stranded and isolated. Without Western funding, the frequency and reach of such seminars and conferences would be considerably smaller; similarly, networking and information exchange would be even more limited.

This fact has important ramifications for the women's movement's ability to affect state policy. In order to produce national-level campaigns, women activists from organizations within and outside Moscow need the opportunity to come together to determine priorities, discuss strategies, and share information. Even with Western funding, such opportunities are limited.

Western organizations also provide technical and program support to a variety of Russian women's groups on a competitive basis. The USAID-funded Consortium, for example, gives out mini-grants (up to $3,000) for Russian women's organizations' initiatives across Russia.[25] Also, several foundations held competitions for individual women activists' travel funding to the UN's Fourth World Conference on Women and the concomitant NGO Forum, held in Beijing in 1995. Without these funds, many of the 200 Russian women who attended would have been unable to afford their trips, keeping the independent Russian women's movement isolated from activists in other countries. This instance of foreign funding has particular resonance in terms of coalition-building. At the behest of Martina Vandenberg (the American coordinator of the Consortium), several foreign foundations decided to hold a joint funding competition, administered by an organizing committee with representatives of the four major women's networks in Moscow: the Women's League, the Union of Russia's Women, the Inform Center of the Independent Women's Forum, and the US–NIS Consortium. According to one of the organizing committee members, this was the "first coalition and first positive collaborative experience of Russia's major women's organizations" (the first three did not tend to work together or to get along, at that time), and she evaluated their work

[25] The Consortium had a grant of $95,000 from USAID, through the Eurasia foundation for "seed grants to NIS women's NGOs to meet program needs, develop a cadre of trained trainers, provide technical services to women's organizations, and improve communication through email and newsletters between NGOs. The Consortium will also work to increase the visibility of women's NGO contributions in the transformation process to a democratic society." See Network of East–West Women (newsletter of group of the same name), Fall 1994, p. 17.

as successful and "friendly."[26] In this case, Western foundations were indirectly responsible for fostering a working relationship between organizations previously on rather unfriendly terms.

The West also funds the development of email networks in Russia. In a society where the cost of long-distance telephone calls is becoming prohibitive, and where mailing information is both expensive and unreliable, email takes on a new importance. The Network of East–West Women initiated the first program to link women in the former communist bloc countries, hooking women's groups throughout Russia and Eastern Europe up to an email conference which lists information about women's groups and events in the United States, Russia, and Eastern Europe. The program is funded by the Ford and MacArthur Foundations, and by World Learning, Inc., and the Eurasia Foundation, which, in turn, are both recipients of USAID monies.[27]

USAID itself has a granting program called Support for Women's Initiatives, the goal of which is to assist in developing a space for NGO-sector activity in Russia, and to build ties between NGOs and the commercial and governmental sectors, in order to enrich the democratic and economic reforms in Russia. According to an announcement of their June 1995 grant competition published in a women's movement newsletter, "The development of a nongovernmental, noncommercial sector, representing a wide spectrum of organizations through which people can express themselves, and guarantee their needs, is a necessary component of the reform process."[28] The ramifications of foreign governments pursuing goals through the funding of indigenous NGOs are far-reaching and complex.

Side effects of Western funding

Despite the obvious benefits of foreign aid, the injection of money into a relatively impoverished system produces a number of side effects bemoaned by activists – beneficiaries and nonbeneficiaries alike. While the money is welcomed, some women have raised concerns about some of its effects on the movement. One problem is equal access. Networking between women's groups and activists does take place, but a frequent critique is that *odni i te zhe* (the same old people) appear at each conference and seminar; in other words, that an "in" clique of women's groups has formed, and that outsiders have a hard time breaking in.

[26] Elizaveta Bozhkova, "Chto dni v Pekine nam gotoviat i chto gotovim my v Pekin?," *Strategii vzaimodeistviia*, October 1995, p. 29.
[27] See *Network of East–West Women*, Summer 1995, p. 1.
[28] *Vestnik*, no. 2–3, 1995.

Information on grants is sometimes published in small-run women's newsletters, which are far from available to everyone. To the credit of Western granting agencies, some, such as the Consortium, have made a clear effort to announce grant competitions at all kinds of women's movement events: at Union of Russia's Women conferences, Women's League events, and Independent Women's Forum events, as well as at Consortium meetings.

Despite efforts to the contrary on the part of some grantors, the most striking side effect of foreign grants is divisiveness. With the exception of travel and research grants, Western granting agencies in Russia give grants to organizations, not to individuals. Usually, it is only the leaders of the recipient organization who will gain a salary from the grant. Thus, in order for as many people as possible to get funding, the logic of the situation demands fragmentation into myriad groups, each boasting their own program. In a rather cynical article on the National Endowment for Democracy and its pretenses to "export democracy" and "promote the growth of what is called 'civil society' in Eastern Europe," David Samuels wrote, "As one might guess, the availability of dollars for NGOs is leading to their proliferation."[29] Foreigners, however, have no monopoly on cynicism. Olga Samarina, an official heading the Ministry of Social Protection's department on women's issues, bluntly argued that the lure of getting a free trip to Beijing for the UN's Fourth World Conference on Women was the cause for women's organizations' proliferation in Russia:

Far from all of the women leaders who run various NGOs formed their organizations in order to solve women's actual problems. Very often they formed in order to solve some concrete problems of the actual woman leader herself, her own problems: acquiring status, social status, political points . . . For example, the Beijing conference is coming up. There's the possibility to get accreditation and go to Beijing. There is a growth of NGOs: because they can form themselves quickly, get accredited, and the leaders go off to Beijing. They form these organizations, they come to the National Council [on Preparation for Beijing]. They speak there. And sometimes . . . it's clear that there's no program there at all. But the woman is there, she's visible. She's there once, twice, ten times: and then, you see, she's become a leader![30]

Similarly, a Russian publicist, long familiar with women's organizing in Russia and the Soviet Union, argued that many of the independent Russian women's groups exist merely to get foreign grants and trips abroad:

[29] David Samuels, "At Play in the Fields of Oppression," *Harper's Magazine*, May 1995, p. 47.
[30] Ol'ga Samarina, interview, March 24, 1995.

These women's groups exist to affirm their own existence. Women's groups have become prestigious, so they're popping up in all the regions. It's like an attempt to copy the social scenery of Europe and the USA. They get grants . . . All these women's groups seek US friends, to travel abroad. They try to deceive people with false impressions of themselves, just in order to go abroad . . . I don't wish to throw stones at the women who want to go to the West. I understand it. But it makes the women's movement into one big cultural exchange program [*moshnyi kulturnyi obmen*].[31]

To the extent that organizations proliferate and undergo a type of meiosis in order to get grants and travel to the West, those that are successful in this endeavor (whether motivated by sincerity or otherwise) are often accused of trying to monopolize the Western contacts that they have acquired. Some activists accuse the Union of Russia's Women (URW) of monopolizing contacts with the West:

It was enough to have the Soviet Women's Committee, which in fact subsumed all the interests of other organizations, personifying them only in itself. And now, the Union of Russia's Women is becoming that type of organization . . . trying to represent all women's organizations in itself. And that's wrong. That organization is significantly bigger than the others, you have to admit that objectively, they have more experience, and a traditional base, but it's a social organization of *regional* significance, and I can't understand why it's precisely *that* organization that's got to represent the whole Russian women's movement in international forums. I am categorically opposed to that. Monopolism hasn't been outlived yet.[32]

Indeed, in an interview, a representative of the Union of Russia's Women explained to me that, although the URW was completely different from the old Soviet Women's Committee, they had maintained the latter's international department, with the express purpose of retaining their international connections:

When the Soviet Union's structures collapsed, and when the republic women's organizations went their separate ways, the only thing left was the Union of Russia's Women (URW) – and it was logical to take over the continuation of the Soviet Women's Committee (SWC) international ties. There was at that time a meeting of the former leaders of the former SWC, to decide what to do with the enormous baggage of these international ties. They decided that it was the URW's responsibility as the inheritor, to continue those ties. And that those who worked in the international division would come and work for the new organization.[33]

Likewise, several interviewees criticized the Moscow Center for Gender Studies – an organization historically counterposed to the Union of Russia's Women – of trying to keep their Western contacts for them-

---

[31] Interview, June 25, 1995.
[32] Galina Sillaste, interview, March 28, 1995.
[33] Interview, February 2, 1995.

selves, of "facing the West" exclusively, publishing primarily in English, in order to maintain contacts with foreign granting sources.[34] These kinds of perceptions make it rather difficult for various women's groups to cooperate, whether out of feelings of jealousy, or out of the belief in maintaining some distance from Western funding.

Russia's political history suggests multiple reasons why Russian women's organizations choose not to collaborate with each other, especially across the main networks in Moscow. Western funding contributes to the lack of cohesion, but does not single-handedly cause it. Some activists do, however, attribute some of the disagreements between organizations and individual activists directly to the influx of funding (whether from foreign grants, or from the state):

Women's organizations saw their differences: some had technology, office space, and weren't badly off in the material sense. Others had no resources at all; lots of women were unemployed . . . Misunderstandings and conflicts began to arise between women's organizations. Outwardly, this was expressed in criticisms of the activity and personalities of other women – usually the active leaders of other groups. Moreover, some women thought that these differences did not need to be discussed. As a result, to this day, many unspoken grudges and resentments remain between women's organizations, which significantly complicates communication and joint activity.[35]

Many of the respondents in Moscow talked about intramovement competition over Western funding, benefits, and trips abroad, and believed that competition over funding detracts from organizations' ability and desire to work together, even when organizations are focused on similar issues. Said one activist:

A lot of it has to do with money. Don't quote me on this or I'll get it from all sides in the women's movement. But it has to do with the economic crisis in the country. Women intellectuals, first and foremost, are hit by the economic problems. The economic problems have led to (1) anxiety (across the country, not just in the women's movement); and (2) the fact that the various groups are in competition with each other for the same Western funding. If the Western foundations support *my* idea, I'll get funding for it. People end up saying, "We're more worthy than *them* – fund *us!*" This creates competition and disunity, which is exacerbated by the conditions of poverty [*nishcheta*].[36]

[34] Mariia Arbatova, interview, April 16, 1995. In 1998 alone, MCGS produced four Russian-language publications under their "Gender Expertise" Project, including: E. A. Balaeva, *Gendernaia ekspertiza zakonadetel'stva RF: reproduktivnye prava zhenshchin v Rossii*; M. E. Baskakova, *Ravnye vozmozhnosti i gendernye stereotipy na rynke truda*; N. P. Kosmarskaia, *"Zhenskoe izmerenie": vynuzhdennoi migratsii i migratsionnoe zakonodatel'stvo Rossii*; and O. A. Voronina, *Gendernaia ekspertiza zakonodatel'stva RF o stredstvakh massovoi informatsii*.

[35] Natal'ia Khodyreva, "Neperenosimost' razlichii," *Vse liudi sestry*, no. 5, pp. 32–33.

[36] Interview, name withheld.

The bottom line is, of course, the paucity of resources available to women's groups. The leader of Tvorchestvo put it bluntly:

Many organizations are afraid that others will hone in on their contacts with foreigners and get information about their grants and their sponsors, and then the field of competition would become broader.[37]

Were the fundraising base for women's organizations wider, the competition might be less intense.

These issues became particularly evident around acquiring funding for travel to Beijing for the UN's Fourth World Conference on Women, held in August–September 1995. Under conditions of limited resources, questions of justice and fair play arise. A discussion at a Consortium meeting in Moscow became quite heated one afternoon, when one activist accused another of already having acquired funding for the Beijing trip from another source.

Pluralism within social movements connotes a healthy diversity, and no one would argue for the need for (or desirability of) creating a single, unitary, all-encompassing women's organization to embody the movement in Moscow. Yet activists there argue that, although organizations might like to cooperate, the presence of foreign funding exacerbates preexisting constraints, and cooperation thus fails to occur. In short, given the frequency and charge of statements made by activists about Western funding, it seems fair to say that, while Western money increased the capacity of organizations to undertake projects, the structure of granting competitions has contributed to the competitive dynamics in the Moscow-based, national-level women's movement during the transition period.

Organizational structures and priorities

Another important concern among activists is that foreign foundations and governments are setting the rules about women's organizations' structures and priorities. One St. Petersburg activist mentioned this in an article on the fractures in the women's movement:

The foundations' strategies also had an influence on organizational structure, and on the choice of tasks. Because of the formal demands by the sponsors, a nonhierarchical organization changed into a traditional one, with hired workers who poorly understood the organization's mission.[38]

Martina Vandenberg, as the American coordinator of the Consortium, was at the center of one monetary distribution process, and also very

---

[37] Tat'iana Riabikina, interview, April 26, 1995.
[38] Khodyreva, "Neperenosimost' razlichii," p. 34.

well connected to the organizations receiving the grants. When asked what she thought about the distorting effect of granting agencies on the agenda of the women's movement, and/or on individual women's groups receiving grants, she responded:

The way the money distorts things is that it creates leadership hierarchies: you need a responsible director, an accountant – not a collective: that's how the granting agencies see it.[39]

An article by two long-standing activists, Marina Regentova and Natalia Abubikirova, further illustrates some of the disagreements over the role of Western funding in the development of the women's movement. In their article, the authors attribute the "schism [*raskol*]" in the Independent Women's Forum (the loose network of women's organizations associated with the First and Second Independent Women's Forums) in part to the presence of foreigners and foreign funding in the Russian women's movement:

Some foreigners, coming here to work, at first try to gather as many women's organizations around themselves as possible and then take it on themselves to administer them, using an open paternalism, instead of the proclaimed partnership. Unfortunately, the very organizations often happily welcome this, sometimes out of a lack of alternatives.[40]

Foreign funding creates a potentially troubling power relationship, not only between the funders and the recipient organizations, but also between individuals and organizations within the women's movement itself. Regentova and Abubikirova dissected the history of one women's advocacy organization, the Inform Center of the Independent Women's Forum, to illustrate the complex issues to which Western funding can give rise. That organization's roots lay in a "global project" ultimately funded by the Ford Foundation, but, in the authors' opinion, with unfortunate results. In short, argued the authors, starting in 1992, Western foundations had created a bureaucratic system in Russia, without intending to do so. Aside from its positive aspects:

The foundation system has in practice replaced the previous state system of ministries and departments, as far as the third [i.e., nonprofit] sector, including women's organizations, is concerned. The foundations' functions include distributing funds. And they act through a bureaucratic apparatus that they created themselves. And it is precisely in this sense that one can speak of the formation today of a new nomenklatura . . . within the women's movement. An example of this can easily be seen in the Inform Center, which called itself the Inform Center of the Independent Women's Forum.[41]

---

[39] Martina Vandenberg, interview (conducted in English), April 20, 1995.
[40] Marina Regentova and Natasha Abubikirova, no title, unpublished typescript, Moscow, 1995, pp. 13–14.
[41] Ibid., pp. 21–22.

The authors then proceed to tell the story of the global project funded by Ford, resulting in the Inform Center's formation. According to their account, a large number of women's organizations agreed to come together on the project, with thirty-seven separate projects. They agreed to a series of conditions, among which was "not to allow money to be concentrated in one person's hands; that there should be a true umbrella system, where power and control were not fixed in the hands of one or two individuals . . . But difficulties arose: the ideas of the project had to be brought into line with the requirements of the Ford Foundation." Those requirements amounted to this: the Ford Foundation would give money "for the institutionalization of the Forum, including the creation of an informational structure to serve it, and for support of real programs oriented toward concrete work with women. There was also supposed to be a link to the Beijing Conference."[42]

The story ended, in Regentova and Abubikirova's view, sadly. After receiving the Ford funding, the result, despite former agreements, was that the organizations that had entered the project lost their financial independence, and that the project's financing was "centralized – the money was concentrated practically in the hands of one person." The imagined umbrella structure had become a hierarchical one, with the Inform Center at its head.[43] Regentova and Abubikirova concluded that the Independent Women's Forum had become the "Dependent Independent Women's Forum," whose dependence "on Western funds alone is cause for alarm."[44] By contrast, the authors pointed out that the First Independent Women's Forum conference, held in March 1991, was sponsored by their organization – SAFO – which had raised money "with great difficulty, from Russian sponsors."[45] The implication was that control could be maintained only under conditions of financial independence from the West.

Western granting agencies have an effect not only on the structure of women's movement organizations, but also on the content of their activities – on women's groups priorities. Such agencies' priorities condition the choices that women's groups' make, when considering what projects might be fundable and, thus, which projects to submit for grants. For instance, activists in Russia have tended not to work on political campaigns for candidates who support women's rights; foreign funding for such work is less available than funds for activities that are not as overtly political. In fact, during the lead-up to Russia's 1995 parliamentary elections, activists were busy eagerly pursuing travel grants to enable them to attend the Beijing conference. Similarly, in

---

[42] Ibid., pp. 22–23.   [43] Ibid., p. 23.   [44] Ibid., p. 26.   [45] Ibid., p. 6.

their article, Regentova and Abubikirova suggested that the fate of the global project might have been different if Beijing had not been an issue: "Perhaps, the energy directed toward writing innumerable projects 'under the rubric of Beijing' would have given a major push toward developing real strategies and tactics for the development of Russian women's organizations, and for their actual inclusion into the international women's movement."[46]

Western funding and intramovement conflict in Ivanovo and Cheboksary

Western foundations and foreign government money are both less of a presence and less of a problem in the provinces. None of the women's groups interviewed in Cheboksary and Ivanovo mentioned any foreign funding source. Nor did any of the respondents in those cities mention any local intramovement competition over Western funding or contacts. Fractionalization, too, was not an issue.

In fact, there was a high degree of organizational cohesion in Ivanovo, with the local city *zhensovet* (women's council) serving as the umbrella organization for three separate organizations – the Committee of Single-Parent Families, the Committee of Multi-Child Families, and the Committee of Soldiers' Mothers – in addition to the four district-level *zhensovety*. The other two women's organizations in the city, the Center for the Social Support of Women and Families (an employment-training organization) and the Businesswomen's Club, were on excellent terms with each other, and also cooperated closely with the city *zhensovet*. The Businesswomen's Club was one of the founders of the Center for the Social Support of Women and Families, and had provided material support to the Committee of Single-Parent Families. The activists seemed quite familiar with each other's work and even family lives.

In Cheboksary, there had been no Western funding until May 1995, when the first internationally sponsored women's training seminar was held in Cheboksary (by American activist Sarah Harder and the Russian women's group Prolog). At that point, a small amount of money was given to the local organizer – the Chuvash branch of the Russian Association of University Women (RAUW) – to pay for the seminar. As in Ivanovo, the city *zhensovet* in Cheboksary played a unifying role, though it had a conflictual relationship with the regional *zhensovet*, largely due to political differences between the chairwomen of each organization. The chair of the city *zhensovet*, Nina Petrova, was among

---

[46] Ibid., p. 23.

the founders of a newly forming club called Women's Initiative, which held its charter conference on May 30, 1995, thus bringing the number of women's organizations in the city to five. The list of club founders and those who attended the conference was quite inclusive. One of the speakers at the conference made favorable mention of the Chuvash branch of RAUW, and the "international seminar" it had sponsored, and said, "Our club will operate relying on the already existing movement and forces here,"[47] a statement that implied a future of collaboration. She also noted the importance of starting a foundation to support the club, based on the support of local factory directors. In addition to the two *zhensovety*, the RAUW, and the Businesswomen's Club, there was a Chuvash women's group supporting ecology and Chuvash culture, called Salam Bi. According to an interview with the co-leaders of that organization, they had sought neither sponsors nor funding from their members. For the most part, the women's movement in Cheboksary was so small that turf conflicts had not arisen, and so isolated that foreign funding had not really reached in to disturb the balance that existed as of 1995 in any significant way.

One cannot attribute the relative smoothness of relations between organizations in Ivanovo and Cheboksary entirely to the absence of Western funding. The cities are considerably smaller than Moscow, and lack the pervasive "politics" endemic to the nation's capital. However, even when asked directly about the obstacles to networking, Cheboksary and Ivanovo women's group leaders did not mention competition over funding. One Cheboksary woman mentioned a potential obstacle (most likely a reference to the city *zhensovet* leader):

Possibly the influence of the older set of women activists, which might hinder the establishment of a truly new kind of organization. If the people who are already in power positions enter this organization [the new branch of the RAUW], it won't come out ahead, maybe. Though it's hard to say. They'd end up making the organization like all the others have already been.[48]

Other group leaders from Cheboksary and Ivanovo stated outright that nothing hindered the development of ties between women's organizations in those cities. Even when asked directly about rivalry, the leader of Ivanovo's Committee of Single-Parent Families flatly denied such a problem, saying, "No, there's no rivalry, just solidarity."[49] This is notable because in Moscow interviewees would bring up the issue of rivalry on their own, and when asked directly about it, would readily

[47] Ol'ga Grigorievna Denisova, speech at Founding Conference of Club "Women's Initiative," May 30, 1995, Cheboksary, author's notes.
[48] Ol'ga Bubina, interview, May 31, 1995.
[49] Larisa Nazarova, interview, April 4, 1995.

expound on the issue. It may be that, in the provincial cities, there are few preexisting conflicts that the injection of funding could potentially highlight.

While the women's movement in Moscow relies to a large degree on Western funds for their projects, the women's movement organizations in Ivanovo and Cheboksary, whose programmatic goals are quite different from those of the Moscow groups, seem to be able to survive without it. The provincial groups are not attempting to maintain and build an extensive communication network across Russia, as is the Inform Center of the Independent Women's Forum, or to arrange Russia-wide conferences with hundreds of attendees. The point is not that the provincial organizations are well funded: according to their leaders, they most certainly are not. However, the funding needs of the organizations in Cheboksary and Ivanovo are smaller-scale, and are met, at least minimally, at the local level.

The point of the contrast between the relative cohesion of the movement in Moscow and that in the provinces is not that private foundations and USAID should cut off funding to the Russian women's movement. Despite the side effects, having the money is far better than not having it at all. Western grants fund salaries for women who might well otherwise be unemployed in today's discriminatory labor market: they fund crisis centers, campaigns against domestic violence, and a variety of other useful projects; they help to familiarize women with bodies of literature, and with international and domestic law pertinent to their concerns; and, finally, they help to foster connections between social movement activists. Without such ties, a civil society has no hope of formation in Russia. However, given the conflicts that some Western funding seems to have exacerbated in the past, it might be wise for foundations and foreign governments to increase their efforts to award funding in ways that would explicitly foster collaboration, or productive competition, rather than the reverse.[50]

The Western role in creating "artificial coalitions": the Consortium

One attempt made by USAID to strengthen the ties between the various networks within Moscow's women's movement was the funding of the US–NIS Women's Consortium. Given the perceptions held by women's

---

[50] Based on research conducted in 1998, political scientist James Richter draws similar conclusions on the complex interaction between Western assistance and women's movement dynamics in Russia. See James Richter, "Citizens or Professionals," unpublished manuscript, 1998.

movement activists in Moscow about coalitions, about Western funding, and about rival organizations' identities vis à vis the Soviet state, the task of uniting these networks was not an easy one. For these and other reasons, the attempts made by Martina Vandenberg, the American coordinator of the Consortium, to create a real coalition during 1994 and 1995 were valiant but not always successful. Vandenberg attempted to bring together activists from the Women's League with those from the Independent Women's Forum's organizations, and described the situation in April 1995 as a rather mixed bag as far as successful coalition-building was concerned:

The fact that this grant exists is what brings people together. The mythology is that we've built ongoing relations. The fact is that they can hear each other talk, with "neutral facilitation." Everyone has access to the same information, which can potentially enrich their work. I think the distortion is small. They're little grants. However, it still exists. But the distortion, in this case, is less in the money than in the people: the Consortium members – it makes for strange bedfellows.[51]

The tensions within the coalition were not only visible to the Americans. In late 1994, one of the Consortium activists, representing the Feminist Orientation Center, voiced her frustration about the lack of collaboration between the Consortium's organizational members: "The barrier to coalition-building is that people can't agree to each contribute one part of the whole. Every organization still wants to do its own thing."[52] This statement was made after a particularly difficult meeting, in which people (especially several of the lawyers present) had refused to take responsibility for working with representatives of other women's groups to write a critique of the Russian government's new and discriminatory draft labor code.

The USAID-funded Consortium, however, was the inspiration for setting up a June 1995 meeting between women's movement organizations and Women of Russia (WOR) deputy Galina Klimantova, then head of the Duma Committee on the Affairs of Women, the Family, and Youth, and Mariia Gaidash, also a WOR deputy. This meeting, described in the introduction to this volume, was a significant milestone in the struggle to establish regular channels of contact between women's groups and policymakers. The meeting was Vandenberg's idea, and it is possible that the reason Klimantova agreed to the meeting was because an American proposed it. In any case, after the meeting, Klimantova sent a letter to the Consortium office and not to the individual women's groups that had attended the meeting. Although the meetings were

---

[51] Martina Vandenberg, interview, April 20, 1995.
[52] Interview, December 7, 1994.

supposed to be regular monthly meetings, only one occurred: the women's groups were told that WOR deputies were too busy with reelection campaigning, and, after the December 1995 elections and WOR's failure to reenter the Duma, the issue was moot.

By March 1996, however, a highly successful instance of coalition work had arisen between Consortium members and others women's groups, without any foreign instigation. A new network, the Association of Independent Women's Organizations (*ob"edinenii*) was created at a December 1995 seminar, financed by foreign sources (Ford Foundation, Eurasia Foundation, and Frauen Anstiftung, a German foundation), and including organizations from both the Independent Women's Forum and the Women's League. Elena Ershova, one of the leaders of the Women's League, pointed to this as an instance of successful coalition-building, aided to some degree by the experience that women's groups had gained in the Consortium:

The women's movement has in the last two years moved away from pyramidal structures, to horizontal ties. Now there's not only the Women's League, but also a new network, the Association of Independent Women's Organizations, which includes organizations from both the Women's League and the Independent Women's Forum. The Consortium helped, in that we were working on an equal basis; this facilitated our work in coalitions. Also the women's organizations have learned how to do advocacy. We sent a letter to the Duma, to remind them that, even though the Women of Russia faction is gone, the women's issue has not been solved; and with the aid of Lena Kochkina and Marina Liborakina, and [the political bloc] Yabloko, hearings were called and held on the labor code.[53]

Elena Kochkina, an activist and scholar then working with the Independent Women's Forum and MCGS, when asked why she and Elena Ershova were now working together, responded directly: "The Consortium."[54] This is interesting, because in the past neither Ershova nor representatives of the Independent Women's Forum had been enthusiastic about collaborating with each other's organizations. Ershova, in April 1995, responded to a question about what hindered the creation of ties and cooperation between women's groups as follows:

A lot of things. If we take the most down-to-earth one [*prizemlennaia*], it's women's ambitions, and the desire on the part of many women to be first. The older women, those who are already ending their life cycle: there are few of us. The majority are young activists, energetic, self-loving – and you shouldn't discount the very strong competition. For instance, the Independent Women's Forum: I read the book that they put out in the USA, in English, and they

[53] Elena Ershova, personal communication, March 1996.
[54] Elena Kochkina, personal communication, March 1996.

simply write about themselves as though they are the only democratic tendency [*napravlenie*] in the entire women's movement.[55]

Similarly ill disposed – but to the Women's League – a representative of the Independent Women's Forum included the following in her answer to a similar question about differences between the various branches of the women's movement, in November 1994:

[The Women's League] is in fact like a parallel network to the Independent Women's Forum. We can't work with them for many reasons: the participants in the League are engaged in small business, and are trying to forge ties with politicians. Their age range is forty-five to fifty; they have a more limited, traditional style of behavior. The Forum's participants are more sincere, they have lower social status, and are real social activists: that's the sense in which the League is more limited. It's a different type of people: in the Forum, people are acting from a personal social basis. Maybe it's not any better organizationally speaking, but it's more sincere. The Forum people know what social reality is, and how to change it. You know you can change the world. It's a different type of people. We do what we do, our social activity, out of deep personal necessity and social necessity. Maybe we do things worse organizationally speaking, but with more sincerity.[56]

It is of course hard to know what made these rather strong opinions change so radically as to enable some of the most prominent women from these two networks to work together, co-authoring appeals to the Duma and articles in major newspapers in 1996.[57] But one thing is starkly clear: both sides mentioned the role of the Western-funded Consortium in their process of moving toward collaboration. In this instance, funding was designed explicitly to foster internetwork collaboration between the politically active women's movement networks in Moscow, and seems to have had a modicum of success.

The language of women's liberation . . . English

The West, particularly the English-speaking West, has played an interesting part in the very expression of women's issues in Russia, not only in agenda-setting and affecting the women's movement's cohesiveness.

---

[55] Elena Ershova, interview, April 18, 1995. Ershova's complaint is a reference to Valentina Konstantinova's typology of women's organizations, in an article in an edited volume: Anastasia Posadskaia, ed., *Women in Russia* (London: Verso, 1994). The Women's League itself does not appear in Konstantinova's typology.

[56] Interview, November 18, 1994.

[57] E. Ershova, E. Kochkina, and M. Liborakina, "Komu nuzhna gendernaia ekspertiza?," *Nezavisimaia gazeta*, February 15, 1996, p. 6; E. Kochkina and E. Ershova, "Diskriminatsia . . . po zakony: zhenshchiny na rynke truda," *Moskovskaia pravda*, April 26, 1996.

While many activists agree that in the early 1990s the Moscow Center for Gender Studies provided the vocabulary for the ensuing debates and discussions about women's rights and status, and about gender analysis in academic research, that vocabulary included some central borrowings from English, such as "gender" (*gender*) and "women's studies," because Russian lacked such terms. Now, not only have terms like "gender" permeated Russian women activists' vocabularies, but, as the movement increasingly tries to affect the policy process, a new series of terms has been borrowed to express activities and ideas that were largely absent from the Soviet political scene – because the NGO sector too was absent – terms like "advocacy" and "lobbying" (*lobbirovanie*). Similarly, the presence of foreign granting organizations has brought terms like "granty," "fandraising," and "treining" into common movement parlance.

A certain amount of backlash has emerged in response to the influx of English terminology, which complicates the transmission of feminist ideas to the general Russian audience. People tire of hearing unfamiliar words, at whose meanings they can only guess. Asked about her feelings on the subject of feminism, Nina Petrova, the 54-year-old head of the Cheboksary *zhensovet* answered the question, defining feminism "probably" as the struggle for women's rights, but then added, in a kindly but firm tone, "We don't like foreign words much. We say, 'Make sense when you talk! [*Govori poniatno!*]' In other words, 'Speak Russian!'"[58] Even English-speaking Russian activists have pointed to the alienation that the use of borrowed terms like *gender, gendernyi* (the adjectival form), and "advocacy" create in the general population. This clearly relates to the problem of issue framing: without being able to express to the general population – in Russian – the need for a "gender analysis" of laws or a "gender approach" to analyzing male and female socialized sex roles, there is little hope for widespread cultural change.

Gender has been a disputed term in Russia since approximately 1990, when the Moscow Center for Gender Studies (MCGS) was created. Anastasiia Posadskaia, then the director of the MCGS described how they chose to use the term "gender" in their name, because there was no equivalent word in Russian to express the socialized (rather than biological) aspects of sex:

Q. Why did you invent a new Russian word – 'Gendernii' [*sic*] – to name the Institute?

A. I know, some of my friends told me it was barbarous. But our problem was that the Russian word for "sex" – *pol* – is in our culture too associated with

---

[58] Nina Petrova, interview, May 29, 1995.

the physical acts, and we lack a term that is distinct from it, which you have in English. So we had to import 'gender'.[59]

The word *gender* has not made many inroads into the provinces. When asked if they had heard of Moscow's Center for Gender Studies (commonly referred to as the "Gendernyi Tsentr"), respondents outside Moscow and St. Petersburg were largely unfamiliar with the institution as well as the word.[60] While the use of English has been beneficial in making connections with Western feminists and researchers, the development of an indigenous vocabulary will be necessary in order for the discussion to reach the general populace, whose tolerance for foreign words may not extend far beyond "Snickers" and other imported brand name items.

The use of English in grant competitions also raises issues of concern among activists. In their article, Regentova and Abubikirova tied the creation of a Western nomenklatura within the women's movement to the use of the English language, which was used as a "means of control and power within the Independent Women's Forum and outside it."[61] They argued that English had acquired such significance because it is the US funding (as opposed to European) which predominates. Under these conditions "the knowledge of English acquires the status of a goal in itself . . . Many people caught on relatively quickly to the situation, and immediately found their way to women's projects."[62] Thus, from this perspective, Western funders partially control the agendas of women's groups, and also inadvertently privilege English-speaking activists, who, in the view of other activists, may not be truly "sincere" about the movement. Neither of these effects is conducive to fostering cooperation between activists and organizations, or between organizations and their potential popular base.

Impact of the international arena on the women's movement and the state

International organizations such as the United Nations, international documents such as UN and ILO Conventions, and international con-

---

[59] Anastasia Posadskaya, "Self-Portrait of a Russian Feminist," *New Left Review*, no. 195 (September–October 1992), p. 11.
[60] All of the Moscow interviewees except two had heard of the Moscow Center for Gender Studies. Seven interviewees outside Moscow and St. Petersburg had never heard of it (one in Ekaterinburg, two in Cheboksary, four in Ivanovo – though a few of the Cheboksary interviewees had learned of its existence at a seminar that took place only a few days before they were interviewed).
[61] Regentova and Abubikirova, no title, p. 14.
[62] Ibid., p. 15.

ferences all play significant roles in the dynamics between the Russian state and the women's movement. Whereas government bodies and women's organizations may have little respect for each other, they both have at least a modicum of respect for the international arena, and both, starting with perestroika, seem to look to the West and to international organizations for standards of behavior regarding women's status, at least in principle. This inclination on the part of the Russian government is perhaps left over from the days of Soviet lip service to the most progressive international documents. Women's groups rely on international documents and their vocabulary in order to attract state attention to women's issues, and find a common language in which to communicate with state representatives.

In their interactions with each other, women's group representatives and state officials alike cite the ILO Convention on Workers with Family Obligations, the UN Convention on the Elimination of All Forms of Discrimination Against Women (CEDAW), and others. In fact, these documents can be central to women's organizations. Elena Ershova noted the importance of CEDAW in the history of the Women's League:

In 1992, after [our founding] conference, we had thirty or so organizations listed, and twenty people signed a coordinating agreement. It said mainly that the signers supported the UN Convention on the Elimination of Discrimination: we all supported it. Other than that, we had nothing.[63]

Similarly, one of the main goals of the women's organization Equality and Peace is, according to one of its leaders, to improve the laws on women in the Russian Federation. As an example she stated that her group wanted the Russian government to sign on to ILO Convention 156, which calls for equal pay for equal work, parental leave, no firings on the basis of the presence of children or pregnancy, and, generally, ending workplace discrimination on the basis of sex.

As the legal heir to the USSR's various and sundry international agreements, the Russian Federation is obliged to abide by CEDAW, which it signed in 1980. It has not, however, ratified ILO Convention 156. Yet, because the Russian Federation has ratified some of these agreements, women's organizations are able to bring the content of these documents to official attention without being open to criticism. The Women's League, for example, in May 1993, initiated hearings in the (then) Supreme Soviet, on Russia's inadequate movement toward fulfilling the UN Convention on the Elimination of All Forms of Discrimination Against Women. "The men present had to agree that Russia was undergoing serious backlash in that area," Elena Ershova

---

[63] Elena Ershova, interview, April 18, 1995.

recalled.[64] The tactic of suggesting that the state should live up to international standards (even when it has not ratified a given convention) goes back to the Soviet period. Elena Kochkina, of MCGS, described the way that her institute wrote a plan for improving women's status, which was approved by the Soviet government, but never implemented (because of the collapse of the Soviet Union a few years later):

In 1989, the *kontseptsiia*, "The State Program to Improve the Status of Women, the Family, and the Protection of Motherhood and Childhood," appeared. This booklet includes the concept of fatherhood [and] the concept of the family's independence from the state, and suggests that the USSR should ratify the [ILO] Convention on Workers with Family Obligations, and so forth. Thus, the system of welfare benefits, rather than going solely to the mother, should reflect the concept of parenthood. In the final analysis, the family should decide on its own who's going to use the resources designated by the state for raising the child: will the family pay for the child to go to a daycare center, will one of the parents stay home, or hire a nanny, or will a grandfather or grandmother do it. In that sense, the fact that the system of Russian state policymaking agreed to this *kontseptsiia*, and adopted it, was an real innovation.[65]

At Duma hearings on the draft labor code in March 1996, a set of amendments to the code was presented on behalf of two major women's organizations: MCGS and the Women's League.[66] The amendments emphasized Russia's responsibilities to abide by more than a dozen international agreements, including ILO conventions, CEDAW, documents from the World Conference on Human Rights (Vienna, 1993), the Declaration and Platform of the UN Fourth World Conference on Women (Beijing, 1995), and a series of new international documents that Russia would be obligated to abide by in order to gain entrance into the European Union. The fact that the activists chose to refer to international documents suggests they believed that the documents provide a certain legitimizing frame for women's movement demands in the eyes of the Russian state.[67] The activists rely on this frame in their paper, stating: "In [these documents] the question of women's rights is posed as an inalienable part of human rights."[68] This insistence on the

---

[64] Elena Ershova, interview, April 18, 1995.

[65] Elena Kochkina, interview, July 22, 1995.

[66] E. Kochkina and E. Ershova, "Komentarii i popravki k proektu federal'nogo zakona 'O vnesenii, izmenenii i dopolnenii v Kodeks zakonov o trude RF' gendernyi podkhod i trudovye prava zhenshchin," presented at Parliamentary Hearings on the Labor Code, March 4–5, 1996.

[67] Women's groups in Britain in the 1980s similarly reached out to the European Community and the European Court of Justice to gain leverage on important policy issues over their domestic government. See Sylvia Bashevkin, *Women on the Defensive* (Chicago: University of Chicago Press, 1998), p. 55.

[68] Kochkina and Ershova, "Komentarii i popravki k proektu federal'nogo zakona," p. 2.

Russian state's obligation to fulfill international norms is also a form of pressure to introduce the rule of law, one of the basic aspects of civil society being demanded by social movement organizations. Naturally, the Russian state (with its various administrative and legislative bodies) is by no means a uniform structure. Some officials respond more favorably to international laws and standards than do others. In this sense, using international documents as a "legitimator" will only work when the state leadership has a vested interest in defining itself as a member of the "Western," "international," "European," "democratic," or "progressive" community.

The use of "international language" on human rights by the Russian women's movement – a language that the Russian state has validated, whether intentionally or not, by signing on to international conventions on women's rights – is a direct result of exposure to international organizations and their documents. That the activists do not hesitate to hold their government up to the standards presented in those documents lends credence to claims by scholars of "world norms" and their diffusion, who suggest that these norms affect not only state institutions, but also "penetrate society itself, and mobilize it to make claims on the state."[69] Thus far, the Russian government has reacted mostly in a declarative fashion, rather than appearing to have been deeply affected in practice or policy by international norms on women's issues, although some inroads have been made by women's organizations.

The importance of Beijing

Not only international agreements, but also international conferences, such as the UN's Fourth World Conference on Women, held in Beijing in 1995, play a special role in the state–social movement relationship. This section focuses on the importance of the Beijing conference, which altered the dynamics between the Russian state and women's movement organizations in several ways.

By early summer 1995, nearly everyone active in a women's organization in Moscow, it seemed, was well aware of the upcoming Beijing conference. In Moscow, even women's groups that existed in nearly complete isolation from the rest of the women's movement were conscious of the event. Natalia Belokopytova, for instance, the chair of the hardline communist Congress of Soviet Women, who had never heard of the Moscow Center for Gender Studies (the most widely known feminist organization in Russia) or of the Women's League, had heard of

[69] Connie L. McNeely, *Constructing the Nation-State* (Westport, CT: Greenwood Press, 1995), p. 146.

the Beijing conference – in particular, she had heard that "the fees to get in are very high."[70] Similarly, Larisa Podgorbunskaia, the head of the International Association of Russian Women-Mothers, an organization rather on the fringe of the women's movement in Moscow, despite its national-level status, answered a question about whether she knew of the Independent Women's Forum or the Women's League, by saying that she knew "about the worldwide meeting in Beijing."[71]

The upcoming Beijing conference motivated a series of local conferences and seminars. The Women's Information Project ADL (Archive–Database–Library), for instance, in conjunction with other women's advocacy organizations (the Inform Center and MCGS) conducted a sequence of seminars in preparation for Beijing, called Strategies of the Independent Women's Forum: Before and After Beijing. These seminars treated both logistical issues (such as how to get travel grants) and substantive topics (preparing for the NGO Forum that would be held parallel to the governmental one; becoming familiar with the international documents; and putting forth amendments to the draft Beijing Declaration and the Platform of Action). The seminars even included representatives of state structures, such as Olga Samarina, of the Ministry of Social Protection, and Valentina Zakharova, a consultant to the Duma Committee on the Affairs of Women, the Family and Youth. Seminars in preparation for Beijing were held outside Moscow as well; one such event took place in Tomsk, Siberia, called The Strategies of Women's Initiatives in the Siberian Region.[72] Governmental bodies as well as women's groups sponsored conferences that addressed issues about the Beijing conference. The Ministry of Social Protection, headed at the time by Liudmila Beslepkina, held one such gathering in mid-December 1994, called Women and Development: Rights, Realities, and Perspectives, and on June 6, 1995, in Moscow, the second All-Russian Women's Congress was held, with the stated goal of preparing for Beijing. Women's organizations were invited to and participated in both conferences, creating a potential opportunity for lobbying and for feedback to the state from women's groups.

Representatives of several women's organizations also flew to New York for a meeting in March 1995, at the UN's 39th session on women's status, in advance of the Beijing event. This provided another opportunity for women's nongovernmental organizations to discuss women's status in their various countries, and to strategize about how to address these issues with their governments. While they were in New York,

---

[70] Natal'ia Belokopytova, interview, May 12, 1995.
[71] Larisa Podgorbunskaia, interview, May 4, 1995.
[72] Vestnik, no. 2–3, 1995, p. 14.

several women's groups (including the Inform Center of the Independent Women's Forum, the Ukraine Center for Women's Studies, the MCGS, and the Moscow-based Association of Women Journalists) held a workshop on Women in Countries Undergoing Economic Transition Periods. Its purpose was to define positions that they could amend to the draft Beijing Declaration and Action Platform. One of the workshop's conclusions was particularly important with regard to the way the issue was framed, reading, "If the significant worsening of women's status in these countries continues, then the entire process of reforms and democratization will be placed in doubt." In other words, the group was posing the issue of women's deteriorating status as one that would make Russia and other transitional countries appear less *democratic* and thus less respectable in the eyes of the international community. In addition to amendments, the group (including representatives from Eastern Europe) also proposed recommendations to their respective national governments, including one suggesting that their governments "regard the reform-support programs proposed by international financial institutions critically, paying attention to their consequences for women."[73] By bringing women together from several countries undergoing similar processes, an international organization had created an opportunity for them to strategize about common problems.

Preparations for the Beijing event provided new opportunities not just for networking and strategizing between women's organizations, but also for contacts between the Russian state and women's organizations, particularly at the National Council on Preparation for Beijing – a special body created in June 1993 by order of the federal government. Several women's NGOs were represented on the National Council, and others were invited to its meetings. There is reason to believe that these meetings enabled the Ministry of Social Protection and certain women's groups to become better acquainted, and more comfortable with one another. In discussing the Independent Women's Forum, Samarina noted that originally it had been difficult for the ministry to work with the Forum, because of their "stress on feminism." It was not until the ministry had started "working with the Forum in the context of preparing for the Beijing conference" that they had found mutual "points of contact." Said Samarina:

For a long time, the Forum said that we have nothing to attract them with, but now they invite us [to their seminars] – there's going to be a seminar they sent me a fax about, a regional seminar about the strategies of the Independent Women's Forum before and after Beijing. They've invited us to speak at the

---

[73] Marina Liborakina, "Masterskaia 'Zhenshchiny v stranakh s ekonomikoi perekhodnogo perioda,'" *Vestnik*, no. 2–3, 1995, pp. 5–8.

seminar, as an equal partner . . . Beforehand, I can't say that we had contradictions or not: we just didn't work together. And now we do.[74]

The women's groups' preparation for the Beijing conference paid off. Approximately 200 Russian women attended the conference, and representatives of several women's organizations were even included in the official government delegation, although only a few were included on the basis of their positions as NGO leaders. Moreover, the results of the Beijing conference provoked controversy in Moscow. Observers on the scene in Beijing suggested that the official delegation was dramatically underprepared for the conference. According to Marina Liborakina, of the Inform Center and Feminist Orientation Center, "representatives of women's NGOs from the CIS, East, and Central Europe spoke out at the plenary session of the Conference, with a resolution from the 'Non-Existent Region' – the twenty-four countries undergoing an economic 'transition period,' where women's status has sharply declined over the last few years. Our governments were silent about this."[75] By contrast, the Russian NGOs came across as being extremely capable and well organized.

In the aftermath of the conference, criticism fell on the official delegation. One member of the delegation was so disgusted with its performance that she felt compelled to write a scathing article about the incompetence of the delegation's leader, Liudmila Beslepkina, the minister of social protection. Apparently, Beslepkina failed to assign members of the delegation to work in either of the two working groups or the main committee working on the draft Platform of Action, where they should have been following the discussions of the document's text, and reporting back to the delegation on a daily basis. The delegation did not even meet as a whole while in Beijing. After a few days, a subgroup of the delegation demanded that Beslepkina gather the delegation and instruct them how to proceed. Beslepkina's only instruction was: "Everyone can go wherever they want." The author pointed out that Beslepkina never even took part in the work of the main committee, or in any of the working groups, during the entire two-week period. Nor, said the author, had Beslepkina ever gathered the delegation together before the conference, in Moscow, "in order to at least meet each other and exchange opinions." The author concluded that, given this information, "it becomes obvious that the conference itself was seen just as an excuse for official receptions and dinners."[76] Meanwhile, given the

---

[74] Ol'ga Samarina, interview, March 24, 1995.

[75] Marina Liborakina, *Obretenie sily: rossiiskii opyt* (Moscow: CheRo, 1996), p. 108.

[76] Alla Iaroshinskaia, "Kak Bezlepkina v Pekine zashchishchala zhenshchin Rossii," *Komsomol'skaia pravda*, October 4, 1995, p. 7.

performance of the Russian women's organizations at and before Beijing, the Russian state was forced into a newfound respect for the women's organizations. Although it is hard to prove that this was a direct result of the Beijing experience, following the conference, an academic affiliated with the Moscow Center for Gender Studies was contacted by the Ministry of Social Protection, asking for a research project; another activist reported that Ekaterina Lakhova (adviser to the president on women's issues, and Duma deputy from the Women of Russia bloc) had become the women's movement's "best friend."[77]

Following the Beijing conference, the Russian government adopted some of the international language used by women's movement organizations. On January 8, 1996, Prime Minister Chernomyrdin's government approved the Ministry of Social Protection's plan (*kontseptsiia*) "On Improving Women's Status in the Russian Federation," and on this basis, called for the creation of an interdepartmental commission, headed by Beslepkina, to coordinate activities designed to improve women's status. The language of Chernomyrdin's decree clearly reflected the Russian state's concern with the international arena, beginning thus: "Being guided by the regulations of the [UN] Convention on the Elimination of All Forms of Discrimination, and by the final documents of the Fourth World Conference on Women's Status, 'Actions in the Interest of Equality, Development, and Peace' (Beijing, September 1995), the Government of the Russian Federation decrees . . ."[78] Similarly, the ministry's plan stated that it had been formulated in accordance with the Russian constitution, Russia's international obligations, and the recommendations of the Beijing conference, albeit "taking into account the actual socio-economic situation in contemporary Russia," a modifier which undermines the stated commitment to the international standards. Several women's organizations were asked for and provided feedback on the plan, though some activists felt that their ideas had not been reflected in the final document. On the other hand, the plan began by stating that it was based on the fact that "women's rights are an inalienable part of human rights" – exactly the same international framing of the issue used by women's rights activists. Moreover, the plan states frankly that while the Russian constitution proclaims that men and women have equal rights and freedoms, and equal opportunities to realize them, "at this point, these constitutional regulations commonly carry a declarative character."[79] Judging from the

---

[77] Elena Kochkina, personal communication, spring 1996.
[78] Pravitel'stvo Rossiiskoi Federatsii, "Postanovlenie ot 8 ianvaria 1996 g. no. 6, g. Moskva, O kontseptsii uluchsheniia polozheniia zhenshchin v Rossiiskoi Federatsii."
[79] "Kontseptsiia uluchsheniia polozheniia zhenshchin v Rossiiskoi Federatsii," pp. 1–2.

approved plan, women's groups and some representatives of the state have discovered a common language that enables them to discuss these issues, particularly when an international presentation by the government is called for.

At a Western-sponsored women's seminar in March 1996, held outside Moscow, Elvira Novikova, an activist who had worked for many years in the Women's Bureau of the Helsinki Citizens Assembly, as well as having worked for the Soviet-era trade union research institute and having been an expert for the UN Committee on the Elimination of All Forms of Discrimination Against Women (1986–90), pointed out that having a document (*bumaga*) to wave at bureaucrats – even an imperfect one like the Ministry of Social Protection's *kontseptsiia* – is better than having nothing at all. Other such documents exist. For instance in 1994, the Russian Federation prepared its Fourth National Report on Fulfilling the Convention on the Elimination of All Forms of Discrimination Against Women,[80] and its National Report for the Fourth World Conference on Women. The latter in particular displayed an unusual degree of state acknowledgment of discrimination against women. All these documents serve as information that can be used by women's groups. Yet these documents and their contents are only known in certain circles. Said Valentina Konstantinova:

Of course [the Ministry of Social Protection] might react to international documents, or prepare national reports for international events, but all that would be far from the real lives of real women. Therefore, I think that for the development of women's consciousness, for the development of their political activity, I think that information needs to get to women. For example: the National Report and National Platform of the Russian Federation for the Beijing Conference was written. Tell me, who knows about it in women's organizations? Practically nobody. Only thanks to the Independent Women's Forum network and various seminars can we get this information out to the common woman. It's the same with laws: the Duma adopts some laws, practically no one discusses them, except the specialists that prepare them.[81]

In order for such information to have an impact on the broader society and on women's perception of their status, women's organizations must find ways to distribute it to the population. Western aid has facilitated this process to some degree.

---

[80] In accordance with CEDAW, Russia, as a state having ratified the convention, is obligated to produce periodic reports (every four years) on the measures being taken to fulfill the convention, and the progress in improving women's status over the previous four-year period. See "Neskol'ko slov o V periodicheskom doklade," in *Strategii vzaimodeistviia*, October 1995, p. 18.

[81] Valentina Konstantinova, interview, July 9, 1995.

Russianization

Russian women's organizations are becoming increasingly aware of the need to operate together, and to focus their attentions at home. There is a certain acknowledgment that Western funding is impermanent, and that a domestic funding base will ultimately be necessary if the women's movement is to expand to the mass level. In 1996 two events took place that seemed to foretell a degree of Russianization of the women's movement: a change in the Consortium's leadership structure, and the participation of women's movement groups' at the parliamentary hearings on the labor code, mentioned earlier.

The parliamentary hearings took place in early March 1996. Called by Duma deputy Iarigina of the Yabloko political bloc, the hearings addressed the current draft of the Labor Code, a revised version of the Soviet-era document. The Russian government had written a new labor code in 1994, but it was found so wanting – particularly on the grounds of equal rights and equal opportunities for men and women in the labor market – that it was rejected in favor of simply reworking the old code. Numerous representatives of women's organizations were present at the hearings, invited through the association Women for Social Democracy, one of whose leaders worked as an aid to a Social Democratic Party deputy (whose party was a component part of Yabloko). At the hearings, representatives of women's organizations were able to distribute their suggestions for amendments to the labor code, as well as an Appeal to the Duma, signed by several dozen women's organizations, and many spoke up with information and recommendations.[82] Although a seminar on the labor code, sponsored by the US League of Women Voters, was held on the eve of the hearings, the hearings themselves and the presence of the Russian women's movement groups at them – without a Western-sponsored mediating body like the Consortium – may indicate a trend toward nativization of the women's movement. The second event points more ambiguously in the direction of increased indigenous control over the movement, namely, the transfer of power from the American coordinator of the Consortium in Moscow to a Russian, Elena Ershova, elected unanimously from among the Consortium's Russian member organizations. Although the Consortium simultaneously was awarded another major grant, through USAID, the change in leadership represents new responsibilities and opportunities for acquiring significant experience in fiscal management of nongovernmental organizations. The new leadership also gives the

---

[82] Transcript of parliamentary hearings on the Labor Code, March 4, 1996, author's files.

Consortium the potential to build a coalition across several of Moscow's indigenous networks without the pull of an American facilitator. A successful coalition-building effort, spearheaded by the Consortium, might help to mend some of the fractures in the national-level Russian women's movement.

Conclusion

The stories relayed by the Russian activists, scholars, and officials cited in this chapter testify to the importance of international influences on Russia's women's movement. Western feminist literature, Western women's organizations, and travel to the West helped inspire some women to activism, while reliance on a foreign terminology that facilitated that access may now reduce the activists' chances to spread their ideas further throughout the population. International influences, from funding to UN documents, affect the relationships among women's groups, and between groups and state officials targeted for lobbying on policy issues. These are only a few of the ways that the international environment has affected the development of the Russian women's movement. While the changes in the Soviet/Russian political opportunity structure and discourse during the transition period allowed for the emergence of the contemporary women's movement, there is no doubt that the shape of that movement would be different were it not for Western influence and aid. This is an issue in many social organizations and movements in the post-Leninist world: labor movements, ecology movements, bar associations, healthcare organizations – anywhere that foreign governments see the potential to undergird manifestations of "civil society." In trying to explain the emergence and development of civil society in the form of social movements under post-Leninist conditions, social theorists ignore the effects of the international environment only at their peril. Indeed, exploring the international opportunity structure and its interaction with the opportunities and obstacles present at the domestic level enriches social movement theory and allows for a more realistic evaluation of the causes and shapes of social movements.

Conclusion

By the mid-1990s, the activists who had created hundreds of Russian women's organizations were calling themselves a women's movement. But where were the demonstrations? Where were the coalitions of groups who worked on similar issues? Where were the leaflets, the national campaigns, the fundraisers, the outreach staff, the membership lists? The foregoing chapters suggested answers to these questions, by drawing attention to the activists' creation of a movement appropriate to their political culture and history, their economic conditions, their political opportunities, and their international context.

Summary of findings

There is no doubt that the political and economic transition period in Russia created conditions enabling the contemporary women's movement to emerge. Increasing political freedoms permitted women to speak out publicly against discrimination and sexist stereotyping; the unfolding economic crisis and its impact on women inspired activism in defense of women's rights in the workplace and the unemployment office. Clearly, the political opportunity structure had changed. Yet, it was not simply that the political transition (from a more to less repressive polity) had paved the way for feminist groups to speak out. The political transition had also allowed for increased exposure to Western ideas and international documents, which, in turn, provided a new standard for Russian state behavior where women's equal rights and opportunities were concerned. Armed with international agreements, activists demanded actions beyond mere hypocritical pronouncements of equality by state officials. Under pressure, the increasingly open Russian state began to render more honest accounts of women's status to the international community, and became slightly more receptive to influence by women's groups.

Likewise, it was not merely that the economic transition created crises and opportunities for women (resulting in the emergence of many pragmatically oriented women's organizations), but also that an entirely new funding source – Western foundations and governments – began to address the resource mobilization needs of the women's movement. This development brought both benefits and unexpected complications, particularly to the Moscow-based groups. There, cooperation between organizations was limited, more so than in the provincial cities, where distance from the West and from Western funding sources helped keep such competition to a minimum. International influences thus helped to explain some of the apparent paradoxes about the movement, including the differential levels of fragmentation in Moscow and the provinces, as well as the organizations' disregard for developing domestic fundraising and outreach strategies.

The impact of political history was no less important in shaping the women's movement. Decades of top-down rule had created a populace shy of hierarchy, wary of coalitions in which their organization might get lost or dominated, and suspicious of organizations and individuals that they believed had ties to the Soviet state and Communist Party. The fragmentation of the women's movement in Moscow could be understood in this context; when added to the fragmentation associated with the process of acquiring foreign grants, the combined effect was striking. Also, recent political history and instability had instilled an aversion to measures perceived as instability-provoking, including mass demonstrations or protests, which suggested an explanation for the movement's preference for less conflictual means of protest. Moreover, the monopolization of the public sphere by the state during seven decades of Soviet rule had nearly silenced civil society; social activism independent of Communist Party control was a new element of public life, emerging tentatively only with glasnost and perestroika.

But even as groups and organizations emerged, voicing their objections to the status quo and making their demands for change, another obstacle came to light. Not only had the political sphere been dominated by the Soviet party-state for decades, but so had the economic realm. Centralized planning of the economy, enforced membership in the state-run trade unions, and mass participation in the faux "civic" organizations sponsored by the party left the new activist population in the early 1990s unprepared for fundraising and the other economic concomitants of grassroots social movement organizing. Moreover, Russia's centralized and inefficient communications infrastructure was weak; access to photocopiers and sometimes even telephones was difficult for social movement groups. Direct mail was an impossibility, checkbook membership in (or support for) movement organizations unknown. In essence, Russia lacked the economic infrastructure necessary to support a civil society, even as political conditions for its emergence were being created. Given such circumstances, the potential for Russian women's organizations to expand their mobilizational base through member outreach was low; organizational outreach was therefore not a priority. Elements of the economic opportunity structure thus contributed to the apparent paradoxes of Russian women's movement organizing.

What can we learn about social movements generally from this analysis of the Russian women's movement? Is Russia simply an oddity, its social movements warped by a unique history? Or might this study contain implications for our understanding of the globalization of social trends and social movements, as well as for the democratization process in Russia?

Implications

Although there are many differences between the Russian context for social movement development and that in other parts of the world, the use of a multi-opportunity structure framework helps illustrate the presence of potential parallels that may provide insight into social movement dynamics overall. Speculation about the implications of this study for understanding other social movements, vis à vis framing (or socio-attitudinal opportunity structure), political opportunity structure, economic opportunity structure, political history, and international opportunity structure follows.

Socio-attitudinal, political, and economic opportunity structures

Each country has its own cultural barriers to the use of particular frames, making some resonant and others anathema. A powerful slogan in one country may give rise to indignation in another. In Russia, for example, the Western women's movement slogan, "The personal is political," would not be a resonant choice. Instead, it might conjure up images of KGB and Communist Party invasions of private space. During the Soviet era, the personal was dragged into the political sphere only unwillingly. Framing is therefore closely tied to political history.

Antifeminist sentiment is another issue with which all women's movements contend. Yet, the reasons for antifeminist sentiment vary, and on that basis so do the frameworks adopted by women's movements. Women's movement activists in Russia, as we have seen, try to avoid triggering antifeminist sentiments instilled by the Bolsheviks, who brought Russian women a double burden under the guise of "equality," and fostered a sharp division of labor within and outside the home. While analysts of issue frames may notice the popular disavowal of feminism per se, in conducting crossnational research into conscious-ness-raising and issue framing, sensitivity to the cultural-historical context of antifeminism is crucial in evaluating the movement's chances for success. Movements may succeed or fail depending on whether they employ consciousness-raising frameworks that overcome (or trigger) antifeminist sentiment.

The Russian case suggests other issues that may also have an impact on social movements' framing choices. Activists in Russia's women's movement, for instance, seek non-English-language terms with which to express feminist ideas, lest they be marked as coopted by foreigners, bringing alien and irrelevant ideas to Russia. A similar situation exists in Mexico, where the women's movement was given impetus by the move-ment in the United States, and where critics claim that the movement's origins lie in "satanic, foreign, colonialist, or imperialist forces."[1] What frames do activists in other countries use to help them handle accusa-tions of foreign cooptation? Might activists in many countries, as in Russia, turn to the international language of the Beijing Platform and United Nations documents, when developing frames with which to discuss their issues? A crosscultural analysis of frames used by women's movements could thus shed light on outreach strategies and pitfalls.

Political opportunity structure, like framing, has been studied quite widely in the social movements of many countries. The Russian case raises some interesting issues, however. For instance, whereas instability in elite alignments has been shown to be one of the determinants for evaluating a social movement's chance of success, analysis of conditions for the Russian women's movement suggests that the instability of elite alignments is not always a boon for social movements. The dimensions of such instability, in regimes undergoing major political transition, may be enough to disrupt the continuity of activists' campaigns, especially their contacts with political structures. Related findings from the former East Germany suggest that this aspect of the political opportunity structure can be useful in understanding some of the limitations on social movements emerging and developing under transi-tional conditions.[2]

Another question suggested by the Russian case is whether inter-

---

[1] Eli Bartra, "The Struggle for Life, or Pulling Off the Mask of Infamy," in Barbara Nelson and Najma Chowdhury, eds., *Women and Politics Worldwide* (New Haven: Yale University Press, 1994), p. 452.

[2] Dieter Rucht, "German Unification, Democratization, and the Role of Social Move-ments: A Missed Opportunity?," *Mobilization*, vol. 1, no. 1 (March 1996), p. 55.

national influences often become increasingly important in other countries undergoing political transition, as seems to have been the case for the Russian women's movement. Might some movements turn inward rather than outward at such transitional moments, and, if so, why? Or is the source of international influence best found outside the domestic political opportunity structure – are some social movements the recipients of international attention not so much by choice, but rather by virtue of the political reputation and "importance" of the countries in which they are located, in the eyes of the world's most powerful states? In other words, might it be easier for Russian activists to get international assistance because other states have an interest in fostering Russian democracy, whereas activists in countries of less strategic importance to the powers of Europe and the United States would be harder pressed to gain attention and aid from the international activist and foundation community? Perhaps this reflects an international component of political opportunity structure.

Social movement theorists have long understood the importance of determining the amount of resources available to a given social movement and, thus, learning something about its potential for success. Equally important, however, for understanding internal social movement dynamics is the infrastructure that allows a movement to collect those resources. In the Russian case, limited infrastructure for the support of social movements drove many organizations to seek their resources abroad, a practice which fit in very nicely with the goals of Western governments and foundations, eager to support signs of life in Russia's nascent civil society.

Economic opportunity structure encourages us to look at the infrastructural conditions that exist in a given society, and how they may affect the fundraising capacity of movements, and, in turn, movements' strategies and tactics. Where the communications infrastructure and the economic infrastructure to support grassroots organizations is weak, as in Russia, outreach to the general population may be weak as well, and the tendency to reach out for support to the international environment may be stronger. This raises questions about the relationship between economic infrastructure and popular outreach in other countries. In countries that lack extensive and reliable postal or telephone communication, do we see social movements using different forms of outreach, different types of communication in the hope of changing popular consciousness (if not immediately gaining material support)? Do we see a tendency to seek foreign support for movement projects? Or some combination of the two? The outreach strategy of activists campaigning to stop the spread of AIDS in Zimbabwe, a country where the technological communications infrastructure is even less accessible to activists than is the case in Russia, involved traveling through rural areas, putting on educational plays in open-air beer halls about AIDS transmission, and giving spontaneous lectures in public buses on proper condom use. The activists' campaign, however, was funded by an international organization.[3]

One implication of external funding sources may be that they help to get social movements started in places where society cannot yet (or is not prepared to) support a movement itself. Yet having a balance of resources skewed toward contributions from foundations and governments is a dangerous strategy, given the potential for sudden changes in foundation priorities and cutoffs of funding. An exploration of how movements jumpstarted by foreign funds survive over the longer term might suggest whether a mix of funding sources is necessary or which mix is optimal. Research on organizing in the United States, for instance, suggests that women's groups, in order to be successful, require a diversified funding base, including membership dues. The latter do not tend to provide a significant source of support for Russia's women's movement organizations; this may be the case elsewhere in the world as well.[4]

Political history

Just as framing is closely tied to political history, so tend to be organizational structures. The Russian case makes clear organizations' dislike for hierarchy, in their desire to avoid a replication of the structures of Soviet-era political organizations. What varied political histories have shaped the organizational structures of movements in other countries? Activists' adoption of consensus decisionmaking, for example, may be a reaction against life in societies that tend overall to make room for powerful voices, and pay less attention to minority opinions.

Fragmentation within social movements is also associated with political history. The basis for fragmentation, therefore, differs from place to place. In Russia, one of the lines of division within the women's movement (and other social movements there) is formed on the basis of charges of affiliation with communists or with the "state." In the United States, by contrast, a parallel basis for fragmentation occurs as a result

---

[3] "Side By Side: Women Against AIDS in Zimbabwe," documentary video (a Villon Films–Harvey McKinnon Production in co-production with the Canadian International Development Agency), 1993.

[4] See Joyce Gelb and Jennifer Leigh Disney, "Feminist Organizational 'Success': The State of the Women's Movement in the 1990s," paper presented at American Political Science Association convention, San Francisco, 1996.

of racism and classism and the concomitant distrust that has accumulated within the US women's movement.[5] Within Russia's women's movement, ethnicity does not seem to play a divisive role. Perhaps this is because the movement is mostly homogenous, or because the historical division within Russia generally between haves and have-nots has been less an ethnicity-defined division than a class division – concretely, between the ruling class and the rest of the population. It is the specificity of Soviet history that produced this division, just as the specific US history of slavery, and of racism within the white-dominated US women's movement, creates a modern-day perpetuation of the division. One interesting issue for crosscultural research thus becomes: do movements in other countries also tend to split along lines predetermined by the political history that surrounds and predates them? Observing intramovement dynamics through the lens of political history may help elucidate both similarities that cut across diverse histories and differences that stem from the historical circumstances peculiar to a given country at a given time.

International opportunity structure and globalization

Much has been made in political science and elsewhere of the globalization of capital, of lending agencies, multinational corporations, and military forces.[6] Yet sometimes, in response or resistance to such global trends, social movements also become galvanized and globalized. Such increasing globalization of civil society in the late twentieth century has led to the proliferation of international organizations, from UN commissions and international NGOs, to informal networks that exist only in the realm of the internet and electronic mail. As transnational networks of activists arise, the social and political borders that separate countries from one another decline and disintegrate.

The globalization of women's movements is part of this trend. As fundamental shifts in transnational society and consciousness take place, nations move toward recognizing an increasing number of women's rights, thereby changing life for men and women alike. As the

---

[5] See Carol Mueller, "The Organizational Basis of Conflict in Contemporary Feminism," in Myra Marx Ferree and Patricia Yancey Martin, eds., *Feminist Organizations: Harvest of the New Women's Movement* (Philadelphia: Temple University Press, 1995), pp. 266–67.

[6] This literature is too copious for thorough citation here. Examples include: Cynthia Enloe, *Bananas, Beaches, and Bases: Making Feminist Sense of International Politics* (Berkeley: University of California Press, 1990); Peter Evans, *Dependent Development: The Alliance of Multinational, State and Local Capital in Brazil* (Princeton: Princeton University Press, 1979); and Thomas Biersteker, *Distortion or Development?: Contending Perspectives on the Multinational Corporation* (Cambridge, MA: MIT Press, 1978).

twentieth century draws to a close, nearly all the countries of the world have women's movements – albeit of differing sizes and degrees of acceptance in their societies – fighting for a diverse spectrum of rights and responsibilities. The changes these movements have made already, and the ones they are still struggling for, fundamentally challenge the realities of daily life at the individual level, as well as the societywide structures of cultural, religious, economic, and political power.

It is for such reasons that social movements are a central key to understanding life in any given society. Often, they prefigure the economic, social, and political changes of the future. What appeared as a radical social movement slogan yesterday (universal female suffrage, for example) becomes the nearly ubiquitous rule of today. The globalization of civil society and social movements speeds these processes, as contacts are made, experiences shared, and tactics diffused across the globe. The information revolution has made all social movements potentially international, making almost instantaneous links possible between movements in multiple countries.

Yet while international linkages facilitate social movement expansion, they may also lead to obstacles and disagreements within the movements, as well as societal apprehension about the movements' indigenous nature. Particularly in the formerly Leninist countries and in the Third World, activists' desire to work on indigenous women's issues may clash with their need to acquire material support. Indeed, literature on the effects of Western feminism and transnational granting agencies on Third World feminism and women's organizing suggests that international funding can shape women's movements in significant ways, from agenda-setting to organizational tactics and structure.[7]

One implication of globalization, then, may be that the issues most important to Western activists and their supporters tend to take on an "objective" importance, and may be imposed on activists elsewhere. In other words, we might expect that, as transnational funding for women's movements grows, a certain set of shared problems common to many countries may achieve an almost canonical status. Other issues, shared across fewer countries, may be ignored at the transnational level, overshadowed by the more common issues. This may have ramifications for activists trying to build grassroots movements; the issues that may be addressed first (or for which international support is available) may be

---

[7] See, for example, Elzbieta Matynia, "Finding a Voice: Women in Postcommunist Central Europe," in Amrita Basu, ed., *The Challenge of Local Feminisms* (Boulder: Westview Press, 1995), p. 395; and Wilhelmina Oduol and Wanjiku Mukabi Kabira, "The Mother of Warriors and Her Daughters: The Women's Movement in Kenya," in the same volume, p. 200.

those most important internationally, but not those most important locally. If so, that can short circuit the growth of women's movements locally; fewer women may be interested in the issues promoted, and local activists may feel disempowered, their interests sidelined.

As this case study of Russia's women's movement shows, the flow of ideas, money, and human resources around the globe affects social movements' emergence and development in a variety of ways. How might the international influences explored in this study affect social movements outside Russia? Certainly, the spread of funding for social movements across borders, whether from one NGO to another or from foreign governments to NGOs located in other countries, adds interesting dimensions to the dynamics of social movements, and suggests questions for future research. Does the advent of foreign funding make the exacerbation of conflicts between organizations inevitable? Is movement fragmentation necessarily a result of funding granted to individual organizations through competitions? Evidence from India suggests that, in Bombay, feminists' receipt of foreign funding led to some fragmentation of the women's movement, wherein increasingly few women were attending the weekly meetings of one feminist coalition group, because women had begun to receive incomes stemming from separate projects.[8] The difficulties that activists encounter when working together (and the difficulties they encounter when working with activists from other countries), and how they relate to the diffusion of funding, deserve further study across the world.

Prospects for the Russian women's movement

Globalization enables movements to find new sources of support, gain leverage over their domestic governments, and accomplish what might otherwise be difficult to achieve when faced with a poorly developed civil society and a weak economic infrastructure for grassroots organizing. Yet, what might be the implications of this aspect of globalization for the Russian women's movement? In combination with the political and economic legacies of the Soviet era, globalization and the diffusion of funding in particular have come to affect the movement's incentive structures, promoting activities that focus on policy analysis, political advocacy, or individual forms of material aid. Meanwhile, relatively less attention is focused on popular outreach, cultural change, or mass mobilization. In short, movement globalization may run the risk of leaving broad segments of the Russian population out of the equation.

---

[8] Raka Ray, personal communication, May 1996.

Yet it is not hard to understand why many activists might prefer a nonmobilizational path. After all, civil society in Russia remains weak, and mass mobilization might be difficult under those circumstances.

Indeed, the Russian case provides us with a laboratory in which to observe attempts to build a civil society, one that remains noninstitutionalized and fragile, culturally, politically, and economically. The cultural practice of organizing into groups from below is still new; the aversion to group formation from above, to hierarchy, and even to coalition formation is strong. And on the political front, although it would probably be no longer feasible for Russia's political rulers to impose a regime that would forbid societal organizing independent of state control, state bureaucrats' near-monopoly over access to information (about proposed legislation, for example) can still make it rather difficult for social movements to operate effectively.

Despite these constraints, the women's movement has done as well as any other social movement in Russia. The hundreds of women's organizations spread across the country are attempting to articulate the interests of diverse groups of women, but are doing so in a rather uncertain economic and political atmosphere, with few tools to assist them. The institutionalization of channels between women's organizations and the state fluctuates between being weak and being nonexistent. But women activists have learned quickly. They are mastering their way around the corridors of power, and maneuvering around the offices of foreign foundations.

They have not yet discovered, however, how best to reach and mobilize the general population. Most of the women's movement's focus has been on organizational maintenance; on contact with state officials (whether to acquire resources, or to lobby for antidiscriminatory policies and laws); on the pursuit of funds to enhance organizational program work; on self-education among the activists, to bring them up to speed with the increasingly transnational women's movements developing around the world; and on informing each other about their ongoing struggles at home. If in the late 1980s the priority was taking small subversive steps to become publicly conscious of sexism and discriminatory stereotypes, and by the early 1990s the priority was trying to save some of the benefits that women had had under the old regime while preventing the imposition of increasingly discriminatory practices in politics and the labor market, then by the mid-1990s perhaps the time had come to enlist the populace in the struggle.

The outstanding question would then be how to do this. How can a population, with decades of sexism and stereotypes entrenched in its views, change, or be guided toward change? Confronted with limited resources and a bad reputation for being under the control of either foreign influences, or former Soviet bureaucrats, attempts by the women's movement to garner adherents in the general population may well pose a challenge. But, should activists so choose, how might the movement transcend some of the barriers that have kept the movement small and, to some extent, disconnected from the masses of women who share a set of problems, but are neither involved in activism nor aware that any is going on? How might the Russian women's movement achieve a more mass-based constituency, and thereby further contribute to building a rooted civil society?

Nearly anything that women's movement activists try to accomplish in Russia will be fraught with difficulty. Indeed, as discussed in previous chapters, activists struggle against a number of obstacles. They come up against sexism in the public sphere, and against essentialist sex roles ingrained before and during the Soviet era, reinscribed by the advent of a market economy. They contend with unstable contacts with people in power. They face a nationwide economic crisis, and fallout from the policies of international lending organizations. They confront a lack of economic infrastructure for nonprofit fundraising, and a limited set of terms with which to discuss feminism with the population at large. And, even if they manage to raise people's awareness of women's issues as shared injustices, they may still have trouble helping people to achieve the second aspect of transformation of consciousness – transcending the belief that action against injustice would have little or no chance of success.

But one thing is clear: there is no lack of subjects with which to make appeals to the population. Russian women's concerns include the struggle for mere survival during the transition period, and despair over the long-standing injunction for women to combine work outside the home with full responsibility for childcare and housework. Both of these concerns could serve as vehicles for consciousness-raising. Although the quotations below are answers by activists to questions about the biggest issues women face in Russia, their responses reflect some of the problems encountered by activist and nonactivist women alike.

Survival issues

The economic and political transition from communism toward a confusing and indeterminate future evokes a particular set of women's concerns. While economic conditions are such that most women must work outside the home, formerly state-subsidized childcare centers are closing, and the cost of private childcare options is increasing beyond reach. The provision of public healthcare is at frightfully low levels, and basic survival issues are at stake. In an attempt to make enough money to keep their families afloat, many women are leaving the professional jobs that they were trained for to take up positions as street traders and other female-dominated low-prestige occupations that arose with the advent of a market-oriented economy.

For some women, this amounts to a choice between survival and self-worth. Explained one activist who worked at an employment-retraining organization: "The women who go into trade, to get money, they lose their [former] qualifications. A woman with a [postgraduate education] can sell bras at the marketplace, but then she stops being a chemist with two academic degrees."[9] As thousands of skilled women left or were forced to leave their jobs for other, better-paying, if less rewarding positions, many likely experienced such a challenge to their identity. This subject could readily lend itself to consciousness-raising, as women consider the structural dimensions that forced them and others into a similar position.

A concern related to the struggle for survival and the search for meaningful employment, voiced by several activists, was that women feel "unnecessary," especially in the new economic order. They also argued that the situation was particularly hard for women because of the dominant propaganda recommending women's "return to the home," making it harder for women to find jobs in general.[10]

Several activists laid blame for women's unemployment squarely on the shoulders of the state. As one activist put it, "Women suffer from vulnerability: it's their main problem. The state leaves them to their fates."[11] Given the Soviet experience of state distribution of goods and services, from apartments to jobs, blaming the state (rather than the market, for example) makes sense. It is possible that women could be roused to act on these feelings, and campaign for changes in government policy.

The difficulty of combining work and family successfully

Women's successful combination of paid work and family "duties," a goal once adopted, at least in theory, by the Soviet/Russian state but now abandoned by politicians, leaves women to balance these roles with little assistance. Activists wonder: how can women feel whole, how can women care for their families, without losing themselves in the process?

[9] Marina Pavlova, interview, April 24, 1995.
[10] Interview, December 1, 1994.
[11] Marina Pavlova, interview, April 24, 1995.

While an activist frame for this issue might involve confronting a patriarchal society and the sex-role stereotyping that prevails within it, some expression of the basic struggle to combine two roles would no doubt resonate within the population.

The "double burden" pervaded activists' analysis of women's problems. Said one activist who worked as a co-counselor:

The main problem [for women] is how to combine what they love to do, with their job, and their family, and their parents, how to find their peace, and take care of all their obligations, too; how to be a good mother, and also improve at work. Men don't have this problem: they don't have to prove themselves to be good fathers. Women will say, "I'm a bad mother . . . " Our goal is [women's] self-realization without damage to their work or their families.[12]

Many activists agreed that the double burden of work within and outside the home was a major source of women's problems. This was especially true (though not exclusively so) among women whose activism brought them into constant contact with nonactivist women. Said one leader of an employment-retraining center in Ivanovo:

One of the basic problems is the high degree of everyday burdens on women . . . women carry out the biggest share of housework, spend more time on the children, and if she also works outside the home . . . nothing has really changed, except that it's become harder to live on the welfare benefits provided by the state.[13]

The head of an organization supporting women's entrepreneurship (herself childless) concurred that the combination of work and family plagued many women:

Besides which, women, as before, have the family. No matter what we say about equal rights, equal opportunities for women to participate with men, women's very nature – to become a mother, and have a husband – everything hangs on her, and this is very disturbing. Women are occupied in industry almost twelve hours [a day], and at home she has to do everything, and express some warmth and affection, and that often leads to illnesses, stresses. The deafness and blindness of the leadership organs regarding this issue simply amazes me.[14]

Women's movement actions geared to spotlight how government and corporate officials ignore (or promote) these problems might spark recognition in many women, and motivate some women to become involved in organizing efforts.

Some activists linked concrete issues of survival to self-esteem and sex-role stereotyping. Said one activist and professor of women's studies:

[12] Interview, November 21, 1994.
[13] Ol'ga Khasbulatova, interview, April 6, 1995.
[14] Tat'iana Maliutina, interview, April 25, 1995.

Society does not see women's problems. Society is trying to tell women that what they ought to do is to sit at home and no one thinks to pay for her housework, even if society isn't going to have someplace she can find work outside the home. The main problem is unemployment, and it's a problem for both men and women, but it's more serious for women. They fire the most qualified women cadres. And it's an economic problem. Also, it's a psychological problem: women feel themselves unnecessary to society, to a larger extent than men feel. For women over thirty-five, it's very hard to find work. They advertise for and hire women who are only used for their bodies.[15]

While some activists shared their dismay at the oppression women experience as a result of living under societal sex-role expectations, much of the population would not make the link between women's daily struggles and questions of self-esteem and sex-role stereotypes. Yet the impossibility of smoothly combining work with nearly full responsibility for the domestic sphere is something millions of Russian women share. And based on their experience of the Soviet state's top-down distribution system, women are also likely to share a belief that the state bears responsibility for solving these questions, and might lend support to campaigns seeking to resolve them.

It is clear enough that survival issues and the difficulty of combining family and paid labor both constitute topics that could be used for the purposes of reaching out to the population, to increase women's familiarity with women's movement organizations, and to garner moral (and possibly material) support for the movement itself. But how exactly might this outreach be accomplished? Political leaders can incorporate calls to solve such pressing issues into their platforms, but what can social movement activists do to get the word out, especially given their resource poverty and limited access to the media?

The ideas that I am going to suggest below reflect my bias as an inhabitant of the civil society-rich United States, as someone who has close ties to activist communities in the United States, and as a scholar who has long taken interest in the ways organizations struggle, fail, and succeed in transmitting their ideas to the general population. I propose the following ideas not to impose them; a dialogue, not a lecture, is intended, lest I fall into the international-imperialist trap that I questioned just a few short pages ago. The ideas emerge from my discussions with activists in the United States and in Russia, particularly from my attempts to listen to Russian activists and their concerns about the lack of financing for their organizations, their awareness of the degree of women's problems in Russian society, and their frustration that these problems are hardly addressed by the media or attended to by the state.

---

[15] Tat'iana Ivanova, interview, May 16, 1995.

The organizing ideas I suggest could provide ways to counteract these problems, to garner popularity for the organizations, and thereby start the process of gaining local support.

Whatever issue activists choose around which to conduct a campaign, it is important to root those actions within the context of a strategy designed to mobilize women, to draw attention to the overall issue, and thereby spark recognition and spur consciousness within the population. Such actions alert previously nonmobilized women to the fact that a women's movement exists, and it addresses their concerns. Campaigns to achieve limited goals, consisting of a series of actions pitched to motivate new people to get involved, can enable the movement to start taking advantage of people power.

To accomplish these goals, the targets of the activism must be decentralized. Actions that focus on parliament may be too remote to spark the population's interest, too centralized to seem relevant to women living outside the capital, and possibly too ineffective (even if successful), given the degree to which laws, once passed, tend to be evaded. Rather than focusing on changing laws or lobbying politicians (centralized actions), the activities could focus on challenging cultural assumptions.[16] This is a formidable task, because cultural resonance must also be maintained, lest actions be dismissed as the behavior of foreign-influenced marginals. For instance, actions that show blatant disregard for essentialist gender roles are unlikely to gain supporters for the women's movement. But actions that point to the injustice of women being expected to have full responsibility for childcare and paid employment, even as public childcare options decline, may have some appeal.

What kinds of decentralized actions might be relevant? In order to involve more women in activities of the women's movement, activists must choose organizing tasks that require, for their success, not money, not access to high-powered politicians, but rather numbers of people – even relatively small numbers. Planning such actions necessitates doing concrete outreach to women, informing them about an event and inviting their participation. Another advantage of engaging in campaigns for specific, achievable objectives is that victories are more likely. In social movements, people are often attracted to organizations that have a track record of concrete achievements.

Examples of potentially effective actions thus might include holding a "take your children to the mayor's office" day, to protest the closure of

---

[16] I am grateful to Sam Diener for sharing his strategic thinking with me on these issues. For more information on planning grassroots campaigns designed to mobilize people, see Ed Hedemann, ed., *War Resisters League Organizer's Manual* (New York: War Resisters League, 1981), pp. 153–56.

childcare centers. Such an action would resonate with many women's sense that the state is shirking its responsibilities. Taking children to work for a day could have a similar effect, although women would be likely to fear losing their jobs if they challenged factory policies directly. Outreach to single-mothers' groups might be one means of attracting participants to such events, which could multiply as women become aware of them. Simultaneously, the women taking part in such an action might be encouraged to form childcare cooperatives (in which women take turns taking care of a group of children), thus addressing the needs of women in a way that might attract more adherents. Meetings of such cooperatives could serve a consciousness-raising function. Meanwhile, one possible demand on local administrations and firms could be to provide space for childcare centers or grassroots cooperatives.

Another target for social movement actions might be firms which make evident their preference for female employees under age thirty-five, as witnessed by job advertisements in newspapers. One potentially effective way to protest against this discrimination would be to mobilize a group of women to picket one such targeted company. If this unusual event could attract media attention (and this might well be the case, at least on a newspaper's "women's page"), it might thereby spark a sense of shared injustice among women who hear about it, and who share the feeling of being discarded and "unnecessary," or who have had trouble finding employment in the market economy.

For some activists, the desire to reach out to more women, with the goal of improving women's lives and attracting them to the movement, is there. On the other hand, as part of a social class, activists may give little thought to women factory workers and rural women, and more to the issues that affect intellectuals or professionals. Yet some of the concerns that the activists voice seem quite universal, and could easily serve to motivate and involve increasing numbers of women in the movement.

Moreover, activists are aware of the potential to create a more mass-based movement, and some see a shift in that direction as desirable. Interviewed in 1995, Tatiana Troinova, an energetic activist with several women's groups in Moscow, herself a relatively recent convert to the cause (as she put it: "I wasn't born a feminist – I was a mathematician!"), believed that the next phase of the movement was slowly coming into view, saying: "It's time for the women's movement to stop focusing solely on our own development, and turn to doing outreach to the population, to the female population, changing women's consciousness."[17]

[17] Tat'iana Troinova, personal communication, April 18, 1997.

Appendix

Table 4. *Surveyed Russian women's organizations officially registered as of 1995, by city*

Name of organization	City	Registration level	Year registered
Cheboksary city *zhensovet* (city branch of URW)	Cheboksary	municipal/city	1991
Chuvash republic *zhensovet* (branch of URW)	Cheboksary	republic	1991
Salam Bi	Cheboksary	republic	1994
Ekaterinburg oblast and city *zhensovet* (URW)	Ekaterinburg	oblast	1991
Urals Association of Women	Ekaterinburg	oblast	1994
Confederation of Businesswomen of Russia (Konfederatsiia Delovykh Zhenshchin Rossii)	Ekaterinburg	interregional	1994
Committee of Multi-Child Families	Ivanovo	within another organization	1991
Committee of Single-Parent Families	Ivanovo	within another organization	1993
City Union of Women (Gorodskoi Soiuz Zhenshchin; branch of URW)	Ivanovo	municipal/city	1991
Center for Social Support of Women and Families	Ivanovo	municipal/city	1994
Klub Delovaia Zhenshchina Ivanovo	Ivanovo	oblast	1992
Klub Garmoniia	Moscow	within another organization	1990
Innovation Fund of Women's Employment and Assistance to Entrepreneurship	Moscow	within another organization	1992
Moscow Crisis Center for Women	Moscow	within another organization	1993
Preobrazhenie	Moscow	municipal/city	1990
Society "Women of Presnia"	Moscow	municipal/city	1991

273

Table 4. *(contd)*

Name of organization	City	Registration level	Year registered
SANTA	Moscow	municipal/city	1991
Center for Women's Initiatives	Moscow	municipal/city	1992
Tolko Mamy	Moscow	municipal/city	1992
Center for Business Assistance to Women Perepodgotovka[a]	Moscow	municipal/city	1993
Congress of Soviet Women[b]	Moscow	municipal/city	1993
Feminist Orientation Center	Moscow	municipal/city	1993
Equality and Peace	Moscow	municipal/city	1994
Inform Center of the Independent Women's Forum	Moscow	municipal/city	1994
Moscow Center for Gender Studies	Moscow	municipal/city	1994
Tvorchestvo	Moscow	interregional	1990
Dzhenklub (Klub Delovykh Zhenshchin)	Moscow	interregional	1991
Association of University Women	Moscow	interregional	1992
Women for Social Democracy	Moscow	interregional	1992
Conversion and Women	Moscow	interregional	1993
Feminist Alternative	Moscow	all-Russian	1990
Association of Women Entrepreneurs	Moscow	all-Russian	1991
Committee of Soldiers' Mothers	Moscow	all-Russian	1991
Union of Russia's Women (URW)	Moscow	all-Russian	1991
Women's Alliance	Moscow	all-Russian	1992
Women's League	Moscow	all-Russian	1993
International Association of Russian Women-Mothers	Moscow	international	1992
International Association of Women and Development	Moscow	international	1992

Notes: [a] Perepodgotovka originated as a similar organization called Vash Shans (Your Chance) two years earlier.

[b] The CSW has branches across the country, and, as of 1995, was in the process of reregistration as an interregional or national organization.

Table 5. *Surveyed Russian women's organizations, by city and year of formation*

Name of organization	City	Year
Cheboksary city *zhensovet* (city branch of URW)	Cheboksary	Soviet era
Chuvashiia republic *zhensovet* (branch of URW)	Cheboksary	Soviet era
Association of Women with a University Education (RAUW), Chuvashiia	Cheboksary	1994
Salam Bi	Cheboksary	1994
Klub Zhenskaia Initsiativa	Cheboksary	1995
Ekaterinburg oblast and city *zhensovet*	Ekaterinburg	Soviet era
Confederation of Businesswomen of Russia	Ekaterinburg	1994
Urals Association of Women	Ekaterinburg	1994
City Union of Women (Gorodskoi Soiuz Zhenshchin; branch of URW)	Ivanovo	Soviet era
Committee of Multi-Child Families	Ivanovo	1991
Klub Delovaia Zhenshchina	Ivanovo	1992
Committee of Single-Parent Families	Ivanovo	1993
Center for Social Support of Women and Families	Ivanovo	1994
LOTOS: Liga Osvobozhdenie ot Obshchestvennykh Stereotipov	Moscow	1987
Tvorchestvo	Moscow	1988
Committee of Soldiers' Mothers	Moscow	1989
Preobrazhenie	Moscow	1989
Association of Women Entrepreneurs	Moscow	1990
Dzhenklub (Klub Delovykh Zhenshchin)	Moscow	1990
Feminist Alternative	Moscow	1990
International Association of Russian Women-Mothers	Moscow	1990
Klub Garmoniia	Moscow	1990
MOLLI: Moscow Organization of Lesbian Literature and Art	Moscow	1990
Moscow Center for Gender Studies	Moscow	1990
SANTA	Moscow	1990
Tolko Mamy	Moscow	1990
Union of Russia's Women (URW)	Moscow	1990
Center for Business Assistance to Women Perepodgotovka	Moscow	1991
Feminist Orientation Center	Moscow	1991
Society "Women of Presnia"	Moscow	1991

Table 5. *(contd)*

Name of organization	City	Year
Women's Alliance	Moscow	1991
Association of University Women	Moscow	1992
Association of Women Journalists	Moscow	1992
Center for Women's Initiatives	Moscow	1992
Conversion and Women	Moscow	1992
Gender Studies Center at the Institute for Ethnology and Anthropology	Moscow	1992
Innovation Fund of Women's Employment and Assistance to Entrepreneurship	Moscow	1992
International Association of Women and Development	Moscow	1992
Klub F-1	Moscow	1992
Radio Nadezhda	Moscow	1992
Women for Social Democracy	Moscow	1992
Women's League	Moscow	1992
Center for Issues of Women, Family, and Gender Studies (Youth Institute)	Moscow	1993
Congress of Soviet Women	Moscow	1993
Equality and Peace	Moscow	1993
Moscow Crisis Center for Women	Moscow	1993
Sofia	Moscow	1993
Women's Liberal Fund	Moscow	1993
Association of Women [Film and Theater] Directors	Moscow	1994
Inform Center of the Independent Women's Forum	Moscow	1994
US–NIS Consortium, Winrock International	USA–Russia	1994

Table 6. *Surveyed Russian women's organizations, by membership size*

Name of organization	Number of individual members (unless noted otherwise)
over 1,000	
Congress of Soviet Women	12,000
Committee of Soldiers' Mothers	several thousand
Urals Association of Women (Ekaterinburg)	3,000, plus collective members
Confederation of Businesswomen of Russia (Ekaterinburg)	2,000, plus 100 collective members
International Association of Russian Women-Mothers	2,000
Tvorchestvo	1,100
200–1,000	
Conversion and Women	500
Association of Women [Film and Theater] Directors	200
Association of Women with a University Education	200
Dzhenklub	200
50–199	
International Association of Women and Development	100
Tolko Mamy	53 women, 62 children
Association of Women Entrepreneurs	50, plus collective members across Russia
Equality and Peace	50
Salam Bi (Cheboksary)	50
Innovation Fund of Women's Employment and Assistance to Entrepreneurship	dozens (individual and collective members)
25–49	
Women for Social Democracy	40
Chuvash republic *zhensovet*	35
Association of Women Journalists	30
Klub F-1	30
Klub Garmoniia	30
Cheboksary city *zhensovet*	25
Feminist Alternative (FALTA)	25
Klub Delovaia Zhenshchina (Ivanovo)	25
Klub Zhenskaia Initsiativa (Cheboksary)	25
Preobrazhenie	25

Appendix

Table 6. *(contd)*

Name of organization	Number of individual members (unless noted otherwise)
under 25	
Sverdlovsk oblast *zhensovet* (Ekaterinburg)	20
SANTA	15
Sofia	15
Ivanovo city *zhensovet*	13, plus two member organizations
Association of Women with a University Education (Chuvash branch; Cheboksary)	11
Committee of Multi-Child Families (Ivanovo)	8, plus 2,329 families (3 children or more)
Committee of Single-Parent Families (Ivanovo)	7, plus 2,300 families
Feminist Orientation Center	7
MOLLI	7
nonmembership organizations	
Center for Business Assistance to Women Perepodgotovka	8 staff
Center for Issues of Women, Family, and Gender Studies (Youth Institute)	3 (researchers/activists/staff)
Center for Social Support of Women and Families (Ivanovo)	8 staff
Center for Women's Initiatives	not a membership organization
Gender Studies Center at the Institute for Ethnology and Anthropology	9 (researchers/activists/staff)
Inform Center of the Independent Women's Forum	15 staff
Moscow Center for Gender Studies	15 (researchers/activists/staff)
Moscow Crisis Center for Women	9 staff
Society "Women of Presnia"	5 staff
Women's Alliance	11 (leaders of subprograms)
Women's Liberal Fund	unknown
networks	
Independent Women's Forum (IWF)	about 200 member organizations
Union of Russia's Women (URW)	115 member organizations
Women's League	over 40 member organizations

Note: All of the membership information presented in the table is approximate. The Committees of Single Parents and Multi-Child Families in Ivanovo consider all the families in Ivanovo with those characteristics to be "members" of their organizations.

Table 7. *Activists' number of children*

Number of children	Number of activists
zero	10 (15%)
one	32 (48%)
two	22 (33%)
three	1 (1.5%)
ten	1 (1.5%)

Table 8. *Activists' education levels*

Level of Education	Number of Activists
Full professor (*doktor nauk*)	4 (6%)
M.A./Ph.D. (*kandidat nauk*)	22 (35%)
College (*vyshee obrazovanie*)	36 (57%)
Vocational school (*srednoe spetsial'noe*)	1 (1.6%)

Table 9. *Data on surveyed Russian women's organization members: age, education, profession*

Name of organization	Demographic data on members
	Cheboksary
Association of Women with a University Education, Chuvash branch	Average age: 35–45. All have higher education; most have advanced degrees.
Cheboksary city *zhensovet* (city branch of URW)	Average age is 40–45. All have a higher education. Various professions: a lawyer, teachers, a doctor, some retired, some housewives.
Chuvash republic *zhensovet* (branch of URW)	"Members of the presidium are on average aged 40. On average, they have a higher education. Most are employed, except the retired ones."
Klub Zhenskaia Initsiativa	Age of the founding members is over 40. Founders are professional women, including republic-level ministers, administrators, and factory directors.
Salam Bi	Average age is 30–35. Most have a higher education. Rural teachers, journalists, doctors, singers, some tutors/governesses. "People who are associated with culture."

Table 9. *(contd)*

Name of organization	Demographic data on members
	Ekaterinburg
Confederation of Businesswomen of Russia	Age 40–50. "All of them have higher education. By profession they are mostly women who changed their professions: they do their own business, or engage in professional activity *plus* having their own business."
Urals Association of Women	Average age is 35–40. "Not everyone has a higher education; it's middle specialized and higher. Probably everyone is employed."
	Ivanovo
Ivanovo Center for Social Support of Women and Families	Average age in the core group is 35. All have a higher education, plus 5 with advanced degrees.
Committee of Multi-Child Families (Ivanovo)	"Average age in the core group is 40 or so. Some have higher education, some do not. All are employed. Among the mothers of the families [the collective members], the average age is 30; most are textile workers, with a high school education. Many, many of them are unemployed."
Committee of Single-Parent Families (Ivanovo)	"Among the mothers of the families [collective members], their average age is around 30, most of them are young. By education most of them have a high school education, or middle specialized, and some with a higher education. Most are in working class jobs. We also have unemployed women."
Klub Delovaia Zhenshchina (Ivanovo)	Average age is 45. "Everyone has a higher education. Some have advanced degrees."
	Moscow
Association of Women [Film and Theater] Directors	The members are theater and film directors; their average age is 35–45.
Association of Women Entrepreneurs	"Average age varies. 99% have a higher education, a lot with higher degrees; one percent or less with a technical high school degree."
Association of Women Journalists★	Average age is approximately late thirties. Members have on average a higher education; they are journalists by profession.
Association of Women with a University Education	Members have a higher education, some with advanced degrees.
Committee of Soldiers' Mothers	The average age in the core group is between

	40–55. They have either a higher education, or technical high school education.
Congress of Soviet Women	Age: "Unfortunately, we have few young people. Maybe 5% are women under 30. About 15% are women between 30 and 40. The rest are 40–60, with about 15% being over 60. Most fall within the 35–55 range. Professionally, there are more white collar workers and intelligentsia than there are blue collar workers."
Conversion and Women	More than 56% of the women in the organization have a higher education. By profession they are in the defense industry.
Dzhenklub (Klub Delovykh Zhenshchin)	"Average age varies. There are some very young entrepreneurs, some are 23–25, already successfully in business. There are some older ones, over 60, maybe over 65. The average is 40–45. Education: most have a higher education, almost exclusively. And probably half have advanced degrees. And professionally, they're all different."
Equality and Peace	Core group has higher education; includes academics, lawyers, theater people, a businesswoman and a woman director of a bank.
Feminist Orientation Center	Members have higher education, advanced degrees in research fields, including psychology and sociology.
International Association of Russian Women-Mothers	Members mostly work at the Academy of the Parliamentary Corps in Moscow and its affiliates, and at scientific-research institutes (NII), especially in the sphere of communal services.
International Association of Women and Development.	Average age, from 40–45; they range from 25 to 60. "Practically all our members have a higher education. About 1/4 of them have a *doktor nauk* degree. About 1/3 have a *kandidat nauk* degree. All of them are employed."
Klub F-1*	Age of those attending meetings varies widely (from late 20s to 60s). Many of those who attend the meetings are journalists by profession; all appear to have higher education, many with advanced degrees.
Klub Garmoniia	Average age is about 30–35. "By occupation, they are women in the creative professions. Mostly, intellectuals. Many are journalists. Most of them work. Some are unemployed."
MOLLI*	Members are lesbians; several in the creative arts.

Preobrazhenie	Several core members have advanced degrees.
SANTA	"Our members are all aged about 45–50. There are no unemployed people in the association."
Sofia	Age of members is 30–56; members are artists and writers by profession.
Tolko Mamy	"Our membership is single mothers with small children, though we also have mothers with teenagers."
Tvorchestvo	"About 35% of the people who come to the training courses [conducted by the organization] have a higher education. 40% of them are unemployed, or fear losing their jobs, especially at scientific research institutes."
Women's Alliance	The core group is aged 40–50. "Mostly the women were unemployed, but we helped them find work; most are women with a higher education and advanced degrees."

Note: Data in this table is taken mostly from interviews. Data derived from participant observation is marked with an asterisk. Nonmembership groups do not appear in the table. Membership data is missing for: FALTA, Innovation Fund, Women for Social Democracy, and the Ekaterinburg and Ivanovo *zhensovety*.

Selected bibliography

RUSSIAN WOMEN'S ORGANIZATIONS' PERIODICALS CONSULTED

Feministskii informatsionnyi zhurnal (FemInf)
Informatsionnyi listok: Informatsionnyi Tsentr Nezavisimogo Zhenskogo
    Foruma
Preobrazhenie
Vestnik zhenskogo informatsionno-obrazovatel'nogo proekta
Vse liudi sestry
Vy i my
Zhenshchina plius
Zhenshchiny Rossii, *Informatsionnyi biulleten'*
Zhenskoe dvizhenie v SSSR (later, Zhenskii diskussionnyi klub)

RUSSIAN NEWSPAPERS AND PERIODICALS CONSULTED

Delovaia zhenshchina
Ekspress-khronika
Izvestiia
Komsomol'skaia pravda
Krestianka
Literaturnaia gazeta
Nezavisimaia gazeta
Novaia zhenshchina
Moskovskaia pravda
Moskvichka
Ogonek
Rabotnitsa
Segodnia
Sudarushka
Vechernaia moskva
Zhenskie dela

ORGANIZATIONS AND PERSONS INTERVIEWED

Interviews between September 19, 1994, and February 2, 1995, were conducted anonymously; hence the names of my informants for those organizations do not appear below. Many individuals were associated with more than one organization. I list them alongside the primary organization for which they acted as informant.

CHEBOKSARY

Association of Women with a University Education, Chuvash branch (Ol'ga Bubina)   .
Cheboksary city *zhensovet* (Nina Petrova)
Chuvash republic *zhensovet* (Iraida Stekol'shikova)
Iuman: City Coordinating Center on Ecological Education (Al'bina Endiuskina)
Klub Zhenskaia Initsiativa (Ol'ga Denisova)
Salam Bi (Lida Suvara, Vera Arseneva)

EKATERINBURG

Confederation of Businesswomen of Russia (Svetlana Kornilova)
Ekaterinburg oblast and city *zhensovet* (Maia Mikhailova)
Library Center, "Women's World" (Mariia Kaurova)
Urals Association of Women (Larisa Volkova)

IVANOVO

Center for Social Support of Women and Families (Marina Mints, Ol'ga Khasbulatova)
Committee of Multi-Child Families (Nina Temnikova)
Committee of Single-Parent Families (Larisa Nazarova)
City Union of Women (Natal'ia Kovaleva)
Ivanovo Employment Services
Ivanovo State University, Department of Social Psychology (German Morozov, Roal'd Gitel'makher)
Klub Delovaia Zhenshchina (Margarita Razina)
Textile Institute (Galina Viatkina)

MOSCOW

Association of Russian Women-Mothers (Larisa Podgorbunskaia)
Association of University Women
Association of Women Entrepreneurs (Tat'iana Maliutina)
Association of Women [Film and Theater] Directors (Elena Demeshina)
Association of Women Journalists
Association "Women and Development" (Galina Sillaste)
Center for Business Assistance to Women, "Perepodgotovka" (Marina Pavlova)

Center for Issues of Women, Family, and Gender Studies, at the Youth
    Institute
Center for Women's Initiatives (El'vira Novikova)
Charity Organization: Society "Women of Presnia" (Nina Tiuliulina)
Committee of Soldiers' Mothers (Valentina Mel'nikova)
Congress of Soviet Women (Natal'ia Belokopytova)
Conversion and Women (Eleonora Ivanova)
Duma Committee on Women, Family, and Youth Affairs/Women of Russia
    political bloc (Galina Klimantova)
Dzhenklub: Klub Delovykh Zhenshchin (Nina Iakovchuk)
Equality and Peace
Feminist Alternative (FALTA)
Feminist Orientation Center
Gender Studies Center at the Institute for Ethnology and Anthropology
Independent Women's Forum (Elena Kochkina)
Inform Center of the Independent Women's Forum (Tat'iana Troinova, Laima
    Geidar)
Innovation Fund of Women's Employment and Assistance to Entrepreneurship
Institute for the Socio-Economic Study of the Population (Natal'ia Rimashevs-
    kaia)
Klub F-1
Klub Garmoniia (Mariia Arbatova)
LOTOS: Liga Osvobozhdeniia ot Obshchestvennykh Stereotipov (Ol'ga
    Voronina)
MacArthur Foundation (Tat'iana Zhdanova)
Ministry of Social Protection (Ol'ga Samarina)
MOLLI: Moscow Organization of Lesbian Literature and Art
Moscow Center for Gender Studies (Valentina Konstantinova)
Moscow Crisis Center for Women
Preobrazhenie (Tat'iana Klimenkova)
Radio Nadezhda (Tat'iana Zeleranskaia, Irina Kovaleva)
SANTA (Nonna Nikonova, Anna Potemkina, Liudmila Iarovaia)
Sof'ia (Nina Gabrielian)
Tol'ko Mamy
Tvorchestvo (Tat'iana Riabikina)
Union of Russia's Women
US–NIS Women's Consortium (Martina Vandenberg)
Women for Social Democracy
Women's Alliance (Tat'iana Ivanova)
Women's League (Elena Ershova, Maia Kaz'mina)
Women's Liberal Fund

ST. PETERSBURG

Petersburg Center for Gender Issues (Ol'ga Lipovskaia)

BOOKS AND ARTICLES

Almond, Gabriel, and Sidney Verba. *The Civic Culture.* Beverly Hills: Sage Publications, 1989.

Alvarez, Sonia. *Engendering Democracy in Brazil: Women's Movements in Transition Politics.* Princeton: Princeton University Press, 1990.

"Women's Movements and Gender Politics in the Brazilian Transition." In Jaquette, *The Women's Movement in Latin America.* Pp. 18–71.

Attwood, Lynne. *The New Soviet Man and Woman.* Bloomington: Indiana University Press, 1990.

Bahry, Donna, and Lucan Way. "Citizen Activism in the Russian Transition." *Post-Soviet Affairs,* vol. 10, no. 4 (1994), pp. 330–66.

Banfield, Edward. *The Moral Basis of a Backward Society.* Glencoe, IL: Free Press, 1958.

Basu, Amrita, ed. *The Challenge of Local Feminisms.* Boulder: Westview Press, 1995.

Beissinger, Mark. "Event Analysis in Transitional Societies: Protest Mobilization in the Former Soviet Union." In Dieter Rucht, Ruud Koopmans, and Friedhelm Neidhardt, eds., *Acts of Dissent: New Developments in the Study of Protest.* Berlin: Sigma Press, 1998. Pp. 284–316.

Berkovitch, Nitza. "From Motherhood to Citizenship: The Worldwide Incorporation of Women into the Public Sphere in the Twentieth Century." Dissertation, Stanford University, 1995.

Berry, Ellen E., ed. *Postcommunism and the Body Politic.* New York: New York University Press, 1995.

Bohachevsky-Chomiak, Martha. *Feminists Despite Themselves: Women in Ukrainian Community Life 1884–1939.* Edmonton: Canadian Institute of Ukrainian Studies, 1988.

Bolt, Christine. *The Women's Movements in the United States and Britain from the 1790s to the 1920s.* Amherst: University of Massachusetts Press, 1993.

Bridger, Susan. *Women in the Soviet Countryside.* Cambridge: Cambridge University Press, 1987.

Bridger, Susan, Rebecca Kay, and Kathryn Pinnick, eds. *No More Heroines?: Russia, Women and the Market.* London: Routledge, 1996.

Browning, Genia. *Women and Politics in the USSR: Consciousness Raising and Soviet Women's Groups.* Brighton, Sussex: St. Martin's Press, 1987.

Buckley, Mary. *Women and Ideology in the Soviet Union.* Ann Arbor: University of Michigan Press, 1989.

Buckley, Mary, ed. *Perestroika and Soviet Women.* Cambridge: Cambridge University Press, 1992.

Post-Soviet Women: From the Baltic to Central Asia. Cambridge: Cambridge University Press, 1997.

Buechler, Steven M. *Women's Movements in the United States.* New Brunswick, NJ: Rutgers University Press, 1990.

Clements, Barbara Evans. *Bolshevik Women.* Cambridge: Cambridge University Press, 1997.

"Concluding Document of the First Independent Women's Forum of the Soviet Union." *Feminist Review,* 39 (Winter 1991), pp. 146–48.

D'Anieri, Paul, Clair Ernst, and Elizabeth Kier. "New Social Movements in Historical Perspective." *Comparative Politics*, vol. 22, no. 4 (1990), pp. 445–58.

Dawson, Jane. *Eco-Nationalism: Anti-Nuclear Activism and National Identity in Russia, Lithuania, and Ukraine*. Durham, NC: Duke University Press, 1996.

Diani, Mario. "The Concept of Social Movement." *Sociological Review*, vol. 40, no. 1 (1992), pp. 1–25.

"Doklad o vypolnenii v Rossiiskoi Federatsii Konventsii o likvidatsii vsekh form diskriminatsii v otnoshenii zhenshchin: chetvertyi periodicheskii doklad (predstavlen v sootvetstvii so stat'ei 18 Konventsii)." Moscow: Ministry of Social Protection, 1994.

Duka, A., N. Kornev, V. Voronkov, and E. Zdravomyslova. "Round Table on Russian Sociology: The Protest Cycle of Perestroika." *International Sociology*, vol. 10, no. 1 (March 1995), pp. 83–99.

Eckstein, Harry. "A Culturalist Theory of Political Change." *American Political Science Review*, vol. 82, no. 3 (September 1988), pp. 789–804.

Edmondson, Linda H. *Feminism in Russia, 1900–1917*. Stanford: Stanford University Press, 1984.

Einhorn, Barbara. *Cinderella Goes to Market*. London: Verso Press, 1993.

Evans, Sara. *Personal Politics*. New York: Random House, 1980.

Feministstkaia teoriia i praktika: vostok–zapad. Konferentsiia 9.6–12.6.95, ed. Iuliia Zhukova, et al. St. Petersburg: Peterburgskii Tsentr Gendernykh Problem, 1996.

Ferree, Myra Marx, and Patricia Yancey Martin, eds. *Feminist Organizations: Harvest of the New Women's Movement*. Philadelphia: Temple University Press, 1995.

Fish, M. Steven. *Democracy from Scratch*. Princeton: Princeton University Press, 1995.

Fisher, Jo. *Mothers of the Disappeared*. Boston: South End Press, 1989.

Freeman, Jo. *The Politics of Women's Liberation*. New York: David McKay Company, 1975.

Friedman, Debra, and Doug McAdam. "Collective Identity and Activism." In Morris and Mueller, *Frontiers in Social Movement Theory*. Pp. 156–73.

From Problems To Strategy: Materials of the Second Independent Women's Forum, Dubna, 27–29 November 1992. Moscow/Hilversum: Center for Gender Studies/Ariadne Europe Fund, 1993.

Funk, Nanette and Magda Mueller, eds. *Gender Politics and Post-Communism: Reflections from Eastern Europe and the Former Soviet Union*. New York: Routledge, 1993.

Gamson, William. *The Strategy of Social Protest*, 2nd edn. Belmont, CA: Wadsworth, 1990.

Gitlin, Todd. *The Whole World Is Watching*. Berkeley: University of California Press, 1980.

Goldman, Wendy. "Industrial Politics, Peasant Rebellion and the Death of the Proletarian Women's Movement in the USSR." *Slavic Review*, vol. 55, no. 1 (Spring 1996), pp. 46–77.

Gorbachev, Mikhail S. *Perestroika: New Thinking for Our Country and the World.* New York: Harper and Row, 1987.

Heitlinger, Alena. *Women and State Socialism: Sex Inequality in the Soviet Union and Czechoslovakia.* Montreal: McGill-Queen's University Press, 1979.

Holland, Barbara, ed. *Soviet Sisterhood.* Bloomington: Indiana University Press, 1985.

"Itogovyi otchet o rabote logo Nezavisimogo Zhenskogo Foruma." Dubna, Moscow, 1991.

Jancar, Barbara. *Women Under Communism.* Baltimore: Johns Hopkins Press, 1978.

Jaquette, Jane S., ed. *The Women's Movement in Latin America: Feminism and the Transition to Democracy.* Boston: Unwin Hyman, 1989.

Johnston, Hank, and Bert Klandermans, eds. *Social Movements and Culture.* Minneapolis: University of Minnesota Press, 1995.

Jowitt, Kenneth. *New World Disorder: The Leninist Extinction.* Berkeley: University of California Press, 1992.

Katsiaficas, George. *The Imagination of the New Left: A Global Analysis of 1968.* Boston: South End Press, 1987.

Katzenstein, Mary Fainsod, and Carol McClurg Mueller, eds. *The Women's Movements of the United States and Western Europe: Consciousness, Political Opportunity, and Public Policy.* Philadelphia: Temple University Press, 1987.

Keck, Margaret, and Kathryn Sikkink. *Activists Beyond Borders: Transnational Advocacy Networks in International Politics.* Ithaca: Cornell University Press, 1998.

Khasbulatova, Ol'ga. *Opyt i traditsii zhenskogo dvizheniia v rossii (1860–1917).* Ivanovo: Ivanovskii Gosudarstvennyi Universitet, 1994.

Zhenskie organizatsii v novykh usloviiakh. Ivanovo: Znanie and Oblastnoi Sovet Zhenshchin, 1991.

Khotkina, Zoia, ed. *Seksual'nye domogatel'stva na rabote.* Moscow: ABA-CEELI, Zhenskii konsortsium, and MCGS, 1996.

Zhenshchiny i sotsial'naia politika. Moscow: Russian Academy of Sciences, 1992.

Klandermans, Bert. "The Social Construction of Protest and Multiorganizational Fields." In Morris and Mueller, *Frontiers in Social Movement Theory.* Pp. 77–103.

Kochkina, E., and E. Ershova. "Komentarii i popravki k proektu federal'nogo zakona 'O vnesenii izmenenii i dopolnenii v Kodeks zakonov o trude RF' Gendernyi podkhod i trudovye prava zhenshchin." Commentary presented at Parliamentary Hearings on the Labor Code, Moscow, March 4–5, 1996.

Konstantinova, Valentina. "The Women's Movement in the USSR: A Myth or a Real Challenge?" In Shirin Rai, Hilary Pilkington, and Annie Phizacklea, eds., *Women in the Face of Change.* London: Routledge, 1992. Pp. 200–17.

"Women's Political Coalitions in Russia (1990–1994)." In Anna Rotkirch and Elina Haavio-Mannila, eds., *Women's Voices in Russia Today.* Brookfield, VT: Dartmouth Publishing, 1996. Pp. 235–47.

Korniak, V. B., ed. *Integratsiia zhenshchin v protsess obshchestvennogo razvitiia.* Moscow: Luch, 1994.

Lapidus, Gail. "Gender and Restructuring: The Impact of Perestroika and Its Aftermath on Soviet Women." In Valentine Moghadam, ed., *Democratic Reform and the Position of Women in Transitional Economies*. New York: Oxford University Press, 1994. Pp. 137–61.

Women in Soviet Society: Equality, Development, and Social Change. Berkeley: University of California Press, 1978.

Liborakina, Marina. *Obretenie sily: rossiiskii opyt*. Moscow: CheRo, 1996.

Lipovskaia, Ol'ga. "New Women's Organizations." In Buckley, *Perestroika and Soviet Women*. Pp. 72–81.

Lissyutkina, Larissa. "Soviet Women at the Crossroads of Perestroika." In Funk and Mueller, *Gender Politics and Post-Communism*. Pp. 274–86.

Liubimova, V. V., ed. *Zhenshchiny v sovremennom mire*. Moscow: Nauka, 1989.

McAdam, Doug. *Political Process and the Development of Black Insurgency, 1930–1970*. Chicago: University of Chicago Press, 1982.

McAdam, D., J. D. McCarthy, and M. N. Zald. "Social Movements." In N. J. Smelser, ed., *Handbook of Sociology*. Beverly Hills: Sage, 1988. Pp. 695–738.

McAdam, Doug, John D. McCarthy, and Mayer M. Zald, eds. *Comparative Perspectives on Social Movements*. Cambridge: Cambridge University Press, 1996.

McAdam, Doug, Charles Tilly, and Sidney Tarrow. "To Map Contentious Politics." *Mobilization*, vol. 1, no. 1 (March 1996), pp. 17–34.

McCarthy, John D., and Mayer N. Zald. "Resource Mobilization and Social Movements: A Partial Theory." *American Journal of Sociology*, vol. 82, no. 6 (1977), pp. 1212–41.

Mamonova, Tatyana. *Russian Women's Studies: Essays on Sexism in Soviet Culture*. Elmsford, NY: Pergamon Press, 1989.

Mamonova, Tatyana, ed. *Women and Russia*. Boston: Beacon Press, 1984.

Marsh, Rosalind, ed. *Women in Russia and Ukraine*. Cambridge: Cambridge University Press, 1996.

Mohanty, Chandra, ed. *Third World Women and the Politics of Feminism*. Bloomington: Indiana University Press, 1991.

Molyneux, Maxine. "Interview with Anastasya Posadskaya." *Feminist Review*, vol. 39 (Winter 1991), pp. 133–40.

"Mobilization Without Emancipation?: Women's Interests, the State, and Revolution in Nicaragua." *Feminist Studies*, vol. 11, no. 2 (Summer 1985), pp. 227–54.

Morris, Aldon D., and Carol McClurg Mueller, eds. *Frontiers in Social Movement Theory*. New Haven: Yale University Press, 1992.

Moskovskii tsentr gendernykh issledovanii: 1990–1995. Moscow: Moskovskii Tsentr Gendernykh Issledovanii, 1995.

Nechemias, Carol. "The Prospects for a Soviet Women's Movement: Opportunities and Obstacles." In Judith B. Sedaitis and Jim Butterfield, eds., *Perestroika from Below: Social Movements in the Soviet Union*. Boulder: Westview Press, 1991. Pp. 73–96.

Nelson, Barbara J., and Najma Chowdhury, eds. *Women and Politics Worldwide*. New Haven: Yale University Press, 1994.

NEZHDI (Independent Women's Democratic Initiative) Manifesto. *Feminist Review*, vol. 39 (Winter 1991), pp. 127–32.

O'Donnell, Guillermo, Philippe Schmitter, and Laurence Whitehead, eds. *Transitions from Authoritarian Rule*. Baltimore: John Hopkins University Press, 1986.

Pilkington, Hilary, ed. *Gender, Generation and Identity in Contemporary Russia*. London: Routledge, 1996.

Posadskaia, Anastasiia. "Gender Studies in the Soviet Union: How We See the Issue." Unpublished typescript, Moscow Center for Gender Studies, 1991.

[Posadskaya, Anastasia,] "Self-Portrait of a Russian Feminist." *New Left Review* 195 (September/October 1992), pp. 3–19.

Posadskaia, Anastasiia, ed. *Women in Russia*. London: Verso, 1994.

Racioppi, Linda, and Katherine O'Sullivan See. *Women's Activism in Contemporary Russia*. Philadelphia: Temple University Press, 1997.

Regentova, Marina, and Natasha Abubikirova. No title. Unpublished typescript, Moscow, 1995.

Rimashevskaia, N., ed. *Zhenshchina v meniaiushchemsia mire*. Moscow: Nauka, 1992.

Zhenshchiny v obshchestve: realii, problemy, prognozy. Moscow: Nauka, 1991.

Rucht, Dieter. "German Unification, Democratization, and the Role of Social Movements: A Missed Opportunity?" *Mobilization*, vol. 1, no. 1 (March 1996), pp. 35–62.

Rueschemeyer, Marilyn, ed. *Women in the Politics of Postcommunist Eastern Europe*. Armonk, NY: M. E. Sharpe, 1994.

Rule, Wilma and Norma C. Noonan, eds. *Russian Women in Politics and Society*. Westport, CT: Greenwood Press, 1996.

"Russia: Neither Jobs Nor Justice. State Discrimination Against Women in Russia." *Human Rights Watch Women's Rights Project*, vol. 7, no. 5 (March 1995).

Russian Federation National Report to the Fourth World Conference on the Status of Women. "Actions in the Interests of Equality, Development, and Peace." Moscow, 1994.

Ruthchild, Rochelle. "Sisterhood and Socialism: The Soviet Feminist Movement." *Frontiers*, vol. 7, no. 2 (1983), pp. 4–12.

Scott, W. Richard, and John W. Meyer. *Institutional Environments and Organizations*. Beverly Hills: Sage, 1994.

Smith, Kathleen E. *Remembering Stalin's Victims*. Ithaca: Cornell University Press, 1996.

Stenogramma Parlamentskikh slushanii. "Zhenshchiny i trudovoe pravo." Moscow, March 5, 1996.

Stites, Richard. *The Women's Liberation Movement in Russia*. Princeton: Princeton University Press, 1978.

Strategii vzaimodeistviia. On the third interregional seminar from the series, "Strategies of the Independent Women's Forum: Before and After Beijing," August 1995. Moscow, October 1995.

Tarrow, Sidney. "Mentalities, Political Cultures, and Collective Action Frames:

Constructing Meanings Through Action." In Morris and Mueller, *Frontiers in Social Movement Theory*. Pp. 174–202.

Power in Movement. Cambridge: Cambridge University Press, 1994.

Struggle, Politics and Reform: Collective Action, Social Movements, and Cycles of Protest. Occasional Paper No. 21, Western Societies Program, Center for International Studies, Ithaca, Cornell University, 1989.

Terekhina, V. A., ed. *O polozhenii semei v Rossiiskoi Federatsii*. Moscow: Iuridicheskaia Literatura, 1994.

Tilly, Charles. *From Mobilization to Revolution*. Reading: Addison-Wesley, 1978.

"Social Movements as Historically Specific Clusters of Political Performances." *Berkeley Journal of Sociology*, vol. 38 (1993–94), pp. 1–30.

Tishkov, V. A., ed. *Zhenshchina i svoboda*. Moscow: Nauka, 1994.

Traugott, Mark, ed. *Repertoires and Cycles of Collective Action*. Durham, NC: Duke University Press, 1995.

Voronina, Ol'ga. "Women in a 'Man's Society.'" *Soviet Sociology*, March–April 1989, pp. 66–79.

"Zhenshchina i sotsializm: opyt feministskogo analiza." In M. T. Stepaniants, ed., *Feminizm: Vostok, Zapad, Rossiia*. Moscow: Nauka, 1993. Pp. 205–25.

Wolchik, Sharon, and Alfred G. Meyer, eds. *Women, State, and Party in Eastern Europe*. Durham, NC: Duke University Press, 1985.

Zakharova, N., A. Posadskaia, and N. Rimashevskaia. "Kak my reshaem zhenskii vopros." *Kommunist*, no. 4, 1989, pp. 56–65.

Zdravomyslova, E., and Anna Temkina, eds. *Gendernoe izmerenie sotsial'noi i politicheskoi aktivnosti v perekhodnyi period*. St. Petersburg: Center for Independent Social Research, 1996.

Zhenshchiny Rossii: statisticheskii sbornik. Moscow: Goskomstat Rossii, 1995.

Index

abortion, 4, 101, 133
Abubikirova, Natalia, 189–90, 195, 237, 238, 239, 246
activists, 34–8
  age, 35, 36, 279–82
  and ambition as a post-Soviet phenomenon, 193–5
  attitudes to feminism, 59–73
  combining work and family, 268–72
  contact with Westerners, 225–7
  and democracy, 93–4
  on economic conditions, 175–6
  education levels, 35, 36, 210–11, 279–82
  on equal rights and equal opportunities, 90–2, 96
  and human rights, 94–5
  on lack of solidarity among women's organizations, 182–3
  leaders of organizations, 36, 210
  marital status, 35
  and mass mobilization, 213, 214–15, 216–18, 266
  numbers of children, 34–5, 279
  occupations, 34, 279–82
  oldtimers and newcomers, 189–92
  and organizational pluralism, 195–6
  and resource mobilization, 169–71
  suspicion and the state, 183–9
  traditionalists vs. feminists, 192–3
  transformation of consciousness, 44, 54, 54–9
  universal concerns of, 272
  and WOR, 119–20, 127–8
ADL, *see* Archive–Database–Library project
advocacy organizations, 29, 30, 31, 41, 146
  and dues collection, 172
  and feminism, 62
  Western influences on, 224, 237
  see also Independent Women's Forum (IWF); Inform Center
Agrarian Party, 117

Aivazova, Svetlana, 76, 126, 127
All-Russian Women's Congress (1995), 250
Almanac group, 101, 102
Almond, Gabriel, 181
ambition, as a post-Soviet phenomenon, 193–5
antinuclear movements, 211
Arbatova, Mariia, 3–4, 7, 84
Archive–Database–Library (ADL) project, 197, 250
Argentinean women, and feminism, 72–3
artistic women, and Tvorchestvo, 4–5, 6–7
Association of Independent Women's Associations, 205, 243
Association of Women Entrepreneurs, 26, 31, 119, 170–1, 280
Association of Women [Film and Theater] Directors, 27, 32, 58, 127–8, 166, 172, 184, 185, 280
Association of Women Journalists, 79, 184, 251, 280
atomization, in women's movement, 196–7
Azhgikhina, Nadezhda, 74, 84

Babukh, Larisa, 127
baby-food production, 154
beauty contests, 78
beauty salons, newspaper advertisements for, 82–3
Beijing conference (UN World Conference on Women), 112, 131–2, 133, 187, 196–7, 248
  importance of, 249–54
  and Western funding, 231, 233, 236, 238–9
Beissinger, Mark, 211–12
Belokopytova, Natalia, 209, 249–50
Berezhnaia, Natalia, 197
Beslepkina, Liudmila, 121, 129, 130, 135, 145, 250, 252, 253
Bobbitt, Lorena, 79

Printed in the United States
119982LV00004B/265-276/A